# REFLECTIONS ON REFORMATIONAL THEOLOGY

# REFLECTIONS ON REFORMATIONAL THEOLOGY

Studies in the Theology of the Reformation, Karl Barth, and the Evangelical Tradition

Kimlyn J. Bender

LONDON • NEW YORK • OXFORD • NEW DELHI • SYDNEY

T&T CLARK
Bloomsbury Publishing Plc
50 Bedford Square, London, WC1B 3DP, UK
1385 Broadway, New York, NY 10018, USA
29 Earlsfort Terrace, Dublin 2, Ireland

BLOOMSBURY, T&T CLARK and the T&T Clark logo are trademarks of
Bloomsbury Publishing Plc

First published in Great Britain 2021
Paperback edition published 2023

Copyright © Kimlyn J. Bender, 2021

Kimlyn J. Bender has asserted his right under the Copyright, Designs and Patents Act, 1988, to be identified as Author of this work.

For legal purposes the Acknowledgments on p. xi constitute an extension of this copyright page.

Cover image: Svetlana Isochenko/Alamy Stock Photo

All rights reserved. No part of this publication may be reproduced or transmitted in any form or by any means, electronic or mechanical, including photocopying, recording, or any information storage or retrieval system, without prior permission in writing from the publishers.

Bloomsbury Publishing Plc does not have any control over, or responsibility for, any third-party websites referred to or in this book. All internet addresses given in this book were correct at the time of going to press. The author and publisher regret any inconvenience caused if addresses have changed or sites have ceased to exist, but can accept no responsibility for any such changes.

A catalogue record for this book is available from the British Library.

Library of Congress Cataloging-in-Publication Data
Names: Bender, Kimlyn J., 1969- author.
Title: Reflections on reformational theology : studies in the theology of the Reformation, Karl Barth, and the evangelical tradition / by Kimlyn J. Bender.
Description: London ; New York : T&T Clark, 2021. | Includes bibliographical references and index. |
Identifiers: LCCN 2021000830 (print) | LCCN 2021000831 (ebook) |
ISBN 9780567678249 (hardback) | ISBN 9780567702258 (paperback) | ISBN 9780567678270 (epub) | ISBN 9780567678256 (pdf)
Subjects: LCSH: Reformation. | Evangelicalism.
Classification: LCC BR305.3 .B455 2021 (print) | LCC BR305.3 (ebook) |
DDC 230/.04409031–dc23
LC record available at https://lccn.loc.gov/2021000830
LC ebook record available at https://lccn.loc.gov/2021000831

| ISBN: | HB: | 978-0-5676-7824-9 |
|---|---|---|
| | PB: | 978-0-5677-0225-8 |
| | ePDF: | 978-0-5676-7825-6 |
| | eBook: | 978-0-5676-7827-0 |

Typeset by Integra Software Services Pvt. Ltd.

To find out more about our authors and books visit www.bloomsbury.com and sign up for our newsletters.

*For John Hiigel and Lee Martin McDonald*
Ministers, Scholars, Friends

"The church (which is a matter of the Spirit) is not born or preserved, it cannot exist, work, conquer, continue, or do any other [suitable] thing unless it is based on its foundation which is Christ alone; that is, the church must have Christ for its ruler, who rules it through faith, the Spirit, and the other gifts of his Spirit. From this it necessarily follows that [only] such preaching and teaching which are concerned exclusively with these matters and these mysteries should be done in the church; for only that should be preached in the church by which alone it is preserved and continues to exist. Therefore one should preach Christ alone and establish him as foundation, and teach the faith and those matters which are related to the faith, as Paul has said above: 'We do not preach ourselves, but Jesus Christ our Lord.'"

Letter from Martin Luther to Margrave Albrecht of Brandenberg,
Grand-Master of the Teutonic Order
December 1523

"History you can read and hear about as about the past; here you can if it so pleases you, judge by the outcome. But Christ's life on earth is not a past; it did not wait at the time, eighteen hundred years ago, and does not wait now for the assistance of any outcome. A historical Christianity is non-sense and un-Christian muddled thinking, because whatever true Christians there are in any generation are contemporary with Christ."

Søren Kierkegaard
*Practice in Christianity*
1848

"If Rudolf Bultmann were surrounded by a church which in its preaching and order, in its politics and relation to state and society, in its whole way of dealing with modern problems, were to put into practice even a little its belief in the Risen Lord, then not only would it be practically immune against the heresies of the Bultmannian conclusions and theses but it would also have in reply to Bultmann the one argument which could perhaps cause him to abandon his basic position, with its tying of the gospel to a pagan ontology, and make him a free expositor of the NT freely speaking for itself."

Letter from Karl Barth to Bishop Theophil Wurm,
President of the Council of the Evangelical Church in Germany
May 20, 1947

"What do I do? I study. Chiefly the Reformation and everything connected with it."

Letter from Karl Barth to Eduard Thurneysen
January 22, 1922

"The secret things belong to the LORD our God, but the revealed things belong to us and to our children forever …."

Deuteronomy 29:29

# CONTENTS

| | |
|---|---|
| Acknowledgments | xi |
| Abbreviations | xii |
| Preface | xiii |

Introduction
CHRIST, THE GOSPEL, AND THE EVANGELICAL VISION ......... 1

## Part I
## THE REFORMATION AND ITS LEGACY

Chapter 1
MARTIN LUTHER AND THE BIRTH OF THE PROTESTANT
ECCLESIAL VISION ......... 7

Chapter 2
THE *SOLA* BEHIND THE *SOLAS*: THE UNITY OF THE FIVE *SOLAS*
OF THE REFORMATION ......... 29

Chapter 3
KARL BARTH ON LUTHER AND CALVIN AS FATHERS
OF THE CHURCH ......... 55

Chapter 4
THE LAST PROTESTANT: KARL BARTH AND THE CULMINATION
OF THE PROTESTANT ECCLESIAL VISION ......... 77

## Part II
## ECUMENICAL CONVERSATIONS BETWEEN DISTANT
## DESCENDANTS OF THE REFORMATION

Chapter 5
KARL BARTH, CONFESSIONALISM, AND A FREE CHURCH TRADITION ......... 157

Chapter 6
KARL BARTH AND PIETISM: TRACES OF A FAMILY RESEMBLANCE ......... 179

Chapter 7
KARL BARTH AND KIERKEGAARD: UNACKNOWLEDGED
DEBTS TO A LUTHERAN EXISTENTIAL PIETIST                              199

## Part III
## CHURCH AND ACADEMY EVER REFORMING

Chapter 8
THE ASCENSION OF CHRIST AND THE PILGRIM CHURCH                      225

Chapter 9
THE CONFESSIONAL TASK OF THE CHRISTIAN UNIVERSITY                   245

## Part IV
## POSTSCRIPT

Chapter 10
THE AMERICAN EXPERIENCE OF A DARKENING AND
RECEDING PROVIDENCE: THE CIVIL WAR AND
THE UNMAKING OF AN AMERICAN RELIGIOUS SYNTHESIS                     263

Name Index                                                          281
Subject Index                                                       286

# ACKNOWLEDGMENTS

The majority of the essays collected in this volume have been published previously in earlier forms, as indicated below. The author and publisher gratefully acknowledge permission to republish:

"Martin Luther and the Birth of the Protestant Ecclesial Vision" in *Perspectives in Religious Studies* 41 (2014): 257–75.

"The *Sola* behind the *Solas*: The Unity of the Five *Solas* of the Reformation" previously published as "The *Sola* behind the *Solas*: Martin Luther and The Unity and Future of the Five *Solas* of the Reformation" in *Evangelical Quarterly* 90 (2019): 109–31.

"The Reformers as Fathers of the Church: Luther and Calvin in the Thought of Karl Barth" in *Scottish Journal of Theology* 72 (2019): 414–31.

"Karl Barth, Confessionalism, and a Free Church Tradition" previously published as "Karl Barth, Confessionalism, and the Question of Baptist Identity" in *Perspectives in Religious Studies* 45 (2018): 49–67.

"Karl Barth and Pietism: Traces of a Family Resemblance" previously published as "Bringing an Elephant and a Whale into Conversation: Karl Barth and Pietism" in *Karl Barth and the Future of Evangelical Theology.* Ed. C. Winn and J. Drury. Eugene: Cascade Books, 2014. 45–66. Used by permission of Wipf and Stock Publishers. www.wipfandstock.com.

"Karl Barth and Kierkegaard: Unacknowledged Debts to a Lutheran Existential Pietist" previously published as "Søren Kierkegaard and Karl Barth: Reflections on a Relation and a Proposal for Future Investigation" in *International Journal of Systematic Theology* 17 (2015): 296–318.

"The Ascension of Christ and the Pilgrim Church" previously published as "The Church as a Pilgrim People: The *Communio Viatorum* of the Risen and Ascended Christ" in *American Baptist Quarterly* 33 (2014): 326–46.

"The Confessional Task of the Christian University" in *Christian Scholar's Review* 48 (2018): 3–16.

"The American Experience of a Darkening and Receding Providence: The Civil War and the Unmaking of an American Religious Synthesis" in *Cultural Encounters* 9 (2013): 109–29.

# ABBREVIATIONS

| | |
|---|---|
| CD | Karl Barth. *Church Dogmatics*. Ed. Geoffrey W. Bromiley and T.F. Torrance. Four volumes in thirteen parts. Edinburgh: T&T Clark, 1936-77. |
| ChrD | Karl Barth. *Die christliche Dogmatik im Entwurf, Vol. 1: Die Lehre vom Worte Gottes, Prolegomena zur christlichen Dogmatik 1927*. Ed. Gerhard Sauter. Zürich: Theologischer Verlag Zürich, 1982. |
| ET | *English translation* |
| GD | Karl Barth. *The Göttingen Dogmatics: Instruction in the Christian Religion*. Ed. Hannelotte Reiffen, trans. Geoffrey W. Bromiley. Grand Rapids: Eerdmans, 1991. |
| KD | Karl Barth. *Kirchliche Dogmatik*. Four volumes in thirteen parts. Zürich: Evangelischer Verlag, 1932-67. |
| LW | Martin Luther. *Luther's Works*. Ed. Jaroslav Pelikan and Helmut T. Lehmann. Fifty-five volumes. St. Louis and Philadelphia: Concordia and Fortress, 1958-86. |
| nt | note |
| NT | New Testament |
| OT | Old Testament |
| TC | Karl Barth. *Theology and Church: Shorter Writings 1920-1928*. Trans. Louise P. Smith. New York/Evanston: Harper & Row, 1962. |
| Unterricht I | Karl Barth. *Unterricht in der christlichen Religion, Vol. 1: Prolegomena 1924*. Ed. Hannelotte Reiffen. Zürich: Theologischer Verlag Zürich, 1985. |
| Unterricht II | Karl Barth. *Unterricht in der christlichen Religion, Vol. 2: Die Lehre von Gott/Die Lehre vom Menschen 1924/25*. Ed. Hinrich Stoevesandt. Zürich: Theologischer Verlag Zürich, 1990. |
| Unterricht III | Karl Barth. *Unterricht in der christlichen Religion, Vol. 3: Die Lehre von der Versöhnung/Erlösung 1925/26*. Ed. Hinrich Stoevesandt. Zürich: Theologischer Verlag Zürich, 2003. |
| WA | Martin Luther. *Martin Luthers Werke: Kritische Gesammtausgabe*. 112 volumes. Weimar: H. Böhlaus, 1883-2009. |
| WGT | Karl Barth. *The Word of God and Theology*. Trans. Amy Marga. London/New York: T&T Clark/Continuum, 2011. |

## PREFACE

Behind this book stands not only an author but so many others from whom he has received much. I remain indebted to more persons than I can name, but here I express particular appreciation to my colleagues at Truett Theological Seminary and Baylor University, of whom Brian Brewer, Stephen Evans, Barry Harvey, and Ralph Wood deserve special mention. I also wish to thank Hannah Boman, Sam Davidson, Jamie McGregor, Jared Patterson, and Jake Raabe for assistance over the years in research and formatting of these chapters in this and their earlier forms. Finally, I am ever grateful for the loving support and patience of my family. They have endured the costs of these labors as much as I have.

# INTRODUCTION

## Christ, the Gospel, and the Evangelical Vision

For I believe that to the very day of judgment we shall wait in vain for an Evangelical Church which takes itself seriously unless we are prepared to attempt in all modesty to take the risk of being such a Church in our own situation and to the best of our ability.

Karl Barth
*Church Dogmatics* I/1
1932

The essays in this collection are all, in one way or another, an attempt to reflect upon the radical and scandalous particularity of the gospel and examine what an evangelical theology might be for the present in light of its past. To speak of an evangelical theology is to speak of the gospel, and it is in this way, first and primarily, that such a term is used here. To speak of the gospel is to speak of God's gracious salvation that has come in Jesus Christ and in which Christians have been enlivened and awakened by the Holy Spirit. To speak of the gospel is to speak of Christ, and to speak of Christ is to speak of the cross, and to speak of the cross points to our own inclusion in Christ's crucifixion and his righteousness, so that, through Christ's death, his glorious resurrection might become ours as well (Gal. 2:19-20; Phil. 3:8-11). Jesus Christ—crucified and risen—was the ground of the gospel Paul proclaimed, and to know Christ—his death, his sufferings, his resurrection—stood as the goal of its proclamation, and the goal of Paul's own life. This gospel, Paul attests, is the foundation of the church, as well as the commission and content of the church's witness.

Second, to speak of an evangelical theology is to speak of one that takes up this message as it is articulated in Scripture and in faithfulness to the distinct Protestant vision that flows from the Reformation into all of its subsequent tributaries and streams. An evangelical theology, without nostalgia or sentimentality, without apology or defensiveness, but in honest and humble acknowledgment of Protestantism's own failures and weaknesses, looks back to the Reformation not as simple tragedy but necessity, and a necessity not only for the past, but for the present.[1] It asks, without polemical acerbity or ecumenical indifference, what an evangelical witness under the Word of God might be and look like today, what it must teach and confess, and how it should be lived. It asks such questions not only for itself and for the clarification of Protestant identity and existence, but for the sake of the wider church, and, ultimately, for the world. At its best, it displays a graciousness to the multitude of the Reformation's children, for it believes that there is an evangelical vision that, despite their differences and past and present disputes, unites them in the end.[2] It extends graciousness beyond the children of the Reformation because it knows that, without trivializing real disagreements, all Christians bear the name of Christ and are called to live by faith in one God, in hope for the same coming Lord, and, empowered by the Spirit, for love that is to be shared not only with those who bear Christ's name but all who walk this earth. It also knows that the lines marking off such an evangelical vision do not today, if they ever did, fall neatly and exclusively along confessional or ecclesial lines. The essays in this book are therefore evangelical in conviction but offered here in ecumenical goodwill to all. They embrace the particular as the way to the universal, and they therefore hold fast unapologetically to convictions of the Reformation and examine how these are embodied in different figures and traditions that have followed in its wake, even as they offer such things for consideration to those who do not identify this vision as their own.

The chapters that follow are dedicated to thinking along such lines of what it means to speak of an evangelical theology. Outlining an evangelical vision for church and theology for the good of the church as a whole is a significant

1. To speak of the Reformation is not to ignore the complexity of the historical issues surrounding it, including what was, and what was not, new with its appearance. Some of these issues will be revisited in the following chapters. For one examination of Luther's continuity and discontinuity in relation to the medieval past, see Gerhard Müller, "Luther's Transformation of Medieval Thought: Discontinuity and Continuity," in *The Oxford Handbook of Martin Luther's Theology*, ed. Robert Kolb, Irene Dingel, and L'Ubomír Batka (Oxford: Oxford University Press), pp. 105–14. It must be emphasized, however, that the Reformation can neither be dissolved into the Middle Ages nor be simply seen as the inchoate precursor of modernity. For a similar judgment, see George Hunsinger, *Disruptive Grace: Studies in the Theology of Karl Barth* (Grand Rapids: Eerdmans, 2000), p. 285. Hunsinger argues that the "relentless focus on Christ himself as the entire substance of our salvation constitutes nothing less, we may say, than the breakthrough that caused the Reformation" (p. 285).

2. This point should be kept ever before the reader of these essays. As Scott Hendrix noted in commenting on the breakdown of agreement and conversation between Luther and Zwingli at their famous meeting in 1529: "The misfortune of Marburg was not that theologians disagreed, rather that they did not agree to disagree while accepting that they stood on common evangelical ground." See Scott H. Hendrix, *Martin Luther: Visionary Reformer* (New Haven and London: Yale University Press, 2015), p. 207. I would extend this assessment of the misfortune not only to the divisions of the original Reformers but to those that have plagued their children and step-children.

part of the exploration of these chapters and provides them with an underlying unity of purpose amid their diversity of topics and themes as well as undoubted shortcomings. Martin Luther and Karl Barth figure prominently in these essays, for Luther stands as the most prominent figure of the Reformation and provides its earliest expression of an evangelical vision for the church, and Barth, one could argue, gave this theology its most comprehensive and ambitious presentation in recent memory. In this sense, Luther and Barth stand as bookends to the studies here provided, especially in the first section of the book which is on the articulation of this evangelical vision. The second section hopes to display the graciousness earlier mentioned, placing Barth into conversation with Baptists, Pietists, and Kierkegaard. The final division of the book turns from historical to constructive questions, addressing an evangelical vision for the church "on the way" and how such a vision might be reflected within the university. It is hoped that readers will witness the themes and questions that unite the chapters, of which of particular importance are a commitment to the radical particularity of the revelation of Christ as the center of the church and its gospel proclamation, the proper ordering of Christ and the church as well as of a substitutionary and exemplarist christology in which both are requisite but the second exists in subordination to the first, and a recognition that the church ever receives and acknowledges the finished salvation of God in Christ enacted through the Spirit before it confesses this and acts in witness to it. The church thus lives ever in the space between humility and confidence as it lives before the world.

This work follows the guiding commitments that were articulated in an earlier collection of essays entitled *Confessing Christ for Church and World: Studies in Modern Theology*. Those commitments were discussed in the introduction of that volume and will not be repeated here, except to say that, like those essays, these have a two-fold purpose. On one level, most of these essays take Luther, Barth, and other theological movements and figures as their objects of study; they are in this respect exercises in historical theology. But they are studies ultimately not only of "looking at" such figures, but of "looking along" with them to what they themselves were attempting to indicate, which was the revelation and salvation of God in Christ proclaimed by the Spirit's power to and for all people.[3] In this sense, the subjects of these essays, such as Luther and Barth, are not simply objects of study in their own right, but witnesses to something, Someone, greater than themselves.

So while these essays no doubt trade heavily in "looking at" Luther and Barth and a number of other ecclesial figures and movements, and in this respect as essays in historical theology have their own integrity, they ultimately aim to "think

---

3. The understanding of the difference between "looking at" and "looking along" is here drawn from C. S. Lewis—see Lewis, *God in the Dock*, ed. Walter Hooper (Grand Rapids: Eerdmans, 1970/1999), pp. 212–15. For a fuller discussion of the importance of this piece for the essays here included along with the convictions that inform them, see Kimlyn J. Bender, *Confessing Christ for Church and World: Studies in Modern Theology* (Downers Grove: InverVarsity Academic, 2014), pp. 11–18.

along" with such figures and beyond them. As exercises in historical theology, they attempt to follow Barth's own instruction when he observed that "history is made up of living men whose work is handed over defenceless to our understanding and appreciation upon their death. Precisely because of this, they have a claim on our courtesy, a claim that their own concerns should be heard and that they should not be used simply as a means to our ends." He then concluded with a word that gives utterance to the aspirations of the essays of this volume: "History is meant to bear witness to the truth of God, not to our own achievements, so that we must avoid any thought that we already know what they have to say and be prepared to hear something new."[4]

The study of history, for the Christian, is on this account not only one of intellectual rigor and academic responsibility, but one of charity and graciousness toward those who have gone before as members in the church. Such recognition should lead the Christian scholar to a present resolution to exercise both "the highest reason and the fullest faith," in the words of J. B. Lightfoot.[5] Christian scholarship should be a diligent and faithful exercise in service not only to the academy or to a discipline but to Christ, the church, and the world. Correspondingly, the discovery of an evangelical theology is something that the Lord alone can grant, for freely and faithfully to confess the freedom and faithfulness of God is to acknowledge a prevenient divine act to which we can only respond. For this reason, Reformational theology signifies not simply a past period of time or a movement, but an aspiration and, truly, an invocation, for renewal in the gospel is not something that ultimately belongs to humanity but to God. For this reason, Luther never called himself a Reformer nor his movement a Reformation: "He didn't and he couldn't—because 'reformation' is God's ultimate intervention."[6]

Here historical narration gives way to invocation and expectation, as history comes to an end as an academic exercise and points to that which it cannot achieve. That academic exercises might serve a larger purpose is but a hope, but one predicated on the larger hope to which evangelical theology must point, a hope beyond itself, a hope that God will not abandon his church to its own dissolution, that God's Word does not return void but renews and calls forth life from dead things. This, too, is an evangelical word.

---

4. Karl Barth, *Protestant Theology in the Nineteenth Century: Its Background & History*, trans. Brian Cozens and John Bowden (London: SCM, 1972), p. 22.

5. Quoted in J. B. Lightfoot, *The Gospel of St. John: A Newly Discovered Commentary*, ed. Ben Witherington III and Todd D. Still (Downers Grove: InterVarsity, 2015), p. 35. I am thankful to Todd Still for drawing my attention to this quotation.

6. Heiko A. Oberman, *Luther: Man between God and the Devil*, trans. Eileen Walliser-Schwarzbart (New York: Doubleday/Image Books, 1992), p. 79.

: Part I

THE REFORMATION AND ITS LEGACY

## Chapter 1

## MARTIN LUTHER AND THE BIRTH OF THE PROTESTANT ECCLESIAL VISION

The Reformation of the sixteenth century was a time of great upheaval for the church in the West. The early magisterial Reformers such as Luther, Zwingli, and Calvin called not simply for the church's moral renewal but for a thorough-going re-formation of some of its central theological convictions, particularly in the area of soteriology.[1] It has been said that in effect what the Reformers did was to trade Augustine's doctrine of the church for his doctrine of grace.[2]

Whether or not this oversimplifies a complex movement of reform and renewal, it is nonetheless true that the energy of the Reformers, and Luther particularly, was directed toward soteriology, and that this soteriological concern was no longer simply set within a larger ecclesiological matrix, but in no small part set against it. In short, and lightly skimming over a complex history of Luther's disputes with Silvester Prierias (1518), Thomas Cajetan (1518), and Johann Eck (1519), Luther came to proffer a new theology not within, but against, a prevailing ecclesiology, providing a nascent formal critical principle (*sola Scriptura*, i.e., the Scripture principle) and an explicit material norm (justification by faith alone, i.e., *sola*

---

1. Calls for the church's moral reform and to address papal excesses and other grievances pre-dated Luther by at least a hundred years, evident in the complaints registered against such papal decadence and overreach at the Council of Constance (1414–18). The Council itself was convened to overcome the papal schism following the Avignon papal exile of the late fourteenth century. Such complaints continued on in the next century as expressed by theologians, ecclesiastical leaders, and various humanists. Such calls for moral reform were overshadowed only with the arrival of the more substantial and extensive reform movement launched by Luther, itself foreshadowed by those attempted by John Wycliffe (1320–84) and John Hus (1369–1415). For the general tenor and events of this period, see Steve Ozment, *The Age of Reform 1250–1550: An Intellectual and Religious History of Late Medieval and Reformation Europe* (New Haven: Yale University Press, 1980), pp. 135–222; and Carlos Eire, *Reformations: The Early Modern World, 1450–1650* (New Haven: Yale University Press, 2016), pp. 1–129.

2. "The Reformation, inwardly considered, was just the ultimate triumph of Augustine's doctrine of grace over Augustine's doctrine of the church." See B. B. Warfield, *Calvin and Augustine* (Philadelphia: Presbyterian and Reformed Publishing, 1956), p. 332; quoted in Diarmaid MacCulloch, *The Reformation: A History* (New York: Penguin, 2003), p. 111.

*fide*, through grace alone, i.e., *sola gratia*) that were used to test and criticize an ecclesiology that, in its teaching on indulgences and other meritorious actions had, in Luther's estimation, twisted the gospel and usurped Christ through papal presumption. Moreover, it had equated obedience to the pope with obedience to Christ such that the voice of the latter was subsumed into the voice of the church itself.[3] In the judgment of the Reformers, the conflation of the voice of Christ and the voice of the church, as well as the subsuming of the salvific action of Christ into the sacramental and penitential practices of the church without remainder so that Christ's action and the church's vicarious action became indistinguishable, entailed that humanity had joined together and, even worse, confused, what God had carefully distinguished.[4] Luther's reform movement opposed such ecclesial presumption and thereby pushed hard against the two pillars of the late medieval church, that is, the mass (with its attendant doctrine of purgatory and correlative understanding of indulgences and meritorious works), and papal primacy (with its incipient understanding of papal supremacy and infallibility).[5]

## *The Word of God as Critical, Constructive, and Constitutive*

What Luther in effect accomplished by setting Scripture over against key components of medieval church tradition and papal primacy was never fully explicated by him in any systematic or comprehensive way, nor did he develop a doctrine of the church in any kind of programmatic and formal manner. Luther's ecclesiological thought was developed as a response to the concrete events of the time and directed against specific abuses in the church of his day.[6] Nevertheless, the debate over Scripture and tradition had deep and far-reaching consequences. This debate, itself played out concretely in a two-fold form as a debate between

---

3. The word "church" here is used to signify what this term signified in sixteenth-century Catholicism, namely, the teaching magisterium of the papacy, in its essence, along with the hierarchical collection of bishops and priests. One of the difficulties of comparing this conception of the church with that of Luther is that the Catholicism of the time and Luther thought of the term along two very different lines—for Catholicism, the church was defined by its essence as a papal hierarchy of bishops and priests, whereas for Luther, the church was the gathered people of God. This distinction will become evident below.

4. Nevertheless, it must be said that for Luther, specifically, Christ's work and the sacraments were not separated, even as they were distinguished. The sacraments remained for Luther, as for Calvin, the means for receiving the Word (or promises) of God. Luther thus replaced the ecclesial framework of the sacraments with a christological one, so that Christ and *sola fide* become the replacements for an ecclesial sacerdotalism, even as Luther retained a central place for sacramental, and even penitential, practices.

5. For a discussion of the centrality of these two pillars, see MacCulloch, *Reformation*, pp. 10-34.

6. The closest thing to a developed and sustained discussion of ecclesiology from Luther may be found in his work *On the Councils and the Church* (1539). See LW 41: pp. 5-178.

Scripture and the contemporary soteriological practices of indulgences and meritorious works and masses on one hand, and between Scripture and the ecclesiological questions of papal primacy, supremacy, and infallibility on the other hand, was, in fact, the (re-)establishment of a relation between Christ and the church that not only had explicit implications for ecclesiology, but also was predicated upon significant though often implicit convictions that Luther only occasionally and only inchoately articulated. In short, the Reformation discovery as played out in ecclesiology involved a rediscovery of the irreversible relation of Christ and the church (in any sense, i.e., whether defined as hierarchy or people of God), a relation in which Christ could not be subsumed into the church but retained a living voice not only within but also over it. This refusal to equate the authority and voice of Christ with the authority and voice of the papacy was, in turn, the Reformation's attack upon the second pillar of the medieval church.

This critical principle for testing doctrine and the church's tradition, as well as papal claims, also had soteriological significance, again tied up with christological convictions. Luther's understanding of Christ and the Word of Scripture entailed that the work of salvation could not be seen as extending from Christ to the church in a straightforward manner such that the salvific agency of the former was simply extended and assimilated within the latter, the church seen as a steward, administrator, and mediator of the grace of Christ in the world, a continuation of his own salvific agency and activity. Luther's discovery of justification within Scripture was constituted by the conviction that this justification came by faith alone through grace alone, and this itself was predicated upon the fact that salvation came from Christ alone (*sola Christus*) and his finished work that could only be received in faith as a gift of God's gracious action, who alone was to be credited with its accomplishment (*sola Deo gloria*). And if all this was so, the authority over the salvation of souls could not be seen as vested in the papacy, for as Luther consistently maintained, Christ *alone* is the head of the church, and this christological conviction had significant implications for the church's soteriological teaching and sacramental practice. This was Luther's attack upon the first pillar of the mass and its attendant sacramental, sacerdotal, and soteriological convictions.[7]

Against, and in place of, both of these pillars—that of the mass and its attendant convictions and practices of indulgences and penitential excess, and that of papal primacy and supremacy—Luther set the Word of God, the dynamic and unhindered reality of God's voice expressed in law and in gospel, in conviction and assurance, both of these framed by and constitutive of the message of the justice and mercy of God demonstrated in the cross of Christ. This reality of God's Word was found

---

7. In the *Smalcald Articles*, summarizing his criticisms of the mass and its attendant abuses, Luther stated: "In summary, we cannot tolerate and must condemn what the mass is, what has resulted from it, and what is connected to it, so that we may retain the holy sacrament in purity and with certainty and may use and receive it with faith according to the institution of Christ." See *The Book of Concord*, ed. Robert Kolb and Timothy J. Wengert, trans. Charles Arand et al. (Minneapolis: Fortress, 2000), p. 306. For Luther, the basis for knowledge of this institution was of course Scripture.

definitively in Scripture but could not be flatly or unqualifiedly identified with Scripture itself, and it was best understood as arising from and discerned within its written form but quintessentially and properly identified and located in its public proclamation.[8] Indeed, when Luther thought of the Word of God, he prioritized the form of proclamation, though this was never separated from and always implicitly included its grounding in Scripture, its written form. Therefore, to sum up this point: against and in place of a sacramental and penitential system entrusted to the stewardship of the church, which, as the practice of indulgences and the interdict demonstrated, was seen as invested within the jurisdiction of papal authority and dispensation, Luther set the Word of God in Scripture and proclamation, placing this Word at the center of the church's liturgical life and doctrinal confession.

The Word of God, and particularly its existence as Scripture, thus served a *critical function* for Luther's ecclesiological thought. The critical function of Scripture is readily evident in how it was wielded to criticize and correct what Luther took to be abuses and indeed heresies in the Roman church. So Luther could assert: "Scripture alone is the true lord and master of all writings and doctrine on earth."[9] In light of their deep forays into Scripture, Luther, along with Zwingli and Calvin, had a very dim view of the predominant image of the church as the steward of a treasury of merits to be dispensed at papal and priestly discretion. Everything that undergirded such a conception of the church—whether the practice of dispensing indulgences, or the administration of a sacramental system that gave intelligibility to a portrayal of the Eucharist as a meritorious sacrifice and that granted credibility to the practice of masses for the dead, or any other meritorious actions on the part of the church as a whole or individuals within it—was, for the Reformers, anathema. Furthermore, Scripture also came to be the critical principle not only to evaluate and condemn specific papal claims and traditions, but to call into question the very notion of a divinely instituted papacy, as well as any strong forms of ecclesial hierarchy, sacerdotalism, and separation of clergy from the laity. So Luther stated in his treatise *The Sacrament of Penance* (1519) that all Christians, and not only bishops and priests, are authorized to pronounce the assurance of pardon.[10]

---

8. Speaking of the Word, Luther provided the following definition in *The Freedom of a Christian*: "The Word is the gospel of God concerning his Son, who was made flesh, suffered, rose from the dead, and was glorified through the Spirit who sanctifies. To preach Christ means to feed the soul, make it righteous, set it free, and save it, provided it believes the preaching" (LW 31: p. 346).

9. LW 32: pp. 11–12; cf. LW 26: pp. 57–8; LW 34: p. 284.

10. "It follows in addition that in the sacrament of penance and forgiveness of guilt a pope or bishop does nothing more than the lowliest priest. Indeed where there is no priest, each individual Christian—even a woman or child—does as much. For any Christian can say to you, 'God forgives you your sins, in the name,' etc., and if you can accept that word with a confident faith, as though God were saying it to you, then in that same faith you are surely absolved. So completely does everything depend on faith in God's word. No pope, bishop, or priest can do anything to your faith" (LW 35: pp. 12–13). This anti-sacerdotalism was accompanied by a rejection of the superiority of spiritual vocations over other vocations, a rejection that in the end effectively eliminated monastic vocations in Protestant understandings of the church.

In this sense, all are in principle able to proclaim the Word of God. Such an understanding had far-reaching effects for conceptions of the ordained ministry.

While Luther traced back his thought on the general priesthood of all believers to the fact that all Christians are priests based upon the external sign of baptism and their inner faith, it is important to see that such a view can take on significance only in light of an understanding of the church where Christ's agency is not seen to be transferred to a select agent or group of agents in terms of a papal vicar or episcopal or priestly hierarchy. Hence even the strong notions of the common spiritual priesthood of all believers in Luther's thought can be traced back, even if not directly, to particular christological convictions that Christ alone is the head of the church, and that this voice of Christ is heard in the proclamation of the Word of God as found in Holy Scripture. Luther thus could equate the voice of God, the voice of Christ, and the testimony of the authors of Scripture.[11]

With Luther we therefore see for the first time in church history a significant and far-reaching movement that concedes that Scripture and church authority cannot, in some cases, be reconciled. In this event, the first must take precedence and correct the second.[12] A corollary of this conviction was that Luther rejected late medieval Catholic conceptions of papal and ecclesial authority and infallibility. In turn, the elevation of the Scripture principle in Protestantism explicitly set forth the positive affirmation that Scripture is the ultimate authority for the church, over not only present papal authority but also past councils. But it also included the negative affirmation that the church itself can err, and when it does so, it must be corrected by Scripture. The discovery of the Scripture principle for Luther was predicated upon both sides of this equation, both the positive affirmation and its negative connotations. It was this negative side of the equation, this critical function of Scripture, this admission that Scripture and tradition may at times irreconcilably conflict rather than exist in a harmonious peace, that was new with the Reformation and Luther's theology specifically.[13]

---

11. See, for instance, Luther's *An Order of Mass and Communion for the Church at Wittenberg* (1523), where the words of God, the institution and law of Christ, and the testimony of the gospels and Paul in Scripture are used almost interchangeably and set over against the authority of a church council (LW 53: pp. 34–6). This ecclesiology of Christ as the sole head of the church, in which the organization of the church should foster rather than hinder the Word of God, was one that Luther shared with John Hus—see Martin Wernisch, "Luther and Medieval Reform Movements, Particularly the Hussites," in *The Oxford Handbook of Martin Luther's Theology*, ed. Robert Kolb, Irene Dingel, and L'Ubomír Batka (Oxford: Oxford University Press, 2014), pp. 62–70 (64).

12. Bernhard Lohse, *Martin Luther's Theology: Its Historical and Systematic Development*, trans. and ed. Roy A. Harrisville (Minneapolis: Fortress, 1999), p. 103. As Lohse states, this is already evident in the *Ninety-Five Theses* of Luther. Lohse claims that Luther was the beginning of a critical tradition within the church that began a new age: "Never before had a theologian dealt so critically with other positions as did Luther in the sixteenth century. The Reformation first made clear that theology exercises a critical function for the church's teaching and preaching" (ibid., p. 9). For Luther's understanding of Scripture as the norm for this critical function, see also ibid., pp. 187–95.

13. Lohse, *Martin Luther's Theology*, pp. 187–8.

As Luther's works progressed, this principle was accompanied by an increasing criticism of the papacy and limitations placed upon its power and authority. While Luther could end his 1517 treatise *Disputation against Scholastic Theology* with the appeal that in it "we wanted to say and believe we have said nothing that is not in agreement with the Catholic church and the teachers of the church," this conciliatory and submissive tone would lessen and give way to invective as Scripture and the church's tradition and magisterial office were no longer seen as in harmonious agreement but in frequent opposition.[14] When considering the abuses of the sacrament of the Lord's Supper and the attacks of his opponents in the *Babylonian Captivity of the Church* (1520), Luther retorted: "Why do they flaunt the authority of the church and the power of the pope in my face? These do not annul the words of God and the testimony of the truth."[15]

The differing views regarding Scripture, tradition, and papal authority during this time can readily be witnessed when Luther is compared to his Roman opponent Silvester Prierias. Prierias opposed Luther and his theology with four basic propositions, the third being the following: "Whoever does not hold to the doctrine of the Roman church and to the pope as the infallible rule of faith, from which also Holy Scripture derives its power and authority, is a heretic."[16] Luther would effectively reverse the place that Scripture takes in this statement with those of the Roman church and the pope. Heresy, for Luther, was not based upon failure to adhere to the church and the papacy but upon failure to follow Scripture. In effect, and contrary to Prierias, it was not the papacy that established the authority of Scripture, but Scripture that was the only normative rule of faith and which established the power and authority of the papacy. In time Luther came to doubt whether it did this at all.

This is not to say that Luther quickly dismissed the papacy *en toto*, but as time wore on, he came to deny its divine ordination, even if he continued to appeal to its specific authority as a representative of the church.[17] Moreover, no longer could Christian faith be equated with membership within the Catholic Church. Luther's reevaluation of the Hussites required that he reconsider the meaning of salvation and ecclesiology, as well as the relationship between them. As Lohse

---

14. LW 31: p. 16.
15. LW 36: p. 22.
16. Quoted in Lohse, *Martin Luther's Theology*, p. 108. Prierias' argumentation for papal supremacy and infallibility was followed and echoed by Cajetan in his debate with Luther, which Luther recounts in his comments on the Augsburg disputation (LW 31: pp. 262–3).
17. As Luther stated in the *Smalcald Articles*: "That the pope is not the head of all Christendom 'by divine right' or on the basis of God's Word, because that belongs only to the one who is called Jesus Christ. Instead, the pope is only bishop, or pastor, of the church at Rome and of those who willingly or through a human institution (that is, through secular authority) have joined themselves to him in order to be Christians alongside him as a brother and companion but not under him as a lord" (*Book of Concord*, 307). See also Lohse, *Martin Luther's Theology*, pp. 121–2.

states: "Though some outside the Western church were excommunicated, in some respects they could more properly be called Christian than members of the Catholic church. What is 'Christian' could not flatly be judged by membership in a church, but rather by Holy Scripture and faith."[18] For Luther this truth deepened as he came to conclude that not only the papacy, but councils as well, could err and contradict one another.[19]

Hence, for both soteriology *and* ecclesiology, the most accurate statement of Luther's position (and one echoed by the Reformation at large) was that Christ was Lord of the church, and that this entailed that the church was not the steward but the servant of the gospel, not Christ's vicar upon the earth in his absence but the gathered fellowship brought into existence through his presence in Word and sacrament. In Luther's terms, *sola Christus*, Christ alone, was the head of the church, its only agent of salvation, and the ultimate voice of authority it must heed. Furthermore, Christ's voice was not to be found today in the magisterium, but in Scripture and in its proclamation through the power of the Spirit. Therefore, while Luther never entirely renounced the papacy as a human institution, he came to renounce its claim to divine right as a presumption that in effect set it against rather than under the authority of Christ and Scripture.[20]

The Word of God in Scripture was for Luther not only the critical principle for testing the contemporary church's teaching and practices, but also the foundation for establishing and reforming the church's faith, worship, and conduct along proper lines. As such, Scripture served as the *constructive norm* for laying down the pattern for the church's confession, liturgy, and life. Indeed, it was the ultimate norm for such things, and this is another aspect of how Scripture shaped not only Luther's soteriological but ecclesiological thought.[21] To Luther's mind, it was precisely because the Word had lost this central and normative place that the problems of the church had arisen, including not only those of its teaching

---

18. Lohse, *Martin Luther's Theology*, p. 126.

19. For instance, not only the wrongful execution of Hus by the Council of Constance, but also the conflicting sacramental instruction between the Council of Constance and the Council of Basel regarding the withholding of the cup from the laity, demonstrated this for Luther. See Luther's comments in *The Babylonian Captivity of the Church* (LW 36: p. 27).

20. See Luther's *On the Papacy in Rome against the Most Celebrated Romanist in Leipzig* (1520) (LW 39: pp. 55–104).

21. Luther's understanding of how Scripture limits and prescribes what can and cannot be retained from the mass and the Catholic liturgy was more conservative and moderate than that of Zwingli, a point succinctly summarized by Justo Gonzalez, who writes that whereas Luther "was willing to retain all traditional uses that did not contradict the Bible," Zwingli "insisted that all that had no explicit scriptural support must be rejected." See Gonzalez, *The Story of Christianity: The Early Church to the Present Day* (Peabody: Prince Press, 2001), p. 50.

on salvation, but also those of its liturgical life, and for Luther, these were not unrelated. In his brief work *Concerning the Order of Public Worship* (1523), Luther wrote:

> Three serious abuses have crept into the service. First, God's Word has been silenced, and only reading and singing remain in the churches. This is the worst abuse. Second, when God's Word had been silenced such a host of un-Christian fables and lies, in legends, hymns, and sermons were introduced that it is horrible to see. Third, such divine service was performed as a work whereby God's grace and salvation might be won. As a result faith disappeared.

In contrast to these abuses, Luther insisted that the Word of God proclaimed, as based upon Scripture, should be placed at the center of the church's life. As he concluded: "Therefore, when God's Word is not preached, one had better neither sing nor read, or even come together."[22] It should come as no surprise, then, that the Reformers set the preaching of the Word alongside, if not over, the sacraments as the center of the church's identity, worship, and life.[23]

But Scripture had greater significance still. Not only was it the means for testing the doctrine and practices of the church (thus serving a *critical function*), and not only did it serve as the norm and source for right teaching and practice (thus a *constructive purpose*), but Scripture as the context from which the dynamic Word of God arose—in all of its revelatory and exhortatory power, and as the ground and content of gospel proclamation—was also the *constitutive basis* for the church. For it is by the Word of God proclaimed, as empowered by the Spirit, that the church is called into existence and through which it is constituted. Once again, this does not entail that the dynamic Word of God for Luther was simply equated with the words of Scripture *simpliciter*. But neither could it be divorced from Scripture, either, for the message of the gospel came to us through this written testimony of Christ which contains and transmits his Word to us.[24] For Luther, Christ himself

---

22. LW 53: p. 11.

23. LW 39: p. 314. That the Word of the gospel took precedence over the physical elements even *within* the sacraments also held for Luther. For instance, as Luther declared already in *The Babylonian Captivity of the Church* in 1520: "We may learn from this that in every promise of God two things are presented to us, the word and the sign, so that we are to understand the word to be the testament, but the sign to be the sacrament. Thus, in the mass, the word of Christ is the testament, and the bread and wine are the sacrament. And as there is greater power in the word than in the sign, so there is greater power in the testament than in the sacrament; for a man can have and use the word or testament apart from the sign or sacrament" (LW 36: p. 44). Some other later separatist Protestant groups more strongly privileged the preaching of the Word *over* the sacraments.

24. For a brief synopsis of Luther's dialectical understanding of the relation of the Word of God and Scripture, see Denis R. Janz, *The Westminster Handbook to Martin Luther* (Louisville: Westminster John Knox, 2010), pp. 14–19; for an extended investigation, see Werner Führer, *Das Wort Gottes in Luthers Theologie* (Göttingen: Vandenhoeck & Ruprecht, 1984).

spoke with saving efficacy through his Word, a Word that the church could proclaim but not claim to control. It was through this Word of Christ enlivened by the Spirit that faith was awakened.[25] Thus for Luther the church could be defined both in relation to the Word and in relation to the faith of those within it. Luther asserted with regard to the former:

> Now, wherever you hear or see this word preached, believed, professed, and lived, do not doubt that the true *ecclesia sancta catholica*, "a Christian holy people" must be there, even though their number is very small. For God's word "shall not return empty," Isaiah 55[:11], but must have at least a fourth or a fraction of the field. And even if there were no other sign than this alone, it would still suffice to prove that a Christian, holy people must exist there, for God's word cannot be without God's people, and conversely, God's people cannot be without God's word.[26]

With regard to the latter, the faith of the people within the church as added to the Word, Luther defined the church in terms of this relation, stating in the *Smalcald Articles* that the reality of the church was apparent even to a seven-year-old child, who knew that the church is "holy believers and 'the little sheep who hear the voice of their shepherd,'" whose holiness does not exist in external adornments, but in "the Word of God and true faith."[27]

It should not be surprising then that Luther defined the church not in geographic or institutional terms such as a hierarchy of pope and bishops, but as a Christian community [*Gemeine*] or a "holy Christian people" [*ein heilige Christenheit*].[28] Again, for Luther this definition of the church is closely related to Christ as its head:

> I believe that there is on earth a holy little flock and community of pure saints under one head, Christ. It is called together by the Holy Spirit in one faith, mind,

---

25. As put in Luther's "Larger Catechism": "Neither you nor I could ever know anything about Christ, or believe in him and receive him as Lord, unless these were offered to us and bestowed on our hearts through the preaching of the gospel by the Holy Spirit. The work is finished and completed; Christ has acquired and won the treasure for us by his sufferings, death, and resurrection, etc. But if the work remained hidden so that no one knew of it, it would have been all in vain, all lost. In order that this treasure might not remain buried but be put to use and enjoyed, God has caused the Word to be *published and proclaimed*, in which he has given the Holy Spirit to offer and apply to us this treasure, this redemption" (*Book of Concord*, p. 436; emphasis added). And the reverse seems to hold as well for Luther: "For where Christ is not preached, there is no Holy Spirit to create, call, and gather the Christian church, apart from which no one can come to the Lord Christ" (ibid., p. 436). In this quotation, we see not only the close relation of Christ, Word, and Spirit in Luther's thought, but also the supremacy and finality of Christ's salvific agency that is set over against the ongoing existence of the church, which itself exists solely as a recipient, rather than mediator, of such salvific action.
26. LW 41: p. 150.
27. *Book of Concord*, pp. 324–5.
28. "The Larger Catechism" in *Book of Concord*, p. 437; cf. also LW 41: pp. 143–4.

and understanding .... I was brought into it by the Holy Spirit and incorporated into it through the fact that I have heard and still hear God's Word, which is the beginning point for entering it.[29]

But the later critique of individualism, to which this description may appear to give occasion, has no real traction at this point or elsewhere in Luther's thought, however much it may fit some later Protestant conceptions of the church. For Luther, the faith of the individual, though a necessary part of the church, cannot be abstracted from the community, for the means by which such faith is awakened and enlivened are within, though not under the control of, the community of faith. As Luther asserts: "Outside this Christian community, however, where there is no gospel, there is also no forgiveness, and hence there also can be no holiness. Therefore, all who would seek to merit holiness through their works rather than through the gospel and the forgiveness of sin have expelled and separated themselves from this community."[30]

### *The Evangelical Understanding of the Church under the Lordship of Christ*

As has been noted above, Luther never developed the relation of Christ, Scripture, and church in a systematic fashion, as his works are almost entirely occasional in nature, addressing the particular questions and immediate issues of his late medieval context. Moreover, it is a common observation that Luther did not write systematic theology, and some have gone so far as to say that Luther's theology calls any such enterprise into question.[31] That Luther was not a systematic thinker is of course true. Furthermore, it is also the case that Luther and his followers often addressed issues in a predominantly critical rather than constructive manner. This fact is readily evident in the very brief section on the church in the *Augsburg Confession* as compared over against the extensive critical engagement of what its authors perceived as abuses and errors of the Roman Catholic Church regarding

---

29. "The Larger Catechism" in *Book of Concord*, pp. 437-8.

30. *Book of Concord*, p. 438. Lohse writes: "In Luther's quest for a gracious God, the individual may be articulated in a new way, but the individualism often declared to be typically Protestant is absent. According to Luther, one may be a Christian only in the fellowship of the church. This does not mean that the church mediates salvation, but it does mean that Jesus Christ has not merely redeemed individuals but called a new people to his discipleship. The church is thus the new people of God or, in another figure, the body of Christ. The individual is set within this fellowship by the message of the gospel. It was inconceivable to Luther that one could be a Christian without being connected to the church" (*Martin Luther's Theology*, p. 281).

31. See, for instance, Oswald Bayer, *Martin Luther's Theology: A Contemporary Interpretation*, trans. Thomas H. Trapp (Grand Rapids: Eerdmans, 2008), p. xv.

matters such as sacramental practice, clerical celibacy, papal claims, and episcopal power, among other such things.³²

Yet while Luther's theology is occasional, complex, and thereby cannot and should not simplistically be reduced down to a single central concept, this reality does not entail that it did not contain a relatively coherent and distinctive theological vision.³³ Nor should the fact that it underwent a distinctive development (which must be appreciated) be seen to undermine its thematic coherence centered around a number of central enduring convictions. Certainly these did not spring *de novo* from Luther's early discovery of his understanding of justification. But his thought is better understood as the development of a committed theological and ecclesial position than a series of circuitous reversals and intractable paradoxes. This remark is not meant to deny real and significant tensions in Luther's thought witnessed in such development.³⁴ Nor does it overlook that these convictions may not have always been consistently followed.³⁵ Yet such tensions should not cause us

---

32. *Book of Concord*, pp. 60–103. The German text of the famous definition of the church in the Augsburg Confession states that the church is the "assembly of all believers among whom the gospel is purely preached and the holy sacraments are administered according to the gospel" (*Book of Concord*, p. 42). The Latin text states, "The church is the assembly of saints in which the gospel is taught purely and the sacraments are administered rightly" (p. 43).

33. Bayer states: "Luther's theology is too lively and too complex to be summarized by a single concept" (*Martin Luther's Theology*, p. xvii). Bayer himself nevertheless posits the dynamic relationship between law and gospel to be "the chromosomal structure within every cell of Luther's theology" (p. xvii).

34. One famous example of this tension is of course that in his battles against the hard objectivism of Roman ecclesiology, Luther emphasized the spiritual nature of the church and the importance of faith. When, however, Luther later argued against those who abandoned almost all such objectivism and sacramental efficacy, Luther emphasized the external means of grace and the objectivity of sacramental action against what he took to be mistaken appeals to internal faith. The former is readily evident in his 1520 treatise *The Babylonian Captivity of the Church* on the Lord's Supper, whereas the second is evident in his debate with the Anabaptists on the question of baptism in his 1528 treatise *Concerning Rebaptism*. This tension was famously expressed as that between "Spirit versus structure" by Jaroslav Pelikan, and more recently as the tension between "institutional positivism" on one hand and "spiritualism" on the other hand. For the former, see Pelikan, *Spirit Versus Structure: Luther and the Institutions of the Church* (New York: Harper & Row, 1968); for the latter, see Janz, *Westminster Handbook*, p. 23. Janz notes that Luther simply failed consistently to apply this distinction between "spiritual, internal Christendom" and "physical, external Christendom." Another parallel and closely related tension is that between the visibility and invisibility of the church in Luther's thought (see Janz, *Westminster Handbook*, p. 25). Another correlative tension is seen in Luther's ambivalent and various answers as to whether the Roman Catholic church is, or is not, a true church (ibid., pp. 25–6).

35. For instance, it is questionable that Luther followed the principle of *sola Scriptura* without exception, with a lapse evident when he fell back upon tradition in his argument with the Anabaptists on the practice of baptism (LW 40: pp. 256–7; see also Janz, *Westminster Handbook*, pp. 15–16).

to make the mistake of denying the existence of this Protestant ecclesial vision, nor to discount it because it may have existed more as an ideal to be striven after than as a reality consistently followed. Moreover, that this vision came to exist within different traditions requires that we of course not ignore the real and significant variations in which it was embodied (for instance, the different Lutheran and Reformed confessions), but neither should this fact cause us to deny its ability to unite such confessions under a common overarching ecclesial perspective with common convictions and commitments, regardless of how great the differences may have been in regard to a number of doctrinal matters such as the understanding of the sacraments (e.g., questions of eucharistic presence) and church government.

For Luther's ecclesiology, if we can call it such, was not in the end simply a diatribe against contemporary abuses, proffering solely a critical and prophetic rebuke of a tradition, a rebuke that offers little of constructive value or promise. Certainly for Luther, as for the other original Reformers, ecclesiological thought was predominantly critical rather than constructive, as we have noted. Yet there were, nevertheless, a number of key convictions that shaped a coherent picture of the church, even if underdeveloped and at times not always consistently practiced. It is therefore appropriate to speak of a Protestant, or Reformation, vision of the church, and one shaped by a few key convictions interlocking one with another.

The chief of these convictions, and the one that seems to lie behind them all, is christological in nature, or perhaps more accurately, Christo-ecclesiological. This chief conviction is that Christ is the Lord and head of the church, and as such, his salvific agency and teaching authority cannot be handed off to or subsumed into a priestly sacramental system or papal teaching office. That Christ is head of the church entails that his lordship continues to be exercised in the present. For Luther, as well as for the other Reformers, this was the case as Christ ruled the church through his Word and Spirit. It was the Word that served as the concrete critical principle by which the church was to test its own doctrine and practice, as well as the constructive norm according to which the church was to order its teaching, confession, worship, and life. Furthermore, the Word was the means by which the church was called into existence, for it was the proclamation of the Word of Christ through the Spirit that constituted the people of God and called individuals to faith within it, as Christ was joined to his body through the Spirit.[36] In short, the church could be simply defined as the people who hear the Word of God and who have been awakened to faith by it, as witnessed above.[37] The Word was thus the basis for the church's teaching and the center of its liturgical life.

---

36. Not only did Luther emphasize the Lordship of Christ over the church, but Christ as the head of the church lived and existed with his body. In other words—and this is crucial—Luther not only distinguished Christ from the church, carefully preserving the priority of the first as lord of the church and sole source and agent of salvation, but he also emphasized that Christ as head existed with his ecclesial body. Yet while Luther could speak of the unity of Christ as head with his body, this never was for him an undifferentiated unity. See LW 39: p. 76.

37. Though for the magisterial Reformers, this included not only those awakened to faith, but also their children, who in turn could be proper recipients of baptism. This of course set them apart from the Anabaptists and later Baptists.

Therefore what Luther and the other Reformers presented was not simply a critique of contemporary ecclesial and salvific abuses, but a radically re-formed theology of the church and of salvation, and one which, for all of its emphasis upon soteriology over ecclesiology, was in fact not the trading of the second for the first, but a new picture of their relationship. The Reformation did not just present a different notion of justification (such that, were this question settled, the Reformation would effectively be "over"). Nor was it simply a reactionary ecclesiology that served a solely critical function but provided no real constructive alternative to the Catholic one. What one sees in the Reformation, rather, is a rediscovery that extends beyond soteriology and ecclesiology to a deeper discovery of christology, namely, that Christ is not absent from the world since the ascension but present to it through the Word proclaimed in the power of the Spirit.[38] For this reason, his voice cannot be replaced in the present with that of the magisterium and his salvific action divested from him and invested and subsumed into a sacramental system that distributes his merits under the church's stewardship, management, and dispensation. More than simply a reactionary protest against sacramental and other abuses (for instance, the controversy of withholding the cup from the laity), what the Protestant Reformation presented was a positive vision for ecclesial life, one that was, without question, developed against a medieval conception, yet one that need not exist only in dependence upon it. The critical element of this vision was the claim that Christ was not simply absent in ascension, but present in the Spirit through the Word, and thus the church could not see itself as his vicar upon the earth in matters of authoritative teaching or in matters of salvific agency. These two pillars had to fall, the Reformers believed, not simply because they were historical abuses and unfortunate examples of ecclesial pride and presumption, but because they undercut the lordship of Christ as the church's singular Savior and Lord and betrayed the heart of the gospel.

Should this claim itself be seen as overreaching, an over-systematization of Luther's scattered and occasional ecclesiological concerns, one need only consider Luther's Open Letter to Pope Leo X affixed to the beginning of his treatise *The Freedom of the Christian* (1520). After setting the authority of the Word of God over against the Roman curia, Luther refused to acknowledge "fixed rules for the interpretation of the Word of God, since the Word of God, which teaches freedom in all other matters, must not be bound (2 Tim. 2:9)."[39] Then, having denied that the pope is "lord of the world" possessing "power over heaven, hell, and purgatory" and having rejected the claims that the pope has an authority that must be recognized for one to be a Christian, Luther stated the following:

---

38. In this sense, the position of Luther, and of Calvin, can rightly be said to be grounded in an "exegetical Christology" of *soli Christo* more fundamental even than *sola fide* and *sola scriptura* themselves, and that which grounds and defines them. See Alister E. McGrath and Darren C. Marks, *The Blackwell Companion to Protestantism* (Malden, MA: Blackwell Publishing, 2004/2007), pp. 6–7.

39. LW 31: pp. 341–2.

See how different Christ is from his successors, although they all would wish to be his vicars. I fear that most of them have been too literally his vicars. A man is a vicar only when his superior is absent. If the pope rules, while Christ is absent and does not dwell in his heart, what else is he but a vicar of Christ? What is the church under such a vicar but a mass of people without Christ? Indeed, what is such a vicar but an antichrist and an idol? How much more properly did the apostles call themselves servants of the present Christ and not vicars of an absent Christ?[40]

Once again, it would be easy to see here simply a reaction against current ecclesiological practice and papal abuses, itself marked by polemical excess. But what is truly offered is a nascent but nonetheless positive ecclesiological vision, one predicated upon the strong christological notions that Christ is not absent from, but present to, the church. As such, he remains the sole agent and source of salvation and singular teacher of truth, both effected in the present time of his ascension by his action through his Word made effective through the power of the Spirit. These two central convictions, namely, that Christ is present, and not absent, and that Christ alone is the head of the church (so that the church cannot take his place in the teaching office or in salvific action), are at the core of this vision. In other words, at its heart is the realization that the relation between Christ and the church is an asymmetrical and irreversible one. Once such an understanding of *sola Christus* is understood, the other convictions of the Reformation fall into place: (1) *sola Scriptura*—Christ's living voice present and active through the Spirit coming through his authoritative witness in Scripture to awaken faith and teach the church, such that tradition is the echo and response to this divine voice, and not the voice itself, and thus tradition can have a relative and limited, rather than parallel or equal, authority with Scripture; (2) *sola gratia*—grace as a free and unmerited application of Christ's sacrifice and its benefits to us through his Word and Spirit effected and preeminently witnessed in the preaching of the gospel; and (3) *sola fide*—the church and the believer always the recipient and not the agent of such grace and salvation, the church being the servant rather than the steward of grace, its witness rather than its mediator.

It is easy to focus on Protestant disagreements among the original Reformers and especially their followers without seeing how much agreement actually was shared on the central tenets of this vision. While disagreements about sacramental practice proliferated (e.g., those between Luther and Zwingli at Marburg in 1529, and the differences between both of them and Calvin), and while the extent and nature of what and how the reform was to be carried out produced tragic and unresolved debates on particulars that became embedded and entrenched in differing traditions (for instance, the falling out of Karlstadt and Luther on the speed and nature of the reform, as well as the even more substantive disagreements between the Lutherans, the Reformed, and the Anabaptists), there was no question among them on Christ's headship over the church or the Scripture principle *per se*—namely, that Scripture ruled the church because it was the means by which Christ's

---

40. LW 31: p. 342.

own lordship was expressed and exercised over the church. This is evident when one compares Luther's equation of the voice of God, the voice of Christ, and the voice of Scripture with Calvin's own understanding of these things (and, one could argue, with later Anabaptist and other Free Church understandings, regardless of their very significant material differences from the magisterial Reformers).[41] Calvin, in his famous debate with Jacopo Sadoleto, presented a picture of the relation of the voice of God, of Christ, and of Scripture that is in no way different from that of Luther himself, while also drawing upon the imagery of the church as those who hear the voice of their shepherd, Jesus Christ, earlier encountered in the *Smalcald Articles*. He wrote to Sadoleto:

> You either labor under a delusion as to the term *church*, or at least, knowingly and willingly give it a gloss. I will immediately show the latter to be the case, though it may also be that you are somewhat in error. First, in defining the term, you omit what would have helped you in no small degree to the right understanding of it. When you describe it as that which in all parts, as well as at the present time in every region of the earth, being united and consenting in Christ, has been always and everywhere directed by the one Spirit of Christ, what comes of the Word of the Lord, that clearest of all marks, and which the Lord himself, in pointing out the Church so often recommends to us? For seeing how dangerous it would be to boast of the Spirit without the Word, He declared that the Church is indeed governed by the Holy Spirit, but in order that that government might not be vague and unstable, He annexed it to the Word. For this reason Christ exclaims that those who are of God hear the Word of God—that His sheep are those which recognize His voice as that of the Shepherd, and any other voice as that of a stranger (John 10:27). For this reason the Spirit, by the mouth of Paul, declares (Eph. 2:20) that the Church is built upon the foundation of the Apostles and Prophets. Also, that the Church is made holy to the Lord, by the washing of water in the Word of life. The same thing is declared still more clearly by the mouth of Peter, when he teaches that people are regenerated to God by that incorruptible seed (1 Pet. 1: 23). In short, why is the preaching of the gospel so often styled the kingdom of God, but because it is the scepter by which the heavenly King rules His people?[42]

Here nearly all the convictions earlier addressed are present in one short paragraph—the critical, constructive, and constitutive aspects of the Word for the

---

41. Whether Anabaptists were or were not Protestants cannot be explored here. Suffice it to say, however, that on these broad Christo-ecclesiological and biblical commitments now outlined, they stood with the Reformers. See, for instance, the *Dordrecht Confession* of 1682 in *Creeds of the Churches*, ed. John H. Leith (Louisville: John Knox, 1982), p. 297. This is not to deny that they, and the later English Separatists, had their own unique and very different vision for the church from that of Luther, Zwingli, Calvin, and their followers.

42. John C. Olin, ed., *John Calvin and Jacopo Sadoleto: A Reformation Debate* (Grand Rapids: Baker, 1976), p. 60.

church; the close relation of Word and Spirit, these the means by which the voice of Christ is present to and rules over the church on earth, and specifically through the central gospel message; the close identification of the voice of God, the voice of Christ, and the words of the prophets and apostles in Scripture, all set over against the church's own confession and teaching; the sanctifying of the church by the power of the Word enlivened by the Spirit which awakens the church to faith and effects its sanctification and holiness; and not least, the centrality of the Word proclaimed that is the center of the church's liturgy and life by which Christ calls and rules his people.

Regardless of specific material differences in their Reformation movements, Luther and Calvin (and their plethora of Protestant followers) were agreed that it was the Word of God that was, in Calvin's terms, the "scepter by which the heavenly King rules His people." It was also the decree by which he saved his people in awakening them to faith. The Word of God was therefore at the center of the Protestant ecclesial vision and was that which united its ecclesiology and its soteriology into one coherent whole. And both of these were predicated upon a central christological principle: that Christ was not absent, but present, in the world today, and the church therefore was not his vicar but his servant, his body under his singular headship. Once again, Calvin stands shoulder to shoulder with Luther on this central point, as when he continued to defend the Reformation understanding of the church against Sadoleto:

> Ours be the humility which, beginning with the lowest, and paying respect to each in his degree, yields the highest honor and respect to the Church, in subordination, however, to Christ the Church's head; ours the obedience which, while it disposes us to listen to our elders and superiors, tests all obedience by the Word of God; in fine, ours the Church whose supreme care it is humbly and religiously to venerate the Word of God, and submit to its authority.[43]

In our day such Reformation writings and the teachings they present cannot appear but as intrinsically polemical, and we often judge the invective and diatribes of the past unfortunate and best left behind. Some would go further, however, declaring the Reformation over, and that in our day we had best "unlearn Protestantism."[44] Yet one cannot unlearn what has not been truly learned and appreciated. For the necessary polemical nature of the sixteenth-century disputes (both between the Reformers and their Catholic opponents, and among the Reformers and their followers themselves) can mask the constructive vision the Reformation offered. It cannot be entirely shorn of its polemical elements (for it did come into existence through opposition to its medieval Catholic rival). Yet one need not see the evangelical vision as intrinsically combative, for more important than its

---

43. Ibid., p. 75. To submit to the authority of Christ and to submit to the authority of Scripture were, for Calvin, the same thing.

44. To borrow the language of Gerald W. Schlabach, *Unlearning Protestantism: Sustaining Christian Community in an Unstable Age* (Grand Rapids: Brazos, 2010).

critical reaction is the fact that it does stand as an alternative to a weighty and historic, and different, conception of the church, and one that continues into our own day.

As but one modern articulation of this different conception, consider a noteworthy passage defining the church by Karl Rahner, one of the most important representatives of Roman Catholic theology in the twentieth century:

> As the people of God socially and juridically organized, the Church is not a mere eternal welfare institute, but the continuation, the perpetual presence of the task and function of Christ in the economy of redemption, his contemporaneous presence in history, his life, the Church in the full and proper sense .... Now the Church is the continuance, the contemporary presence, of that real, eschatologically triumphant and irrevocably established presence in the world, in Christ, of God's salvific will .... The Church is the official presence of the grace of Christ in the public history of the one human race. In its socially organized form the people of God as in fact redeemed by Christ, receives his permanent presence through history. And when we examine what this one reality implies, it means a presence, as it were an incarnation, of the truth of Christ in the Church through Scripture, tradition and magisterium; a similar embodiment and presence of Christ's will in the Church's teaching when it announces Christ's precepts in her pastoral office and her constitution; and a presence and embodiment, again analogous to the incarnation, of the grace of Christ, for the individual as such, through the sacraments. Viewed in relation to Christ, the Church is the abiding promulgation of his grace-giving presence in the world. Viewed in relation to the sacraments, the Church is the primal and fundamental sacrament.[45]

Here we face a very different ecclesiology than the Reformation one, though one that on the surface does seem to speak of presence rather than absence: with regard to the conception of the relation of Christ and the church, one of organic unity and symmetrical relation between Christ and church, rather than a strict differentiation between them marked by irreversibility and subordination; one emphasizing sacramental mediation, rather than sacramental reception; one where hierarchical and juridical organization overshadows the common priesthood of all; one where Scripture, tradition, and magisterium bleed one into the other on a continuous spectrum, rather than one in which the first is the ruling scepter above the others; one that equates the voice of Christ and the voice of the church's pastoral office, rather than a commandment given by the first echoed by a response in the second; one in which the sacraments are central and accompanied by Scripture, rather than one in which the Word is central and accompanied by the sacraments; and one in which the Catholic Church is the "primal and fundamental

---

45. Karl Rahner, *The Church and the Sacraments*, trans. W. J. O'Hara (New York: Herder and Herder, 1963), pp. 13, 18, 19. It may be asked, if all this is true, how Christ and the church can ever really be distinguished, and in what way his agency and life and voice have been preserved without being subsumed into, and thus replaced by, that of the church.

sacrament," differing from the understanding of Luther, who stated that, if one stuck closely to Scripture, one would have "only one single sacrament," Christ himself (cf. 1 Tim. 3:16 in the Vulgate), "with three sacramental signs," again displaying a distinction, rather than organic unity, between Christ's sacrifice and the sacraments themselves.[46] Here Christ seems to be present by being subsumed into the church itself, which is the extension of his own presence, with little said of their demarcation.

If one were to object that Rahner is a single example of excess, it could be admitted that others articulating this Catholic vision could be more circumspect in their ecclesial and sacramental reflection and echo Luther's words a bit more closely. But they also nonetheless offer a quite different way of thinking on the church than those of the Reformers. This is readily evident in one of the preeminent Catholic ecclesiologists of the twentieth century, Henri de Lubac, when he writes:

> If Christ is the sacrament of God, the Church is for us the sacrament of Christ; she represents him, in the full and ancient meaning of the term; she really makes him present. She not only carries on his work, but she is his very continuation, in a sense far more real than that in which it can be said that any human institution is its founder's continuation.[47]

Leaving aside all polemical considerations, it is nevertheless difficult not to conclude that were Luther to read Rahner's, or even de Lubac's, description of the church, he would not be encouraged that much had changed.[48] Such lofty language of the church might for Luther be deemed a theology of glory that warrants a second *Heidelberg Disputation*. Apart from such speculation, we are still left with the rather unavoidable conclusion that we have here two distinct ecclesial visions present before us. It is not the case that one is simply the reaction to the other or parasitic upon it. These are, rather, two coherent and compelling visions for ecclesial life, yet they are difficult to reconcile with one another, not only theologically, but liturgically and even architecturally. To note this fact does not entail that these visions necessarily fall solely along confessional lines. For

---

46. LW 36: p. 18. Indeed, the Reformers with one voice opposed any conception of the mass as a sacrifice or replication of Christ's sacrifice in the present.

47. Henri de Lubac, *Catholicism: Christ and the Common Destiny of Man*, trans. Lancelot Sheppard and Elizabeth Englund (San Francisco: Ignatius Press, 1988), p. 79.

48. Escape from this dilemma also cannot be found by retreating to the official documents of Roman Catholicism. For instance, the beautiful and extraordinary document *Lumen Gentium* states, in reference to papal infallibility: "For that reason, his [the Roman Pontiff's] definitions are rightly said to be irreformable by their very nature and not by reason of the consent of the church, in as much as they were made with the assistance of the Holy Spirit promised to him in blessed Peter; and as a consequence they are not in need of the approval of others, and do not admit of appeal to any other tribunal" (Ch. 3, Art. 25; see the rest of this Article, as well as Art. 28). This finality is the very definition of a statement being canonical, and thus a *norma normans non normata*.

instance, Friedrich Schleiermacher's ecclesiology, in which the agency and spirit of Christ are indistinguishable from the agency and spirit of the church, and in which Christ's agency is subsumed into the agency of the community, is itself a quite "Catholic" conception of the church in spite of his Reformed dogmatic commitments.[49] Likewise, some Roman Catholics have in reality gravitated more toward a "Protestant" vision.[50] Moreover, there are attempts to mediate between them.[51]

Regardless of where ecclesiological discussions may go in an ecumenical future, at the very least they must begin with the acknowledgment that Protestant ecclesiology presents not merely a reactionary corrective, but an alternative proposal, for ecclesiastical life. It is not predicated simply upon a doctrine of soteriology or a prophetic critique of ecclesial excess, but upon a christological commitment, namely, that Christ is the Lord of the church, and that as such he is unique and present through Word and Spirit, and that all called to faith and baptized in his name are priests in and for the world. Christ is unique in that his salvific work cannot be subsumed into but can simply be received by Word and sacrament, and his relation to the church is one marked not only by a freely elected unity but an irrevocable distinction. Christ is present in that his voice is still heard where the Word is proclaimed, and this Word, as found in Scripture, is the test and norm of the church's response in its tradition and confession, these latter standing under the canon, rather than over it or even alongside it on the same plane—though they do, contrary to misreadings of *sola Scriptura*, have a real though relative authority and proper place. Indeed, for the children of the Reformation, to embrace *sola Scriptura* did not *undermine*, but *required*, that the church must be a church of confession, the church confessing before the world what it has heard in the proclamation of the gospel and witnessing to what it has found in Holy Scripture, and that it do so in conversation with the church of the past.[52] Hence the proliferation of Protestant confessions.

For Luther, the distinction of Christ and church was central to such confession and entailed that "the church is the creature of the gospel, incomparably less than the gospel."[53] Moreover, just as the church is less than the gospel, so it cannot be equated with the Kingdom of God, Reformation ecclesiology thus displaying

---

49. It should therefore not be surprising that Karl Barth's criticisms of Schleiermacher's understanding of the church and those of the Roman Catholicism of his day were essentially the same criticisms. See Kimlyn J. Bender, *Karl Barth's Christological Ecclesiology* (Aldershot: Ashgate, 2005; repr., Eugene, OR: Cascade, 2013), pp. 17–58.

50. See, for instance, Hans Küng, *The Church* (London: Burns & Oates, 1967).

51. Such attempts mark the "evangelical catholic" movement. See Carl E. Braaten, *Mother Church: Ecclesiology and Ecumenism* (Minneapolis: Fortress, 1998); *The Catholicity of the Reformation*, ed. Carl E. Braaten and Robert W. Jenson (Grand Rapids: Eerdmans, 1996).

52. Such conversation could be affirming and appreciative, not only critical, seen for instance in the Reformers' affirmation of the early church's trinitarian definitions and their indebtedness to Augustine.

53. WA 2: p. 430.6–7; as cited in Lohse, *Martin Luther's Theology*, p. 280.

not only christological convictions but a distinctive eschatological reservation. Evangelical ecclesiology thus denies all attempts to see the church as an extension of Christ's salvific agency in the world or as a prolongation of the incarnation into the present. To assert such is to confuse the unique person and work of Christ as Savior and Lord with the real if circumscribed task of the church as those who live by and proclaim Christ's finished and unique action. Thus for the ecclesiological vision of the Reformation, to say that (1) Christ as head is distinguished from his ecclesial body, and that (2) the gospel of Christ precedes and grounds the church (logically if not chronologically), and that (3) the canon stands over against all later tradition, is to say one thing in a three-fold form. These convictions remain pivotal for any ecclesiology to be deemed faithful to the Reformation vision and designated as evangelical.

## Attending to the Past for the Sake of the Future

In the end, regardless of the relation of Augustine's soteriology to his ecclesiology and how the Reformers appropriated them, it is best to see the Reformation not as a trade of one for the other, but as an emphasis upon a soteriology which included deep ecclesiological implications, and that lying behind both was a new christological understanding of what it meant to say that Christ was the head of the church.[54] When this fact is discerned, one can in fact speak coherently of a Reformation (i.e., Protestant) vision that, while certainly not always consistently applied or developed, while embodied in traditions often fragmented by other material disagreements, and while suffering from its own internal problems that should not be romantically or polemically papered over (as the Catholic one suffers from its own), is nonetheless shared among these various confessional traditions.

Whatever an evangelical theology of this sort might offer for the future—and this remains an open question—its adherents in the different Protestant traditions that embrace it need at least to attend to its past. And attending carefully to its past entails that its commitments be seen as more than provisional and reactionary, but as principled, rooted in a particular christology (and attendant pneumatology), and with distinctive soteriological and ecclesiological convictions and implications. Indeed, this evangelical vision was not a trading of ecclesiology for soteriology, but one in which both were taken up into a larger christological

---

54. An even-handed way to state this relation, one that retains the Reformation emphasis upon soteriology without overstating it, has been given by Lohse, who maintains that what is new with Luther and his reform was that "of all the questions with which theology must deal, the aim and goal in any given instance is the question of salvation. Questions about the doctrine of God, about the sacraments, about ecclesiology, can be dealt with only when this aspect is seen from the outset" (Lohse, *Martin Luther's Theology*, p. 35). What I have argued here is that such soteriological concerns themselves are, when fully explored, grounded in particular christological convictions and accompanied by specific ecclesiological entailments.

framework, a vision that, however underdeveloped and unsystematic it may have been, was nonetheless remarkably coherent and fecund. It would be profitable not only for those in the Lutheran and Reformed traditions, but for all direct and indirect heirs of the Reformation, to review this vision and to ask themselves if they still adhere to it.[55] For if they do, then they would not only have a point by which to consider their identity and to conduct ecumenical discussions with those who do and do not share this vision, but may once again rediscover their own confessional heritage set against what has too often devolved for many into a non-confessional theological subjectivism or moralism. This development can be illustrated by considering one final example and question. It might be asked whether the contemporary loss of the theological, associational, and missional cohesion of so many heirs of the Reformation, having been replaced by a kind of *hyper*-congregationalism (or worse, subjective individualism), is not itself ultimately traceable back to a loss of a broadly shared confessional identity and understanding of this evangelical ecclesial vision. In other words, Protestants of various stripes might ask whether the only answer to subjectivism is a retrieval of an ill-defined catholic substance, or whether the best and proper answer to a narrow and authoritarian confessionalism is no confessionalism at all.

---

55. Or, at the very least, whether they have incorporated its central tenets into their own.

## Chapter 2

## THE *SOLA* BEHIND THE *SOLAS*: THE UNITY OF THE FIVE *SOLAS* OF THE REFORMATION

The 500th anniversary of the Reformation naturally marks an occasion to revisit the essential questions surrounding the rise of Protestantism and its ongoing witness. One way of doing this is, of course, to reexamine the five *solas*: *sola fide*, *sola gratia*, *sola scriptura*, *solus Christus*, and *soli Deo gloria*. That these terms and the ideas they express were and remain causes not only of doctrinal coalition but conflict is of course undeniable, yet the question may be asked what ongoing role they should play for those who claim the Reformation heritage in our time, and here it may be helpful to look not first to their future but to their origin. Such terms and their ensuing doctrinal convictions are evident throughout Protestant literature from the Reformation onward, yet for the sake of limiting the range of purview we might examine their initial appearance in the thought of Martin Luther. In an important sense, the *solas* as they came to be developed and affiliated with one another are only anachronistically applied to Luther, yet each can be readily witnessed in their incipient form in his corpus if we remember that the concept of each *sola* is not limited to the actual use of the formal term.[1] Having examined Luther, we can move on to draw some provisional conclusions about how the *solas* might continue to function for Protestant confession and theology.

1. Here it must be admitted that the history of the *solas* is a complex one. In their mature and grouped form, first as three, then four, and finally five, they are a later development from the time of Luther. This point is made by Henk van den Belt, who argues that *sola gratia*, *sola fide*, and *sola scriptura* were grouped together as a triad to serve as an expression of the "theological core of the Reformation" only in the past century—see Van den Belt, "The Problematic Character of *Sola Scriptura*," in *Sola Scriptura: Biblical and Theological Perspectives on Scripture, Authority, and Hermeneutics*, ed. Hans Burger, Arnold Huijgen, and Eric Peels (Leiden: Brill, 2017), pp. 38–55 (39–40). Such an observation, however, does little to affect the current study, which does not argue that Luther: (a) grouped these terms together in a formal way, or even, (b) relied heavily on these terms themselves as a summary of the gospel. Nor does it ignore that there were precursors to such ideas before Luther—for example, arguments similar to Luther's regarding the supremacy of Scripture can be found already in the patristic age and explicitly in persons like Wyclif and Hus, though not as sharply articulated as his own—see Vítor Westhelle, *The Church Event: Call and Challenge*

## Christ Alone and Faith Alone

Luther's break from both the medieval sacramental system and the supreme authoritative claims of the papal hierarchy was rooted in discoveries that highlighted the unique and singular place that faith and Scripture were growing to have in his thought.[2] That such discoveries were revolutionary for Luther is evident in his own estimation and is well-attested in his later reflection.[3] It may well be that the epitome of the *solas* is most aptly attributed to Luther's insertion of the word "alone" [*solum*] after the word "faith" in Romans 3:28 in his translation of the New Testament published in 1522. Luther, in an open letter of 1530, reflected back upon his translation decision:

---

*of a Church Protestant* (Minneapolis: Fortress, 2010), pp. 47-57; also Heiko Oberman, *Forerunners of the Reformation: The Shape of Late Medieval Thought*, trans. Paul Nyhus (New York: holt, Rinehart, and Winston, 1966), esp. pp. 53-66. The modest argument here made, rather, is that the concepts that the terms represent can be readily evidenced in Luther's writings and are indeed integral and interrelated. Moreover, the current examination of Luther moves to a constructive argument of how such concepts might be understood not only in Luther's thought but set forth to serve a theological purpose in our own day. In brief, whether Luther himself intentionally conjoined these terms or systematically coordinated these concepts is not fundamental to the argument here presented, and thus any charge of anachronism is simply misplaced.

2. Diarmaid MacCulloch, *The Reformation* (New York: Penguin, 2003), ch. 1. MacCulloch identifies the two pillars of the late medieval church as the mass (with its corresponding doctrine of purgatory accompanied by distinctive understandings of indulgences and merit) and papal primacy (with its incipient understanding of papal supremacy and infallibility)—see ibid., pp. 10-34. Scott Hendrix also speaks of the centrality of papal authority for medieval Catholicism but designates a different second pillar than MacCulloch: "The two buttresses of the Roman system were the papal claims to divine authority and the monastic claims to the perfect or nearly perfect Christian way of life that laity ought to emulate." See Hendrix, *Martin Luther: Visionary Reformer* (New Haven/London: Yale University Press, 2015), p. 13. Whether designated as pillars or buttresses, Luther attacked all three of these foundational elements of the medieval world—papal authority, the sacramental system, and practiced monasticism.

3. Luther remarked in the early 1530s looking back upon his life: "When I was a monk, I wearied myself greatly for almost fifteen years with the daily sacrifice, tortured myself with fastings, vigils, prayers, and other very rigorous works. I earnestly thought to acquire righteousness by my works, nor did I think it possible I should ever forget this life. Now, by God's grace I have forgotten it. Even today I recall these torments, but not in such a way as to consider returning to that prison. To speak according to the flesh, it was not a prison but a soft kind of life, free from all the innumerable annoyances of civil government and domestic affairs. Yet it was a prison to good men who did not think simply of their bellies but longed for salvation" (LW 12: p. 273). He could also later state: "Why did I undergo excessive hardships in the monastery? Why did I torture my body with fasts, vigils, and cold? Certainly because I was trying to be sure that through these works I would get forgiveness of sins" (LW 4: p. 165; cf. LW 23: p. 348).

Now I was not relying on and following the nature of the languages alone, however, when in Romans 3[:28] I inserted the word *solum* (alone). Actually the text itself and the meaning of St. Paul urgently require and demand it. For in that very passage he is dealing with the main point of Christian doctrine, namely, that we are justified by faith in Christ without any works of the law.[4]

Here Luther made a judgment of translation (without question predicated on his theological convictions) that had in turn not only exegetical but also hermeneutical and indeed far-reaching theological significance. These convictions pertaining to faith alone in Christ as the basis of justification were not restricted to his interaction with Pauline texts but marked and shaped the entire range of his biblical and theological commentary. A few examples may serve the purpose of illustrating this claim.

In his lectures on Genesis proffered in the mid-1530s, and therefore in his mature period, Luther instructed his readers:

Learn, therefore, not to attribute righteousness to your love or to your works and merits; for they are always unclean, imperfect, and polluted. Consequently, they call for a confession of our unworthiness and for humbling ourselves with a prayer for forgiveness. But attribute your righteousness to mercy alone, to the promise concerning Christ alone, the promise which faith accepts and by means of which it protects and defends itself against conscience when God sits in judgment.[5]

What is apparent in this quotation is not only Luther's emphasis upon faith over against human works, but also that this theme of faith is for him deeply interwoven with others, such as divine mercy alone and the promise of Christ alone. Already in his Psalms lectures in his earlier period, long before his mature theology of justification had fully coalesced, Luther contrasted the justification that came through Christ alone with that of human works, distinguishing the divine work of God and the human response of "faith and the obedience of faith."[6] Such soteriological convictions ran along parallel scriptural ones, for the authority of his claims for faith alone and Christ alone was predicated upon a view of Scripture that took precedence over all other theological and ecclesial authorities.[7] So in his

---

4. LW 35: p. 195.
5. LW 3: p. 25.
6. LW 10: p. 130; also ibid., p. 145; cf. LW 13: p. 290; LW 16: pp. 129, 305; LW 17: p. 215.
7. Bernard Lohse states: "It would be an exaggeration to speak of a Scripture principle in those first Psalms lectures, but what is striking is the extraordinary earnestness with which he [Luther] aimed at the christological sense of the psalm texts." See Lohse, *Martin Luther's Theology: Its Historical and Systematic Development*, trans. Roy Harrisville (Minneapolis: Fortress, 1999), p. 51. For the development and centrality of christology to Luther's hermeneutics and entire theology, see Marc Lienhard, *Luther: Witness to Jesus Christ—Stages and Themes of the Reformer's Christology*, trans. Edwin H. Robertson (Minneapolis: Augsburg, 1982).

lectures on Isaiah chapter 53 reflecting upon the Suffering Servant, Luther set the singular sufficiency of Christ's sacrifice and righteousness over against the law and human merits which "do not justify," and he did so with an explicit appeal to Paul over against the papacy, predicating such claims solely on biblical grounds. The conclusion he drew was conveyed in a tight and terse syllogism: "Christ alone bears our sins. Our works are not Christ. Therefore there is no righteousness of works."[8] Luther set both Christ alone and faith alone against a salvation of works, and it is apparent that saying one of these things implicates the other.[9] We can further perceive this connection when we take up the themes of Christ and of faith in turn.

First, Luther could attribute salvation solely to Christ and his work without remainder. Nowhere is this singular agency and sufficiency of Christ for the salvation of sinners and his unique and unrivalled existence as the revelation of God so clearly set forth as in Luther's sermons on the Gospel of John, where Luther upholds not only the sufficiency of Christ as the sole savior of grace for the church, but also his unrivalled authority as the unique revelation of God and the church's sole teacher of truth.[10] These two works of Christ as savior and revealer are in fact often intermingled in Luther's thought, and both themes are evident in these sermons. In the first role, Christ is the unique Savior, the one whose sacrifice and merits are the sole basis for salvation. Luther stated that if a person is to find mercy,

> Christ alone must be the means. He alone makes us paupers rich with his superabundance, expunges our sins with His righteousness, devours our death with His life, and transforms us from children of wrath, tainted with sin, hypocrisy, lies, and deceit, into children of grace and truth. Whoever does not possess this Man possesses nothing.[11]

In the second role, Christ is the only revelation of the invisible God, the only place where God is to be found, and in turn the singular teacher of divine verities.[12] He alone is the Way, the Truth, and the Life, the only way to the Father.[13] Luther put this point with remarkable starkness:

> Even if God Himself were to speak to me, as Münzer boasted that God had communicated with him, or if all the angels were to address me, I would still not give ear to a single word concerning my salvation; yes, I would plug up my ears

---

8. LW 17: pp. 222–3; cf. LW 27: p. 17; LW 30: p. 294.

9. So, for instance, in his lectures on Zechariah published in December of 1527, Luther stated: "The unique glory of the Christians, however, lies in Christ alone, in whom they believe and whom they trust" (LW 20: p. 28).

10. LW 22: pp. 130–1; also ibid., pp. 255–6; 272; 443; 487. For the significant place of the Gospel of John in Luther's christological thought, see Dennis Ngien, *Luther's Theology of the Cross: Christ in Luther's Sermons on John* (Eugene: Cascade, 2018).

11. LW 22: pp. 130–1.

12. LW 23: p. 117; cf. LW 26: p. 396.

13. LW 24: pp. 31–56.

with lead. In worldly matters I am willing to be credulous. But in this matter I would not believe the voice of God, even though it were heralded with drums and fifes. I am resolved not to believe or hear anything save Christ alone. I will not regard anything else as the voice of God. For God has ordained that He would not communicate with man through any other medium than Christ alone.[14]

This theme of Christ alone in both of these salvific and revelatory capacities is absolutely foundational to Luther, and this christological concentration deeply stamps his theology. Yet this focus upon Christ is complemented with an equally prominent emphasis upon faith as the effective element of salvation. Moreover, if Luther's christology is primarily shaped by the Gospel of John, his conception of faith, as well as grace, cannot of course overlook the unique influence of Paul. In his Galatian lectures published in 1535, Luther expounded upon the interrelated themes of the sufficiency of Christ, grace, and faith, and he set them in opposition over against a person's own righteousness, holiness, works, and merit.[15] Christ can be taken hold of by faith alone, and the only faith that is effective is that which takes hold of nothing but Christ alone.[16] For this reason, the law must be distinguished from both faith and Christ. That Christ and faith are for Luther indivisibly united is evident in his thought: "Therefore victory over sin and death, salvation, and eternal life do not come by the Law or by the deeds of the Law or by our will but by Jesus Christ alone. Hence faith alone justifies when it takes hold of this."[17] Later he wrote that Christ has overcome "the Law, sin, death, the devil, and hell," yet

> we must accept this blessing of Christ with a firm faith. For just as what is offered to us is neither the Law nor any of its works but Christ alone, so what is required of us is nothing but faith, which takes hold of Christ and believes that my sin and death are damned and abolished in the sin and death of Christ.[18]

Christ is therefore the inalienable object of the believer's faith, though Luther could at times also refer to God's promise as this object of faith. Yet this seeming shift in the referent of faith should not deter us from seeing that this too is in truth christologically grounded. In commenting upon Abrahams's faith in God's promise in Genesis 15:6, Luther asserted: "The only faith that justifies is the faith that deals with God in His promises and accepts them."[19] But even in dealing with

---

14. LW 23: p. 348.
15. LW 26: p. 40. Luther does this throughout his writing and in various ways throughout his adult life—see, for example, LW 44: pp. 286–93; 297–303; 318–20.
16. LW 26: pp. 88–9.
17. LW 26: p. 138; cf. LW 35: pp. 196–7. Luther writes that "there is no repentance, no satisfaction for sins, no grace, no eternal life, except by faith alone in Christ, faith that he has given full satisfaction for our sins, won grace for us, and saved us" (LW 52: p. 253).
18. LW p. 26: 160; cf. LW 31: pp. 346–7; LW 34: p. 91.
19. LW 3: p. 24. The centrality of the theme of divine promise for Luther's "reformational" turn is documented by Oswald Bayer, *Martin Luther's Theology: A Contemporary Interpretation*, trans. Thomas H. Trapp (Grand Rapids: Eerdmans, 2008), pp. 44–58.

this Old Testament text, Luther read it through a New Testament lens, and soon thereafter stated that "every promise of God includes Christ; for if it is separated from this Mediator, God is not dealing with us at all."[20] Furthermore, in a sermon on the third chapter of John's Gospel, he summoned the vivid image of marriage as the appropriate illustration for the relation between the believer and Christ: "Faith is the engagement ring which betroths us to Christ," and that by which we "take hold of Christ."[21] Moreover, to take hold of Christ is specifically to take hold of him in his death and resurrection: "Faith alone, indeed, all alone, without any works, lays hold of this death and resurrection when it is preached by the gospel."[22]

Luther's mature understanding was of course that we are justified by faith in Christ alone, apart from the law or works of any kind.[23] Christ and faith are therefore intricately conjoined in Luther's thought, and he could attribute forgiveness and justification to Christ alone as effortlessly and sincerely as he could attribute them to faith alone. And yet, and this is of course crucial—Christ and faith cannot be collapsed for Luther, either. Our faith requires an object, and for all of his encomiums to faith, Luther in circumspect and nuanced moments emphasized that in truth faith has no intrinsic power or sufficiency to allow one to approach God, for we can only approach God through Christ alone. It is in him our faith must rest, for faith has its value only in its object.[24] And so while both Christ and

---

20. LW 3: p. 26.

21. LW 22: p. 334; cf. LW 31: p. 352; LW 26: p. 132. In 1521 in his criticisms of monastic vows, Luther stated: "Faith brings Christ to us, makes us one flesh with him, bone of his bones. Faith causes us to have all things in common with him so that our conscience glories in him and on account of him. We live as justified men solely because of his blood and merits, and we shall live redeemed in eternity, without any works of our own or the works of others." He later continued: "Now faith establishes us on the foundation of the works of Christ without our own works, and transfers us from the exile of our own sins into the kingdom of his righteousness. This is faith, this is the gospel, this is Christ" (LW 44: pp. 286, 287). And so: "This is the definition of being a Christian: simply believing you are justified by the works of Christ alone without any works of our own, believing you have been freed from your sins and saved" (ibid., p. 287).

22. LW 35: p. 197. Luther already said something similar in "The Babylonian Captivity of the Church" (1520), where not Christ, but the mass itself as a promise of God, is grasped by faith alone: "If the mass is a promise, as has been said, then access to it is to be gained, not with any works, or powers or merits of one's own, but by faith alone" (LW 36: pp. 38–9). In time, Luther's estimation of the mass would in fact change considerably.

23. LW 4: pp. 163–71; LW 22: pp. 275–6; LW 23: pp. 105–9; LW 26: pp. 87–92; 136–8; 154–64; 202–16; et al. In its basic form, this position was already in place in his early discussion of salvation by faith rather than works in "On the Freedom of a Christian" of 1520 (LW 31: pp. 343–77).

24. See LW 25: p. 286. This point must be qualified, however, in light of the fact that Luther could also speak of faith as "the creator of the Deity," or "faith creating divinity" ["*fides est creatrix divinitatis*"] (WA 40/1: p. 360; cf. pp. 359–62; LW 26: p. 227). Yet this statement itself must be seen in light of its immediate qualification by Luther that such faith

faith are constitutive for justification in Luther's thought, there is a proper ordering of these and a required subordination of the latter to the former, even while he could uphold the necessity of each, for salvation could no more become a matter of a christological metaphysics apart from the believing response of the human subject than it could become a matter of subjective existentialism, a kind of faith in faith itself. As he wrote in his lectures on Romans: "Therefore those who approach God through faith and not at the same time through Christ actually depart from Him .... For this reason it is necessary to emphasize both points: 'through faith' and 'through Christ,' so that we do and suffer everything which we possibly can in faith in Christ."[25] Luther would not place Christ and faith in such contrastive terms in later years, but he would nevertheless always distinguish them, even as he saw both Christ and faith in intricate union in God's gift of justification.

## Faith Alone and Grace Alone

From faith and Christ we can turn to other themes pertinent to our investigation of the *solas*, beginning with grace. While faith alone (as a single concept) served as the lodestone for Luther's doctrine of justification, the theme of grace is readily

---

constitutes us rather than God, and it must furthermore be seen in the larger context in which for Luther faith itself is tied to God's promise in Christ. Thus, rather than a statement akin to later modern idealism and its God-creating and in turn atheistic tendencies, it too serves a larger christological purpose. Finally, such a statement must be understood in view of Luther's other firm pronouncement in the Galatian lectures: "Therefore faith acknowledges that in this one Person, Jesus Christ, it has the forgiveness of sins and eternal life. Whoever diverts his gaze from this object does not have true faith; he has a phantasy and a vain opinion" (LW 26: p. 88; see also LW 13: p. 88 nt. 21). It is of course true that later idealism could point back to Luther, and Feuerbach's project is often traced back to Luther himself—see Hans-Martin Barth, "Fides Creatrix Divinitatis," *Neue Zeitschrift für Systematische Theologie und Religionsphilosophie* 14 (1972), pp. 89–106; and Oswald Bayer, "Gegen Gott für den Menschen: Feuerbachs Lutherrezeption," in *Leibliches Wort: Reformation und Neuzeit im Konflikt* (Tübingen: J. C. B. Mohr Siebeck, 1992), pp. 205–55. But such an appeal is established upon a highly selective reading of Luther. As Gregory Walter notes with regard to Feuerbach's reference to Luther's phrase as implying the creation of God: "All of this misses the correlation of faith and promise. If one isolates the statement and then interprets it alongside of the identity-thinking that idealism generates, Luther's statement will immediately support the idea that theology is subjectively generated by human consciousness alone. This could not be further from Luther's sense." See Walter, "On Martin Luther's Statement, 'Fides Creatrix Divinitatis,'" *Dialog* 52 (2013), pp. 196–203 (197). No small part of Karl Barth's purpose in the first volume of the *Church Dogmatics* was in fact to correct this misreading of Luther in both the tradition of idealism and what Barth discerned to be the trajectory of his own theological contemporaries.

25. LW 25: p. 287.

evident and closely affiliated and correlated with the theme of faith itself. Here too, there are distinctions of grace and faith but no absolute divisions. In his lectures on Genesis (1539/40), Luther sought to understand the expulsion of Hagar and Ishmael in terms that salvaged a larger purpose of hope from the situation's seemingly tragic character. He therefore judged their banishment as ultimately serving a larger mercy shown toward them: "This is the purpose of such pitiful expulsion: God wants to teach us that we are saved by grace alone or by faith alone. Faith takes hold of the grace that is set before us in the promise."[26]

While Luther's exegesis and interpretation of this story of Hagar and Ishmael are intriguing on their own, for current purposes what is important to register is that here Luther attributes salvation to both grace alone and faith alone, almost indifferently ("we are saved by grace alone or by faith alone"), though he immediately draws a distinction with his gloss that faith takes hold of the grace of the promise, language reminiscent and familiar to us by now in light of his statements that faith is that which "takes hold of Christ." Here the language of grace is akin to that describing Christ himself, and points to their own at times functional equivalence in Luther's thought, even if not systematically developed or fully integrated.

So while Luther usually spoke of faith and of the work of Christ as the means by which sins are forgiven and persons are justified, he could also attribute this salvation to grace itself, which, in a sermon on the Gospel of John, he succinctly defined and identified with Christ's own benefits:

> You have heard truth and grace defined before; however, it will not be amiss to touch on these again briefly, for a good song bears repetition. "Grace" means that God is merciful to us, that He deals graciously with us for the sake of Christ our Lord, forgives us all our sins, and that He does not impute them to us or punish us with eternal death. Grace is the forgiveness of sin for Christ's sake, the covering of all sin. That is grace.[27]

Grace is therefore the divinely enacted mercy, forgiveness, and justification we receive "for Christ's sake" which is actualized in the act of faith. Luther therefore had no difficulty stating that "grace alone justifies," even though he more frequently stated that faith alone does this.[28] As he wrote in his Lectures on First Timothy: "We assign righteousness not to the Law and its works but to grace alone, which is offered to us through Jesus Christ."[29] We might say that for Luther justification is attributed to grace alone when justification is considered from the perspective of what is divinely offered in Christ, and it is attributed to faith alone when considered from the perspective of the human trust in the promise of God that comes in this offer of grace. Like Christ and faith, so also grace and faith are not

---

26. LW 4: p. 60.
27. LW 22: p. 139.
28. LW 25: p. 242; cf. LW 28: p. 236.
29. LW 28: p. 234; cf. p. 236.

identified, but neither are they divided for Luther. They roughly and respectively correspond to the objective salvific work of God that comes to us *extra nos* in Christ, and the salvific work that is enacted within us by the Spirit of God. The first points, as Luther recounted, to God's mercy shown and extended to us, whereas the second corresponds to the human act of trust in the grace offered concretely in Christ, even as this faith is itself a divine work within us. Hence grace and Christ are aligned in a way analogous to the way that faith and the Spirit are aligned, though the first pair lends itself to an identification in Luther's description in a way that the second pair does not. Moreover, within the pairs, Luther gravitates to the language of Christ rather than that of grace, and to the language of faith itself rather than to the work of the Spirit within us that gives rise to faith.

## Grace Alone and God's Glory Alone

We can turn next from the relation of faith and grace in Luther's thought to the relation of grace and God's glory. As Luther could inextricably enjoin Christ as the object of faith with faith itself, and in turn entwine God's grace with faith, attributing our salvation to our faith penultimately and to Christ and God's grace ultimately, so he could seamlessly move between referencing God's grace and God's own glory. Examining Isaiah 48:11 in his lectures on that book, he gave particular attention to the phrase attributed to God, that is, "My glory I will not give to another." He observed:

> Here you see that a self-righteous person is a thief of the divine glory and also an idolater, because he lays claim to God's glory for himself. He does not pray, "Hallowed be Thy name." Aspiring to the glory of divinity is a most grievous monstrosity. Here you see the battle between God and the self-righteous concerning glory. The outward glory of this world is nothing compared with it. The self-righteous want to rob God of His glory. And God will not permit this. The self-righteous man thinks that God will give him rewards for fasting and labor. He thinks that without these God will give him nothing. He thinks precisely that God is someone who will save him through his works, not for the sake of free grace. To this fiction, "God will save me through my works," he attributes salvation. This is the most persistent struggle and battle of the world against God. No one wants to rely on *God's glory alone* and repudiate all his own merits. For that reason there are so many examples in Scripture which invite us to look to *grace alone*, whether we eat or whether we drink. So there are endless examples of sins, such as of the robber, that draw us to *God's grace alone*.[30]

In this passage we again see a number of intriguing associations. First, Luther has a robust notion of God's glory and, like Augustine before him and Calvin and

---

30. LW 17: p. 162 [emphasis added].

Barth after, contrasts it to a form of idolatry of the self.[31] But what is also of great interest for our inquiry is that Luther here seemingly equates God's glory and God's grace in his soteriological reflection. To spurn God's grace and to set our works in its place are effectively to rob God of his glory. Conversely, if the self-righteous person stands in opposition to God's glory, then the meritorious works offered to God by such a person stand in opposition to God's grace. Indeed, God's glory is here for Luther nothing but the exercise of his grace. "No one wants to rely on God's glory alone and repudiate all his own merits," Luther concludes, but he immediately goes on to speak of God's grace alone to which Scripture drives us. It appears that to rely on God's glory alone and to rely on God's grace alone are here for Luther the same thing.[32] Indeed, to proclaim God's grace alone is to give glory to God alone.[33]

These affinities of grace and glory are mirrored in others between faith and glory, shifting the referent from God's own intrinsic glory to the glory that is ascribed to God by the human person. Luther could speak of attributing glory to God with the same terminology and conceptual underpinnings with which he described having faith in God. In his Galatian lectures, Luther stated that those who have faith offer a pleasing sacrifice to God and "ascribe glory to God; that is, they regard Him as just, good, faithful, truthful, etc., and believe that He can do everything, that all His words are holy, true, living, and powerful. This is the most acceptable allegiance to God. Therefore no greater, better, or more pleasing religion or worship can be found in the world than faith."[34] In short, to have faith in God is to ascribe glory to God, and justification therefore occurs by faith alone even as it is due to God's intrinsic glory alone and is also, correspondingly, the ground for giving glory to God alone. Glory thus has a three-fold objective, communicative, and subjective character—that is, glory that which God intrinsically possesses, what God in turn graciously communicates and salvifically effects, and what God then rightfully receives in faith from the forgiven sinner. Obversely, to trust in one's own works is to withhold giving glory to God alone, to insult God's glorious work of salvation, and to impugn God's intrinsic glory and very character, denying God's mercy, truth, and faithfulness. In doing this, Luther stated, such persons "despise God, accuse Him of lying in all His promises, and deny Christ and all His blessings. In short, they depose God from

---

31. For a discussion of Augustine, Luther, and Barth on this score, see Matt Jenson, *The Gravity of Sin: Augustine, Luther and Barth on* "homo incurvatus in se" (London/New York: T&T Clark/Continuum, 2006).

32. LW 17: p. 162.

33. LW 17: p. 324. Moreover, Luther placed the glory of Christ and the glory God in an apposition that suggests a close affinity and even identity: "The Holy Spirit convicts the whole world of sin (John 16:8) and proclaims the righteous Christ and His glory alone. It is the office of an evangelical preacher to proclaim the glory of God alone" (LW 17: pp. 172–3). This will be revisited below.

34. LW 26: pp. 228–9. As Lohse writes: "Only those who humble themselves honor God, while those who would exalt themselves deny God honor …. It is faith that ultimately gives God the honor" (*Martin Luther's Theology*, pp. 60–1).

His throne and set themselves up in his place," and thus neglect and despise God's Word.[35] Notice here—to oppose works to *faith* is in effect to renounce *Christ*, to deny *grace*, to impugn *God's glory*, and to despise *God's Word*.

## *God's Glory Alone and Christ Alone*

We can now bring all of these themes full circle, for God's glory is not only God's grace, but God's grace is, in its actual concrete form, that which Christ alone brings to us, and Luther spoke interchangeably of the grace of God and the grace of Christ, even as he spoke interchangeably of their glory.[36] He could even directly equate Christ *with* the glory of God, though this was quite rare.[37] Similarly, he could equate Christ with God's grace itself, though he was much more prone to speak of Christ as the bearer of God's grace, the one through whom such grace comes, or the one on account of whom it is given to us.[38] In this sense, grace is not only the basis for the gift of Christ but the gift itself. In his final judgment on the medieval church in 1539 in "On the Councils and the Church," he stated:

> If the council grants us that the grace of *Christ alone* saves us and does not also grant us the conclusion and deduction that works do not save us, but maintains that works are necessary for satisfaction or for righteousness, then the first that was granted to us is thereby again taken from us, namely, that *grace alone*, without works, saves us.[39]

For Luther, to say that grace alone saves us, and that Christ alone saves us, and that faith alone saves us, is to say one thing in an irreducibly three-fold form, for each is not identified with the other (and particularly the first two with the last), but each implies the other when one is speaking of God's salvation of humanity.[40] Moreover,

---

35. LW 26: p. 229; cf. LW 13: p. 185.
36. LW 12: p. 271.
37. LW 11: p. 207.
38. "Christ is God's grace, mercy, righteousness, truth, wisdom, power, comfort, and salvation, given to us by God without any merit on our part" (LW 14: p. 204).
39. LW 41: p. 139 [emphasis added].
40. When these interrelations in Luther are thereby understood, arguments like Van den Belt's that the conjunction of the *solas* is a late invention far removed from the Reformation are greatly attenuated and in need of their own qualification (see Van den Belt, "The Problematic Character of *Sola Scriptura*," pp. 39–42). The recognition of such interrelations no doubt lies behind Vítor Westhelle's characterization of Luther's "Copernican revolution": "The *solus Christus*—reappearing in *sola gratia, sola fide, sola scriptura*—was the sun (*sol*) that regimented the orbits of the theological, ecclesial, and political 'planets.' As Copernicus placed the sun at the center of our gravitational system, so did the Reformer with the *solae* for systems of theology and ecclesial autarchies." See Westhelle, *Transfiguring Luther: The Planetary Promise of Luther's Theology* (Eugene: Cascade, 2016), p. 2. This language of Luther's "Copernican Revolution" is not new—see Heinrich Boehmer, *Luther and the*

to recognize each and properly esteem them is to acknowledge the glory of God as grace and to ascribe glory to God in faith, as well as rightly to perceive this glory as concretely displayed yet hidden in Christ.

## Christ Alone and Scripture Alone

Lastly, we might turn to Scripture. Not only are faith, grace, and God's glory tied intricately to Christ for Luther, but so also is Scripture, though in a somewhat different way. In his 1522 treatise "Avoiding the Doctrines of Men," Luther commented on the law of Moses and insisted that while books beyond those of Moses have been written, they have not overturned Moses' injunction in Deuteronomy 4:2 not to add anything to his words, for all later biblical books and their messages are already present in insipient form in the words of Moses themselves. Luther concluded: "For this much is beyond question, that all the Scriptures point to Christ alone."[41] Indeed, Luther's famous definition of Scripture was whatever books proclaimed, set forth and inculcated Christ [*was Christum treibet*].[42] Luther's particular understanding of this led, of course, to some of his most controversial canonical decisions, particularly his disparagement of the Epistle of James, as well as of Hebrews and Revelation.[43] Yet this christological rule was the one by which he read not only all of the New Testament but the Old, for the gospel "teaches nothing but Christ, and therefore Scripture contains nothing but Christ."[44] Alternatively, the opposite holds true as well: "Take Christ out of the Scripture, and what will you find left in them?"[45]

*Reformation in the Light of Modern Research*, trans. E. S. G. Potter (New York: Dial Press, 1930), p. 80; Philip Watson, *Let God Be God!: An Interpretation of the Theology of Martin Luther* (London: Epworth, 1947), pp. 33-8; and Anders Nygren, *Agape and Eros*, trans. Philip S. Watson (Chicago: University of Chicago Press, 1953), pp. 681-4.

41. LW 35: p. 132.

42. LW 35: p. 396; WA Deutsche Bibel (Weimar: H. Böhlaus, 1931/1968) 7: pp. 384-5; cf. LW 25: p. 405; LW 34: p. 112; LW 52: p. 173.

43. With regard to the Revelation of John, Luther baldly asserted: "My spirit cannot accommodate itself to this book. For me this is reason enough not to think highly of it: Christ is neither taught nor known in it" (LW 35: p. 399). Yet he did not argue for its removal, and indeed in time his attitude toward it softened and grew more positive, such that he could state in the second preface to it (in contrast to the first) that if rightly interpreted it could serve with profit and be made of good use for Christians (LW 35: p. 409). The later Lutheran confessions were more circumspect and less critical still in their canonical judgments—see Edmund Schlink, *Theology of the Lutheran Confessions*, trans. Paul Koehneke and Herbert J. A. Bouman (Philadelphia: Muhlenberg Press, 1961), p. 9. For Luther's canonical judgments on such matters, see Denis R. Janz, *The Westminster Handbook of Martin Luther* (Louisville: Westminster John Knox, 2010), pp. 16-17. It must also be remembered that whatever criticisms Luther may have had of individual books, he nonetheless affirmed the inspiration of Scripture in its entirety—see Paul Althaus, *The Theology of Martin Luther* (Philadelphia: Fortress, 1966), p. 50.

44. LW 52: p. 207; LW 35: p. 396; LW 13: p. 309.

45. LW 33: p. 26.

These christological convictions were at the heart of all Luther said and believed formally and materially about Scripture, and they shaped not only his ontology of Scripture but his hermeneutical program, these themselves indivisible in his theology.[46] Explicating Christ's comparison of himself to the bronze serpent of the Old Testament in Jesus' conversation with Nicodemus in John chapter three, Luther remarked:

> In this way the Lord shows us the proper method of interpreting Moses and all the prophets. He teaches us that Moses points and refers to Christ in all his stories and illustrations. His purpose is to show that Christ is the point at the center of a circle, with all eyes inside the circle focused on Him. Whoever turns his eyes on Him finds his proper place in the circle of which Christ is the center. All the stories of Holy Writ, if viewed aright, point to Christ.[47]

Whether under the rubric of soteriology or that of authority, Christ alone and Scripture alone are intricately connected in Luther's thought.[48] Just as Christ's sacrifice was sufficient and required no repetition, so that its effects and benefits come to the sinner simply through its proclamation received in faith, so also Scripture served as the locus of the authoritative Word of this gospel announcement and therefore was the sole arbiter and judge of all ecclesial claims and the critical

---

46. Hans-Martin Barth, *The Theology of Martin Luther: A Critical Assessment* (Minneapolis: Fortress, 2013), pp. 443-6. For Luther's doctrine of Scripture with an eye toward his understanding of *sola scriptura* and its implications, see Jörg Baur, "Sola Scriptura—historisches Erbe und bleibende Bedeutung," in *Sola Scriptura: Das reformatorische Schriftprinzip in der säkularen Welt*, ed. Hans Heinrich Schmid and Joachim Mehlhausen (Gütersloh: Gütersloher Verlagshaus Gerd Mohn, 1991), pp. 19-43.

47. LW 22: p. 339.

48. Luther spoke of Scripture as the written Word of God in letters just as Christ is the eternal Word of God hidden in the veil of flesh (WA 48: p. 31). For the relation of the Word of God as Christ and Scripture and the proclaimed gospel in Luther's thought, see WA 48: p. 31; also David W. Lotz, "*Sola Scriptura*: Luther on Biblical Authority," *Interpretation* 35 (1981), pp. 258-73; for an extensive examination of Luther's understanding of the Word of God in these relations, see Werner Führer, *Das Wort Gottes in Luthers Theologie* (Göttingen: Vandenhoeck & Ruprecht, 1984). Of course, for Luther the spoken Word was accompanied by the Word proclaimed in the sacraments, though he set the proclaimed gospel even above these (LW 39: p. 314; see Janz, *The Westminster Handbook to Martin Luther*, pp. 27; 121; also Führer, *Das Wort Gottes in Luthers Theologie*, pp. 120-33). This accompaniment of proclaimed Word with the sacraments was of course articulated by Karl Barth as well, regardless of Barth's significant sacramental differences from Luther (CD I/1: pp. 56-7). There is therefore a line from this three-fold form of the Word in Luther to Barth's own exposition of the Word of God in the first volume of the *Church Dogmatics*, and Luther figures prominently there throughout.

norm against which they were to be tested.[49] For this reason, just as Christ could not be replaced with a vicarious priest, so also could Scripture not be replaced with the authority of the papacy. In his early treatise "On the Papacy in Rome," Luther stated that Christ cannot have a vicar in the church, which is why "neither pope nor bishop can ever be, or be allowed to become, Christ's vicar or regent in this church."[50] Furthermore, as the singular Savior of sinners, Christ alone could be the head of the church. The church was built upon him, not upon the papacy.[51] He is the church's sole foundation, and therefore the only one who should be proclaimed by the church.[52] Christ thus stood alone, for Luther, as the savior, teacher, and lord of the church. With this christological conviction in its three-fold priestly, prophetic, and kingly form, Luther, in Samson-like fashion, pushed out what Diarmaid MacCulloch has called the two pillars of the medieval church, the Mass and papal primacy, and with them an ecclesial world came crashing down.[53]

---

49. Lohse, *Martin Luther's Theology*, pp. 187–8. Lohse contends that Luther emphasized the proclaimed Word over the written one when speaking of God's encounter with us (ibid., p. 189; see also LW 52: p. 206; cf. LW 35: p. 123; also Baur, "*Sola Scriptura*—historisches Erbe und bleibende Bedeutung," pp. 30–1). Yet though Luther emphasized the spoken Word of the gospel, it is nevertheless true that for him Scripture accompanied the proclaimed Word and served as the source and content of the contemporary church's proclamation, so that Bayer asserts: "When it comes to understanding the gospel, the verbal proclamation is not given pride of place over against the written proclamation" and notes that while these are distinct, they are not rivals in Luther's thought (Bayer, *Martin Luther's Theology*, p. 79; see pp. 78–9). For Luther, then, there were two intertwined witnesses to Christ: Scripture and the spoken word (ibid., p. 79; see also LW 52: p. 205).

50. LW 39: p. 72.

51. LW, 49: pp. 61–8.

52. LW 49: pp. 63–4.

53. MacCulloch, *The Reformation*, p. 10; cf. pp. 10–34; see also note two above. Luther's discovery was therefore not simply a new view of faith and justification, but an attack upon all attempts to subsume Christ into the church, and specifically, into its sacramental system with its priestly class and into its tradition with its teaching office. What Luther proposed was not only a different doctrine of faith but a different christology, with its own soteriological and ecclesiological ramifications. Hence as Willem van Vlastuin states: "Luther did not deny the importance of the church as the body of Christ, but he accepted the implications of his understanding of the authority of Scripture by making a distinction between the authority of the body of Christ and the Word of Christ, so that the ultimate authority lies with scripture and not with the church, without rejecting the tradition of the interpretation of scripture." See Vlastuin, "*Sola Scriptura*: The Relevance of Luther's Use of *Sola Scriptura* in *De Servo Arbitrio*," in *Sola Scriptura: Biblical and Theological Perspectives on Scripture, Authority, and Hermeneutics*, ed. Hans Burger, Arnold Huijgen, and Eric Peels (Leiden/Boston: Brill, 2017), pp. 243–59 (247); cf. Führer, *Das Wort Gottes in Luthers Theologie*, pp. 135–7. This in no way should be taken to imply that the church became marginal in Luther's thought, for God's Word and God's people could not be separated—see LW 41: p. 150; also Scott Hendrix, "Open Community: The Ecclesial Reality of Justification," in *By Faith*

In light of this relation of Christ's own sole sacrificial sufficiency and sole teaching authority on one hand, and with Scripture's own correspondent salvific content and instructional authority on the other hand, it should not be surprising that Luther portrayed Christ not only as the center of the content of Scripture but also attributed Christ's own revelatory and teaching authority to Scripture. The authority of Scripture is thus the authority of Christ himself, such that *sola Scriptura* is best understood with regard to Luther not as a formal principle but, like justification, as an implication of *solus Christus*.[54] In the 1521 defense of his articles of the Reformation in the face of his excommunication (*Exsurge Domine*, 1520), Luther went so far as to call the Scriptures "the spiritual body of Christ."[55] Scripture is that to which other writings appeal for verification, the ultimate standard that pronounces a "verdict and judgement" upon them all: "Scripture alone is the true lord and master of all writings and doctrine on earth."[56] Therefore, just as Christ alone is Lord of the church, so Scripture alone is the lord of all ecclesial dogma and tradition.[57] Later, Luther could associate not only Christ's authority but his salvific efficacy with Scripture when he asserted that "the Holy Scriptures constitute a

---

*Alone: Essays on Justification in Honor of Gerhard O. Forde*, ed. Joseph A. Burgess and Marc Kolden (Grand Rapids: Eerdmans, 2004), pp. 235–47 (238). Yet Führer is certainly correct to note that the Reformation of the church that Luther called forth was not predicated on testing the current church against an ecclesial ideal retrieved from the ancient church or against a golden age of the past, but solely against the Word of God as the standard for the church's renewal (Führer, *Das Wort Gottes in Luthers Theologie*, p. 138).

54. Führer, *Das Wort Gottes in Luthers Theologie*, pp. 112–13. "Both justification and the doctrine of Scripture are explicated Christology and complement each other by unfolding what is decided in 'solus Christus'" (ibid., p. 113). Hendrix similarly comments: "Historically and theologically, justification and ecclesiology are derivatives of Christology" ("Open Community," p. 237).

55. LW 32: p. 11.

56. LW 32: pp. 11–12; cf. LW 26: pp. 57–8; LW 34: p. 284. A few years later (1525), in his famous debate with Erasmus, Luther declared that proper disputation was to be carried out not "by appealing to the authority of any doctor, but by that of Scripture alone" (LW 33: p. 167). In the much later preface to the Wittenberg edition of his German writings, he commended Augustine as his exemplar for being "the first and almost the only one who determined to be subject to the Holy Scriptures alone, and independent of the books of all the fathers and saints." Luther concluded: "And if the example of St. Augustine had been followed, the pope would not have become Antichrist, and that countless mass of books, which is like a crawling swarm of vermin, would not have found its way into the church, and the Bible would have remained on the pulpit" (LW 34: p. 285; cf. LW 41: p. 25; LW 44: p. 205; LW 52: pp. 176, 191).

57. This authority extended not only over the papacy but over church councils themselves—see Luther's "On the Councils and the Church," LW 41: pp. 51–2; cf. pp. 9–178; also Christa Tecklenburg Johns, *Luthers Konzilsidee in ihrer historischen Bedingtheit und ihrem reformatorischen Neuansatz* (Berlin: Töpelmann, 1966), pp. 144; 183; cf. pp. 179–98; and Lohse, *Martin Luther's Theology*, p. 117. Johannes Zachhuber concludes regarding Luther's view of the ecumenical councils: "Luther situated his Christology within the

book which turns the wisdom of all other books into foolishness, because not one teaches about eternal life except this one alone."[58] Of course, it should be clear by now that to speak of eternal life was for Luther but another way of speaking of Christ who secured this eternal life for us.

It must be acknowledged that with regard to Scripture Luther thought of Christ most often in terms of the content of Scripture rather than as its subject, with the message of God's grace and glory offered in Christ the central message found in its pages, to be received in faith. Nevertheless, as Calvin and others would do, he also set forth Christ as the ascended Lord who wields Scripture for his own witness, rule, and self-attestation.[59] In his Galatian lectures of 1535, he spoke of Scripture ruling as queen of the church, even while emphasizing later in those same lectures that Scripture is also servant to Christ who rules as the king of the church and is Lord even over the Scriptures.[60] In short, Luther's view of Scripture

Chalcedonian tradition, but his attitude toward this tradition was more flexible because he perceived doctrinal decisions as ultimately deriving from scripture and therefore in need of justification in light of the biblical testimony." See Johannes Zachhuber, *Luther's Christological Legacy: Christocentrism and the Chalcedonian Tradition* (Milwaukee, WI: Marquette University Press, 2017), p. 103. Yet whether Luther was always consistent in the application of this *sola Scriptura* principle can be questioned—see Janz, *The Westminster Handbook to Martin Luther*, pp. 15–16. Nevertheless, it is because of Luther's position on the final authority of Scripture that the later Scripture principle of the Reformation is generally regarded to have its origins [*Ursprünge*] in Luther's theology—see Bengt Hägglund, "Evidentia sacrae scripturae: Bemerkungen zum 'Schriftprinzip' bei Luther," in *Vierhundertfünfzig Jahre lutherische Reformation 1517–1967: Festschrift fur Franz Lau zum 60 Geburtstag* (Göttingen: Vandenhoeck & Ruprecht, 1967), pp. 116–25 (117). This is not to say, however, that there are not difficulties with speaking of a Scripture "principle" in Luther if such is not carefully defined in theological rather than philosophical categories. For Luther, Scripture was not so much a foundational epistemological principle as a living and effective Word whose truth is communicated to faith. Scripture is not for Luther a book of self-evident axioms understood through reason, but a living Word which enlightens and gives understanding to the reader or listener by the power of the Spirit (see ibid., pp. 119–20).

58. LW 34: p. 285.

59. Calvin famously depicted Christ as Scripture's subject, the one who wields and speaks through Scripture such that the proclamation of the gospel is "the sceptre by which the heavenly King rules his people." See John Calvin and Jacopo Sadeletto, *A Reformation Debate*, ed. John C. Olin (Grand Rapids: Baker Books, 2005), p. 60. Such imagery was not entirely foreign to Luther, who in his first lectures on the Psalms commented: "*Rod of iron* is the holy Gospel, which is Christ's royal scepter in His church and kingdom" (LW 10: p. 35).

60. LW 26: pp. 57–8; 295. See Lotz, "*Sola Scriptura*: Luther on Biblical Authority," pp. 263–4; also Arnold Huijgen, "Alone Together: *Sola Scriptura* and the Other Solas of the Reformation," in *Sola Scriptura: Biblical and Theological Perspectives on Scripture, Authority, and Hermeneutics*, ed. Hans Burger, Arnold Huijgen, and Eric Peels (Leiden/Boston: Brill, 2017), pp. 79–104 (95). Huijgen writes: "Typically, Luther says on the one hand that scripture alone must rule as queen in the church, and on the other hand that scripture is servant and Christ is king" (ibid., p. 95).

was established upon Christ from first to last, and Luther saw the proclamation of the gospel, attested in Scripture, as the living Word through which the risen and ascended Christ continues to speak.[61] It therefore is rightly said that "all Scripture must be read and interpreted from and toward Jesus Christ."[62]

## A Constructive and Modest Proposal

Having surveyed these themes in Luther's thought, one can safely conclude that for Luther, the consummate meaning and significance of faith, of grace, of God's glory, of Scripture, and of Christ, are deeply and mutually implicated. In an important respect, there are not five *solas*, but one *sola* that seems to stand behind them all. As William Lazareth incisively comments:

> For Luther the biblical message of salvation is a tension-filled unity which can be viewed from the perspective of any of its constitutive elements. He can speak of "grace alone," "Christ alone," "Scripture alone," or "faith alone," and mean thereby the same saving Event in terms of its eternal source, historical expression, apostolic witness, or personal appropriation.[63]

In view of this conclusion, and our earlier findings, we might proffer some constructive judgments, though briefly outlined. First, each element, each *sola*, when properly understood, contains the whole, for grace includes within it both the objective work of Christ and the subjective work of the Spirit, and this all for God's purposes and glory, so that these can only be received by faith as they are

---

61. Lotz writes that for Luther "the gospel is not only a message *about* Christ but is above all the living Word in and through which the Lord Christ himself is *still acting* as savior and redeemer in the present, as he once acted in the past in the flesh .... The gospel as spoken Word of God, in short, is nothing else than the real presence of the exalted Christ, the living Lord of the church" ("*Sola Scriptura*: Luther on Biblical Authority," p. 262). Rounding out his discussion of Luther's understanding of Christ and gospel and Scripture, Lotz later concludes: "While Scripture, therefore, is properly designated Word of God, it holds this dignity because it witnesses to Christ the Word who is in Scripture as its matchless content and because it contains the gospel through which the risen and exalted Christ still speaks and acts redemptively on behalf of his church" (ibid., p. 263).

62. Lohse, *Martin Luther's Theology*, p. 195. Paul O'Callaghan likewise states that "for Luther *sola Scriptura* means *solus Christus*, or at least leads us directly to this principle." See O'Callaghan, "*Solus Christus* and *Sola Scriptura*: The Christological Roots of Martin Luther's Interpretation of Scripture," *Annales Theologici* 31 (2017), pp. 459–71 (467). In truth, however, there is a sense in which *sola Scriptura* precedes *solus Christus* in the order of knowing, though *sola Scriptura* follows from *solus Christus* in the order of being and in the ordering of God's economy, for Christ does not exist for the sake of Scripture, but Scripture exists for the sake of Christ and in service and witness to him.

63. LW 44: p. xii.

attested in Holy Scripture. That each contains the whole is not, however, to collapse all into a single undifferentiated divine work, for not only do divine and human distinctions of course remain, but also such distinctions as that between Christ as the object of faith and faith itself, as well as that between Christ and Scripture, cannot simply be set aside. Yet all of the *solas* taken alone and together point to a single movement within the divine economy of works, a unified divine act in which Christ alone is the incomparable savior and teacher and head of the church, himself authoritatively attested in Scripture alone, proclaimed in the Word alone (*sola verbo*), and received in faith alone, and all of this the expression of God's glory alone and effected by God's grace alone, for all is grounded in this glorious and gracious disposition and declaration of God. All of the *solas* taken together point beyond themselves to one movement from God to humanity, and every single *sola* taken with seriousness unfolds to include all of the others. In this sense, the *solas* are not isolated polemical principles (though historically such polemics both during and after the Reformation were of course largely at play in the usage of the *solas*), but rather explications of facets of the one divine salvific economy.[64]

Second, this examination of Luther raises the question of whether the five *solas* themselves are best approached and explicated in view of a particular order. While each can be taken up as the initial point for examining the others in turn, it is the lens of Christ alone that provides the ground for rightly explicating all and prevents their definition from wandering into speculation and abstraction. This is so because God's grace and glory, as well as faith and Scripture, cannot be rightly understood except insofar as these are defined and delineated by the salvific, revelatory, and royal work of Christ. If so, then the concrete definition of the terms themselves, as well as the explicit exclusions they espouse and the implicit relations they enjoin, are only rightly understood in this light.

To unpack this claim entails the following. If the *solas* are to have a continuing felicitous place in theological description, then a guard must be placed against particular forms of distortion and abstraction. The *solas* serve poorly when they are established as independent doctrinal topics, when they are isolated one from the other, and in turn their deep connections lost. They themselves are poorly served when their order of movement is collapsed into an indifferent independence of attention and explication, when their terms are defined apart from the strict determinations and constrictions of christology, and where their singular

---

64. Once again, the constructive proposal here given for the *solas* is not negated nor dependent upon the historical contingency that the *solas* served and were conjoined for a particular polemical purpose—see Van den Belt, "The Problematic Character of *Sola Scriptura*," p. 40. This history of course must be acknowledged, but the full meaning of the *solas* is not captured by their past or present polemical usage. Kevin Vanhoozer thus sets forth the retrieval of the five *solas* as constituting "the *material principle* of mere Protestant Christianity insofar as they summarize the economy of the gospel." See Vanhoozer, *Biblical Authority after Babel: Retrieving the* Solas *in the Spirit of Mere Protestant Christianity* (Grand Rapids: Brazos Press, 2016), p. 25; cf. p. 28. As such, they serve a positive theological articulation even as they include an ineluctable polemical element.

exclusionary claims fail to push on to attend to the deeper relations they suppose. There will without question always be a place for the rejections that the *solas* uphold.[65] The *solas* were and continue to be appropriate lenses through which to view God's singular work of salvation and revelation, and they therefore continue to serve as forms of exclusion, demarcating God's work of grace alone, in Christ alone, for his glory alone, attested in Scripture alone, and received by faith alone.[66]

Such exclusions are a necessary first word that the *solas* speak and they can be further elucidated. The *solas* importantly uphold that human efforts are excluded from all proper matters of divine salvation and that human doctrines are excluded from the authority of divine disclosure. In short, both reconciliation and revelation are centered and fulfilled in Christ such that human moral works and ecclesial doctrinal teachings are responses to, rather than constitutive of, the salvation and the revelation Christ brings, which themselves are both received as one act of God's glory and grace alone, and thus received according to the testimony of Scripture alone and by faith alone.[67] These are the claims that the

---

65. As when the Formula of Concord states that questions of good works "must be completely excluded from any questions of salvation." See Robert Kolb and Timothy J. Wengert, eds., *The Book of Concord: The Confessions of the Evangelical Lutheran Church* (Minneapolis: Fortress, 2000), p. 498. Yet even here what might be required is an articulation of the exact nature of this exclusion, and on what terms, and how such does not eliminate the proper place for a life of active praise, thanksgiving, and good works "which God prepared beforehand to be our way of life" (Eph. 2:10 NRSV; cf. Rom. 12:1).

66. The *solas* have been the object of criticism as well, of course, but much of the criticism fails to grasp the rich and dialectical nature of the *solas*, which were never meant to be flat-footed assertions of exclusion and negation. For instance, *sola Scriptura* did not mean for the Reformers a rejection of tradition outright, but a proper ordering of tradition under the authority of Scripture. For an insightful discussion of *sola Scriptura* aware of such distortions and criticisms, as well as of its relation to the other *solas*, see Arnold Huijgen, "Alone Together," pp. 79–104. Huijgen pays particular attention to the fact that while the authority and revelation of Scripture follow and are dependent upon Christ's own, Christ himself is only known through Scripture, and he pushes back against a Christocentrism that would be set against Scripture, maintaining that the Christ worshipped by the church is none other than the Christ of Scripture (p. 95). Here we see ordered, reciprocal, and dialectical relations of Christ and Scripture that are largely implicit in Luther yet which would greatly occupy later Protestant thinkers such as Barth.

67. In "The Babylonian Captivity of the Church," Luther extended this argument even to the sacraments themselves. Having iterated that there are three sacraments, that is, baptism, penance, and "the bread," rather than seven, as held by the Roman curia, Luther continued: "Yet, if I were to speak according to the usage of the Scriptures, I should have only one single sacrament, but with three sacramental signs" (LW 36: p. 18). Luther referred to Christ himself as this *sacramentum* (LW 29: p. 123). A developed position along the lines here intimated was provided by Karl Barth, who maintained that Christ was the only sacrament—see CD IV/1: p. 296; CD IV/2: p. 55; cf. CD IV/2: p. ix; CD IV/4; and Barth, *The Christian Life*, trans. Geoffrey W. Bromiley (Grand Rapids: Eerdmans, 1981), p. 46.

*solas* serve and continue to uphold at the heart of the ongoing Reformation witness. They thereby preserve the careful order and distinction between the singular office and work of Christ and the commissioned vocation and witness of the church and the Christian.[68]

Yet if this word of exclusion is the first word that the *solas* speak, it cannot be the last one. The *solas* in truth have limited constructive and ecumenical promise if simply posed in terms of rejection, for what is implied in all of them is not only an exclusion but also a relation and affirmation. In effect, what the *solas* ultimately signify and articulate is not oppositional but ordered relations. If the witness of the *solas* is to be more than insular confession and protest, and instead is to be one of constructive understanding and even ecumenical promise, then such explicit exclusions must push onward to explore and articulate the intricate and irreversible relations that these *solas* implicitly uphold, for it is with an ever-deepening appreciation of the mysteries of these relations that unity in Christ may be hoped. These relations are tacit in each of the *solas*, and the ultimate goal of each *sola* is not so much to set forth an exclusion but a proper ordering of these relations at the heart of "so great a salvation." This mystery of salvation is myriad in its implications and inexhaustible in its wonders: first—that God has chosen to display his glory not only in opposition to fallen humanity but preeminently through his Son and the reconciled and redeemed humanity joined with him, such that it can rightly be said, when properly and christologically framed, that "the glory of God is the human person fully alive"[69]; second—that Christ sovereignly and incomparably reigns even as he has singularly saved and revealed God to us, but he reigns even as he also now lives in union and fellowship with his church, which truly is his bride and body; third—that Scripture stands over tradition and reason but is not opposed to their proper consultation and exercise, for they too need not be in utter opposition to revelation but can be redeemed and sanctified to be attendant and properly servile to it in confession and reflection; fourth—that God's grace is unassisted but nevertheless calls forth a requisite form of gratitude that includes a fitting celebration of creation and estimation of nature; and fifth—that faith excludes our works in the establishment of our salvation but not in its lived expression and indeed, as Dietrich Bonhoeffer delicately insisted, in its actual instantiation, for such works are, as Luther himself contended, of real necessity, for love of God and others must take concrete and tangible expression in the obedience of faith.

---

68. For Luther, this division was predicated on a right understanding and ordering of Christ's substitutionary (sacramental) and exemplary work: "Therefore he who wants to imitate Christ insofar as He is an example must first believe with a firm faith that Christ suffered and died for him insofar as this was a sacrament. Consequently, those who contrive to blot out sins first by means of works and labors of penance err greatly, since they begin with the example, when they should begin with the sacrament" (LW 29: p. 124).

69. Irenaeus, *Against Heresies* 4.20.7.

In short, the five *solas* find their proper end not in the judgment of exclusion they make (which is a necessary first word), but in the gracious affirmation they confess, an affirmation dependent upon a proper ordering of divine and human relations and activities.⁷⁰ It is in the ordering of these relations, more than in the polemical rejections, where the ongoing promise of the *solas* rests. It is also where

---

70. Once again, such a claim does not ignore the polemical element of the *solas*. But their negations serve a larger affirmation, and thus they present a constructive and positive vision of these relations of: (1) divine glory and human dignity; (2) Christ and the church (and the Christian); (3) Scripture and tradition (and reason); (4) grace and gratitude (and nature); and (5) faith and works. The *solas* when rightly articulated preserve rather than preclude such nuanced and ordered relations between these pairs. In contrast, Van den Belt states: "Whoever, then characterizes the Reformation by the *sola*-triad, allows Tridentine theology to determine the agenda and ignores the fact that the Catholic theology of the Middles [*sic*] Ages was more nuanced and diverse than later Roman Catholicism .... As a matter of fact, the Reformation did not reject tradition as such, but the idea that tradition was an extra-biblical source of revelation" (Van den Belt, "The Problematic Character of *Sola Scriptura*," p. 41). These two statements are problematic respectively. The first sentence is an assertion without warrant or necessity (and see note 40 above). The latter sentence is a truism that merits no real argument—*sola Scriptura* rightly understood (either in its earliest form in Luther's setting forth the authority of Scripture against papacy and tradition, or in its mature concept in later Protestantism) did not entail a necessary biblicism that eschewed *all* tradition, even if it was taken by some Christians to be such. Nor need it become a formal objective stance that "can easily erase the appreciation of the interrelationship of Word and Spirit"—it certainly did not do so for Luther or Calvin (see ibid., p. 50). Much less should it mean that any constructive proposal for retrieving the *solas* is simply allowing "Tridentine theology to determine the agenda" (ibid., p. 41). In his strict point, Van den Belt is of course correct that the actual position of the Reformers is misconstrued if *sola Scriptura* is meant to say that Scripture excludes all tradition. But the rightful understanding of the term as put forward here and in consonance with its actual use by the Reformers is not a matter of excluding all appeals to tradition but of preserving the qualitative status of Scripture as the singular witness to God's revelatory and salvific action centered in Jesus Christ, and in turn the norm that stands against all later tradition. In the end, if *sola Scriptura* can only be taken to mean an ahistorical biblicism, then it is best jettisoned. But there is no reason to limit it to such a flat construal. And if the term is rejected, the concept of the superiority of Scripture over later tradition would still require articulation. This qualitative difference between Scripture and tradition is underplayed in Van den Belt's essay (see, for instance, ibid., p. 44), though he does affirm that "Scripture contains all the truth necessary for salvation and there is no higher court to appeal to" (ibid., p. 50). In conclusion, Van den Belt is correct that *sola Scriptura* requires a nuanced understanding. What is less clear is why it needs to be discarded. He notes that it can be misunderstood and requires qualification—though this may simply be the fate of any short theological summation. Yet his own preferred term of *scriptura prima* itself requires qualification such that Scripture's primacy in relation to later tradition is not simply chronological or functional but a

the Good News finds its full voice, for the negation of improper human striving and idolatry turns at its end to the affirmation of humanity's true and proper worship, service, and redeemed existence. The exclusions of the *solas* are thus necessary but of circumscribed utility, for they must give way to an explication of the relations they attempt to set to rights.[71] Therefore, the Reformation vision they together serve to articulate is not simply a polemical protest but a constructive theological proposal set forth before the entire universal church.[72] The *solas* when treated as atomistic, simplistic, and provocative bumper sticker slogans stripped of all context and nuance cannot serve the richness of this exposition. But when rightly appreciated as facets of a far richer mystery of God's movement toward humanity "for us and for our salvation," they can in fact serve such a positive evangelical articulation, and one that did not originate with Luther, yet found in him its most articulate witness in his time.

This witness hangs, in the end, on the christological heart of all of the *solas*. So many problematic distortions preserved or newly invented—whether of grace as a transactional substance mediated through ecclesial channels rather than a divine disposition that sends the Son and establishes a relation by and with him with its accompanying pronouncement and gifts of the Spirit; or of faith as a subjective or existential topic in its own right torn from its object rather than trust in a name, that of Jesus Christ; or of divine glory as a triumphalistic power isolated from rather than defined by Christ's cross and his form as a servant and revealed in his resurrection and ascension; or, finally, of Scripture as an epistemological principle standing before all dogmatic topics rather than the means of Christ's own self-announcement in the economy of redemption whose content and center are

---

qualitative and absolute one (see ibid., p. 52). Hence as he acknowledges, primacy itself requires definition through debate (ibid., p. 53). More helpful is Huijgen who simply states that "*sola scriptura* is meant as a statement that the scriptures are the final, not the sole, authority" ("Alone Together," p. 85; also p. 87); the same point is made by Anthony N. S. Lane, "*Sola Scriptura*? Making Sense of a Post-Reformation Slogan," in *A Pathway in the Holy Scripture*, ed. Philip E. Satterthwaite and David F. Wright (Grand Rapids: Eerdmans, 1994), pp. 323–7. Kevin Vanhoozer dispatches common objections to *sola scriptura* as themselves caricatures of it—see Vanhoozer, "*Sola Scriptura* Means Scripture First! A 'Mere Protestant' Dogmatic Account (and Response)," in *Sola Scriptura: Biblical and Theological Perspectives on Scripture, Authority, and Hermeneutics*, ed. Hans Burger, Arnold Huijgen, and Eric Peels (Leiden/Boston: Brill, 2017), pp. 335–58; esp. pp. 338–9.

71. In other words, the "No" they pronounce is entirely in the service of a larger "Yes," their word of condemnation taken up into a larger gospel. See Vanhoozer, "*Sola Scriptura* Means Scripture First!," pp. 339–41.

72. Vanhoozer argues that the Reformation was itself a retrieval of the biblical gospel, "particularly the Pauline articulation, but also, secondarily, of the church fathers" (*Biblical Authority after Babel*, pp. 22–3). What must be added is that what was inherent and decisive in this retrieval was the rediscovery of the distinction of Christ and the church, and thus in turn the distinction between Scripture and the papacy, as well as later tradition.

Christ himself—all of these are due to an abstraction of grace, of faith, of glory, and of Scripture, from a christological center and from the single movement of God in the divine economy.[73] In essence, evangelical theology *is* christological theology. Put negatively, theology that is not christologically defined is not evangelical

73. With regard to grace, such distortions are particularly due to a separation of Christ from his benefits, and where the means of grace are rendered to be means of grace's dispersal rather than pronouncement. With regard to faith, such distortions follow in the train of seeing faith as a virtue or element of a general existential religiosity. With regard to Scripture, perhaps no one has articulated such distortions as succinctly and incisively in recent times as John Webster. Webster bemoans the shift of Scripture from its true home in "the saving economy of the triune God" to a "relatively isolated piece of epistemological teaching" as it was forced "to migrate to the beginning of the dogmatic corpus." He concludes: "The extent to which this process is a natural result of the Reformation insistence upon *sola scriptura* is debatable; it is, I believe, more plausible to see it as the result of the abstraction of *sola scriptura* from the other Reformation exclusive particles *solus Christus, sola gratia* and *solo verbo* (all of which are extensions of the primary principle *solus Deus*), which, in effect, tied Reformation teaching about Scripture to a wider set of doctrinal materials and thereby ensured its integration into the scope of dogmatics." The canon is thus shorn of its connections to christology, soteriology, and pneumatology. See Webster, *Word and Church* (Edinburgh/New York: T&T Clark, 2001), pp. 9-10. When such connections are fully appreciated, *sola Scriptura* is seen to be the acknowledgment of the singular witness of Scripture to Christ, and not, as has at times been attempted, as a legitimation for our own confessional identities. Maarten Wisse rightly points out the problematic nature of such uses of *sola Scriptura*—see Wisse, "Contra et Pro Sola Scriptura," in *Sola Scriptura: Biblical and Theological Perspectives on Scripture, Authority, and Hermeneutics*, ed. Hans Burger, Arnold Huijgen, and Eric Peels (Leiden/Boston: Brill, 2017), pp. 19-37 (22-3). But such misuses need not, of course, entail the necessity of abandoning the concept altogether. Wisse recognizes that *sola scriptura* at its heart points to Scripture as the singular witness to the unique revelation of God in Christ and entails the irrevocable distinction of Christ and his church, and thus in turn "a very clear distinction between the holy scriptures and other scriptures" (ibid., pp. 32-4). He therefore perceptively argues that "the consequences of the understanding of *sola scriptura* for ecclesiology are more profound than those for the doctrine of scripture" (ibid., 35). In truth, these are mutually implicated, for *sola Scriptura* as a doctrine of Scripture is predicated upon christological convictions and entails particular ecclesiological positions regarding the relation of Christ and the church. Put positively, *sola scriptura* upholds the lordship of Christ not only within but also over the church, as well as the insistence that it is the Word that makes the church and not the church the Word (see LW 36: pp. 144-5; cf. LW 54: p. 119). Put negatively, it is the recognition that the church can err (see Lane, "Sola Scriptura?" p. 324). The latter was a fundamental discovery for Luther—so Lohse, *Martin Luther's Theology*, pp. 187-8. In other terms, *sola Scriptura* attests the firm resolution that the gospel takes precedence even over the church. So Lane succinctly comments: "The root issue was one of ecclesiology: does the church define the gospel or vice-versa?" See A. N. S. Lane, "Scripture, Tradition and Church: An Historical Survey," *Vox Evangelica* 9 (1975), pp. 37-55 (42).

theology but betrays its central vision.[74] For while all of the *solas* are intimated in the others, it is Christ alone who gives them proper definition and form.[75] And only Christ crucified allows us to call all such things by their proper names, for all things are known rightly only through the cross alone (*sola crux*).[76] Indeed, Luther could go so far as to say that "the cross alone is our theology," for *sola crux*

---

74. If this is understood, the christocentric concentration of evangelical theology is properly seen not as a development within modernity but residing within the DNA of the original Reformation vision, and, as one might argue alongside Luther, as residing at the heart of the New Testament itself. Indeed, in the New Testament Christ is not simply the herald but the content of God's grace and the instantiation of his kingdom, and this too provides the warrant for grounding all of the *solas* in that of Christ alone (in comparison to Vanhoozer, who argues for grace as the starting point—*Biblical Authority after Babel*, p. 37; though see ibid., p. 149, where Vanhoozer defines "Christian theology" as "the conceptual indication of what is in Christ").

75. It might rightly be said in another regard that the *solas* must be understood in light of God's triune identity, as Graeme Goldsworthy has stated: "It is important to grasp that the four 'alones' really take their essential characteristic from God as Trinity. Consequently, none of the 'alones' can exist without the others." See Goldsworthy, *Gospel-Centered Hermeneutics: Foundations and Principles of Evangelical Biblical Interpretation* (Downers Grove: IVP Academic, 2006), p. 50. Certainly this is true, for Christ is the revelation of the Father and God's grace and glory, and the awakening of faith occurs only through the Spirit just as Scripture is Spirit-inspired, such that one could state that the *solas* must also be understood pneumatologically as well as christologically. Yet as Barth so rightly knew, the doctrine of the Trinity takes its rise chronologically and logically from the revelation Christ brings, just as, Barth maintained, it is the second article that is the key to understanding the first and the third. When this is forgotten, theology untethered from this center becomes susceptible to forms of deism or pantheism, straying into philosophical theism or mysticism. Moreover, as both Luther and Barth never failed to insist, the Spirit cannot be separated from the Word, even as the Son testifies to the Father. It is for the same reason that one must understand the *solas* christologically, for it is in the light of Christ that they find their grounding and determination. In short, it is this focus on Christ that prevents all abstract speculation: "Everything that deserves to be called knowledge in the Christian sense lives from the knowledge of Jesus Christ"—see Barth, *Dogmatics in Outline* (New York: Harper & Row, 1959), pp. 67; 65-7. In saying this, Barth was not the paragon of modern theology but simply a faithful disciple of Luther: "I am resolved not to believe or hear anything save Christ alone. I will not regard anything else as the voice of God. For God has ordained that He would not communicate with man through any other medium than Christ alone" (LW 23: p. 348).

76. As stated in Luther's "Heidelberg Disputation" (LW 31: p. 45). Ngien comments on this work: "To know God aright is to know him in his opposites: in the folly of the world rather than in wisdom, in weakness rather [than] in strength, in suffering rather than in power, in humility rather than in majesty" (*Luther's Theology of the Cross*, p. 5; cf. pp. 3-8; see also Lienhard, *Luther: Witness to Jesus Christ*, pp. 98-100).

is not only a particular soteriological intensification of *solus Christus*, but also its proper interpretation, for the Christ the church worships is a crucified and risen Messiah.[77] Divine salvation comes to us bearing a name, and that name is Jesus Christ. This movement of God in Christ to us is the *sola* that stands behind them all. For in the end, it is not God alone, but God with us, Emmanuel, that is the heart of the gospel.[78]

---

77. "CRUX sola est nostra theologia" (Commentary on Psalm 5, WA 5: p. 176). Luther can add that "the cross tests everything" [Crux probat omnia] (WA 5: p. 179).

78. CD I/2: p. 257. "It is a fundamental rule of Christian theology that a doctrine of God which is *only* a doctrine of God is not a Christian doctrine of God." See John Webster, *Holiness* (Grand Rapids: Eerdmans, 2003), p. 53.

Chapter 3

KARL BARTH ON LUTHER AND CALVIN
AS FATHERS OF THE CHURCH

In the academic discipline of textual criticism, it is often said that manuscripts should be weighed and not simply counted. What this means is that in attempting to determine the original wording of the Greek text of the New Testament, the number of manuscripts that witness a particular reading is not as important as the age and significance of the manuscripts that give this wording. In brief, many extant manuscripts might possess the same reading, but they may all have been later copies that include a demonstrably mistaken transcription of an even earlier text. In this regard, a few earlier manuscripts may be much more significant for determining a reading than many later ones, for numerous later copies are less important than the existence of early documents closer in time and fidelity to the original. The point is simply that number does not overshadow substance, and the quality of references is more significant than their quantity.

Something similar should be remembered when one looks at Karl Barth's evaluation of Luther and Calvin. If one were simply to assess the most important engagement with Luther by Barth in the crude terms of frequency of references to Luther himself, then the most important work by Barth on Luther would be the lectures he gave very early in his academic career in Göttingen in the winter semester of 1922–3 for a course on Zwingli, with his lectures on Calvin in the previous summer semester of 1922 a distant second.[1] With regard to references to Calvin, these two works could simply be reversed, with *The Theology of Calvin* lectures containing the most references to the Reformer, and the *Theology of Zwingli*

---

1. By far the most direct references to Luther are found in *The Theology of Zwingli* with *The Theology of John Calvin* a distant second. See Barth, *Die Theologie Zwinglies 1922/1923*, ed. Matthias Freudenberg (Zürich: Theologischer Verlag Zürich, 2004); and Barth, *The Theology of John Calvin*, trans. Geoffrey W. Bromiley (Grand Rapids: Eerdmans, 1995). The third source for most mentions of Luther and for Calvin alike is the 1923 lectures on the Reformed Confessions. See Barth, *The Theology of the Reformed Confessions*, trans. Darrell L. Guder and Judith J. Guder (Louisville: Westminster John Knox, 2002).

lectures coming in second.² Barth's early historical and theological attention to Luther and Calvin as figures in their own right would never be replicated on the scale or with the intensity of these early lectures. Yet Barth's mature understanding of Luther and Calvin far outstrips these lectures in significance of judgment even while demonstrating lines of continuity in assessment. In truth, Barth's early lectures were, by his own later admission, the result of feverish work to master the foundational thinkers of Reformed theology—a tradition that he belonged to in name but which he did not truly know.³ Hence, his first theological lectures were historical studies of Calvin, Zwingli, and the Reformed Confessions (and the Heidelberg Catechism) in order to understand the Reformers themselves and the Reformed heritage. This is what occupied him during his early years in Göttingen.⁴

For all of the importance of Barth's examination in these course lectures of Luther's interaction and influence with regard to Zwingli and Calvin, it would be a mistake to see this early period as the one where Barth was most indebted to Luther for his own thought and where Luther displayed the most influence upon his work. In these early lectures on Zwingli and Calvin, Barth was learning a tradition, and his engagement with Calvin and Zwingli entailed a new concentration on the theology of Luther as well, for, as the preeminent first-generation Reformer who influenced both, his significance could not be ignored. Barth wrestled with Luther's thought especially in the Zwingli lectures as he examined the debates on the Lord's Supper that came to a head at the Marburg Colloquy in 1529 and pondered the inability of Zwingli and Luther to reach agreement there on sacramental questions. In a very important respect, at this juncture Luther was for Barth primarily a character in a debate with Zwingli, and

---

2. The vast majority of references to Calvin are unsurprisingly in *The Theology of Calvin*, with *The Theology of Zwingli* a distant second. By themselves, of course, such numbers mean very little. George Hunsinger is correct when he states: "What Barth learned from Luther cannot be appreciated through statistical calculations." See Hunsinger, *Disruptive Grace* (Grand Rapids: Eerdmans, 2000), p. 280 nt. 2. Again, it is the quality and use of references, not their frequency, that is of importance.

3. Barth remarked in an interview late in his life that though he had read Luther and Calvin before his first academic appointment, he was not a true confessional Reformed person (*konfessioneller Reformierter*) when he entered it, and that upon assuming this position he had to engage with the thought of Reformed theology with seriousness for the first time ("Jetzt mußte ich mich gründlich mit reformierter Theologie beschäftigen, zum ersten Mal eigentlich"). It was during this period that he studied Zwingli, Luther, and Calvin with concentrated intensity—a time, as he recalled, of tremendous labor. See Karl Barth, "Interview von H. A. Fischer-Barnicol, Südwestfunk (5.5.1964)," in *Gespräche 1964–1968*, ed. Eberhard Busch (Zürich: Theologischer Verlag Zürich, 1996), pp. 131–66 (151).

4. See Barth's letter to Eduard Thurneysen of January 22, 1922 in *Barth–Thurneysen Briefwechsel 1921–1930*, ed. Eduard Thurneysen (Zürich: Theologischer Verlag Zürich, 1974), pp. 27–34 (29).

thus a foil for the Reformed tradition that Barth was attempting to learn and make his own. His research led not only to the production of these Zwingli lectures, but also to the important essay of 1923, "Luther's Doctrine of the Eucharist: Its Basis and Purpose," where he brought to culmination his reflections on Luther's position on the Lord's Supper and connected these sacramental convictions to other important theological questions that would continue to haunt his lifelong reflection on Luther and the Lutheran tradition.[5]

Just as significant for understanding Barth's estimation of Luther as these extensive interactions with him in the Zwingli and Calvin lectures are his weighty (if brief and passing) references to him in the ensuing years. These references portray Luther not predominantly as a historical character in a debate with Zwingli, but as a figure in his own right that turned the course of history in the Reformation and stood not only as the foremost representative of its accomplishment, but in a line of faithful witnesses to God and God's revelation.

This assessment of Luther was prefigured in Barth's famous commentary on Romans. In the preface to the second edition (1921), Barth famously mentioned the apostle Paul, Franz Overbeck, Plato, Immanuel Kant, Søren Kierkegaard, and Fyodor Dostoevsky as significant influences upon his thought.[6] Notably absent from this initial list was either Luther or Calvin. Yet elsewhere in the commentary (as well as in prefaces to later editions) the early importance of both Reformers for Barth is evident, and the reason for this is their exposition of Scripture. What Barth discovered in Luther and Calvin was an approach to Scripture that engaged the subject matter of the text in a way that was not limited to the historical questions and methods of his contemporaries. In the preface to the second edition, Barth lauded Luther and Calvin's insight into reading Scripture in contrast to the historical critics of his own time, citing "that creative energy which Luther exercised with intuitive certainty in his exegesis; which underlies the systematic interpretation of Calvin; and which is at least attempted by such modern writers as Hofmann, J. T. Beck, Godet, and Schlatter."[7] Similarly, in the preface of the third edition (1922), Barth could commend not only Calvin's exegesis but also his understanding of the inspiration of Scripture that gave coherence to his exegetical practice.[8] These comments and others show that Barth valued Luther and Calvin for both their exegetical approach and their theological understanding of Scripture's importance during this period, although their absence from his list of significant influences in the preface to the second edition remains noteworthy.

In a short time, however, Barth's list of important persons began to change. It became a list not of idiosyncratic and eclectic theological (and philosophical?)

---

5. Barth, "Luther's Doctrine of the Eucharist: Its Basis and Purpose" in TC, pp. 74–111.
6. Karl Barth, *The Epistle to the Romans*, trans. Edwyn C. Hoskyns (Oxford: Oxford University Press, 1968 [1933]), pp. 3–4.
7. Ibid., p. 7; cf. p. 22.
8. Ibid., pp. 18–19.

influences, but of theological heritage and confessional continuity—a theological genealogy of faithful witnesses to God's revelation extended through church history.[9] A year after the publication of the *Römerbrief*, for example, in the lecture "The Word of God as the Task of Theology," Barth provided a list of persons that was now marked by the intentional identification of a historic line of faithful witnesses to divine revelation. This is evident in his placement of Luther and Calvin in a theological genealogy of true theological paragons in which Barth hoped also to situate himself: "I would like to conclude this discussion with a historical footnote. If my reflections here are decisive in any way, then the line of ancestors upon which we have to orient ourselves runs through *Kierkegaard* to *Luther* and *Calvin*, to *Paul* to *Jeremiah*. Many are used to calling upon these familiar names."[10] As Barth emphasized, this list does not include Schleiermacher.[11] Indeed, Barth was working to identify not only those who belonged in this faithful line of witnesses, but also those who did not, and particularly those who in his view had betrayed the decisive insights of the Reformers.

It should be noted that in time Kierkegaard would drop in Barth's estimation and would not be included on the same plane as the others in this list of faithful witnesses, but of most importance for our present purpose is to register that Barth here holds Luther and Calvin in the highest regard and places them in the same ancestral line as the prophet Jeremiah and the apostle Paul. Yet despite this straightforward commendation of Luther and Calvin, Barth also circumscribes their dignity, demarcating their witness to the truth of God's revelation from revelation itself, insisting that, regardless of their faithfulness, even they can only point to what God alone can do, for "our goal is the speaking of *God himself.*"[12] This was another conviction Barth would hold to the end, and it was a thoroughly dialectical one. On the one hand, the Reformers were of preeminent importance,

---

9. In point of fact, this type of list was already prefigured in the Romans commentary, but there it was more a list of association than of ancestry. See ibid., pp. 57, 117; cf. p. 137.

10. Barth, "The Word of God as the Task of Theology," in WGT, pp. 171-98 (182; cf. 183).

11. Barth believed that Schleiermacher represented the end result of the betrayal of the Reformation, a conviction he expressed to his students in Göttingen: "Protestantism has not in fact had any greater theologian since the days of the reformers. But this theologian has led us all into this dead end! This is an oppressive and almost intolerable thought. How can it really be reconciled with confidence in Protestantism's power of truth? Or should we in fact say that this was and is the normal and legitimate continuation of the Reformation, the completion of the work of Luther and Calvin: this doctrine of the feeling of absolute dependence or of the universum and all that is connected with it? If it were, for me the right thing to do would be to become a Roman Catholic again." See Barth, *The Theology of Schleiermacher: Lectures at Göttingen, Winter Semester of 1923/24*, ed. Dietrich Ritschl, trans. Geoffrey W. Bromiley (Grand Rapids: Eerdmans, 1982), p. 259.

12. Barth, "The Word of God as the Task of Theology," p. 196.

standing in the line of Jeremiah and Paul. Yet on the other hand, they had no true importance except insofar as they gave witness to God's revelation, pointing beyond themselves to this Word that comes from God in their attendance to Holy Scripture. This recognition of the Reformers as exemplary witnesses to God's revelation by virtue of their service as preeminent expositors of Holy Scripture is the basis of Barth's understanding of Luther and Calvin as church fathers. It is also the basis for his distinction between them and prophets and apostles like Jeremiah and Paul, who, as biblical witnesses, possess an authority Luther and Calvin do not.[13]

Though Barth treated Luther and Calvin as a pair with regard to their importance for the Reformation and their practice of faithful exegesis of Scripture, he nevertheless did draw distinctions between them and the respective confessional traditions that followed in their wake. In his lectures on Calvin in 1922, Barth emphasized the singular role that Luther played for the church's Reformation, writing:

> The man who thought out first, and with most originality and force, the basic antimedieval and, as we saw last time, the basic antimodern thought of the Reformation, that of the theology of the cross, was neither Zwingli nor Calvin but Luther. Both Zwingli and Calvin learned from Luther, not without at once contradicting him, not without giving their own shape to what they learned, yet learning from him at the decisive point. Luther's Reformation was not the whole Reformation. It was not even the source or place of origin of the whole Reformation. Nevertheless, it initiated the movement which characterizes the whole and of which the Reformation of Zwingli and Calvin was primarily a repetition, even though a second turn was given to the Reformation in and with the repetition.[14]

---

13. It is important to note, however, that Barth had at this point not yet elaborated the technical distinction between primary and secondary witnesses to God's revelation, which came only with his reflections upon apostolicity and canon in his Göttingen theology lectures, which commenced in 1924.

14. Barth, *The Theology of John Calvin*, p. 70; cf. pp. 80–1. Barth continued soon thereafter: "A good member of the Reformed communion must begin by simply recognizing Luther's unique position in the Reformation, not moving away from or forsaking Luther, nor, in following the hints of Zwingli and Calvin, feeling compelled to go a step beyond him; but instead, while consciously following those hints, constantly coming back to him. At the outset we distinguish ourselves from Lutherans in this way. As disciples of the most loyal disciples of Luther, we do not detract from Luther any more than Lutherans do, whereas they for their part can never manage to promote regard for Luther without open or concealed polemics against Zwingli and Calvin" (ibid., pp. 70–1).

Barth also, however, praised Calvin for moving beyond Luther, stating that Calvin emphasized not only justification as Luther did, but also sanctification; not only faith, but obedience; and thus not only the vertical but the horizontal elements of the Christian life.[15] Moreover, Barth could look awry at what he esteemed to be Luther's emphasis upon faith and subjectivity,[16] as well as what Barth esteemed were Luther's casual demarcation and even confusion of revelation and the creaturely medium taken up for God's self-manifestation.[17] Nevertheless, Barth

---

15. See Barth, *The Theology of John Calvin*, pp. 81-2; cf. pp. 87-90. These are distinctions between Luther and Calvin that Barth would hold for his entire life. See Barth, "Gespräch mit Rheinischen Jugendpfarrern (4.11.1963)" in *Gespräche 1963*, ed. Eberhard Busch (Zürich: Theologischer Verlag Zürich, 2005), pp. 235-333 (260); cf. Barth, *The Theology of the Reformed Confessions*, pp. 43-4 and 80-1; and also CD IV/2: p. 509. These estimations changed little over Barth's lifetime, evidenced in Barth's comments in 1965: "Luther and Calvin are essentially always concerned with two great things: Luther teaches the freedom of the Christian person as one who believes in the Word of God. Calvin teaches the majesty of God, which gives us the freedom to have faith and to render obedience. These are, so to speak, the two poles of the Reformation. Luther is more human-oriented and Calvin more oriented to God. One should not make this out to be a contradiction between them, but it is a difference." See Barth, "*Interview von G. Puchinger (15.4.1965)*" in *Gespräche 1964-1968*, pp. 184-96 (193) (author's trans).

16. See Barth's 1923 lecture "The Substance and Task of Reformed Doctrine," in WGT, pp. 199-237 (223; cf. 231). There Barth stated: "The Reformed confessions [over against the Lutheran ones] did not lay the emphasis on the fact that the human is justified through *faith* instead of through *works*, but, rather, that it is *God* and not the *human* who completes this justification" (ibid., p. 223). Gerhard Ebeling judged this criticism of Luther's subjectivity as the foundation of all Barth's later criticisms of Luther. See Gerhard Ebeling, "Über die Reformation hinaus? Zur Luther-Kritik Karl Barths," *Zeitschrift für Theologie und Kirche*, Beiheft 6: Zur Theologie Karl Barths: Beiträge aus Anlaß seines 100 Geburtstags (1986), 33-75 (36-37; cf. 47).

17. In other words, Barth judged that for Luther the indirect identity of revelation and the creaturely medium of revelation was flattened into a direct one, such that the Creator and creature distinction was jeopardized. Therefore in reference to christology and sacraments, Barth wrote in his 1923 essay on Reformed doctrine: "The Lutherans went so far as to make a *direct*, miraculous, but earthly identity out of the indirect identity between the heavenly and earthly gifts that are only perfected in God himself, between the thing and the sign, between witness and revelation. Thus they made a direct mediation out of revelation, which, if it is real, is always a veiling. They constructed a religious 'givenness'" ("The Substance and Task of Reformed Doctrine," p. 227; see also "Luther's Doctrine of the Eucharist," in TC, pp. 74-111 (99; 108-11); cf. CD I/2: pp. 163-71; CD IV/2: pp. 51-2; 75-7). Even more pointedly, Barth worried that Luther's emphasis on subjectivity and the intermingling of the divine and human natures of Christ in christology, which in turn failed to maintain the irreversibility of their relation, opened the way for Feuerbach's critique of religion as the divinization of the human. See Barth's lecture of 1920, "Ludwig Feuerbach," in TC, pp. 217-37 (230-1). In later years Barth criticized Luther along a third major line, specifically, as the source for a law and gospel distinction that Barth maintained played into German nationalism.

also maintained in his early lectures that Luther and Calvin, and their respective emphases, were both necessary and complementary for understanding the Reformation accomplishment and for evangelical witness to the gospel.[18]

If in fact there was a substantive advantage to the Reformed tradition over the Lutheran one in Barth's estimation, it was composed of two primary elements: first, that whereas Luther discovered a material principle (justification by faith) in Scripture, Calvin emphasized the formal principle of Scripture as the rule of all faith and life; and second, that whereas Luther's focus was upon questions of salvation and faith (i.e., soteriology), Calvin's was upon questions of God and truth (i.e., theology proper), and this in turn protected the Creator-creature distinction more carefully than Luther had done, as well as prioritizing christology over anthropology. In truth, Barth's estimation of Luther was always marked by both deep appreciation and an undeniable ambivalence.[19] Yet, Barth's ultimate judgment was that Luther and Calvin were, in the end, partners in a common project of church reformation. What Paul, Luther, and Calvin all have in common, Barth consistently argued, is a recognition of and insistence upon the movement of God to humanity that must precede and frame any talk of our movement and obedience toward God.[20] It was, even more fundamentally, a recognition of the lordship of God in all matters of salvation, a recognition that in turn demanded a decision.[21] It is this common declaration of God's singular lordship by Luther and Calvin, along with their corresponding confession of the singular authority of Scripture, that makes them fathers of the church.[22] Barth articulated this exact conviction more than a decade later in the weightiest passage that he provides on Luther and Calvin as paired Reformers, to which we will now turn.

18. Barth, *The Theology of John Calvin*, 90.
19. For an intensive account of Barth's relation to Luther traced over time, including details and criticisms beyond those considered here, see Gerhard Ebeling, *Lutherstudien*, Vol. 3, *Begriffsuntersuchungen—Textinterpretationen—Wirkungsgeschichtliches* (Tübingen: J. C. B. Mohr [Paul Siebeck], 1985), pp. 428–573. For a succinct summary of the central criticisms, see Bernhard Lohse, *Martin Luther: And Introduction to His Life and Work*, trans. Robert C. Schultz (Philadelphia: Fortress Press, 1986), pp. 227–8.
20. See Barth's 1922 essay, "The Problem of Ethics Today" in WGT, pp. 131–70 (168).
21. See Barth, "Reformation als Entscheidung," in *Vorträge und kleinere Arbeiten 1930–1933*, ed. Michael Beintker, Michael Hüttenhoff, and Peter Zocher (Zürich: Theologischer Verlag Zürich, 2013), pp. 516–50 (532–5).
22. As Barth would later write in his Gifford Lectures of 1937/38, the fundamental fact of importance regarding the Reformers, regardless of any problematic elements of their thought, was that "the revival of the gospel by Luther and Calvin consisted in their desire to see both the church and human salvation founded on the Word of God *alone*, on God's *revelation in Jesus Christ*, as it is attested in the Scripture, and on faith in that Word." See Barth, *The Knowledge of God and the Service of God according to the Teaching of the Reformation: Recalling the Scottish Confession of 1560*, trans. J. L. M. Haire and Ian Henderson (Eugene: Wipf and Stock, 2005 [1938]), pp. 8–9.

## Barth's Mature Estimation of Luther and Calvin

While Luther and Calvin are important interlocutors in Barth's *Church Dogmatics*, the most sustained and significant discussion of them in their own right occurs relatively early in that massive work. In the second part of the first volume, Barth examines Holy Scripture in three sections (§19–21). In the second of these, he discusses the authority of Scripture and the corresponding authority of the church. He locates three specific areas where the authority of the church is exercised under the authority of Scripture: first, in confessing the parameters of the biblical canon and thus effectively setting forth its constituent books; second, in recognizing exemplary expositors of the Bible and holding them up before the church for her instruction as authoritative teachers; and, third, in producing confessions of a common faith and establishing them as formal articulations of what has been heard in Holy Scripture, these confessions thus possessing a relative authority under the authority of Scripture itself.[23] Barth's discussion of Luther and Calvin occurs in the second of these three sections, where he begins simply by acknowledging the existence of such teachers:

> We assume that between the Church now and here and the Church then and elsewhere there exists a unity of confession in respect of the authority of the word of specific ecclesiastical teachers, i.e., specific expositors and preachers of the Bible, whose word has in fact emerged from all the words of other expositors and preachers and spoken to the Church of their day and of a later day, and still speaks to the present-day Church, in a way which cannot be said of other teachers of their own or other periods.[24]

While the existence of such teachers is not a theological necessity for Barth, he nevertheless notes that the church recognizes "that there are 'Church fathers' and that these fathers have a definite ecclesiastical authority."[25] He argues, however, that such figures are not to be thought of in the same sense as church fathers are reckoned in Catholic thought. The Reformation did not recognize earlier prestigious teachers as part of a rigid hierarchical ranking of theological authority or as a "second source of revelation."[26] Nevertheless, the evangelical tradition does recognize church fathers when these are rightly defined; moreover, Barth's remarkable claim is not just that there are church fathers, a claim with a long ecclesial pedigree, but that these fathers are, preeminently and singularly, Luther and Calvin themselves. They are, for Barth, the quintessential church fathers, for reasons we will examine below.

This identification of Luther and Calvin as church fathers does not entail, however, that their persons are held to be of particular interest. Indeed, Barth

---

23. These three areas are found in CD I/2: pp. 597–603, 603–20, and 620–60, respectively.
24. CD I/2: p. 603.
25. Ibid.
26. Ibid., p. 604.

expresses a concern that the Lutheran tradition especially placed too much emphasis upon the person, personality, and life of Luther.[27] With regard to this focus upon Luther's person, Barth writes:

> Certainly the firm popularity which has been retained by the figure of Luther even in modern developments, and in particular the estimation as an apostle of freedom of conscience or a religious personality or a German which he has been accorded more recently on every possible or impossible count, is no substitute for a recognition of his ecclesiastical signification as a Reformer and Church teacher.[28]

These were no idle words when Barth published them in 1938, for while Luther had been esteemed a towering spiritual personality and religious genius in the nineteenth century, it was during the 1930s that he especially came to be considered as a hero of the German *Volk* and a nationalist figure.[29] In Barth's estimation, Luther was misunderstood if identified and thought significant as a religious personality or pious genius, a soldier of reason against medieval superstition, or a national hero or "great German."[30] Barth had quite simply no interest in Luther as understood in any of these roles, although he well recognized the recurrent temptation to cast

---

27. Although Barth acknowledged that these tendencies could also be found in the Reformed tradition, he held that the latter was in general more circumspect, esteeming Calvin, for example, solely for his ecclesiastical instruction. See ibid., pp. 604–5.

28. Ibid., p. 606.

29. For an understanding of Luther in light of the developments in Germany from the time of the Reformation, through the Enlightenment and the liberalism of the nineteenth century, up until Barth's own time, see Peter Opitz, "'Wer darf sich ernslich auf die Reformation berufen?' Die gefeierte Reformation und Karl Barth," *Zeitschrift für Dialektische Theologie* 32 (2016), pp. 7–34. Opitz recounts how with the 450th anniversary of Luther's birth in 1933 renewed attention was given to Luther, but now in the context of a rising National Socialism and its portrayal of Luther as "the great German" (ibid., pp. 8; 10). For Barth's reactions against this celebration of Luther as a religious or national personality during this period, see his 1933 essays, "Luther" and "Reformation als Entscheidung," in *Vorträge und kleinere Arbeiten 1930–1933*, pp. 478–87 and 516–50, respectively; see also Opitz, "Wer darf sich ernslich auf die Reformation, berufen?," pp. 9–10; and Ebeling, *Lutherstudien*, Vol. 3, pp. 395–404. Opitz traces a long-standing line of development tying Luther to German nationalism and shows that this nationalistic emphasis intensified during the rise of National Socialism. One example of such extreme nationalism was the church historian Hans Preuss, who paired Luther and Adolf Hitler as great "German leaders" (*deutsche Führer*) who stood above their contemporaries even while suffering in struggle for them against the foes of their respective times. Preuss asserted that both men achieved comparable and parallel monumental accomplishments, Luther translating the Bible while in exile at the Wartburg and Hitler writing *Mein Kampf* while in prison in Landsberg, each one deeply united with God before the people of their nation (see ibid., p. 21). Such views were not peripheral in Germany at the time but are widely attested (ibid., pp. 21–2).

30. Barth, "Luther," pp. 485–6.

him into the image of the contemporary age.[31] Yet to know Luther in truth was simply to acknowledge him for what he not only was in his time but continues to be: a teacher of the church, who was best not celebrated but heard.[32]

One of the things Barth learned from Kierkegaard that never left him was that there is all the difference in the world between a "religious genius" and an apostle.[33] Barth did not think of Luther and Calvin as apostles, of course, as their writings were not to be included in the canon of Holy Scripture. Yet as preeminent biblical expositors and teachers, and therefore as church fathers, they were, in their own way, the true heirs of the apostles in that they pointed away from themselves to Scripture, just as the apostles of Scripture pointed away from themselves to Christ.[34] It is therefore accurate to conclude that, for Barth, Luther and Calvin are fathers of the church because of this analogous relation to the apostles: they are exemplary witnesses to the singular witnesses of the prophets and apostles. It was this unique role, and not the Reformers' personality, that was decisive. Indeed, Barth had no place for hero worship and already in 1923 wrote in regard to a witness to revelation: "The human does not come into consideration, not even as a prophet, never mind as a Christian hero but rather as a minister, as a *servant* of the divine Word."[35]

This attitude meant that Barth put very little weight upon anniversaries commemorating the Reformers. He had little time for a nationalist "Deutschen Luthertag" (German Luther Day) or the 450th anniversary celebrations of Luther's birth in 1933. Nor did he have any real regard for similar celebrations of Calvin's anniversaries. Toward the end of his life, Barth wrote a short piece entitled "Thoughts on the 400th Anniversary of Calvin's Death," and he found it no accident (and in fact quite appropriate) that Calvin's grave had been allowed to slip into oblivion but a few years after his passing.[36] Calvin was not a hero, Barth insisted, and should not be worshipped as one. He was, rather, a witness, a servant of the Word of God—and for Barth, who considered John the Baptist as the paragon of the Christian's vocation of indication, this was the highest compliment he could

---

31. Ibid., p. 486.

32. Ibid., p. 487; cf. Barth, "Reformation als Entscheidung," pp. 528-9.

33. Søren Kierkegaard, The *Book on Adler*, ed. and trans. Howard V. Hong and Edna H. Hong (Princeton: Princeton University Press, 1998), pp. 173-88.

34. Thus, Barth recounts, when Luther died it was said in the Evangelical Church of the Reformer that "a prophet like Elijah or John the Baptist was among us, a man of God, a bearer of the light, a theologian whose theology came directly from revelation" ("Reformation als Entscheidung," pp. 530-1). In a similar way, Calvin's *Institutes* was esteemed by his own respective church tradition as a book the likes of which had not been seen since the writings of the apostles themselves (ibid., p. 531). The Reformers were and thus are rightly recognized as singular church fathers, teachers of the church. What the Reformers are not, Barth insists, are "poets, philosophers, or kings" (ibid., p. 526).

35. Barth, "The Substance and Task of Reformed Theology," p. 215.

36. Barth, *Fragments Grave and Gay*, ed. Martin Rumscheidt, trans. Eric Mosbacher (London: Collins, 1971), p. 105.

in fact give Calvin.[37] As with Luther, Barth had no romanticism when it came to Calvin or his Geneva, nor with the Reformation in general. His criticisms of Calvin could in fact be trenchant, as when in this brief essay he stated that Calvin was "undoubtedly stronger when he spoke about faith and obedience than about love and hope," and was "not only a child of his time, but also the prisoner of certain rigidities in his own basic ideas."[38] Still, Barth could nevertheless conclude by saying of Calvin that, despite all such "necessary criticism and corrections, there is hardly a better teacher, apart from the biblical prophets and apostles, than he."[39] In this regard, Barth's estimation of Calvin was no different in 1964 than it was in 1923 when he bemoaned the rise of hero worship with regard to Calvin in the Reformed church.[40]

In summary, for Barth what made Luther and Calvin church fathers was not their forceful and unique personalities, or even the eventfulness of their lives and distinctive accomplishments. What made them church fathers was their divine call exemplified in their vocation as teachers of Holy Scripture. This focus on their role as preeminent expositors of the Bible, and thus as witnesses to that which Scripture attested rather than as religious personalities, made all of the difference in how they were to be understood. Their importance hinged on the fact that they were called and used by God to restore his word for the church, to teach that word to the church, and to bring about the church's renewal. So although it is true that for Barth to say Reformation was to say Luther and Calvin, they were for him church fathers only because of this call and use. One could say that what Barth valued so much about them was their utter *transparency* before the Word of God in Scripture.

The Reformers are therefore not only positioned by Barth in relation to and under the prophets and the apostles, and thus Holy Scripture (what we might call a vertical relation), but also situated by Barth as witnesses among a cloud of church witnesses (what we might call a horizontal relation). He notes that while Holy Scripture stands over all secondary tradition, it is nevertheless the case that Scripture speaks to every generation and individual as it finds itself within the company of the church, among those fellow pupils of Scripture who include all of its members. We therefore hear the echo of Scripture not first in our own voice but in the voice of others who precede us in the faith. Yet while that company of teachers may appear boundless, Barth proffers that not all voices are to be heard in the same way, for some witnesses speak in such a way that "others had and still have to listen to them." He continues, "And basically the older and more experienced fellow-pupil is simply the Church teacher."[41] Preeminent among these teachers are Luther and Calvin.

---

37. Ibid.
38. Ibid., p. 109.
39. Ibid.
40. Barth, "The Substance and Task of Reformed Doctrine," pp. 213–15.
41. CD I/2: p. 607.

Not only must such teachers therefore be identified, they must be heeded, though not slavishly obeyed or mimicked. To refuse to listen to such exemplary voices in a kind of emancipated biblicism, Barth contends, is not to read the Bible in freedom but to succumb to a captivity of our own subconscious convictions in our interpretation. To read the Bible freely is, ironically, the reading of it under the tutelage of church teachers.[42] In this light, it becomes clear that Barth rejects not only a traditionalism that saw the Bible and tradition as two parallel sources of truth, but also a biblicism that cut itself off from all tradition and prior voices altogether. As he writes:

> In actual fact, there has never been a Biblicist who for all his grandiloquent appeal directly to Scripture against the fathers and tradition has proved himself so independent of the spirit and philosophy of his age and especially of his favourite religious ideas that in his teaching he has really allowed the Bible and the Bible alone to speak reliably by means or in spite of his anti-traditionalism.[43]

In contrast, the biblicism of the Reformers, for all of their calls for the supremacy of Scripture, differed from this modern biblicism, and "not in spite but in application of the Evangelical Scripture principle it kept itself free from this anti-traditionalism."[44]

We might assess Barth's position as follows: what made the evangelical (i.e., Protestant) church unique was not its recognition of an ecclesiastical authority expressed in "specific teachers of the church," but rather its definition of a church father predicated on singular witness to the truth of Scripture rather than antiquity, along with the claim that it was the *Reformers* who rightly received this title. It goes without saying that such judgments are contentious and thus may be contested. Important for our purpose here is simply to register that Barth holds in tension the absolute authority of Scripture and the relative authority of the Reformers in a nuanced dialectic that judges the quality of Christian witness not on antiquity

---

42. For Barth, this entailed that the spiritual authority of the Reformers took precedence over our own individual reading (CD I/2: p. 620). This did not mean, however, that Barth subjugated his own reading to the Reformers when he took their interpretation to be contrary to the witness of Scripture itself, as is especially evident in his break with Calvin on the question of election (CD II/2). Barth could put this approach in quite frank terms: "Holy Scripture is the object of our study, and at the same time the criterion of our study, of the Church's past. As I read the writings of the 'Fathers,' the witness of Holy Scripture stands continually before my eyes; I accept what interprets this witness to me; I reject what contradicts it. So a choice is actually made, certainly not a choice according to my individual taste, but according to my knowledge of Holy Scripture." See Barth, *Credo* (Eugene: Wipf and Stock, 2005[1962]), p. 183.

43. CD I/2: p. 609. Barth also asks: "Will those who will have the Bible alone as their master, as though Church history began again with them, really refrain from mastering the Bible?" (ibid., p. 609).

44. Ibid.

but on something akin to Kierkegaard's notion of contemporaneity with Christ, yet one effected from God's side. In the time of the Reformation, God called forth Luther and Calvin for the church's renewal through a fresh and decisive hearing of the Word of God. This estimation is evident when Barth writes:

> If our Churches confessed that they were reformed by the Word of God and not simply by Luther and Calvin, their reformation did take place by the witness borne to them by Luther and Calvin. Therefore the witness of Luther and Calvin is decisive and essential for their existence as this Church, as the Churches reformed in this way, and therefore for the whole contingency of their existence as the Church of Jesus Christ.[45]

Barth then concludes: "If they free themselves from this witness they are no longer these Churches and therefore no longer contingently the Church of Jesus Christ."[46]

Barth's argument here hangs on a delicate balance and decisive distinction between absolute and relative authority, as well as one between necessity and contingency. It is also predicated on a firm sense of ecclesiality grounded in a divine election and providence that calls not only the church, but also its very teachers and reformers, into existence. His claim is not that the Reformers Luther and Calvin hold the same authority as Scripture, for Scripture possesses an absolute authority, but rather that this absolute authority is always expressed in any time through the teaching of a relative authority, and for the evangelical churches, this is preeminently the teaching of Luther and Calvin. While the existence of such teachers is not necessary for the act of revelation itself, revelation nevertheless in actual fact comes to establish such teachers to serve as witnesses to it; and their appearance is not simply the result of the contingent fact of their historical genius, but rather is grounded in the necessity of God's eternal election and providence. Moreover, while the church is necessarily predicated on its founding by Jesus Christ and his rule of it through Holy Scripture, this too takes place through the contingencies of history, such that the evangelical church cannot be recognized for what it is, nor understood as a church of Jesus Christ, apart from the witness—found preeminently in Luther and Calvin—to the exemplary teaching of Scripture that provides its bearing and identity. It is in this circumscribed yet crucial way—as a relative and contingent yet real, concrete, and indeed providentially ordered authority—that the witness of Luther and Calvin stands over the other teachers and traditions of the evangelical churches.[47]

Of course, the fact that such authorities are not absolute but relative requires that they are themselves open to correction in light of the Word of God, and Barth's esteem of Luther and Calvin did not lead him to an uncritical reverence for them, as we have seen. Moreover, that they are relative authorities entails the

---

45. Ibid.
46. Ibid.
47. Ibid.

possibility that they could in time be superseded.[48] Yet while theoretically possible, Barth judges this eventuality practically unlikely (and, indeed, difficult to imagine, because he has grounded their appearance in divine providence). He therefore states that, despite the calls of modern skeptics, Luther and Calvin have rightly retained their central place for the Protestant churches.[49] They set the standard for the recognition of other church fathers past and present, because they correctly taught the Word of God and were used and confirmed by God in the reformation and renewal of the church at a decisive turning point in its history. For this reason, other teachers are judged in light of their teaching.[50]

This supremacy of Luther and Calvin does not mean, however, that the list of teachers of the church is closed. At the same time, although for Barth there is every reason to expect the emergence of church teachers beyond Luther and Calvin, he maintains that very few teachers are in truth church fathers like them; for, as he writes, "This real guidance of the Church, as it was exercised by Luther and Calvin, is a rare thing."[51] Thus, rather than identifying actual examples of further teachers, Barth lists four criteria that must be met for a person to be recognized as a teacher of the church of this magnitude. First, such a person must be an expositor of Holy Scripture who, like the Reformers, has helped the church rightly understand the Word of God; second, such a person must be in accordance with the confession of the Reformation, for the Reformers set the standard for such confession; third, such a person must speak as a teacher to and for the whole church and not simply for a segment of it; and finally, such a person must, in agreement with the Reformers and with responsibility to the church, speak a word of decision for the church and call it to confession.[52]

As we have already witnessed, Barth dialectically balances recognition of the real authority of such teachers with a great wariness regarding attention that is to be paid to them as persons. He hints that an overenthusiasm for church teachers raises the same specter of danger as the angel worship warned about by Paul in Galatians 4. Moreover, he holds that when the Reformers are revered as persons, the church may become more Lutheran and Calvinist, but it will then become, correspondingly, less Christian and evangelical.[53] In the end, "the authority of a human doctor of Holy Scripture" can

---

48. Barth notes that this question parallels his earlier judgment that while the canon is open in principle, it is closed in practice, since a change in the canon would require an agreement of the universal church (see CD I/2: pp. 597–603; also CD I/1: pp. 99–111). In a similar manner, Barth holds that until the (evangelical) church receives new truth resulting in a new confession and the replacement of the authority of the Reformers with that of new teachers, it is to accept the previous and ongoing confession of the church, including its recognition of the ecclesiastical authority of Luther and Calvin. It therefore should "not play truant from the school of Luther and Calvin until we are better instructed, but to learn in it what there is to be learned. It is a matter of instruction in understanding Holy Scripture, when and to the extent that the Reformers are genuine teachers of the church" (CD I/2: p. 612).
49. CD I/2: pp. 609–12.
50. CD I/2: p. 613.
51. Ibid.
52. CD I/2: pp. 613–16.
53. CD I/2: p. 617.

be predicated not of the person but only of his task, which is "to acquaint his pupils not so much with himself as with the object which is his and their concern, to point and bind them not so much to himself as to this object."[54] And just as it is the object of the message and not the voice of the teacher that is of ultimate importance, so also, similarly, the voice of the teacher is not ultimately his own, but the voice of the church of his time. Such a teacher speaks for the church, for Scripture and the confession of the church are not judged by the standard of the teacher, but the teacher by the standard of Scripture and the church's confession.[55] We pay teachers their proper due, Barth insists, precisely when we honor God and not them, and thus when we place ourselves under them insofar as they themselves are placed under Scripture and witness to what it attests: God's very revelation which calls forth our faith and decision—the same decision impressed upon and made by the Reformers themselves.[56]

With all of these observations in view, it should not surprise us that Barth refused to equate faithfulness to Luther and Calvin with simple repristination of their theology.[57] What is required to honor the Reformers is not mimicry but reflection, interpretation, and, if carefully understood, translation—perhaps even correction: "Not those who repeat the doctrine most faithfully, but those who reflect upon it most faithfully so that they can then expound it as their own doctrine, are their most faithful pupils."[58] This means that, for Barth, *ad fontes* could never entail a simple preservation and repetition of the past:

> The Church of to-day would not be accepting them if it were simply accepting or reproducing them in their historical form. It would be accepting them not as the Church of to-day, not obedient to its own calling along the lines of the Reformation, but as an institute of antiquities—the worst dishonor of which it could be guilty for all its well-meant veneration.[59]

Years later in a conversation, Barth asserted that Luther and Calvin were not "museum directors," and that he had no interest in being one himself.[60] Along with the ecclesial confession, the teacher of the church exercises a real if circumscribed

54. Ibid.
55. CD I/2: p. 618.
56. See Opitz, "Wer darf sich ernslich auf die Reformation, berufen?," p. 23.
57. Barth did not think that one could simply solve theological challenges of the present by parroting the Reformers. As he stated: "'Back to ... ' is never a good slogan" (CD IV/1: p. 372). Earlier in 1935 he could more pointedly state with regard to simple retrieval of the past: "Repristination is nonsense" (Barth, *Credo*, p. 182).
58. CD I/2: p. 619.
59. Ibid. Late in life, Barth stated to his conversation partners that in the face of a vibrant Catholicism what was needed was that Protestants "must rediscover the work of Luther and Calvin, but not be prisoners of their work." See Barth, "Interview von H.-Ch. Tauxe, Gazette de Lausanne (20.4.1965)," in *Gespräche 1964–1968*, ed. Eberhard Busch (Zürich: Theologischer Verlag Zürich, 1996), pp. 197–202 (199); cf. p. 571 (author's trans.).
60. Barth, "Was bedeutet uns Barmen heute?, 1954," in *"Der Götze wackelt": Zeitkritische Aufsätze, Reden und Briefe von 1930 bis 1960*, ed. Karl Kupisch (Berlin: Käthe Vogt Verlag, 1961), pp. 162–4 (163).

and qualified authority.[61] Yet that authority is one not so much possessed as witnessed, and thus is best exercised when never claimed, and most honored when consulted but not simply imitated. As Barth later iterated this point in his short piece reflecting upon Calvin's death: "It is not worth while really to become a 'Calvinist', but it certainly is almost singularly worth while to become Calvin's free pupil."[62] In fairness, Barth held the same standard for himself. If you meet a Barthian, he could later say, tell them that I am not one.[63]

There are nevertheless a number of tensions that remain in Barth's explication of the role and authority of church teachers. Certainly the fact that the Reformers are both contingent historical persons whose viewpoints could be corrected in light of further reflection upon Scripture, yet also at the same time persons whose appearance was grounded in a providential and divine ordination, creates complexity in understanding the nature of their authority—an authority Barth situates precisely between unquestioned obeisance and indifferent dismissal. He esteemed church tradition as both necessary and relative, even if others esteemed it as entirely contingent or as absolute. His articulation of the authority of Luther and Calvin displays a precarious balance between an abandonment and an absolutizing of tradition, both of which he rejected.

Another area of dialectical tension is that Barth had a somewhat circuitous understanding of ecclesial authority with regard to individual teachers and church confessions. The logic of his communal understanding of confession, which stands over individual teachers and believers, is such that one might have expected him to elucidate the authority of confessions before that of the Reformers. Yet he sees the confessional task of the Protestant churches as made possible by the initial renewal to which Luther and Calvin called the churches, and he thereby treates them in his discussion of church authority before taking up the question of the authority of the confessions. Here Barth seems to follow a chronological rather than ontological ordering of the authority of the confession and the individual teacher: in truth, confessions have an authority that exceeds that of the individual reformer or theologian; but for Barth the church fathers Luther and Calvin stand before the confessions in the sense that they made such confession of the church possible in their wake. In this, Barth may be less consistent with his dogmatic ordering of relative authorities but nevertheless more honest in his assessment of the Protestant confessions themselves with regard to the circumstances of their actual historical appearance.

## The "End" of Historical Study

Perhaps no person has been as laudatory of the Reformers' ecclesiastical role while being relatively disinterested in their actual material lives as was Barth. This may make him a reluctant historian of the Reformers, but it does not jeopardize his faithful

---

61. CD I/2: p. 620.
62. Barth, *Fragments Grave and Gay*, p. 110.
63. Eberhard Busch, *Karl Barth: His Life from Letters and Autobiographical Texts*, trans. John Bowden (Grand Rapids: Eerdmans, 1994), p. 417.

witness to their actual intention and spirit. In effect, he wanted to understand the Reformers as they understood themselves. This entailed attending to what they themselves attended rather than fixating upon them as historical figures. Even as a confessional Reformed theologian and church member, Barth had no interest in esteeming Calvin simply as an ancestor of his own tradition.[64] Commenting on the meaning of Reformed confessional identity in 1923, Barth concluded:

> Remaining true to the Fathers must mean, then, adhering precisely to history the way they themselves adhered to it: letting history speak but only as an indication beyond itself to revelation, not confusing age with originality, and not confusing the authority that is given to the Church with the authority by which the church was founded.[65]

The most important thing about Luther and Calvin for Barth was therefore not the material content they provided on specific theological questions (as important as this may be), but the exemplary role they played in calling the church back to the Word of God and the supremacy of Scripture. In this regard, the fact that Barth had so little interest in them as historical figures is understandable: he saw them as exemplary solely because they displayed unwavering focus upon the subject matter that had captured their lives and compelled their testimony in speech and life. He had no regard for Luther or Calvin as historical geniuses but only as secondary witnesses to the primary witness of Scripture in attesting God's revelation.[66] This was the path he followed in his own work.[67]

---

64. Barth, "The Substance and Task of Reformed Theology," p. 206.

65. Ibid., p. 208. Barth added that this kind of confessional stance "does not bow down before any hat propped on a stick, even it is the hat of Calvin himself" (ibid., pp. 208–9). As earlier noted, Barth thought that in this respect the Reformed were more circumspect than their Lutheran counterparts (ibid., p. 214). In his lectures on Reformed theology, Barth stated: "The well-known Wittenberg saying, 'God's Word and Luther's teaching will not perish now or ever' (*Gottes Wort und Luthers lehr vergehen nun und nimmermehr!*) could never be uttered by a Calvinist. To put Calvin in the first line, pairing it with God's Word, would be impossible for even the most enthusiastic Calvinist" (Barth, *The Theology of the Reformed Confessions*, p. 21).

66. "But interpretation of the confessions or of the writings of Luther and Calvin is just as little the special task of dogmatics as is biblical exegesis. It cannot become merely a report on various doctrines of the fathers, or have as its aim, even its subordinate aim, their rehabilitation. The theology of the fathers and the confessions must be used as a pattern only in proper subordination to the Word of God attested in Scripture. It must never allow an appeal to them to replace the thinking for which it is directly responsible to Scripture. It is not by referring to the fathers and confessions and reproducing their doctrine, but only by actually learning from them, that it maintains its confessional attitude. We can be confessional only κατὰ πνεῦμα. If we try to be so κατὰ σάρκα, we shall not be so at all" (CD I/2: pp. 837–8).

67. John Webster has put this point succinctly: "Genuine and fruitful theological work on Barth's account is always objective, in that it takes its rise in astonishment at the *Sache* by which the mind is seized." See Webster, *Karl Barth's Earlier Theology: Four Studies* (London/New York: T&T Clark, 2005), p. 9.

Barth's stance amounts to a rejection of hagiography of historical figures, but its significance runs much deeper and is much more disturbing: it is ultimately an attack not only upon uncritical historical hero worship, but upon historical science itself when it is set forth as an academic discipline for its own sake and forsakes the theological setting and purpose of its practice. Barth's construal of historical investigation is, in short, a rejection of any independent discipline of church history that does not find its place in the richer conception of the church's theological task that moves from explication (biblical theology), to meditation (dogmatic theology), to application (practical theology).[68] His understanding and estimation of Luther and Calvin are thereby predicated upon and indeed reveal the underlying rationale of his insistence that church history is indeed necessary but can only be an ancillary theological discipline that does not stand alongside of but must rather serve biblical, dogmatic, and practical theology. Historical study is never for the church an end in itself, because its service, however necessary, is always merely preparatory to the ultimate task of the church's proclamation and confession.

This estimation of historical study when approaching figures of the church's past is in fact parallel to and in perfect accordance with Barth's views on historical criticism and its place in biblical interpretation.[69] Church history, like historical criticism, is an indispensable and preparatory though subsidiary discipline that must push on to richer theological investigations that do not make either the historical world of the Bible or the figure of church history ends of study in themselves, but which rather serve the subject matter of the divine revelation to which both Scripture and its teachers testify.[70] Just as Barth denounced an objective historical criticism when esteemed by its practitioners to be the self-sufficient and final method to understand Scripture, so he also undermined any field that makes Luther and Calvin objects of historical interest and fails to take account of their proper vocation as witnesses and church fathers. To treat Scripture or such later witnesses to the gospel in this way is, in Barth's parlance, to treat them as abstractions: not for what they truly are in the divine economy, but as independent objects of a study. For this reason, Barth read the Reformers analogously to how he read the Scriptures: not as interesting objects

---

68. "What is called church history does not correspond to any independently raised question concerning Christian talk about God, and it cannot therefore be regarded as an independent theological discipline. It is an auxiliary science indispensable to exegetical, dogmatic and practical theology" (CD I/1: p. 5; see also CD I/2: pp. 722–40).

69. Barth's engagement with historical criticism exceeds what can here be examined. For a magisterial introduction to this topic, see Richard E. Burnett, *Karl Barth's Theological Exegesis: The Hermeneutical Principles of the Römerbrief Period* (Grand Rapids: Eerdmans, 2004).

70. As Barth already observed in 1924, purely historical biblical research is a possible and meaningful thing, but it takes place outside of the discipline of theology, for "The concept of history is not a theological concept." See Barth, "Menschenwort und Gotteswort in der christlichen Predigt 1924," in *Vorträge und kleinere Arbeiten 1922-1925*, ed. Holger Finze (Zürich: Theologischer Verlag Zürich, 1990), pp. 426–57 (454).

of historical investigation in their own right, but as witnesses that point beyond themselves to the subject of their witness.[71]

However much Barth's approach to historical investigation may grate against modern critical and academic sensibilities, it provides a challenge precisely because of such marked iconoclasm. It is difficult to deny that in the contemporary age much historical research has become the examination of trees with little consideration of the forest—an examination that, in turn, dissects the trees themselves into a multifarious array of ever-more particulate source material. In such a world, not only texts but their authors are dissolved into a viscous amalgam of background sources and constitutive tributaries of prior influences, with meaning itself often dissolved in the process. We live in a world of scholarship that is trained to look *at* things and refract them into a seemingly endless number of dispersed constituent background elements, not to look *along* with them to what they indicate.[72]

In pushing against this way of approaching Scripture and history, Barth was pushing hard against much of the modern age and its dominant historiography. Correspondingly, what made Luther and Calvin of interest to Barth was not their lives and accomplishments but the object of their work, and what he shared with them was an undivided commitment to look *along with* rather than *at* the witnesses of the church's past and to read them akin to how he read Scripture: to think *after* them (*Nachdenken*), to face the subject matter (*die Sache*) with which they were confronted, and to feel and take the weight of their decisions upon his own shoulders.[73] Once again, Barth's stance here with regard to Luther and Calvin is entirely consonant with Kierkegaard's distinction between a religious genius and an apostle or witness. A religious genius displays the brilliance of an inner insight, the discovery of a truth within the self, the product of an incandescent intelligence

---

71. Barth thereby attempted to read the Reformers along the lines of their own self-understanding. One of the necessary ironies of church history as an academic enterprise is that it makes objects of those who would have been horrified by this occurrence, and this is truer for Luther and Calvin than for most. Nothing illustrates Luther's fear of this more than the preface to his German writings—LW 34: pp. 283–8. Luther did not want persons to be called "Lutherans" but "Christians" and saw his importance only in his witness to the content of his teaching, not in his own personal accomplishments. See Oswald Bayer, *Martin Luther's Theology: A Contemporary Interpretation*, trans. Thomas H. Trapp (Grand Rapids: Eerdmans, 2008), p. 8. The same was true of Calvin, for whom all good things achieved by anyone could only be attributed to the gospel and to God's grace—see, for example, Calvin, *Institutes of the Christian Religion*, Vol. 1, ed. John T. McNeill, trans. Ford L. Battles (Philadelphia: Westminster Press, 1960,) p. 306.

72. No one in the modern period has drawn this distinction and detailed its ramifications as succinctly as C. S. Lewis in his essay, "Meditation in a Toolshed," in *God in the Dock*, ed. Walter Hooper (Grand Rapids: Eerdmans, 1999), pp. 212–15.

73. Burnett, *Karl Barth's Theological Exegesis*, pp. 58–9. We might say that *Nachdenken* is that which unites Barth's reading of Scripture with his reading of its witnesses, and then extended to all reading of all persons. It is that which unites his special and general hermeneutics (see CD I/2: pp. 457–72).

or other religious capacity of feeling or conscience. Modern scholarship may seek to deconstruct the genius into a collection of prior historical influences, questioning the very idea of a single individual who turns history. A witness like Luther or Calvin, however, points away from himself and from prior history to that which he did not discover on his own. He is rather imposed upon, commissioned, indeed burdened, with a message he not only did not create or discover but would not even have chosen.[74] He can only report it and point to it. This is not the celebration of imagination or of intelligence, though both may be present in a witness. It is rather the rapt attention to a message that overshadows the messenger and applies to him as much as to all who hear it. Historical study may illumine this message, but it does injustice to both the message and messenger if it attempts to drown them both in the ever-flowing stream of historical occurrence and its relativizing waters. For both Kierkegaard and Barth, this particular practice of historical contextualization was in fact a subtle way to evade the confrontation of the truth to which the witness testifies and the decision it places before us.

Two things remain for us to ponder in light of Barth's counter-witness to our modern age. First, we are left with the decision whether or not to confront our seemingly irresistible urge to reduce witnesses to geniuses or to historical instantiations of prior sources, rather than to accept the far greater challenge of honestly facing the questions raised by the actual witnesses themselves.[75] The second is reckoning with the undeniable fact that today theology has largely become the practice of church history with but few exceptions. Unlike Luther and Calvin, and Barth himself, we do not live in an age of exemplary witness as much as in a golden age of the historical investigation of prior witnesses. There may have been a time when one could justifiably bemoan a "retreat to commitment" as the greatest danger to Christian vitality.[76] But now, the retreat is not to commitment but to historiography itself as a safe enclave of dispassionate respectability: we are all historians now. Perhaps prior ages were wary of an ascendant philosophy that might overshadow theology's rightful tasks, but philosophy itself has succumbed to the relativism of historical consciousness. It is not philosophy, but history, which now sets the rules for respectability and the game to be played. Trying to understand what has been lost with the triumph of history as the queen of the biblical and theological sciences is no direct slight of critical historical investigation, nor warrant to overlook or dismiss the real gains achieved by its ascendancy, but the question remains valid and pressing nonetheless. One place where such questioning may begin is with the recovery of Barth's understanding of church history as a subordinate and supplementary discipline that can serve,

---

74. One cannot help but think of how Luther and Calvin were thrown into their role as Reformers apart from and even against their own desires and choices.

75. For the dangers of doing this to Barth specifically, as well as for others more generally, see Webster, *Barth's Earlier Theology: Four Studies*, pp. 7–10.

76. William W. Bartley III, *The Retreat to Commitment* (LaSalle/London: Open Court Publishing, 1984).

but not overtake, the constructive and confessional task of theology in every age. For Barth, historical science, like historical criticism, is not to be abandoned, much less practiced shoddily, but it is not the final word, and it must instead find its rightful place in a larger theological framework of meaning and practice. Barth's own hope for resisting the acids of historicism, however, did not lie in a methodological reorientation but a waiting upon God to speak anew through his witnesses of Scripture and church—all of which simply reinforces our suspicions that Barth, though very much a modern theologian, stands in this respect far closer to Luther and Calvin than to our own age of critical (and ironic) distance and its commitment to the superiority of convictional neutrality and scientific method.

Perhaps the greatest irony is that Barth's objections to the historicist readings of Scripture, which he pressed so adamantly in the 1920s, could now simply be translated into arguments against how we read witnesses to Scripture, whether the Reformers or others. We should not ignore the strange paradox that Barth himself has often been treated in this way, though he would have been as dismayed and likely appalled by this as would Luther or Calvin. Yet if Barth has a future beyond a narrow field of academic investigation, it will not be because of a renewed interest in his life for its own sake. It will be because of the manner in which Barth himself disappears and becomes transparent before the witness of Scripture, enabling his theology to serve church reform, renewal, and confession rather than historical commemoration. For the church lives not by commemoration, but by hope and expectation.

Historical study must take account not only of means but of ends, and the ends one chooses will be perennially contested, though the act of choosing cannot be avoided. If studies of Barth like this one, as well as studies of Luther and Calvin, and of church history generally, are to fulfill their fitting and proper end, they must dare to climb up from the plateau of academic scholarship and respectability to a yet higher level of exploration—or, at the very least, point to it. If we as theologians cannot help to be, and perhaps must be, historians as well, then we might begin to fulfill and transcend this latter vocation and fulfill our theological one when we are not afraid to climb to a higher plane of inquiry and pull the ladder from our historical investigation up after us. But this is meaningful, and indeed possible, only if a ladder has already been dropped down to us from above.

## Chapter 4

## THE LAST PROTESTANT: KARL BARTH AND THE CULMINATION OF THE PROTESTANT ECCLESIAL VISION

In approaching a significant intellectual figure from the past, there are various ways to contextualize his or her thought and trace its development, as well as to proffer reasons for its particular form, character, and material commitments. One dominant way to do this, of course, is to look for the origin of the concepts and ideas that may lie behind his or her writings, and this form of investigation has been predominant in historical studies of the prior two centuries. Such forms of genetic investigation and source criticism not only stand behind much of the critical biblical studies of the modern period, but also extend to investigations of the work of any historical figure. Such is true of course with Karl Barth.[1] Much of past and current scholarship is dedicated to tracing the background influences upon his thought, some readily apparent and generally accepted, others more indirect and controverted. This practice, a kind of conceptual archaeology, has its value and necessity, even while possessing weaknesses and limitations. At its best, it opens up new vistas to understand the range of Barth's thought and reveals nuances that may lie behind his doctrinal description, but at its worst, it appears forced and loses Barth's own distinctive theological voice and argument in a search for trees most at home in other forests, mistaking distant allusions or passing reference for things of central and constitutive importance, or even dissolving Barth into his background and culture and thus explaining him away.[2]

---

1. For a brief summarization of current trends in Barth research (*Barth-Forschung*) today, see Michael Beintker, "Barth-Forschung heute," in *Barth Handbuch*, ed. Michael Beintker (Tübingen: Mohr Siebeck, 2016), pp. 7–11.

2. No one has so succinctly listed such limitations and dangers of developmental study and source criticism in general and in relation to Barth in particular as John Webster: "There are the familiar problems of genetic analysis (the difficulty of distinguishing a source from an association; the danger of reductionist 'explanation' of Barth out of putative 'background'; the near-impossibility of determining in detail how Barth reacted to much of what he absorbed from his reading; the ease with which the most obvious and omnipresent source—Scripture—can be overlooked). And there is another, less tangible, difficulty, one not uncommon in scrupulous readings of Barth's early work. This is the danger of over-expounding Barth and

There is another way to contextualize a person's thought, one more modest and less ambitious, but with its own value (and limitations). It is to take with seriousness a thinker's description and contextualization of his or her own life and work within the person's narrated historiography of a discipline or tradition. In this case, it is to ask the simple question—how did Barth understand his work within a historiography of his own construal, if indeed he did articulate such? Such a question is worth pursuing because to read Barth with historical and exegetical sensitivity is not solely defined by an attempt to register and catalog historical influences through tracing their appearance, ascendancy, and decline, but also requires attention to how he understood ecclesial and theological history itself, including his understanding of its meaning and his place within it. This is the difference between focusing upon conceptual borrowing and focusing upon historical narrative or historiography, though the latter need not ignore the former, as will be seen below.

To discover such historiography, one must look across the range of Barth's works and correspondence, and when this is done, his own understanding of his project contextualizes and casts light upon his formal and material theological decisions over time. It particularly provides insight into the distinctive character and shape of his final prolegomena to theology in the first volume of the *Church Dogmatics*. Before turning to that work at the end, Barth's historiography and self-understanding found within it can be traced across his development, beginning with his relation to the liberal tradition in which he was educated and to which he

his sources, on the assumption that he was a maximally attentive reader whose texts are full of reverberations from his reading. The effect is not simply that of making the interpretation of Barth depend on detective work, but more that of portraying Barth as complex in the wrong way, a kind of highly sensitive register of the ideas of others, and so less vividly and solidly and confusingly himself." See John Webster, *Barth's Earlier Theology: Four Studies* (London/New York: T&T Clark, 2005), pp. 7–8. Noteworthy also is the judgment of Scott Kirkland: "Developmental studies have shown ... that there is no single way up the mountain that is Barth's corpus. They provide helpful, but not absolutely constraining, guides." See Kirkland, *Into the Far Country: Karl Barth and the Modern Subject* (Minneapolis: Fortress, 2016), pp. 5–6, nt. 15. Martin Westerholm adds: "The heavily diachronic readings that are de rigueur amongst Barth scholars have yielded considerable insight; yet they tend to attract attention to an entrenched set of categories that obscure important features of Barth's thought." He continues: "Barth engages too many questions on too many different fronts to suppose that one set of questions holds the key that unlocks all doors." See Martin Westerholm, *The Ordering of the Christian Mind: Karl Barth and Theological Rationality* (Oxford: Oxford University Press, 2015), pp. 12 and 17; cf. pp. 10–19. Finally, it is worthwhile to remember the warning of Stephen Sykes: "Nothing in the history of the interpretation of Barth hitherto should lead one to suppose that any one scholar has the 'key to Barth' secreted in his robes." See S. W. Sykes, "The Study of Barth," in *Karl Barth: Studies of His Theological Method*, ed. S. W. Sykes (Oxford: Clarendon Press, 1979), p. 2.

reacted. In setting forth such a historiography, strict and fine-grained demarcations of periodization recede into the background, as consistent and enduring judgments and convictions come to the fore.[3]

## Barth and Liberalism: Personal Historiography

The first thing to note is that Barth consistently understood himself in the moment and in later reflection upon the past as breaking and having broken with the theology of his formal education and his teachers, and thereby with the liberal tradition itself, a tradition he traced back to Schleiermacher as its source and which he identified as Protestant modernism [*protestantische Modernismus* or *modernistisch-protestantische Theologie*] or Neo-Protestantism [*Neuprotestantismus*]. Certainly there are debates over how much Barth retained from his past and this tradition, for all historical study is perennially entrenched in attempts to delineate both the continuity and discontinuity of a figure or movement with that which has come before them and their proximate background and context.[4] But there is no question how he understood his own theology, seeing it to be a break from the immanentism of the nineteenth century and a specific break from the forms of historicism, psychologism, and (significantly) the christology of

---

3. It was Wittgenstein's great achievement to reveal that "simple" and "composite" are not contrasting and exclusive concepts but are relative to a system of signification and reference, i.e., something is "simple" or "composite" based upon the question asked. A tree, for example, is one "simple" thing if the frame of reference is a forest, but it is a "composite" thing composed of many other things (leaves, roots, trunk, branches, etc.) if the frame of reference is the tree itself with its own constituent parts (*Philosophical Investigations* §47). Something similar pertains to Barth's timeline of development. Divisions of periodization differ based upon the topics and questions under investigation. To ask, "What are the divisions, or periods, of Barth's development?" is a question that requires a second, namely: "In relation to what question?" There is no reason to think that all theological, ethical, ecclesiological, philosophical, social, and political questions progressed in the exact same manner for Barth, though there are of course broad correspondences between them, even as there are events and occurrences in his life that did have wide-ranging and lasting consequences. In this study, however, the focus is upon broad historiography and enduring judgments and convictions, rather than discrete and decisive periods and periodization.

4. One can think, for example, of Augustine as standing between the classical and Christian ages, or Luther between the medieval and the modern one, with debates about both figures as to how each stood in continuity and discontinuity with their inherited and immediate past as well as with their own prior lives in view of their respective conversions. One can also think of how the Reformation is understood in relation to such movements and periods as medieval scholasticism and the Renaissance before and Protestant orthodoxy and the Enlightenment after. Such debates are intrinsic to historical study and its demarcation of periods in light of determinations of what is continuous with the old and what marks the new.

the nineteenth-century Protestant liberal tradition in general and his teachers such as Wilhelm Herrmann and Adolf von Harnack specifically.[5] Such an outlook of a taking-leave from the past is readily attested in his letters and debates of the teens

5. These arguments Barth had with his teachers (that do not need to be rehearsed here) were in time extended to his own contemporaries and theological compatriots in the so-called dialectical movement such as Emil Brunner, Rudolf Bultmann, Friedrich Gogarten, and Paul Tillich, for even in the time of their greatest allegiance in the early 1920s, deep theological differences separated Barth from each of them, with christological differences separating Barth from both Paul Tillich and Rudolf Bultmann specifically. With regard to Bultmann and Barth, Christoph Chalamet asserts: "The most important point of disagreement between the two theologians was over christology" (Chalamet, *Dialectical Theologians: Wilhelm Herrmann, Karl Barth and Rudolf Bultmann* (Zürich: TVZ, 2005), p. 141). This disagreement could be framed in different ways, from differences over the relation of christology and anthropology to differences over the relation of theology to philosophy (see below). Barth and Bultmann also differed in their understanding of the primary task of theology, which for Barth was singularly oriented to the church, and for Bultmann was primarily oriented to critical reflection upon Christian existence. This difference is one reason that Bultmann favored Friedrich Gogarten over Barth to fill a systematic theology vacancy at Marburg in 1929. See Konrad Hammann, *Rudolf Bultmann: A Biography*, trans. Philip Devenish (Salem, OR: Polebridge, 2013), pp. 166–7. It is not incidental that while Bultmann was (at times) an active participant in the church's life, his favorite venue for preaching and worship was the academic worship of the university in Marburg, and that both Barth and Bultmann, while agreeing in principle on the centrality of the sermon for theological activity, disliked each other's sermons (ibid., pp. 337–40). Barth outlined reasons for the break-up of the dialectical school in 1933, though the fissures of the dissolution appeared significantly earlier. What brought these persons together in the beginning, Barth stated, was their shared opposition to the liberal theology of Neo-Protestantism and their commitment to a theology of the Word of God grounded in Scripture and the Reformers. Nevertheless, to his mind, this commitment was not uniformly shared and so their theological partnership could not last—see Barth, "Abschied," in *Vorträge und kleinere Arbeiten 1930–1933*, ed. Michael Beintker, Michael Hüttenhoff, and Peter Zocher (Zürich: Theologischer Verlag Zürich, 2013), pp. 492–515 (496–7). Barth first articulated his reservations of this alliance publicly three years earlier in "Die Theologie und der heutige Mensch 1930" in *Vorträge und kleinere Arbeiten 1930–1933*, pp. 8–43 (see esp. 36–43). In the end, the overarching reason for his break with his colleagues such as Brunner, Gogarten, and even Bultmann was his judgment that they had not truly broken with the liberalism of the nineteenth century, evident in their ongoing interest in anthropology and in natural theology. With regard to Gogarten specifically, Barth found his flirtation with German nationalistic theology and his identification of the law of the German people with the law of God especially otiose (ibid., p. 502). He considered this theology of Gogarten shared with the German Christians to be nothing other than the "last, most perfect, and worst outburst" of Neo-Protestantism's being (ibid., p. 504). In brief, he took leave of his colleagues in the dialectical school precisely because he did not see them as having broken with liberalism as (to his mind) he had done. And if Barth could not make peace with Brunner, who, as both Reformed and

and early twenties of the twentieth century.⁶ That Barth saw his own development as entailing an abandonment (and not simply a revised continuation) of the theology of his teachers is apparent regardless of allowance for an occasional conscious or unconscious re-writing of his own past, and of the continuity that may in truth have existed, some of which he implicitly acknowledged in his nuanced estimation of Herrmann especially. In truth, Barth's greatest break was not with his teachers, but with his own earlier theology expressed in his own work.⁷ He must of course

---

a dogmatician, was closest to him among his dialectical colleagues, he certainly could not make peace with the nineteenth-century liberal tradition or those whom he believed followed in its wake—see John W. Hart, *Karl Barth vs. Emil Brunner: The Formation and Dissolution of a Theological Alliance, 1916-1936* (New York: Peter Lang, 2001), p. 220. Barth would treat Bultmann (and, in the end, Brunner too) with more sensitivity in his later reflections upon that time, but his judgments did not truly change. In sum, he set the Reformation over against Bultmann's project, as well as the theological project of modern Protestantism in general. See Barth, "Rudolf Bultmann—An Attempt to Understand Him" in *Kerygma and Myth: A Theological Debate*, ed. Hans-Werner Bartsch, trans., Reginald H. Fuller, V. I and II combined (London: SPCK, 1972), V. II, pp. 83-132 (esp. 88-91).

6. As but one famous example, consider the pointed debate between Barth and his former teacher Harnack carried out in 1923. Their exchange can be found in James M. Robinson, ed., *The Beginnings of Dialectical Theology*, trans. Keith R. Crim and Louis De Grazia (Richmond: John Knox, 1968), pp. 165-87.

7. Nothing makes this clearer than reading Barth himself from this early time and comparing it with his own later theology—for but one example, see Karl Barth, "Der Christliche Glaube und die Geschichte 1910," in *Vorträge und kleinere Arbeiten 1909-1914*, ed. Hans-Anton Drewes and Hinrich Stoevaesandt (Zürich: Theologischer Verlag Zürich, 1993), pp. 149-212. Nothing that Barth would come to hold of Christ, of the church, of the canon of Scripture, of his understanding of Luther and the Reformation, and of Schleiermacher and religion, would remain the same and be untouched from this essay, and no specific date need be determined for this turn from one way of thinking to the other for it to be evident. In this respect, Simon Fisher is warranted to claim that Barth's later criticisms of Schleiermacher's christology would equally apply to his own earliest one. See Simon Fisher, *Revelatory Positivism?: Barth's Earliest Theology and the Marburg School* (Oxford: Oxford University Press, 1988), p. 231; cf. pp. 271-2; 277-8. Barth's later polemical arguments against a range of thinkers, from Augustine to Descartes to Schleiermacher, polemics predicated on and united by a rejection of their immanent understandings of religion, were thus in no small part a rejection of his own early theology. He stated the principle of such a rejection of immanentism in his prolegomena of the CD: "Karl Holl once formulated as follows the fundamental principle that is 'common to all men' and that constitutes 'the plumb-line of their religion.' 'Nothing,' he said, 'is to be recognised as religiously valid but what can be found in the reality present to us and produced again out of our direct experience.' This principle is in fact the principle of Cartesian thinking, which is quite impossible in theology. On the basis of this principle there is no knowledge of the Word of God. For we do not find the Word of God in the reality present to us. Rather—and

be understood as a person in history drawing upon his immediate context and not appearing out of nowhere, but there are certain significant truths that an overemphasis upon his continuity with the past distorts.

*Barth and the Inheritance of Herrmann*

To take the most determinative influence upon Barth's mature theology to be that of the late nineteenth-century liberal theological tradition, and to do so specifically through the lens of Herrmann, his teacher, reveals but also conceals much of Barth's own thought. It is often noted, for instance, that Barth retained the anti-speculative, anti-metaphysical, and anti-apologetic themes inherited from Herrmann and that these remained constitutive of his theological program. What is often not registered, however, is that in the formative decade of his work in Göttingen and then Münster, such convictions were preserved by Barth but were entirely translated into and grounded upon newly discovered and distinct Reformation commitments that deeply shaped his theological character for the rest of his career. Whatever their origin, Herrmann had very little part to play in Barth's explicit articulation, preservation, and eventual formulation of such commitments.

For example, Barth retained an anti-apologetic stance, but he no longer framed this issue in terms of the independence (*Selbständigkeit*) of religion or experience, but rather in relation to the singular revelation of God in Christ and the self-authentication of Scripture (*autopistia*) as articulated superlatively by Calvin. In effect, arguments for the independence of religion which undergirded the anti-speculative and anti-apologetic stance of Herrmann's understanding now migrated to and were indeed transformed by the Protestant loci of revelation and Scripture as Barth found these articulated in the Reformation legacy in general and his Reformed heritage in particular, all accompanied by and indeed wedded to an intensive study of Scripture.[8] In effect, such inherited arguments were entirely reconstituted and undergirded by Reformed theological convictions of the singular and self-authenticating character of *Deus dixit* and the revelation in Christ attested

---

this is something quite different—the Word of God finds us in the reality present to us" (CD I/1: pp. 195–6). This statement represents a rejection not only of Holl (or Herrmann) but of Barth's own earlier appeals to such immanent understandings of religion (see Fisher, *Revelatory Positivism?*, p. 271; cf. pp. 277–8). Bruce McCormack summarizes Barth's break with his early theology succinctly. It is comprised "in the abandonment of the liberal axiom of a 'God in us' in favour of a new conception of the speaking of God which was better calculated to protect the sovereign freedom of the divine Subject in the process of revelation." See Bruce L. McCormack, *Karl Barth's Critically Realistic Dialectical Theology: Its Genesis and Development 1909–1936* (Oxford: Clarendon, 1995), p. 107; cf. pp. 124–5.

8. Barth was becoming a Reformed thinker in identity already as early as his time as an associate pastor in Geneva but truly came into his own as a Reformed theologian in his first professorate. See Chalamet, *Dialectical Theologians*, pp. 69; 167–8; 196.

in Scripture and proclamation (as well as in the christological convictions of the early church).⁹ We can consider this passage from his lectures on Calvin in 1922 as but one example of such discovery and translation:

> We cannot be experts in Reformed theology unless we are aware of Calvin's sense of responsibility, the keenness of his gaze on every hand, his need constantly to sharpen up and delimit his own insights and statements, his feeling that he was always on the watch. If we call this thrust in Calvin apologetic, however, we should note that it is not an apologetics that seeks to justify Christianity before courts outside itself, for example, philosophy or science. The standard by which Calvin's theology measures itself in justification lies instead within itself. It is its own generating principle, holy scripture, which, of course, is related so closely to reason, and therefore to true philosophy and science, that no need for external vindication can exist. The power of Calvin's apologetics, so far as it has any, consists of the fact that basically it is simply a conversation with itself. Its initial premise is that there are not two truths but only one, and hence from the very first it feels no temptation to barter. It proceeds with the silent summons: Those who have ears to hear, let them hear! [Mark 4:9].¹⁰

In truth, this passage is not simply an exposition of Calvin's theology, but also a revelation of Barth's discovery and viewpoint that he now embraced, inclusive of a number of themes of growing importance for his theology, some of which were already prefigured and inherited from Herrmann, but all now re-framed along explicitly Reformed lines: the refusal to justify theology in front of foreign philosophical or scientific courts of appeal with their demands that it meet their criteria; the centrality and supremacy of Scripture as the standard for all theological and doctrinal reflection and articulation (i.e., the Scripture principle, the importance of which can scarcely be overestimated for Barth's theological development); and the task of dogmatics as the articulation of theology's own internal convictions which is in turn the most cogent and powerful form of apologetics. For Barth, apologetics was now framed not primarily as a problem in light of philosophical convictions arising in modernity, but as a practice the Reformers had already rejected as a "theology of glory."¹¹ Moreover, his anti-speculative (and in this sense anti-metaphysical) stance came to be grounded not in a strict adherence to Kantian restrictions on knowledge, but in allegiance with the

---

9. Barth provided in the GD a short list of the "decisive marks of the Reformed school" (gleaned from a study of Calvin and the Reformed confessions) which served as the central convictions that shaped his dogmatic work, what he called "the main rules [*Hauptregeln*] of a Christian, Reformed dogmatics" (Unterricht I, pp. 355–6; ET: GD, p. 284). These rules (with some minor modifications) are evident in all of Barth's later theology and provide guidance and structure to his formal and material discussions of doctrine.
10. Karl Barth, *The Theology of John Calvin*, trans. Geoffrey W. Bromiley (Grand Rapids: Eerdmans, 1995), p. 159.
11. Barth, *The Theology of John Calvin*, p. 53.

Reformers' own rejection of scholasticism and speculation and their indifference to philosophical proofs, as well as their basic and foundational dedication to the particularity of revelation in Christ and Scripture.[12] In effect, one can watch Barth's mature theological convictions being forged in his lecture courses in the early 1920s on Zwingli, Calvin, Schleiermacher, and the Reformed confessions, as well as in his biblical exegetical lectures, while simultaneously witnessing the remnants of his early theology either being re-cast in this new Reformation idiom or disappearing. This does not mean that all of the past is left behind, of course, but nothing was left as it was and simply carried across the theological ledger to a new column unchanged. Even his understanding of being a dialectical thinker came to be identified not with his membership in a contemporary movement but as intrinsic to the character of being a Reformed theologian.[13]

To register this migration and transformation of such arguments problematizes the often-noted continuity of Barth's anti-speculative and anti-apologetic positions as if they were straightforward inheritances from Herrmann and the Ritschlian

---

12. "This incarnate Word then, and not, as we are sometimes told, the so-called historical Jesus, is what Luther rediscovered" (Barth, *The Theology of Calvin*, p. 62). Barth stated that Calvin's theology was determined by christology and not by "a general metaphysical, philosophical view" and asserted that for Calvin "Christ is from the first the key with which he unlocks the whole. Christ is that unspoken original presupposition in terms of which we see God a priori as the ground and goal, the one who judges us and shows us mercy, and in terms of which we see ourselves a priori, when measured against God, as sinners, and are thus pointed to grace. Looking from Christ at God, we have knowledge of God, or, as it is put later, knowledge of God the Creator. Looking from Christ at us, we have knowledge of ourselves, out of which arises later knowledge of God the Redeemer" (*The Theology of John Calvin*, p. 164). Whether or not this is a worthy summation of Calvin's theology, it is a strikingly insightful one of Barth's own trajectory and foreshadows his later thought. His mature christological concentration (in which God's identity and our own are known in Christ) is already encapsulated by such a comment in 1922. A year later in his lectures on the Reformed confessions he maintained that questions of the Father and the Spirit are "secondary and derived questions" that can only be "posed from this center, from the revelation of the Son." See Barth, *The Theology of the Reformed Confessions 1923*, trans. Darrell L. Guder and Judith J. Guder (Louisville: Westminster John Knox, 2002), p. 164. It is not unwarranted to conclude in light of these observations that Barth was on the road to some form of christocentric concentration even before the GD, and that christology as interpreted through his biblical exegesis and the Reformed tradition was the key to his mature anti-speculative conviction and rejection of natural theology. Barth's christology and his anti-speculative attitude were two sides of one coin, or two poles of one reality—the first positive, the second negative.

13. Barth, *The Theology of the Reformed Confessions*, p. 122. For this reason, in comparing the confessional history that flowed from the Reformation, Barth stated that "Reformed theology, particularly in its position on contingent revelation, but from that central point throughout, was in principle a *dialectical* theology" (ibid., p. 179). It was so, he insisted, more consistently than the Lutheran theology of the time (ibid., pp. 179–80).

tradition. In truth, all such inheritances were re-formed and re-articulated in a new dogmatic framework that re-situated them, and one deeply shaped by Barth's scriptural and Reformational discoveries. The same might be said of his conceptions of the revelation and hiddenness of God, notions which, it may be true, were inherited from Herrmann, but which in the years of his first professorate were entirely redefined with new explicit footings in Luther and the Reformation tradition, and these new foundations were only solidified with time.[14] Finally, but not least in importance, there were more radical breaks with his past. Barth embraced the cross in a way that Herrmann never did, and he came to have no regard for Herrmann's emphasis upon the "inner life" of Jesus.[15] His understanding of revelation and of christology, as well as of the task and purpose of theology itself, took a very different direction from that of his teacher.[16] Moreover, with regard to the liberal tradition more broadly conceived, Barth abandoned its philosophy of history and its historicism, as well as prevalent understandings of theology's scientific [*wissenschaflich*] character that so shaped the German theological tradition from F. C. Baur to Ernst Troeltsch.[17]

---

14. For the argument that these were inheritances of Herrmann, see Chalamet, *Dialectical Theologians*, p. 73. Whether this was or was not the case, when Barth spoke of them, he grounded them in the works of Luther explicitly, rather than Herrmann, and while this is evident already in the GD, it is nowhere more evident than in the first volume of the CD.

15. "Do we stand on the ground of the *theologia crucis*? This appears to me to be the question of destiny that is posed to our Protestant church today, where we have the real opportunity to see what the cross is." See Karl Barth, "The Need and Promise of Christian Proclamation 1922," WGT, pp. 101–29 (126).

16. It is questionable whether the theology of Herrmann and Harnack should even be called christocentric at all in light of their understandings of the synthetic quality of religion as a confluence of God, Christ, and the individual. See Fisher, *Revelatory Positivism?*, p. 214. He states: "In view of the fact that each element of the relational synthesis was of equal importance, it is perhaps better to affirm that these theologies were Christo-morphic in character with the symbol, image, or *Bild* of Christ receiving the status of a cipher or conceptual simulator of personal religious experience" (ibid., p. 214). Whether or not this is overstated or entirely captures the views of Herrmann, Harnack, or even the very early Barth, it does correctly point to the fact that the christocentrism of Herrmann and that of Barth from the GD onward were of an entirely different nature and explains why Barth, in light of this immediate past, declared that "both dogmatics and preaching which follows it must dare to be less christocentric" (see GD, p. 91).

17. For this tradition, see Johannes Zachhuber, *Theology as Science in Nineteenth-Century Germany: From F. C. Baur to Ernst Troeltsch* (Oxford: Oxford University Press, 2013). Zachhuber has a nuanced view of Barth's continuities and discontinuities with the liberal tradition (ibid., pp. 291–2; cf. p. 136). See also Thomas A. Howard, *Protestant Theology and the Making of the Modern German University* (Oxford: Oxford University Press, 2006). If Barth did have a predecessor for his understanding of the character of theology, it was, ironically, Schleiermacher (and Ritschl), but this in regard to one specific matter, namely, that theology

That Barth largely abandoned Herrmann's project and many of the central goals of the nineteenth-century theological tradition (to a degree that Bultmann did not, in spite of his disagreements with it)[18] should lead us to question simple lines

was a practical discipline ("positive science") that was carried out within and for the Christian church with concrete acknowledged presuppositions rather than a presuppositionless discipline ("pure science") of the academy (whether philosophical or historical). In this sense, he stood closer to Schleiermacher than to figures like Fichte, Hegel, or D. F. Strauss (see Zachhuber, *Theology as Science in Nineteenth-Century Germany*, pp. 287–8). Barth in fact found the idea of a totally presuppositionless exegeis "comical" (see CD I/1: p. 469). Zachhuber traces the identification of "scientific" with an "absence of presuppositions" back to Strauss, who in turn joined it explicitly to a rejection of all miracles (Zachhuber, *Theology as Science in Nineteenth-Century Germany*, pp. 79; 91; see also pp. 86–95).

18. That Bultmann did not understand his own theological project to consist in a radical break from his early theology and that of his teachers is evident in his self-evaluation. At the end of his life he noted that he had been a part of the dialectical movement and shared with it a conviction that "Christian faith is the answer to the word of the transcendent God that encounters man," maintaining this stance even against his own teacher Herrmann in his adoption of Barth's standpoint in the *Romans* commentary. Nevertheless, he insisted, this judgment "never led me to a simple condemnation of 'liberal' theology; on the contrary, I have endeavoured throughout my entire work to carry further the tradition of historical-critical research as it was practiced by the 'liberal' theology and to make our more recent theological knowledge fruitful for it." See Rudolf Bultmann, *Existence and Faith: Shorter Writings of Rudolf Bultmann*, ed. and trans. Schubert M. Ogden (New York: Meridian Books, 1960), p. 288; see also Robert Morgan, "Ernst Troeltsch and the Dialectical Theology," in *Ernst Troeltsch and the Future of Theology*, ed. John Powell Clayton (Cambridge: Cambridge University Press, 1976), pp. 33–77 (38). Not only was Bultmann more faithful to the critical historical side of the liberal tradition than Barth, but Morgan notes that he also "remained theologically closer to Herrmann than Barth did, and found it a small step from Herrmann to Heidegger" (ibid., p. 38). As Bultmann asserted, "But just because I learned from Herrmann I was prepared for Heidegger" ["Aber eben, weil ich bei Herrmann gelernt habe, war ich für Heidegger vorbereitet"]. See *Barth-Bultmann Briefwechsel 1911–1966*, ed. Bernd Jaspert (Zürich: TVZ, 1994), p. 186; ET: *Karl Barth-Rudolf Bultmann Letters 1922/1996*, ed. Bernd Jaspert, trans. and ed. Geoffrey W. Bromiley (Edinburgh: T&T Clark, 1982), p. 99. Such a comment signals that Bultmann considered his theological project as one marked as much by continuity as by discontinuity with the teachers of his past, and he could continue to quote his former teacher Herrmann with approval. See Rudolf Bultmann, *Jesus Christ and Mythology* (New York: Charles Scribner's Sons, 1958), pp. 72–3; cf. Hammann, *Rudolf Bultmann*, pp. 232; 437. He also had a much higher estimation of Schleiermacher as a faithful interpreter of Christian faith and Scripture than Barth did (see *Karl Barth-Rudolf Bultmann Letters 1922/1996*, p. 6). Moreover, it is evident that Bultmann could not have followed Barth into dogmatics and found Barth's move to embrace its task deeply disappointing, even as Barth never shared Bultmann's dedication to the prevalent academic convictions of historical criticism akin to Troeltsch. As Bultmann stated already

of inheritance and continuity.¹⁹ It is certainly true that Barth retained lessons and positions from Herrmann, such as an aversion to "traditionalism, rationalism,

in 1905: "At the moment my biggest annoyance is dogmatics .... What nonsense is being retained about 'revelation,' 'Trinity,' 'miracles,' 'divine attributes'—it is horrible" (quoted in David Congdon, *The Mission of Demythologizing: Rudolf Bultmann's Dialectical Theology* [Minneapolis: Fortress, 2015], p. 83. Bultmann never abandoned his aversion to dogmatic thinking, and all attempts to draw similarities between Barth and Bultmann in reference to theological method or "dialectical theology" stumble when such differences are taken into account (see Morgan, "Ernst Troeltsch and the Dialectical Theology," p. 40; cf. pp. 59–60). Nevertheless, Bultmann was the most enigmatic member of the dialectical school, trying to walk a fine line between the apologetic strategies of Gogarten and Brunner and the complete rejection of such strategies by Barth. Hammann gives a balanced judgment of Bultmann's intentions in his essay of 1930 on natural theology: "Bultmann took up a completely solitary position with respect to the controversy then going on among Barth, Brunner, and Gogarten. He pleaded for a theology that would accept the primacy of and remain within the framework of revelation and faith, and would take account of the modern person's experience of reality" (Hammann, *Rudolf Bultmann*, pp. 237–8). In this, Bultmann might be seen as the confluence of the projects of Herrmann and Troeltsch, themselves opposed. See Brent W. Sockness, *Against False Apologetics: Wilhelm Herrmann and Ernst Troeltsch in Conflict* (Tübingen: Mohr Siebeck, 1998), p. 214.

19. That Barth in fact only retained elements from Herrmann because they were in harmony with his new theological commitments and their Reformation precedents, and jettisoned the rest, demonstrates that he had no intrinsic commitment to Herrmann's programmatic convictions for their own sake. With this in mind, as well as his systematic dismantling of his inheritance, if Barth is not understood to have "broken" with liberal theology, then one is left to wonder what would constitute such a break. Kenneth Oakes astutely notes that to speak of a break with liberalism depends upon the persons one is identifying as liberals and the definition and features of liberalism being considered, and also rightly observes that Barth's differences with his predecessors were about more than epistemological concerns and included exegetical and even political ones. Yet if, as he avers, Barth can be called not only "orthodox and modern" but "orthodox and liberal," it is legitimate to ask if the term "liberal" has lost all descriptive power when it is so broadened that it can catch up figures as variegated as Schleiermacher, Ritchl, Herrmann, Troeltsch, and especially Barth, and one may wonder what is really left of the term's usefulness or meaning. See Kenneth Oakes, *Karl Barth on Theology and Philosophy* (Oxford: Oxford University Press, 2012), pp. 22; 52; 58–9, and 58 nt. 160; cf. Zachhuber, *Theology as Science*, pp. 136; 291–2. The same problems occur when, like "liberal," the term "dialectical" is used for a theological description that catches up very different figures such as Herrmann and Barth. While Herrmann indeed might be portrayed as a "dialectical" theologian when comparisons are made on a quite formal, methodological level, such says little of the actual and very real material differences between Herrmann and Barth after Barth's renunciation of the theology of his teacher. This is one of the nagging questions remaining regarding speaking of Herrmann, Barth, and Bultmann as all "dialectical" theologians—see Christoph Chalamet, *Dialectical Theologians*. Persons are indeed complex, and Herrmann's theology

[and] mysticism," yet even the first of these was greatly transformed, for while Barth never embraced a positivistic orthodoxy, he found a place for doctrine and the inheritance of the early church in a way that Herrmann (and Bultmann), with their disdain for objectification, dogma, and doctrinal assent, never did.[20] Barth also entirely abandoned the private internal faith of Herrmann that Bultmann

no doubt cannot simply be dismissed or fully grasped by a straightforward summation of it with the word "liberal." This is especially true due to his fight against psychologism and historicism, though perhaps with less success against the former due to a fundamental stress upon the experience of revelation rather than revelation itself (see ibid., pp. 12; 11-19; 40-5; 54-60). Yet all of the ambiguity of "liberal" also pertains to "dialectical." And when the material commitments of Barth and Herrmann are compared, placing Barth and Herrmann under the umbrella of "dialectical" (or "christocentric" much less "liberal") theology does not do full justice to an appreciation of their significant differences regarding their respective understandings of revelation and christology; it also leaves the question of whether "reorientation" is truly a strong enough word to convey Barth's departure from Herrmann's theological convictions (see ibid., p. 89). Chalamet in fact later speaks of Barth "departing from the theology of the preceding generation," including that of Herrmann (ibid., p. 96; cf. p. 109). And a departure is, of course, a break from something that came before and not simply a "reorientation." Nevertheless, nothing here said should detract from the brilliance of Chalamet's study which does set forth differences in the dialectical thought of all three thinkers, nor from the excellent study of Oakes which traces Barth's thought regarding philosophy in relation to theology.

20. Barth, "The Principles of Dogmatics According to Wilhelm Herrmann," in TC, pp. 238-71 (248). Another way to express this point is that Barth had a place for doctrine, tradition, and ecclesiology in theology that neither Herrmann nor Bultmann had nor could due to their understanding of revelation and religion as profoundly interior and experiential realities and their aversion to and rejection of any aroma of a *Lehrgesetz*, an aversion Barth strongly renounced (ibid., p. 270). Barth had his own aversions, and particularly a reaction to any attempt to ground theology in an immanent experience of the individual, which he understood to be central to Herrmann's theological project: "There is no word more significant for Herrmann's theology than the word 'self'" (ibid., p. 254). This marks another gulf between their theologies, for whereas for Herrmann (like Schleiermacher) the Trinity was merely a "reflection of faith" to be assigned to a latter supplementary addendum of dogmatics but peripheral to religious experience, for Barth theology was first and foremost about a triune God who speaks, such that "a wholly different 'Self' has stepped into the scene with *his* own validity" (ibid., p. 256). Such made a correct doctrine of the Trinity an imperative in Barth's estimation. See *Revolutionary Theology in the Making: Barth-Thurneysen Correspondence 1914-1925*, trans. James D. Smart (Richmond: John Knox, 1964), pp. 176; 185. Such differences only solidified with time, such that both Trinity and church take a precedence in the first volume of the CD (already prefigured in the GD) in a way that contrasts sharply with Herrmann's understanding of both in his *Dogmatik*. In light of such divergences, the debate between Herrmann and Troeltsch, for all its personal and professional fervor, came to be seen by Barth not as a life or death struggle between the two great theological alternatives

## 4. Karl Barth and the Protestant Ecclesial Vision        89

continued to espouse and that was wedded to an anti-dogmatism that made doctrine itself suspect as a betrayal of justification by faith alone.[21] Moreover,

of his student years, but as a tempest in a tea pot between two mistaken rivals, such that he was comfortable to dispatch the central concerns of both (whether fairly or not) in a single passage (see "The Principles of Dogmatics According to Wilhelm Herrmann," pp. 255-6). For the nature of the tempest, and for the relation of these figures to Barth and dialectical theology with more appreciation for both Herrmann and Troeltsch (and in turn for the older Ritschlian school and the opposing newer history of religions school) than Barth displayed, see Brent W. Sockness, *Against False Apologetics: Wilhelm Herrmann and Ernst Troetlsch in Conflict*; and Morgan, "Ernst Troeltsch and the Dialectical Theology," pp. 41-2. For a balanced and incisive account of the tempest, see Hendrikus Berkhof, *Two Hundred Years of Theology: Report on a Personal Journey*, trans. John Vriend (Grand Rapids: Eerdmans, 1989), pp. 143-62. In a sense, the famous debate between Barth and Harnack in 1923 over historical criticism and its validity and limitations with regard to theology and faith was prefigured in the debate between Herrmann and Troeltsch. In this regard, Barth certainly remained closer to Herrmann than Troeltsch in a thorough-going rejection of historicism, insistence upon revelation's independence, and an unquestionable commitment to the uniqueness and unsurpassability of Christ, though it must be noted that Troeltsch too could speak of the independence of religion (*die Selbständigkeit der Religion*). But with regard to how Christ was understood, Barth and Herrmann stood on entirely different planes. This was, unsurprisingly, even more true with respect to Barth's differences with Troeltsch, who in the end was pushed toward subsuming Christ and Christianity into the river of historical relativity and religious consciousness: "In the long run Troeltsch found the idea of ranging Christianity within the history of religion inescapable." See Hans-Georg Drescher, "Ernst Troeltsch's Intellectual Development," trans. Michael Pye, in *Ernst Troeltsch and the Future of Theology*, ed. John P. Clayton (Cambridge: Cambridge University Press, 1976), pp. 3-32 (7). It was this relativization that was perceived by the older Ritschlians as the greatest threat posed by Troeltsch and the younger scholars of the history of religions school, namely, the latter's "calling into question the uniqueness and absoluteness of Christian revelation," and thus "the unique historical revelation of God in Christ" (Sockness, *Against False Apologetics*, pp. 27; 21; cf. pp. 36-40; see also George Rupp, *Culture Protestantism: German Liberal Theology at the Turn of the Twentieth Century* [Missoula, MT: Scholars Press, 1977], pp. 18-19; also pp. 37; 43; 49; 51). Barth saw this approach of the history of religions school as a dead-end for dogmatics.

21. In contrast, Barth concluded in his estimation of Herrmann: "The Church should always present the revelation to men in 'doctrine'.... And it should always present it with the claim that this doctrine 'is to be accepted as true'.... For that purpose the Church is here; it is that which the Church can do in relation to the revelation; it can teach what man should accept as true" (Barth, "The Principles of Dogmatics According to Wilhelm Herrmann," p. 270). Herrmann, in contrast, held that Luther's own adherence to the early church's christological dogma of the two natures of Christ and "reverence for dogma" in general was a remnant of Catholicism that needed to be abandoned. See Herrmann, *The Communion of the Christian with God*, ed. Robert T. Voelkel, trans. J. Sandys Stanyon and R. W. Stewart (Philadelphia: Fortress, 1971), p. 52; see pp. 48-56. Bultmann's own project of demythologizing was understood by him to be an extension of Paul and Luther's doctrine of justification by faith alone into the area of epistemology (see Hammann, *Rudolf Bultmann*, p. 449; also Congdon, *The Mission of Demythologizing*,

not only were these inheritances greatly re-shaped or abandoned, but the ones that Barth retained were often not those regularly noted.[22] His departure from

pp. 369–70, 496; cf. 570–1; 674–5). The purpose of this extension was to eliminate any false security that would ground faith in assent to external dogma or any apologetics that might provide proof of belief. Barth also wanted to extend the doctrine of justification to epistemology, but whereas for him it entailed that God is known by God alone through grace alone such that natural theology must be renounced, for Bultmann it entailed the rejection of dogma entirely in a radicalization of the doctrine of faith alone such that the content of faith was sacrificed. The great difference on this score, rarely noticed, is that Bultmann saw adherence to doctrine as a (mistaken) prerequisite of faith and therefore a mark of works-righteousness, whereas Barth saw it as part of the obedience of faith, such that theological confession gives articulation in witness to the grounds of faith itself, i.e., the God who is revealed in Jesus Christ through the Holy Spirit, reflected in the movement to us in revelation, Scripture, and proclamation. To Bultmann (echoing Herrmann) this appeared to be a return to a staid orthodoxy that in the modern world hindered faith due to an objectification of revelation. At its worst, it was a form of re-submission to law and works. To Barth in turn Bultmann appeared to succumb to a doctrinal docetism that collapsed the grounds and divine agency behind faith into faith itself in a thorough-going subjectivity, losing all content to faith in the process of subsuming christology into soteriology. His rejection of dogmatic confession betrayed a doctrinal antinomianism. See Barth, "Rudolf Bultmann—An Attempt to Understand Him," p. 111; see pp. 83–132. Barth's Reformed sensibilities shaped his position, as Bultmann's distinctive Lutheran ones did his, though one might conclude that whereas Barth's program was to bring the Reformation into consistency with its own central insights, Bultmann's own (following Herrmann) was to radicalize those insights such that any claim to normative doctrinal knowledge and assent were stripped away from faith as pure trust, and to do this not in line with, but against the Reformers' own self-understanding. Bultmann cast these differences between the theologians gathered together under the banner of dialectical theology as due to unresolved tensions between the Lutheran and Reformed traditions. Barth concurred, and concluded that such might lead to an eventual explosion within their journal *Zwischen den Zeiten* (see *Karl Barth-Rudolf Bultmann Letters 1922/1966*, p. 32). In time, the alliance, and the journal, would not survive.

22. "The enemy front towards which Herrmann's concept of religion and revelation faced is not the anti-Christian position of modern philosophy and of natural and historical science. (That position is merely addressed occasionally and with ironical superiority.) The real enemy's position is on the right, within Christian theology itself" (Barth, "The Principles of Dogmatics According to Wilhelm Herrmann" p. 248). This conviction that the greatest threat to Christian truth comes from within, rather than without, the Christian church is, along with a principled rejection of historicism, perhaps the most unchanged and persistent inheritance Barth maintained from Herrmann, and one that best describes his own theological program as articulated in the first volume of the CD. On this point he truly was a faithful disciple of his teacher. Another lesser inheritance was the proclivity to radicalize an argument by embracing a seeming foe to one's position as a way to undercut any appeal to historicism or psychologism in religion—hence, both Herrmann and Barth embraced the radical historical skepticism of Strauss as an ally in the fight against historicism itself. There were also more problematic shared practices. As Brent Sockness notes: "Herrmann typically

Herrmann was thus profound even as he remained guardedly appreciative, as in his essay on the theology of his former teacher in 1925.[23] Barth could treat Herrmann dialectically, embracing and commending Hermann's appeal to a knowledge of God "without weapons" (e.g., unapologetically), but judging his definition of this knowledge as the "expression of individual experience" as "not good." Even the anti-apologetic stance of Herrmann was reframed by Barth as due not to the independence of religion but the freedom of God.[24] As he asked: "How would it be if the datum with which dogmatics has to begin were not man—in his

---

sees in his opponents instances of one or more of the following types of misunderstood faith: mysticism, rationalism, moral idealism, or orthodoxy" (Sockness, *Against False Apologetics*, p. 26). This use of broad types is something that is perhaps inescapable and not simply a Herrmannian (and earlier Ritschian) practice, but Barth, following Herrmann, readily embraced it. Such trading in types comes with rhetorical power, but it also entails the ensuing problems of large general judgments against at time thinly defined things like "rationalism" and "mysticism." This was certainly true of Barth's general dismissal of "pietism." He was more nuanced in his conversations with actual pietists later in his life.

23. To think coherently that Barth did not "break" with the liberal tradition would require that one maintain that: (a) Barth did not fully understand the theology of his teachers (e.g., Herrmann and Harnack); (b) that they did not understand him (for they took his new trajectory as both a break with and a threat to their legacy—evident in both their correspondence with Barth, as well as in public debate, such as the famous one of 1923 between Barth and Harnack); and that (c) Barth did not rightly understand his own theology (which he explicitly took to be and stated to be a break with the past). Such would entail an implausible amount of misunderstanding. The question of Barth's break with the liberal tradition is better understood when the explicit persons representing it are named—and when named, Barth's turn from them becomes clearer than speaking about an abstraction such as "liberalism" however necessary it may be. It is also a distorting practice when the discontinuities in his own thought are over-estimated and those between him and the tradition of his teachers under-estimated. Such an underestimation can only thrive when comparisons are limited to general statements about "the liberal tradition" as an abstraction rather than based upon detailed examinations of Barth's differences from specific persons such as Harnack, Herrmann, or Troeltsch. Such downplaying of differences is also only plausible when the comparisons are made on a highly formal level of method and abstract conceptuality, but its viability flounders when material matters (of revelation, of christology with its attendant doctrines of incarnation, cross, atonement, resurrection and ascension, as well as the doctrine of the Trinity, of ecclesiology, the normativity of church tradition, etc.) are actually taken into account (and this is as true of Schleiermacher as of these latter figures). When such material matters are examined, what comes to light is that Barth left no theological stone unturned from Herrmann or Harnack even if he was willing to retain some of the stones in the building of his new theological edifice. Yet even there, all of the stones were re-chiseled before use, and this already by the GD. For a similar judgment, see Bruce L. McCormack, *Karl Barth's Critically Realistic Dialectical Theology*, p. 68.

24. Barth, "The Principles of Dogmatics According to Wilhelm Herrmann," pp. 259-60.

experience as little as in his thinking—but again God himself in *his* Word?"[25] Most conclusively, his judgment upon Herrmann was rooted in a pointed rejection of his teacher's view of revelation and christology, which, because of their centrality to his new theological program, signified that any remaining continuities between himself and Herrmann could exist only on the level of broad and formal theological generalities.[26]

After this essay in 1925, Herrmann recedes into the background and almost entirely disappears from Barth's writings, with but a few very minor exceptions in the CD. In light of Barth's own development, this is unsurprising. He renounced Herrmann's understanding that theology's task was, in Herrmann's words, to set a person "face to face with the reality of religion" (as "his own unrecognized craving for religion emerges into consciousness") so that he can be enabled to discern "the working of a God in the events of life," a theological viewpoint in which revelation and this personal experience of religion become coterminous.[27] Barth broke entirely with such a conception of revelation and dogmatics. To maintain that Barth straightforwardly took over from Herrmann (or other liberal theologians of the time) a "christocentrism" or an aversion to natural theology and metaphysics or a concern with ethics or an acceptance of historical criticism

---

25. Barth, "The Principles of Dogmatics According to Wilhelm Herrmann," p. 260. Barth's understanding of Scripture thus differed greatly from Herrmann's own (see ibid., pp. 269–70). Chalamet notes Barth's turn from the language of the experience of God to the knowledge of God already in 1915 (*Dialectical Theologians*, pp. 92–3). Oakes maintains that this turn from experience was directly tied to Barth's rejection of appeals by Martin Rade and Herrmann to experience to provide explanation and warrant for Germany's participation in the Great War. See Oakes, *Karl Barth on Theology and Philosophy*, pp. 45–51.

26. "Orthodox Christology is a glacial torrent rushing straight down from a height of three thousand metres; it makes accomplishment possible. Herrmann's Christology, as it stands, is the hopeless attempt to raise a stagnant pool to that same height by means of a hand pump; nothing can be accomplished with it" (Barth, "The Principles of Dogmatics According to Wilhelm Herrmann," p. 265; see pp. 264–5). For a discussion of this passage and an examination of Barth and Schleiermacher's christology along similar lines, see Kimlyn J. Bender, *Confessing Christ for Church and World: Studies in Modern Theology* (Downers Grove: IVP Academic, 2014), pp. 353–84. Barth judged Schleiermacher's christology to be as deficient as Herrmann's, and for the same reasons. Speaking of Schleiermacher's christology in his 1923/24 lectures, Barth concluded: "His Christology is the incurable wound in his system." See Barth, *The Theology of Schleiermacher: Lectures at Göttingen, Winter Semester of 1923/24*, ed. Dietrich Ritschl, trans. Geoffrey W. Bromiley (Grand Rapids: Eerdmans, 1982), p. 107; see pp. 103–7. He in effect said the same of Herrmann. Correspondingly, in his lectures on the Reformed confessions in 1923, he asserted: "Can there be any more urgent task for a theologian than *Christology*?" This was, Barth notes, the opinion of the Reformation. See Barth, *Theology of the Reformed Confessions*, p. 160; also Barth, *The Theology of Calvin*, p. 164.

27. Wilhelm Herrmann, *Systematic Theology (Dogmatik)*, trans. Nathaniel Micklem and Kenneth A. Saunders (London: George Allen & Unwin Ltd, 1927), pp. 19; 20; 34–6.

papers over and conceals more than it reveals of a true comparison of them.[28] In this as in all things, shared terminology says little about shared conviction or content. Barth and Herrmann simply mean different things when they speak of revelation or christology.[29] Acknowledging this is to respect them both, even as it makes no final claim about the ultimate referent of their discourse about Christ.

---

28. Marking such similarities, Berkhof concludes that Barth is a "Hermannian of a higher order" (*Two Hundred Years of Theology*, p. 201), which Chalamet references approvingly (Chalamet, *Dialectical Theologians*, p. 19); as do McCormack, *Karl Barth's Critically Realistic Dialectical Theology*, p. 68 nt. 71; and Oakes, *Karl Barth on Theology and Philosophy*, pp. 22; 245-6. The issue remains, however, whether such similarities mitigate the differences, or whether the differences predominate over the similarities. When such matters are taken up line by line in material commitments rather than comparing formal and terminological similarities, it is reasonable to conclude that the differences tip the scales in their favor, for broadly formal methodological similarities should not overshadow real and significant material differences. Chalamet is aware of the difficulty and ambiguity of the judgments. Speaking of Herrmann and Barth, and Barth's relation to the liberal project in general, he concludes: "There were discontinuities, of course … but there were also some continuities. Scholars have so far shown difficulty in keeping both aspects in mind" (ibid., p. 90; cf., however, p. 177). Such is true, and such continuities need to be noted and weighed and not, as often in the past, simply dismissed. But the correction to a past wrong is not to err on the other side. Therefore while continuities must be given their due, they cannot be allowed to paper over or discount real differences—and such differences made all the difference for Barth's project and its execution, as well as his own evaluation of it.

29. It is of no small importance that nearly all of the things that Oakes mentions as inheritances from Herrmann are things that Barth in turn came to ground in convictions of the Reformation rather than in liberal commitments (see Oakes, *Karl Barth on Theology and Philosophy*, p. 22; cf. p. 252): (1) Barth did in fact not straightforwardly embrace a christocentric theology in the GD precisely because he rejected the particular christocentric theology of the liberal tradition (see GD: pp. 91; 120; cf. CD I/2: pp. 350-2), though he did immediately turn to develop a very different christological theology more specifically indebted to the patristic and Reformation convictions regarding the incarnation; (2) his rejection of natural theology was predicated on the *sola gratia* and *sola fide* of the Reformation, along with its rejection of *theologiae gloriae*, rather than predicated on an argument for the independence of religion or a Kantian rejection of philosophical arguments for God's existence; (3) the seriousness of ethics came to be grounded in Calvin and the Reformed tradition more generally, evident in Barth's early lectures on Calvin (1922), and not in a commitment to Herrmann's (or Kant's) ethical program; and (4) the "critical freedom" he had toward confessions was articulated in terms of differences between the Reformed and Lutheran understandings of the nature and normativity of confessions, evident in his early lectures on the Reformed confessions (1923), rather than in Herrmann's suspicion of doctrinal orthodoxy. In truth, only Barth's "judicious acceptance of historical-critical methods and the natural sciences" marks his liberal inheritance on its own terms, and even here, his debates with Adolf von Harnack on the first (following upon his choice

*Barth in Light of the Nineteenth Century's Understanding of the Canon*

A few additional observations might be mentioned that further illustrate other important differences between Barth and his nineteenth-century inheritance. First, a common and consistent theme of the broad liberal tradition out of which Barth emerged was a reductionistic understanding of the canon—namely, that a critical principle was hermeneutically necessary to discern the meaning and essence of Christianity and its enduring significance which in turn relativized segments of the canon. Barth pushed against this tradition with his firm embrace of the canon as a theological category that rejected such reductions (whether displayed in the critically derived reductive gospel of Harnack or the *Sachkritik* of Bultmann) even while recognizing relative canonical differences of importance and clarity and embracing a firm christological lens through which the whole was to be read. This view is present in his first dogmatics of the mid-1920s and fully developed in the CD, evident in passages from each:

> No matter what our attitude to the words and the historical aspect of the witness may be, we have to regard them as transparencies through which a light shines. It shines with varying degrees of brightness and clarity—no one need argue that Jude is as powerful a witness as Romans—yet it is always a light, *the* light. Everything relates to this light, everything that we might view as a transparent medium pointing us in this direction. Even Jude is in its own way a witness to Jesus Christ and not to someone or something else. In this sense—and again the understanding of the historical element is a secondary concern—everything is truth.[30]

of Calvin over modern interpreters of Scripture, as famously stated in his second and third prefaces to the *Romans* commentary) and with Heinrich Scholtz on the second (in CD I/1) demonstrate that with regard to these as well he did not simply accept a liberal (or Herrmannian) inheritance without revision. What is important to take away from such observations is that Barth framed all of these matters in light of Reformation convictions rather than solely Hermannian or modern ones. Of course, it must be noted that Herrmann himself was intentionally standing in the tradition of the Reformers—though Barth saw his project and Neo-Protestantism in general not as a rightful progression of the Reformation, but as a deeply flawed development in Protestantism, as examined below.

30. GD, p. 254. Barth earlier stated, commenting on Calvin: "If in principle it is seen to be right to listen to the Bible, then we should listen to the whole Bible" (*The Theology of Calvin*, p. 391). For the development of Barth's understanding of the biblical canon, see Bender, *Confessing Christ for Church and World*, pp. 145–77. In his acceptance of the diversity of the canon without anxiety, allowing it to speak in witness to one Lord rather than to carve off those parts that did not fit a reductive conceptual or systematic interpretation, Barth remained closer to the decisions of the early church which canonized such diversity, as well as anticipated recent scholarship. In this sense, he prefigured the way that biblical studies would take in the latter part of the twentieth century and into the twenty-first rather than remain fixed in the nineteenth. His view of the canon thus resonates with Larry Hurtado's contention regarding differing biblical accounts that "this deliberate

When we have to do with Scripture, i.e., canonical Scripture, the Scripture which the Church has defined and we in and with the Church have recognized as canonical, when we have to do with Holy Scripture as a witness, in fact the witness of divine revelation, we have to do with the witness of Moses and the prophets, the Evangelists and the apostles.[31]

Scriptural exegesis rests on the assumption that the message which Scripture has to give us, *even in its apparently most debatable and least assimilable parts*, is in all circumstances truer and more important than the best and most necessary things that we ourselves have said or can say.[32]

Such a view of the canon was both derived from and shaped a very different understanding of revelation and Christ than that of the tradition out of which Barth came. One could state that here too it was his Reformed convictions that shone out over Lutheran ones with the latter's proclivity for a canon within the canon. But that would be to admit, once again, that he was shaped as significantly if not more so by Reformation categories than by specifically nineteenth-century ones and that he saw his position as breaking with the latter's central convictions and programs, whether those of Harnack or Herrmann.

Finally, most nineteenth-century understandings of Scripture in the broad liberal and critical theological tradition out of which Barth came were particularly ambivalent about the Old Testament. This was as true of Schleiermacher as it was of F. C. Baur, of Harnack as it was of Bultmann (though Ritschl's case is a more

---

incorporation of diversity in the New Testament canon reflects an early Christian view that there is something to be gained from them all and that *for theological purposes* they are best read in conversation with one another, their various emphases preserved and their diversity seen as enriching the scriptural resources for theology and Christian life." See Hurtado, "Christology and Soteriology," in *Beyond Bultmann: Reckoning a New Testament Theology*, ed. Bruce W. Longenecker and Mikeal C. Parson (Waco: Baylor University Press, 2014), pp. 193-209 (201; see also 208-9). Such a view is markedly different than Bultmann, for example, for whom John and Paul were the only theologians of the NT of any real importance, and for whom the canon displayed only a "relative unity" overshadowed by a diversity that had to be overcome through "content criticism" (*Sachkritik*). See Angela Standhartinger, "Bultmann's *Theology of the New Testament* in Context" in *Beyond Bultmann*, pp. 233-55 (248).

31. CD I/2: p. 481. These four mentioned (e.g., "Moses and the prophets, the Evangelists and the apostles") are obviously inclusive of the entire canon of the OT and NT in Barth's usage.

32. CD I/2: p. 719 (emphasis added). Barth recognized that this does not entail that Scripture presents an undifferentiated witness: "Holy Scripture has always been defined in the Church with varying degrees of emphasis on the constituent parts" for it "does not in fact and practice treat all parts of the Bible alike" (CD I/2: p. 478). But in the end, the witness as a whole attests to one thing, not many. This is foundational to Barth's understanding of the canon as canon. See Bender, *Confessing Christ for Church and World*, pp. 179-205.

complicated exception).³³ If Barth had done nothing else than firmly uphold the centrality and unquestionable status of the OT within the canon and its irrevocable importance for Christian theology and the church against both nascent indifference and explicit calls for its marginalization or removal, he would have stood out as a beacon against the broad liberal tradition from which he came.³⁴

---

33. See Anders Gerdmar, *Roots of Theological Anti-Semitism: German Biblical Interpretation and the Jews from Herder and Semler to Kittel and Bultmann* (Leiden/Boston: Brill, 2009). Such negative sentiments were quintessentially expressed by Harnack: "The rejection of the Old Testament during the second century A.D. would have been a mistake, which the great Church rightly refused to make. Its retention in the sixteenth century was a fate from which the Reformation was not yet able to extricate itself. Its conservation as a canonical document for Protestantism since the nineteenth century is the consequence of a religious and ecclesiastical paralysis." See Harnack, *Marcion* (Leipzig: J. C. Hinrichs Verlag, 1924), p. 217; quoted in Rumscheidt, *Revelation and Theology: An Analysis of the Barth-harnack Correspondence of 1923* (Cambridge: Cambridge University Press, 1972), p. 98. Barth came to read Scripture entirely differently, as a rich narrative tapestry of expectation (OT) and fulfillment (NT), evident in his reflections upon the time of expectation and that of recollection in the first volume of the CD, marking him off not only from Harnack but also Bultmann. Bultmann differed from Barth not only because of his ambivalent estimation of the Old Testament due to seeing it almost exclusively under the negative category of law, but also because of the OT's striking unimportance in his estimation for understanding the essence of Paul's theology. Barth for his part judged that Bultmann had an "inability to make anything of the Old Testament" (Barth, "Rudolf Bultmann—An Attempt to Understand Him," p. 111). For Bultmann's understanding of the Old Testament, see Rudolf Bultmann, *Primitive Christianity in Its Contemporary Setting*, trans. R. H. Fuller (London: Collins, 1960); also Rudolf Bultmann, "Prophecy and Fulfillment," trans. James C. G. Grieg, in *Essays on Old Testament Hermeneutics*, ed. Claus Westerman & James L. Mays (Richmond: John Knox, 1964), pp. 50-75. Quintessential is Bultmann's following judgment: "For the person who stands within the Church the history of Israel is a closed chapter ... Israel's history is not our history, and in so far as God has shown grace in that history, such grace is not meant for us ... The events which meant something for Israel, which were God's Word, mean nothing more to us." See "The Significance of the Old Testament for Christian Faith," in *The Old Testament and the Christian Faith*, ed. B. W. Anderson (New York: Harper and Row, 1963), pp. 8-35 (p. 14). Bultmann's project is criticized for such a stance toward the OT by Richard Hays, "Humanity Prior to the Revelation of Faith," in *Beyond Bultmann*, pp. 61-77. For a more sympathetic account of Bultmann's project than Hays, see John Barclay, "Humanity under Faith," in ibid., pp. 79-99; for a defense of Bultmann's view of the OT as in fact essential for NT understanding and theology, see Hans Hübner, "Rudolf Bultmann und das Alte Testament" in *Kerygma und Dogma* 30 (1984), pp. 250-72; cf., however, Gerdmar, *Roots of Theological Anti-Semitism*, pp. 373-411.

34. In this regard, Barth was much closer to persons like Friedrich Tholuck and J. T. Beck than to his predecessors in the liberal tradition. See Gerdmar, *Roots of Theological Anti-Semitism*, pp. 195-212.

## Barth and Modernity: The Historiography of the Present Age

If the first historiography that Barth provides is that of his own theology as a break with that of his formal education and modern liberal Protestantism, itself echoed in the description of his taking leave from the majority of his colleagues within the dialectical movement, the next and broader historiography is how Barth speaks of his own time and describes its place in relation to the history of Christianity and the church. Here too his nuanced understanding of modernity can be overshadowed by an attempt to see him in the context of his time and to define him by its concerns such that he is portrayed as predominantly or even singularly exercised with the challenges of modernity.

### Theology and Epistemology

Insofar as the modern period is marked by an emphasis upon epistemology (in light of Descartes, Locke, and Kant, as but three significant examples, with the last of particular theological importance), Barth's own theology is often construed as preoccupied with answering epistemological concerns, and specifically, answering the question of the possibility of the knowledge of God in light of the challenges of a post-Kantian world. For this reason, Barth's project is often framed as primarily concerned with the knowledge of God (*Gotteserkenntnis*). There is particular interest in past decades of examining Barth drawing upon and responding to the "idealism" of his age, and specifically the Kantian and Neo-Kantianism of his context. Here again the method of understanding him is composed of discerning the influence of such sources upon his thought, as well as framing his project as one that overcomes the challenges of the modern period, and specifically, the limitations placed upon knowledge by Kant. In turn, the central question that he attempted to address is construed in terms of the knowledge of God and theological epistemology.

It is of course the case that Barth was steeped in and conversant with the questions of modernity.[35] His preoccupation with Schleiermacher is but one instance of this, and he thought of Schleiermacher as being intentionally modern in his identity as a Christian theologian coupled with a distinctively Prussian

---

35. The attempt to read Barth not as primarily shaped by Scripture and the Reformation tradition but definitively according to the questions and themes of modernity was put forth by Trutz Rendtorff—see Rendtorff, "Radikale Autonomie Gottes: Zum Verständnis der Theologie Karl Barths und ihrer Folgen," in *Theorie des Christentums: Historisch-theologische Studien zu seiner neuzeitlichen Verfassung* (Gütersloh: Gütersloher Verlaghaus Gerd Mohn, 1972), pp. 161–81; see esp. pp. 162 and 164. Rendtorff argued that Barth was not best understood as a theologian of the Reformation tradition but as a proponent of liberal theology and of a new Enlightenment that translated the autonomous subject of modernity into the radical autonomous subjectivity of God. For a measured and careful response to such readings of Barth by Rendtorff, as well as others such as Falk Wagner and F. W. Graf and the "Munich school" to which they belong, see Stefan Holtmann, *Karl Barth als Theologe*

national consciousness.³⁶ This awareness of the challenges of modernity is also evident in Barth's engagement with the theology of the eighteenth and nineteenth centuries.³⁷ This engagement included not only recognizable theologians of the period, but also the thought of figures as diverse as G. E. Lessing, Franz Overbeck, and Ludwig Feuerbach, and was extended to the general philosophical and cultural questions of the age.³⁸ It is also indisputably true that Barth engaged the question

*der Neuzeit: Studien zur kritischen Deutung seiner Theologie* (Göttingen: Vandenhoeck & Ruprecht, 2007), esp. pp. 11-19; see also John Macken, *The Autonomy Theme in the* Church Dogmatics: *Karl Barth and His Critics* (Cambridge: Cambridge University Press, 1990), esp. pp. 109-53. What unites such readings is a refusal to take Barth on his own terms and to apply a hermeneutic of suspicion to his work, such that his theology, grounded and expressed explicitly in and through biblical exegesis and evangelical (i.e., Reformational) and other theological convictions, is reckoned to be but a cover for a hidden modern (and, according to Wagner, insidious and tyrannical, even fascist) agenda that needs to be de-coded. A brief but incisive rebuttal to such readings was articulated by Eberhard Jüngel, *Karl Barth: A Theological Legacy*, trans. Garrett E. Paul (Philadelphia: Westminster, 1986), p. 14. For a more circumspect and measured argument for Barth as a distinctly modern theologian than those figures of the Munich school mentioned above, see Bruce L. McCormack, *Karl Barth's Critically Realistic Dialectical Theology*; and the essays in McCormack, *Orthodox and Modern: Studies in the Theology of Karl Barth* (Grand Rapids: Baker Academic, 2008), esp. chs. 1, 3, 5, and 6; also McCormack, "Der theologiegeschichtliche Ort Karl Barths," in *Karl Barth in Deutschland (1921-1935): Aufbruch—Klärung—Widerstand*, ed. Michael Beintker, Christian Link, and Michael Trowitzsch (Zürich: TVZ, 2005), pp. 15-40. In the latter, McCormack, in contrast to Rendtorff and others, states that Barth's theology is not simply a new orientation within the liberal (i.e., Neo-Protestant) tradition, but a true break with it, even as elements of this tradition may have had a lasting influence upon him long thereafter (p. 21).

36. Karl Barth, "Friedrich Schleiermacher: Zum 100. Todestag am 12. Februar 1934," in *Vorträge und kleinere Arbeiten 1934-1935*, ed. Michael Beintker, Michael Hüttenhoff, and Peter Zocher (Zürich: Theologischer Verlag Zürich, 2017), pp. 145-56 (149).

37. See Karl Barth, *Protestant Theology in the Nineteenth Century: Its Background & History*, trans. Brian Cozens and John Bowden (London: SCM, 1972). Commenting on these lectures on Protestant theology in the nineteenth century, John Webster states: "It is precisely as he struggles to come to terms with the dominant figures of modern theology that Barth shows himself in very important respects a modern theologian, taking up modernity's questions even when he turns inside out the answers developed with such skill by his forebears, and, above all, feeling responsible to shoulder (not evade or dismiss) its tasks as a responsible participant in its history" (*Barth's Earlier Theology*, p. 93).

38. Some of the most significant thinkers of modernity who shaped Barth's thought were those who stood as enemies of religion and who thereby served as his allies in his opposition to it. Prominent examples in this regard are Feuerbach, who attacked the arguments for religious psychologism and immanence, and Strauss, who attacked the arguments for historicism as a foundation for faith. See Barth, "The Word in Theology from Schleiermacher to Ritschl 1927" in TC, pp. 200-16, esp. pp. 212-14; see also Karl Barth, "Fate and Idea in Theology (1929)," in *The Way of Theology in Karl Barth*, ed. H. Martin Ruscheidt (Eugene, OR: Pickwick, 1986), pp. 25-61 (34). Katherine Sonderegger summarizes Barth's CD as the work of one steeped in

the preoccupations of the modern age: "Throughout the *Dogmatics* Barth intended to address his contemporaries, to take up the critical problems the human sciences presented, and to acknowledge the standards of coherence, rationality and historical warrant that university faculties honoured. We could never explain the long, detailed excurses on academic debates from anthropology, psychology, and sociology; the retention of Idealist concepts such as dialectic, limit, autonomy, and heteronomy; the detailed exegeses of philosophers such as Nietzsche, Heidegger, and de Beauvoir; reflections on historians and higher critics of all kinds. From these can we not see that Barth was a child of his generation, and a full member of the academy. To the measure that dogmatics was an exercise of the intellect, it must share, acknowledge and conform itself to the standards of intelligibility imposed on reader and writer alike. To that measure, Barth remains a true heir of nineteen-century German academic theology." All that is true—but what she then says is of utmost importance: "But Barth breaks decisively with his inheritance when he moves the discussion of theological method from the formal to the material task of dogmatics. Here Barth shows himself to be not the academic but, rather, the Church theologian, committing himself to the particular freedom that proclamation of the gospel gives, not in that way repudiating his standards of rationality, coherence and intelligibility, but rather deepening them. The distinctive note of *spaciousness* in Barth's theology—the ability to range freely over doctrines, to survey a wide field of history and the arts, to speak in the mixed idiom of Scripture, of high and low culture and, above all, to speak confidently and fearlessly without academic scrupulousness and anxiety all stem from Barth's recognition that method *follows*, and does not precede, content." See Sonderegger, "Et Resurrexit Tertia Die: Jenson and Barth on Christ's Resurrection," in *Conversing with Barth*, ed. John C. McDowell and Mike Higton (Aldershot/Burlington: Ashgate, 2004), pp. 191–213 (194–5). What must be added and modified is that this freedom pertained not only to the material, but even to the formal, questions of method, and that Barth's challenges to the norms of the academy went deep. He simply was not overly concerned with meeting the modern "standards of intelligibility" beyond its most general requirements. Such is evident in his striking dismissals of such standards. When listing the requirements of scientific method as articulated by Heinrich Scholz, he acknowledged the accuracy of Scholz's description of the definition of what constitutes a modern scientific discipline—"It is still the proper concept of science for our time"—but then curtly replied: "And theology can only say point-blank that this concept is unacceptable to it" (CD I/1: 9). This rejection includes a blunt dismissal of the inviolability of even those most basic axioms of science and logic such as the law of non-contradiction. It is this striking indifference to meeting some of the most basic and general expectations of the science and academy of his day that I am not certain Sonderegger's brilliant synopsis fully captures in discussing his acknowledgment and general adherence to the "standards of coherence, rationality and historical warrant that university faculties honoured." Barth was not only materially, but formally, and at time shockingly, iconoclastic. Harnack recognized this full well, as did Scholz, to whom Barth exclaimed that academic theology is founded and dependent upon the resurrection of Jesus Christ from the dead. See Eberhard Busch, *Karl Barth: His Life from Letters and Autobiographical Texts*, trans. John Bowden (Grand Rapids: Eerdmans, 1994), p. 207. Finally, Sonderegger insightfully adds that Barth's assertion that obedience is a theological method is jarring to academic theologians, "because method, to these theologians, is a specimen of epistemology" (Sonderegger, "Et Resurrexit Tertia Die," p. 196). That he was so freely breaking down the neat modern divisions of intellect and will, of epistemology and ethics, is a tell-tale sign that he was not playing by the dominant modern rules, as will become apparent below.

of the knowledge of God and made God's lordship not only in reconciliation but also in revelation (as two sides of one coin) a central element of his theology.[39] Moreover, Barth was influenced by Kantian (and Neo-Kantian) forms of thought in his early theology as he worked through such questions.[40] One can

---

39. For one example, see KD 1/1: pp. 155; 323-4; ET: CD 1/1: pp. 149-50; 306-7. H. J. Iwand notes that just as for the Reformers the doctrine of justification was preeminent, so for modernity it is the doctrine of revelation which is so. See Iwand, "Der Prinzipienstreit innerhalb der protestantischen Theologie," in *Um den rechten Glauben: Gesammelte Aufsätze*, ed. K. G. Steck (München: Chr. Kaiser, 1965), pp. 222-46 (231); quoted in Michael Weinrich, "Theologischer Ansatz und Perspektive der Kirchlichen Dogmatik Karl Barths: Trinitarische Hermeneutik und die Bestimmung der Reichweite der Theologie," in *Karl Barth in europäischen Zeitgeschehen (1935-1950): Widerstand—Bewährung—Orientierung*, ed. Michael Beintker, Christian Link, and Michael Trowitzsch (Zürich: Theologischer Verlag Zürich, 2010), pp. 15-45 (16); see esp. pp. 15-20.

40. Such concepts include Barth's use of *Ursprung* with various iterations of meaning in the two editions of the *Romans* commentaries (though whether such were gleaned directly or first mediated by Herrmann or Barth's brother Heinrich Barth is not as clear). See Johann F. Lohmann, *Karl Barth und der Neukantianismus: Die Rezeption des Neukantianismus im "Römerbrief" und ihre Bedeutung für die weitere Ausarbeitung der Theologie Karl Barths* (Berlin/New York: Walter de Gruyter, 1995), esp. pp. 229-36; 280-306; and 388-91. Even in the Romans commentary such use of this concept was not strictly governed by a philosophical tradition, and Barth's use of it was idiosyncratic in character (see McCormack, *Karl Barth's Critically Realistic Dialectical Theology*, p. 149; Oakes, *Karl Barth and on Theology and Philosophy*, p. 65). Nevertheless, pertaining to the second edition, McCormack states: "Barth's theological epistemology in *Romans* II stands everywhere in the long shadow cast by Immanuel Kant" (see McCormack, *Karl Barth's Critically Realistic Dialectical Theology*, p. 245). He contends that there Barth drew expressly and copiously upon the Kantian notion of "the Unintuitable" (*das Unanschauliche*) to speak of God as hidden and revealed (ibid., p. 249). There is nevertheless in truth a deep tension in McCormack's references to the place of Kantianism in Barth's theology. He can state that Barth's Kantian idealism was foundational and necessary for his theology such that his particular brand of theological realism would have been "unthinkable" without it (see McCormack, *Karl Barth's Critically Realistic Dialectical Theology*, p. 130; cf. pp. 226; 235; 465-6). Yet he also states that "At every point, his [Barth's] theological concerns governed his use of philosophy," and that his theology was eclectic in its use of philosophical and other sources such that philosophy was ancillary to more fundamental theological convictions (ibid., pp. 42; 225; see also McCormack, *Orthodox and Modern*, pp. 125-6; cf. pp. 159-60). It is a valid question to ask whether the reality of the second claim must not soften the firmness of the prior one. It is moreover reasonable to ask if the neo-Kantian influence on Barth especially has been exaggerated, and whether Barth's theology really would have been "unthinkable" without Kantian critical idealism. The first regarding Neo-Kantianism might be cautiously answered affirmatively, and the second regarding the necessity of Kantianism negatively. One of the difficulties, it seems, is that McCormack almost exclusively frames the problem Barth is concerned with as that of knowledge of God (ibid., p. 125; also pp. 207-8). But the problem with which Barth was

see this particularly in Barth's *Romans* period, and Bultmann could recognize (and criticize) this indebtedness upon reading Barth's second edition of *Romans*.[41] Yet even in the commentary, his primary interest was expounding Paul, with Kant's philosophy subordinate to the exegetical task.[42] Moreover, it also must be admitted that Barth's theological interests always ranged beyond narrow epistemological ones, and that his use of philosophical and specifically Kantian concepts for theological descriptions of revelation was always eclectic.[43] In truth, an interest in these concepts burned off fairly quickly, and this already by the writing of Barth's first dogmatics in Göttingen.[44] Certainly a case might be made that such philosophical conceptions continued to exert some influence beyond the *Romans*

engaged seems rather how God's lordship was to be maintained in every aspect of divine and human encounter such that God could not be domesticated in thought, in culture, in the church, or in the ethical agency of the individual. Thus, if "God is God," then God is the Lord not only of human knowledge (theological epistemology), but of human society (politics and culture), and specifically, Lord of the church (ecclesiology), and Lord of human action (ethics). To read Barth's writings across the 1920s is to see him engaged with all of these concerns, and not only those pertaining to epistemology and the problem of *Gotteserkenntnis*. Certainly the question of knowledge took a prominent place, but it did not take the only place.

41. Oakes makes the following judgment regarding the second edition of the Romans commentary: "At several points Barth assumes that Kant's critical philosophy provides an admirable limitation and restriction of the pretensions of speculative reason" (*Karl Barth on Theology and Philosophy*, p. 78). For Bultmann's comments and criticisms of Barth on this score with specific reference to Neo-Kantianism, see James M. Robinson, ed., *The Beginnings of Dialectic Theology*, pp. 119-20.

42. Not only was this clearly Barth's stated intention at the time of the commentary's appearance, but also his judgment upon later reflection, evidenced in a conversation with Reformed clergy in 1963. Admitting the importance of Kant for his very earliest theology as a student and then fledgling pastor, he nevertheless concluded: "Be that as it may, I was there, as are all of you, and my task was chiefly to preach the Bible. As I read the Bible, the God of Immanuel Kant and these other great idealists began to recede in importance .... To be sure, I discovered that St. Paul was a little more interesting than Kant." Nevertheless, Barth expressed an ongoing affinity for Kant in philosophical (rather than theological) matters. See Karl Barth, *Barth in Conversation: Volume 2, 1963*, ed. Eberhard Busch, trans. Karlfried Froehlich, Darrell Guder, Matthias Gockel et al. (Louisville, KY: Westminster John Knox, 2018), pp. 134-5.

43. Oakes, *Karl Barth and on Theology and Philosophy*, pp. 87-8; cf. p. 62.

44. So while "*unanschauliche*," to give one prominent and previously mentioned example, occurs nearly 100 times in the 1922 *Römerbrief*, it almost entirely disappears after 1923, with but a handful of uses. "*Das Unanschauliche*" occurs over twenty-five times in the commentary, but only twice in Barth's corpus in all the years after 1922 (in the provisional searches I have been able to conduct). Berkhof astutely notes that Barth in the writings immediately before and after the Romans commentary had in fact no consistent philosophical terminology, casting about for diverse terms from various philosophers

commentary.[45] Yet such things should not be overstated, for the lines of derivation and descent of such discrete and defined conceptions become in fact more and more tenuous and unclear as time passes. Whatever theological positions Barth earlier sought to develop with the assistance of such philosophical concepts, he

and philosophical schools in service to his theological purposes. After the commentary, Berkhof states, "the philosophical terminology totally disappears. In subsequent years Barth devoted his energies particularly to exegesis. In the instances where he still occupies himself with philosophy there is definitely no question any more of an identity of concern" (*Two Hundred Years of Theology*, p. 196; see pp. 194–8). One might here add that even if the terminology did not totally disappear, it had lost all of its prior significance (as will be seen below—though Kierkegaard's terminology is a more complicated case). He concludes: "If at this point we now look back upon the approximately five tumultuous years after the publication of the first edition of the *Römerbrief*, we cannot help noticing how intensely Barth searched for clarity in different directions. Hardly any two of his writings from this period move within the same terminological sphere. He employed side by side ideas from biblical theology, systematic theology, and philosophy. In the process philosophical concepts played a subordinate role" (ibid., pp. 196–7).

45. That Barth continued to speak during his life of a dialectical relationship between realism and idealism, displaying Kant's synthesis of the empiricist and rationalist traditions, as well as his interest in seeing theology as a science and his use of transcendental deductive forms of argumentation to set forth the conditions for the possibility of revelation—all of these are taken to be evidence that he remained a Kantian thinker, as argued by Joseph C. McLelland, "Philosophy and Theology: A Family Affair (Karl and Heinrich Barth), in *Footnotes to a Theology: The Karl Barth Colloquium of 1972*, ed. Martin Rumscheidt (Waterloo, Canada: Canadian Corporation for Studies in Religion, 1974), pp. 30–52. McCormack sees Barth's Kantianism as having a continuing influence on his understanding of the dialectic of veiling and unveiling in revelation, supposing that it is questionable that Barth would have been so fascinated with the patristic anhypostatic-enhypostatic christology if he had not been "prepared" for it by his Kantianism, and takes such Kantianism to be a "factor of great influence" ("Der theologiegeschichtliche Ort Karl Barths," p. 20; see pp. 15–23; see also Lohmann, *Karl Barth und der Neukantianismus*, pp. 338–61; 361–75). Lohmann, however, notes the difference in Barth's understanding of philosophy by the time of the GD, where, though it continues to have a place, is no longer fundamental but illustrative in its concordance with Barth's more theologically grounded positions, for "the speech regarding the retrospectively-confirming function of philosophy shows that a shift of emphasis has occurred. There is no longer any talk of a 'philosophical police' that forms an eventual corrective for theology" (ibid., p. 339). By the first volumes of the CD, even these congruences disappeared and philosophy, and idealism particularly, had no constitutive purpose for Barth's argumentation or description of God's lordship in revelation or reconciliation: "The end point of the path of abandoning the congruence thesis are the elaborations of a purely revelation-theological epistemology in the first three volumes of the *Church Dogmatics*" (see ibid., p. 353). As Barth stated there, he had attempted to wipe away thoroughly all anthropological, existential, and philosophical starting points for theological reflection which still clung to the *Christliche Dogmatik* (CD I/1: p. xiii; see also Karl Barth, *Karl Barth: How I Changed My Mind* [Richmond: John Knox Press, 1966], pp. 42–3).

quite rapidly moved beyond them and replaced them with explicit justifications and warrants drawn from the findings of his work in Scripture, the classical patristic tradition, and the Reformation heritage. A few things might be set forth as warrants for this claim.

First, to say that Barth was influenced by Kant or is responding to Kant needs delimitation. Barth had no interest in reducing religion to an element of practical reason or ethics (even though he could at times find limited positive correlations between elements of Kant's ethics and his theological claims). He was deeply suspicious of Kant's absolutizing of the human will.[46] He certainly did not follow Kant's understanding of religion, faith, or christology. Rather, the question is best framed in the narrow terms of the limitations of Kant's *First Critique*, that of pure reason, and thus of the limitations of knowledge of metaphysics, and specifically, of God, that Kant imposed. In a broad sense, Barth accepted Kant's rejection of straightforward metaphysical arguments for the existence of God, as well as an acknowledgment that theological claims did not fall under the jurisdiction of theoretical reason. Yet even here, he was not dependent upon Kantian categories for the theological arguments he was making, always seeing them more as matters of supplementation and primarily serving critical rather than constructive purposes, and if this was true already in the *Romans* period, it was all the truer from Barth's first professorate onward, and readily evident in his first dogmatic cycle.[47]

That Barth there generally accepted Kant's criticisms of metaphysics and natural theology and could even find these criticisms of some limited value is to be granted, but they were not of great interest.[48] For Barth, Kant was simply bringing into focus something that should have been apparent and consistently

---

46. Karl Barth, "The Problem of Ethics Today 1922" in WGT, pp. 131–69 (146–7). Barth there asserted: "A personality whose will is governed by the idea of humanity, and who therefore has a *pure, autonomous, good* will, and *moral* personality, who has stepped over the threshold of the world of freedom into our world, has never existed anywhere, and will never exist anywhere" (p. 147). He was much more impressed by a "Pauline-Reformation line of thinking" than such a modern, Kantian one (ibid., p. 163; also pp. 157 and 168; cf. p. 190).

47. Congdon, who places significant weight on the effects and importance of modernity and its questions for Barth, nevertheless notes that all that Barth (and Bultmann) wanted to say theologically was already grounded in Reformation commitments and convictions and that dialectical theology cannot be reduced to matters of epistemology (or ontology)—see *The Mission of Demythologizing*, pp. 290–1; cf. McCormack, *Karl Barth's Critically Realistic Dialectical Theology*, p. 42.

48. See Unterricht I, p. 13; ET: GD, p. 10; and Unterricht I, pp. 26–7; ET: GD, pp. 20–1. See also Unterricht II, pp. 45–6; ET: GD, pp. 349–50. For a nuanced examination of similarities and differences between Kant's understanding of epistemology and Barth's theological reason, see Westerholm, *The Ordering of the Christian Mind*. Westerholm's study is particularly strong with regard to the seriousness with which he takes the importance of Barth's exegetical work for his theological development. Yet even he at times can draw lines of relation between Barth and Kant that appear to be based on discerning broad general

held by the Reformers, but was not—i.e., that God is revealed solely in Christ and his Word, and this is the basis for church proclamation and teaching. He was much less concerned to solve a modern epistemological dilemma in the light of Kant and the Enlightenment than to bring the Reformation into conformity with itself and its best insights regarding revelation and reconciliation by grace alone. Revelation was thereby a question of God's lordship in the reality and particularity of his Self-giving rather than the explication of human limitations that might set forth the conditions of its possibility or that had to be overcome.[49] Moreover, his understanding of the relation of God hidden and revealed, a God veiled in God's assumed medium of revelation, such that "in his revelation God is the hidden God," was itself something that was in the GD deeply shaped by the classical tradition and especially patristic christology (and specifically one framed along anhypostatic-enhypostatic lines), the Reformation debates between the Lutheran and Reformed, and even the christological conceptuality of Kierkegaard, rather than presented as the conclusion of a modern philosophical argument regarding the limitations of human knowledge.[50] Even if Kant played some role in Barth's

similarities, as when he writes regarding transcendental arguments: "Kant and Barth are thus both to be found establishing particular standpoints by deploying transcendental inquiries into the conditions that permit a particular reality to be conceived" (ibid., p. 120). Westerholm is aware of the limitations of such arguments and concedes: "I mean in this context only to show that, on a formal level, Barth's account of a standpoint constructed around the resurrection mirrors Kant's account of a standpoint constructed around freedom" (ibid., p. 120 nt. 121). Such qualifications of course mitigate any sense of Barth's reliance on Kant for this similarity and in effect replace it with indirect association. It is precisely when Westerholm turns from a description of Barth's exegesis of Paul to a positing of possible philosophical sources that Barth may be drawing upon in the background that the argument appears more speculative and tenuous.

49. As Lohmann puts this point succinctly: "Weil Gott der Herr ist, ist er nur dort zu erkennen, wo er sich zu erkennen gibt—in seiner Offenbarung" ["Because God is the Lord, he can only be known where he gives himself to be known—in his revelation"] (*Karl Barth und der Neukantianismus*, p. 375).

50. As Barth wraps up his chapter on the incarnation, he writes: "In this fourth subsection, as in the third, I have followed closely ... the ancient dogma and even the older orthodox dogmatics" (Unterricht I, p. 206; ET: GD, p. 167). Not to be overlooked, in addition to the Chalcedonian language and that of Protestant orthodoxy, is the conceptuality of Kierkegaard, whose notions of "concealment" [*Verborgenheit*], "contradiction" [*Widerspruch*], the divine "incognito," "indirect communication" [*indirekte Mitteilung*], "contemporaneity" [*Gleichzeitigkeit*] as well as his antipathy of speaking of revelation as "historical," play a role in shaping Barth's understanding of God's revelation hidden in the veil of flesh—see all of Unterricht I, pp. 163–73 and 174–87; ET: GD, pp. 134–41 and 142–52. Here some circumspect and modest judgments on sources can be made if only insofar as such conceptuality is explicitly present. Whether gleaned directly from Kierkegaard or elsewhere, such conceptions can be found all the way into the first volume of the CD and its initial paragraphs on revelation (particularly

CD §§4 and 5), to which is added the notion of the elect and the disciples as "witnesses at second hand" (CD II/2: p. 424; also CD III/4: p. 487; this concept too is already present much earlier—see Barth, "Menschenwort und Gotteswort in der christlichen Predigt 1924," in *Vorträge und kleinere Arbeiten 1922-1925*, ed. Holger Finze (Zürich: Theologischer Verlag Zürich, 1990], pp. 426-57 [451]). These sections in the GD are shot through, not with the conceptuality of Kant, but of Kierkegaard (and Barth mentions him explicitly). Indeed, one must strain to glimpse Kant in this section, but the conceptuality of Kierkegaard is everywhere apparent. For important passages in Kierkegaard on these concepts, see *Practice in Christianity*, trans. and ed. Edna H. Hong and Howard V. Hong (Princeton: Princeton University Press, 1991), pp. 123-44; esp. p. 125; see also Kierkegaard, *Philosophical Fragments*, ed. and trans. Howard V. Hong and Edna H. Hong (Princeton: Princeton University Press, 1985), pp. 23-48 and 55-71. Of course, it must be said that there certainly are significant differences between Barth and Kierkegaard— these concepts serve for the latter not only as descriptions of God's revelation in Christ but also have different applications for human subjectivity and existence, and Barth had little interest in Kierkegaard's preoccupation with subjectivity. Barth's concern was with the subjectivity [e.g., lordship] of God in revelation, not with human subjectivity per se. But this transplantation and restriction of Kierkegaard's concepts to the objective revelation of God is in fact a common move in Barth's use of Kierkegaard—conceptions that Kierkegaard could use for both descriptions of the objectivity of revelation and of human subjectivity (e.g., contradiction) Barth took up solely for the former (even though in the GD he can yet speak of revelation as the divine answer to "the contradiction of human existence"—see Unterricht I, p. 190; ET: GD p. 155). A similar move is made in Barth's appropriation of the concept of "contemporaneity," which for him signifies not how we are made contemporaneous with Christ, as it did for Kierkegaard, but how Christ becomes contemporaneous with us through the taking up of the words of Scripture (canon) and the church's proclamation (preaching). It should therefore not be surprising that this language of contemporaneity shows up in the GD when Barth discusses the canon: "The church does not make revelation contemporary with us who come later, nor does it make us contemporary with revelation. Scripture itself does this as the witness of the prophets and apostles to revelation inasmuch as in it and over against it the Spirit speaks to spirit. Scripture does it as God's Word. This is the scripture principle of Protestantism" (Unterricht I, p. 277; ET: GD, p. 227; see also Unterricht I, pp. 245-58 and 321-9; ET: GD pp. 201-11 and 265-72). In sum: Barth's understanding of revelation and of the incarnation were shaped by Kierkegaard's conceptuality for their articulation, most succinctly put in Barth's statement that revelation is "indirect communication" and "indirect communication means God's incarnation" (Unterricht I, p. 185; ET: GD, p. 151). This remains true even if, again, Barth had little use for Kierkegaard's emphasis upon human subjectivity. For a discussion of Kierkegaard in Barth's work, see Lee C. Barrett, "Karl Barth: The Dialectic of Attraction and Repulsion," in *Kierkegaard's Influence on Theology, Tome I: German Protestant Theology*, ed. Jon Stewart (Surrey/Burlington: Ashgate, 2012), pp. 1-41; see esp. p. 27; also pp. 26-34. Barrett directly attributes the language of veiling and unveiling to Kierkegaard (p. 27). For a further discussion of Barth's relation to Kierkegaard, see Chapter 7 below.

early reflections on the hiddenness of God, Barth did not rely on Kant to provide him what he needed for the dialectic of veiling and unveiling. The indirectness of revelation and the veiling of God were things Barth received (either directly or indirectly) in the near distance from Kierkegaard and in the far distance from Luther if Barth's actual explicit attributions and descriptions are to be accepted.[51] They were also intrinsic in his Reformed understanding of the Creator-creature distinction, and he was appreciably shaped by this Reformed tradition even before his time in Göttingen.[52] Even more concretely, they were intrinsic to the incarnation itself as he understood it. In short, God's revelation posed for Barth the question of displaying the conditions of God's lordship that made such revelation possible

---

51. See Chalamet, *Dialectical Theologians*, pp. 136–8, and esp. p. 137 nt. 195; cf. pp. 184 and 269. Chalamet writes: "In his interpretation of Kierkegaard's terminology, Barth (in a typical move) was transferring Kierkegaard's discourse about existence from the human subject to God himself in his revelation" (ibid., p. 138). In light of the prior note, that is exactly correct. Specifically, whereas Kierkegaard asked how the believer might become contemporaneous with Christ, Barth set forth how Christ is contemporaneous with the church and the Christian through the witness of the prophets and apostles in Scripture and the proclamation of the gospel. In this regard, Hart is half right when, comparing Barth's appropriation of Kierkegaard with that of Brunner, and noting Brunner's appropriation of Kierkegaard's works on human analysis and subjectivity that Barth did not share, he concludes that "Barth and Brunner learned different things form the Dane: Barth heard the *critical* Kierkegaard whereas Brunner heard the *existential* Kierkegaard" (Hart, *Barth vs. Brunner*, p. 32; cf. p. 53). But whereas Barth eventually lost interest in the first, what he truly gleaned from was the christological Kierkegaard, for it was Kierkegaard's descriptions of Christ and revelation that had an enduring imprint on Barth's christological articulation (and no work of Kierkegaard made a deeper impression on Barth than *Practice in Christianity*). Finally, it is worth noting that the language of God's veiling of himself in Christ is already present in Luther, who states that Scripture is the Word written, or "formed in letters," just as "Christ is the eternal Word of God veiled in human nature." See WA 48: p. 31; also found in Martin Luther, *Sämmtliche Schriften*, ed. Joh. G. Boltsch (St. Louis: Concordia, 1881): V. 9: p. 1770. In light of all we have seen, McCormack's statement that "In the Göttingen lectures, the Kantian assumptions with which Barth works in explicating this point of view [regarding God's veiling and unveiling in revelation] are especially clear," is not self-evident (see *Orthodox and Modern*, p. 111). It is also not entirely clear why the notion of divine personal Self-revelation is thus taken to be an exclusively "modern" characteristic of revelation (see ibid., p. 31 nt. 24). Arguably its telling mark as modern is the delimitation of revelation exclusively to the personal—but Luther seems to prefigure this as well. It seems what is most specifically modern, in fact, is the move (in Hegel, in Strauss, in Schelling, though decisively not in Kierkegaard) to make this personal divine revelation not a matter of the particular incarnation in Christ but of a divine self-manifestation or realization in humanity and the world or world-process.

52. This is substantiated with Barth's own recounting of his history in an autobiographical reflection of 1927—see *Karl Barth-Rudolf Bultmann Letters 1922/1966*, p. 156.

(both objectively and subjectively) and set the question for the distinction between God's revelation and the medium (or veil) of its event, a question more central and fundamental for him than an epistemological one considering the limitations of knowledge pertaining to the human subject. As Barth put this matter:

> God is hidden then, not because of the relativity of all human knowledge, but because he is the living God who reveals himself as he is, the triune God, inexhaustibly living, immutably the subject, from himself and not from us. It is not a much too skeptical philosophy that makes him the hidden God. If we could learn something better from philosophy, moving on perhaps from critical idealism to critical realism, from Plato to Aristotle, from Kant to Hegel or back to Thomas, who would not gladly accept such instruction? But even the most basic epistemological teaching can give little or no help if God is the hidden God precisely because he is the living God, the self—revealing God, the God before whose Godhead we can neither flee from transcendence to immanence nor vice versa, the one who is never so distant as when he is near, the one who, because he is God can never be an object.[53]

For Barth, the inability of knowing God is therefore not a truth dependent upon a philosophical discovery (ancient or modern) of human epistemological limitations, but upon a theological understanding of the implications of revelation itself.[54] Correspondingly, the question of a human ability (or inability) not only to know but also to speak of God is not predicated upon a philosophical conception or specifically Kantian discovery, nor is it preeminently concerned with overcoming a Kantian question:

---

53. Unterricht I, p. 165; ET: GD, p. 135; see also Unterricht II, p. 54; ET: GD, p. 356; cf. CD II/1: pp. 183 and 248. Barth's conviction was that the particularity of revelation as self-authenticating did not require a pre-understanding of humanity's (epistemological or moral) crisis for its occurrence or understanding. In light of this, Brunner stood closer to a Kantian framework than Barth, for whom philosophy was in the GD at best illustrative but not constitutive of such knowledge gained solely through revelation. See John W. Hart, *Karl Barth vs. Emil Brunner*, p. 74. In general, Brunner was much more dedicated to providing a Kantian theology, explicitly incorporating Kant's distinction of the noumenal and phenomenal into his doctrine of revelation, and he even stated that dialectical theology was a return to the "truly critical scientific concept of transcendental Idealism" (quoted in Hart, *Barth vs. Brunner*, p. 32; see pp. 32–6; cf. pp. 117–19). Brunner consistently held up Kant and critical idealism as explicit complements to the theological task, while Barth chided him for his Kantian foundationalism, even while conceding its helpfulness (see ibid., pp. 74–80). Hart concludes: "Brunner's fundamental and consistent commitment to Kantianism decisively influenced his theological development, as it was philosophical issues, rather than dogmatic ones, which continually engaged his attention" (ibid., p. 211). This simply cannot be said of Barth.
54. Unterricht II, p. 11; ET: GD, p. 325.

The question that dogmatics has to put to preaching would be there even if philosophy could without contradiction accept or proclaim God as an object of possible intellectual or intuitive experience. The doubt that dogmatics would have to raise even were there no critique of pure reason rests on the recollection that, according to the definition of preaching what ministers say about God is supposed to be God's Word.[55]

On this account, all that we can say of human limitations regarding the knowledge of God is something that is given to us through revelation, just as is the reality of the knowledge of God: "We do not achieve it from a consideration of human nature or an examination of the transcendental presuppositions of human knowledge" [which are of course those of Kant], even if it may agree in some negative points with it.[56] In the *Christliche Dogmatik* this point only became more sharp: God is hidden from us not because of the "relativity of human knowledge" or "philosophical skepticism" but because God is the Lord whose very hiddenness is revealed. The question as to what kind of philosophy one holds, Barth asserted, is therefore entirely unimportant, and an "epistemological conversion to a critical realism, for example, would be completely meaningless in view of the fact that God is a hidden God exactly because he is the revealing God."[57] If Kant posed a challenge, it was one more directed to his own age, pointing out the limitations of its hubristic aspirations, than one posed to theology itself.[58]

---

55. Unterricht II, p. 12; see also pp. 54–5; ET: GD, p. 326; see also pp. 356–7. The original German eliminates any doubt as to the explicit reference to Kant here: "Das Bedenken, das die Dogmatik geltend zu machen hätte, auch wenn es keine «Kritik der reinen Vernunft» gäbe, ist begründet in der Erinnerung, daß das Reden der Pfarrer von Gott laut Bestimmung des Begriffs Predigt *Wort Gottes* ist bzw. sein soll" (Unterricht II, p. 12). Barth would make a similar point in the CD: "True knowledge of God does not need to be called to order by any critical theory of knowledge to remember the inadequacy of all human views, concepts and words" (CD II/1: p. 217).

56. Unterricht II, p. 31; ET: GD, pp. 340–1. Such a passage undercuts McLelland's claim that Kant's philosophy serves as a type of natural theology for Barth ("Philosophy and Theology—A Family Affair," p. 46).

57. ChrD, pp. 221–2.

58. Both in content and in tone, this is the substance of Barth's evaluation of Kant in his lectures on nineteenth-century theology. Barth esteemed Kant not as posing a challenge to a true theology of the Word of God but to an age that attempted to circumvent that Word for a natural religion and corresponding theology. Kant's challenge to theology was not so much epistemological but, like others of the modern age, the absolutizing of the self as the locus of the divine and as the standard by which revelation itself is judged. For this reason, Kant had to be opposed rather than accepted and overcome. Moreover, Barth focused less upon the effects of Kant's epistemology in the *Critique of Pure Reason* than upon the question of the relation of a theology of revelation and its relation to a universal religion of reason, and more intently engaged with Kant's work *Dispute of the Faculties* and *Religion within the Limits of Reason Alone* than with the *Critique of Pure Reason*. In the end, what he chiefly

In an essay of the same year as the commencement of the GD lectures, Barth maintained that Kant's *Critique of Pure Reason* was only the negative approximation of what was already long known from reflection upon Exodus 3:14, namely, that "God reveals his name by concealing it"—in truth, by veiling it ("Gott offenbart seinen Namen, indem er ihn verhüllt"). Moreover, he continued, even the older Protestant orthodox theologians and Kant's only rival Thomas Aquinas already knew that God is incomprehensible in his revelation, and especially so there.[59] Barth's language in this passage of describing Christ and the Word in proclamation is not that of Kant and his categories, or of the "intuitable" or "unintuitable," but of Kierkegaard's "paradox" and of the cross of Calvary "to which Luther so often and rightly referred." The Protestant church, Barth exclaimed, dares to place this "paradox" at the center of the church.[60] As it speaks, it recognizes both God's own Word spoken and its own human words, but it also recognizes that there is here an indirect but nevertheless true and necessary identity between the divine Word and the human one. And as earlier noted, this indirectness in revelation was explicitly grounded in patristic and Reformed christology, the Reformed Creator-creature

opposed or even engaged in Kant was not his epistemology (which had its philosophical place and limited theological uses) but his Augustinian *anamnesis* and immanentism which speaks of a "God within ourselves" that stands via reason in judgment over revelation—see Karl Barth, *Protestant Theology in the Nineteenth Century*, pp. 266-312 (282). To read Barth himself on Kant in this most important piece after reading so much secondary literature on Barth and Kant can be disorienting; what one finds there is unexpected. In brief, Kant is treated not as one who poses philosophical challenges to theology, but one who falls into a line of a problematic theological historiography, not least because of his christology, where reason stands in judgment over Christ himself, as well as for his failure to uphold a Reformational understanding of grace and justification (ibid., pp. 287-8 and 303). Yet Barth treats Kant with remarkable sensitivity as well, even if, in the end, he is neither to be simply accepted (as Ritschl and Herrmann had done), nor accommodated even if critiqued (as Schleiermacher had done). Rather, Barth's adopted third option is that Kant should be dismissed in his fundamental demands for reason's jurisdiction over revelation. This ultimate indifference to such demands in which theology follows its own path, one in which theology must "stand on its own feet in relation to philosophy," is his final answer to how theology should proceed in light of Kant. For Barth, Kant's greatest service to theology, however malicious or unintentional, was in fact pointing out this fork in the road between philosophy and "biblical" theology (ibid., p. 307; see pp. 306-12).

59. See Barth, "Menschenwort und Gotteswort in der christlichen Predigt 1924," pp. 432-3. Barth states that the authority of the Bible is not in any way predicated on any mish-mash of norms derived from "Lutheranism and idealism" or other "modern" ideas or inclinations (ibid., p. 437).

60. See Barth, "Menschenwort und Gotteswort in der christlichen Predigt 1924," 432-3. One sees in this essay not only Barth's continuing appropriation of the insights and convictions of the Reformation, but also a growing awareness of their differences from those of Catholicism (see, for example, ibid., pp. 436-7 and 442).

distinction, Luther's theology of the cross, and even Kierkegaard's notion of indirectness and incognito, rather than upon Kant's phenomenal and noumenal distinction.⁶¹

In short, Barth's doctrine of revelation was already in the GD thoroughly theologically contrived. Even if Kantianism had a part to play in some of Barth's original reflection on the problem of revelation in the *Romans* commentary, it had little significance for Barth's dogmatic work, serving at most an ancillary rather than programmatic role. As with his inheritances from Herrmann, Barth replaced whatever he had made use of earlier from Kant's critical philosophy in thinking through revelation with scriptural and Reformational convictions, so that what Kantian critical philosophy remained was illustrative and secondary to Barth's understanding of revelation rather than constitutive and primary for it in the GD and beyond.⁶² This is further substantiated when it is remembered that his later rejections of natural theology were not framed in terms of Kantian objections directed against metaphysics or philosophical arguments for the existence of God but in Reformational terms and arguments against violations of the singular and utterly gracious nature of God's revelation as given by grace alone through faith alone. Such arguments are evident in both his polemical works (such as his diatribe against Brunner in 1934's "*Nein!*") and his constructive work, such as his Gifford lectures in 1937–8, in which natural theology was addressed (insofar as it was addressed) by an exposition not of Kant's *Critique of Pure Reason* but of the Scots Confession.⁶³ Whether or not such applications of Reformational arguments were or are valid when put to use against natural theology, or whether or not they became increasingly important due to the challenges Kant provided,

---

61. For the problems of thinking of Barth's Creator-creature distinction in revelation in terms of that of Kant's noumenal-phenomenal distinction, see D. Stephen Long, *Saving Karl Barth: Hans Urs von Balthasar's Preoccupation* (Minneapolis: Fortress, 2014), pp. 112–20. One does not have to accept every element of Long's broader argument to recognize the truth of the central claim: "Whether Kant teaches idealism or epistemic humility is irrelevant to the fact that his phenomenal/noumenal distinction provides a very inadequate context in which to understand Barth's theology" (ibid., 118). Arguments along similar lines are made by Kirkland (*Into the Far Country*, pp. 4–6; pp. 24–30; pp. 30–5). In sum, to see the noumenal/phenomenal distinction in epistemology as akin to the God-world distinction (or to that between the hidden and revealed God) is a category mistake.

62. In the first volume of the CD, even this illustrative use of Kant had almost entirely disappeared, and references to Kant are for the purpose of seeing him both as a source of the Enlightenment's problematic turn to the subject and as a critic of such Enlightenment pretensions as well—see Oakes, *Karl Barth on Theology and Philosophy*, p. 171.

63. Moreover, Barth explicitly linked his arguments against the forms of natural theology he discerned in modern Protestantism to prior Reformation disagreements with Roman Catholicism. So in 1927, Barth stated that modern Protestantism's problematic teaching on religion and history was nothing but a renewal of the Roman Catholic doctrines of grace and of the church. See Barth, "Gottes Offenbarung nach der Lehre der christlichen Kirche 1927," in *Vorträge und kleinere Arbeiten 1925–1930*, ed. Hermann Schmidt (Zürich: Theologischer Verlag Zürich, 1994), pp. 215–95 (281).

such does not nullify the fact that Barth was driven to frame such arguments along the lines of the Reformation and its rejection of all *theologiae gloriae* in light of his embrace of a theology of the cross and in terms of a doctrine of revelation by grace alone.[64] Correspondingly, he held that natural theology such as philosophical

64. Morgan finds Barth's use of such biblical and Reformational arguments against natural theology unpersuasive and indeed due to Kant's influence: "The appeal to Paul will not support an attack on natural theology in principle—and Luther did not intend it as such. It was given that function later in order to make a virtue of necessity, following the destruction of the old natural theology by Kant" (Morgan, "Ernst Troeltsch and the Dialectical Theology," p. 56). Morgan also notes that such a move of using Luther's theology to frame arguments against natural theology preceded Barth in the work of Ritschl and Herrmann (ibid., p. 56). Yet what must be noted is how Barth's rejection of such arguments for natural theology was more consistently and rigorously grounded in a theology of the Word that came from outside of us than the theologies of either Ritschl or Herrmann, both of whom were much more concerned with the independence of religion than with the distinctive and singular reality of the Word as Barth was. Morgan asserts: "Natural theology cannot be banished in principle by appeal to Paul or Luther" (ibid., p. 57). Barth held that while it had not been consistently banned, the logic of Paul's gospel and the Reformation commitments of salvation entailed that it should be so banned, for revelation and reconciliation are two sides of one movement. He extended the Reformation commitments of salvation by God alone through grace alone to the realm of the knowledge of God, such that God is known by God alone through grace alone. He therefore applied all such Reformation convictions of soteriology to the question of the knowledge of God and indeed to every aspect of human life. A "religious a priori" was therefore something he rejected, whether that of Schleiermacher or Troeltsch, along with any form of a *potentia obedientialis* or *analogia entis*. When this is understood, his similar arguments against Protestant liberalism and Roman Catholicism in the CD become readily intelligible. Moreover, for Morgan to think that Barth's theology of the Word was marked by a turn to the "personal and private sphere" and had little or nothing to say to "political, social and economic reality" as did Troeltsch, is simply mistaken (ibid., p. 63). The great difference between Barth and Troeltsch was not, as Morgan avers, the severing by Barth of the relation of theology and the "real world," but the particularity and character of their understanding of revelation and christology, and thus the terms on which the "real world" should be engaged (ibid., p. 65). It is therefore significant that Gogarten charged Troeltsch with replacing Christianity with "Europeanism," a charge anticipated by Herrmann. See Robinson, *The Beginnings of Dialectic Theology*, p. 349; see also Sockness, *Against False Apologetics*, p. 196. It is also telling that Morgan takes the "real world" simply as a given to which theology must respond, rather than one that must first be theologically defined. Nevertheless, he is not unaware of the problem of christology for Troeltsch and the liberal tradition in general: "But the real weakness of liberalism was in its christology" (Morgan, "Ernst Troeltsch and the Dialectical Theology," p. 68). What he does not seem fully to grasp is that the problems of christology and natural theology are inextricably related (ibid., p. 68). In the end, no comparisons of similarities in method can overshadow the chasm created between Barth and Troeltsch in the latter's rejection of the doctrines of the Trinity and the incarnation (see ibid., p. 69). Where Troeltsch and Barth may in fact have agreed was in the conviction that the liberal project of the Ritschlian school could not in the end stave off the criticisms of Feuerbach regarding the integrity of religion (ibid., pp. 56–7).

proofs for God's existence should be rejected for theological reasons rather than for philosophical ones, even though in the GD he cautiously posited a place for them as illuminations following, rather than causing, faith, even as he maintained that they should still be excluded from dogmatics at least in the present.[65] Even Barth's arguments against Protestant orthodoxy and its doctrine of Scripture were not made in terms of the principles of modernity or the objections of historical criticism but rather according to the convictions of the Reformation, with orthodoxy portrayed by Barth not as opposed to modernity, but as its earliest stage and precursor, making the way possible for the very liberalism that later opposed it.[66]

Therefore, if Barth had to choose between the Christian theological tradition and modern philosophy as setting the conditions for dogmatic discussion, Barth trusted the tradition and the Reformers, and even the post-Reformation theologians, in terms of their basic insights: "Even without Kant they knew something of the distance that we must keep here, of the dialectic that is at work here. The same might be said of the Aristotelianism of Roman Catholic dogmatics, naïve though at first sight it may seem to be to us."[67] In short, Barth held that nothing of the dialectical nature of revelation depends on Kant or any other modern philosopher or thinker for its discovery or its articulation—its nature was present in the past and must now be considered in the present.[68] Moreover, revelation is not a matter of overcoming the limitations of human cognitive capacities determined by transcendental philosophical examination, but the

---

65. "Superstitious faith in the proofs ... arose only when there was no longer any idea what revelation is. Nor do I think it any reproach against the proofs that on other presuppositions of thought they have obviously been refuted by Kant"—Unterricht II, p. 41; see pp. 41–3; ET: p. 347; see pp. 347–8. Here too, Barth's later work on Anselm is already anticipated.

66. Barth's arguments against Protestant orthodoxy's understanding of revelation, Scripture, and inspiration were not predicated on the findings of modern historical criticism but put in terms of a betrayal of the dynamic and christological understanding of the Word of God that Barth saw in the Reformers. See CD I/1: pp. 123–4; 168; CD I/2: pp. 522–6. None of this should be taken to imply that his criticisms of orthodoxy were in every respect fair or above reproach. For an investigation in this regard, see Rinse H. Reeling Brouwer, *Karl Barth and Post-Reformation Orthodoxy* (Surrey/Burlington: Ashgate, 2015), esp. pp. 245–6.

67. Unterricht II, p. 38; cf., however, pp. 45–6; ET: GD, p. 345; cf., however, pp. 349–50.

68. Despite arguing for the importance of Kantianism for Barth's theological development, McCormack in the end does not want to make the validity of Barth's doctrine of revelation dependent upon Kantianism or its veracity, for its ultimate ground is in the doctrine of the Trinity and christology (see McCormack, *Karl Barth's Critically Realistic Dialectical Theology*, pp. 327–8; pp. 350–8; pp. 358–67; cf. pp. 370–1). Nor, McCormack avers, is this doctrine's "critical" aspect dependent upon a critical philosophy, but upon a divine critical judgment in revelation—see "Der theologiegeschichtliche Ort Karl Barths," p. 39. It is therefore significant when he states: "Philosophical epistemologies have come and gone, but Barth's theology is even more impressive now than it was at the time of its appearance" (ibid., p. 40). The question that remains is how determinative Kantianism was for Barth's dogmatic theology at all when in the GD he can appear so indifferent to it.

sovereignty of God who overcomes not only the divide between the Creator and the creation but the chasm that separates them because of human sin.⁶⁹ With his emphasis on the latter, Barth's understanding of the knowledge of God is shown to be shaped much more by theological than philosophical concerns. He was more exercised with the question of how divine revelation overcame human sin than human finitude, and he had no intention of being any more indebted to Kant than to Heidegger in approaching this ultimate human predicament.

*Theology and Philosophy*

In addition to the limitations of singling out Kant's philosophy as uniquely significant for illuminating Barth's understanding of revelation, there is the matter of the relation of theology and philosophy more generally.⁷⁰ Even in the specific sphere of knowledge, the truth is that Barth's concerns were always theological in nature rather than philosophical. While he drew upon philosophical terminology and conceptuality (and early on, particularly upon the Platonic and Kantian tradition) to frame his theological positions and proposals, at no stage, and certainly not after his turn to his work in Göttingen, was he strongly interested in a consistent philosophical program or even singular conceptuality to underpin such positions, a point of contention between Barth and Bultmann as evidenced in their correspondence.⁷¹ A careful

---

69. See, for instance, Barth's "Fate and Idea in Theology," p. 54. See also Kirkland, *Into the Far Country*, p. 29 and pp. 29–30, nt. 94.

70. The following comments are not meant to be exhaustive, and they recognize the complexity of this topic. They nevertheless point to the enduring general convictions of Barth's understanding of the relationship of theology and philosophy. For an examination of the specific development of Barth's understanding of this relation across his career, see Oakes, *Karl Barth on Theology and Philosophy*. Oakes rightly notes that even Barth's definition of "philosophy" in his work was not consistent and that his discussion of it ranged over a number of themes and concerns (p. 19).

71. For Barth's acknowledgment of his earlier indebtedness to Plato and Kant, see GD, pp. 258–9. For the disagreements with Bultmann on the relation of theology and philosophy, see *Karl Barth-Rudolf Bultmann Letters 1922/1966*, pp. 38–42. In face of Bultmann's charge that his philosophy was unexamined, outdated, and unsystematic, Barth curtly replied: "It might also be that what you want of me in relation to philosophy is not for me" (ibid., p. 38). He added: "It is also a fact that I have come to abhor profoundly the spectacle of theology constantly trying above all to adjust to the philosophy of its age, thereby neglecting its own theme" (ibid., p. 41). Barth makes similar points in correspondence with Brunner in 1925, as documented by Chalamet in *Dialectical Theologians*, pp. 215 and 253; see also Hart, *Karl Barth vs. Emil Brunner*, pp. 70–80. Barth could iterate that these differences between Bultmann and himself were rooted in differences in understanding the relationship between christology and anthropology (see *Karl Barth-Rudolf Bultmann Letters 1922/1966*, p. 84). He never changed from this conviction that theology had no need of a systematic or

look at Barth's actual writings on philosophy (and upon the philosophical problems of modernity) displays an ad hoc rather than systematic approach to the use of philosophy, noting both the inevitability of its use and the relativity of its usefulness, as well as insisting upon its provisional nature.[72] Here again a number of general observations can be made.

First, Barth rejected the premise that philosophy provides the questions which theology is obligated to answer or satisfy.[73] Theology does not rely upon the competence of philosophy to set forth the questions it must address or to determine what is the acceptable principle and standard of knowledge and action—and insofar as this concession to philosophy has occurred, it has been the (regrettable) hallmark of modern Protestant apologetics. The only criterion for knowledge in dogmatics is the content of dogmatics itself: the Word of God. Philosophy has no determinative function, for the Word is the content of knowledge precisely as it is the very ground of cognition itself ("Es ist Erkenntnis*gegenstand*, indem es Erkenntnis*grund* ist"). Theology pertains and is based only on the ground of "God's self-revelation and faith."[74] This does

---

modern philosophy even as it necessarily borrowed in an *ad hoc* manner from philosophy (of any age) for its articulation. See Barth, "Rudolf Bultmann—An Attempt to Understand Him," pp. 111-17. Oakes notes the overarching consistency of Barth's position throughout his life on this point despite a diversity of individual judgments (*Karl Barth on Theology and Philosophy*, pp. 244 and 245). His conclusion provides a succinct and judicious summation of Barth's understanding of this relation (pp. 245-50).

72. This is also evident in Barth's correspondence with Bultmann, confirming Berkhof's earlier judgment: "In *Romans* and now in the *Dogmatics* my path has in fact been that, with reference to the matters that I saw to be at issue in the Bible and the history of dogma, I have reached out on the right hand and the left for terms or concepts that I found to be the most appropriate without considering the problem of a preestablished harmony between the matter itself and these particular concepts, because my hands were already full in trying to *say* something very specific" (*Karl Barth-Rudolf Bultmann Letters 1922/1966*, p. 41). He acknowledged that to Bultmann this could only appear to be a "terrible dilettantism," but he remained undaunted: "My own concern is to hear at any rate the voice of the church and the Bible, and to let this voice be heard, even if in so doing, for want of anything better, I have to think somewhat in Aristotelian terms" (p. 42). That Barth would mention Aristotle (rather than Kant, or Hegel, or Heidegger, or any other modern thinker, for that matter) shows just how indifferent he was to address or resolve pressing modern philosophical concerns.

73. Barth, "Theologische und philosophische Ethik 1930," in *Vorträge und kleinere Arbeiten 1925-1930*, ed. Hermann Schmidt (Zürich: Theologischer Verlag Zürich, 1994), pp. 542-65 (552-3).

74. Barth, "Theologische und philosophische Ethik 1930," p. 553. Moreover, philosophy cannot be foundational for how Scripture should be read or understood, even if the presence of philosophical presuppositions when approaching Scripture is inescapable (CD I/2: pp. 727-36).

not entail, Barth insisted, that theology somehow stands over philosophy as a supra-human endeavor—but it is a different endeavor, with both theology and philosophy as human areas of investigation that stand under, rather than over, the Word of God.[75] Theology cannot be subordinated to, but also cannot be isolated from, philosophy, for both are areas of human examination (nor can they be simply combined into a complementary whole). Nevertheless, while there can be no absolute separation between theology and science or philosophy (diastasis), neither can there be a combination and equivocation of their methods and concerns (synthesis).[76]

Moreover, theology is free to borrow terms (like "noetic" or "ontic") from philosophy but has no obligation to use them in the way they were found to be of service to philosophy originally.[77] In essence, Barth upheld both the independence of theology and the unavoidability of its conscription of philosophical concepts.[78] His own use of terms borrowed from philosophy can only be described as makeshift and theologically pragmatic but philosophically imprecise. He had no intention of systematizing his philosophical conceptions or vocabulary and he had little interest in maintaining strict accuracy of terminology in relation to the philosophical schools that provide it. Moreover, he held that the concepts themselves, in the form in which theology is interested in them, predate their formalized philosophical use. So even when he used such terms as "realism" and "idealism" and "dogmatism" and "critical" in his dogmatics and writings of the period, and thus displayed a general borrowing from a Kantian (and Fichtean?) inheritance, he did not use such terms with the exact connotations or meaning as the philosophy of the time, nor did he have

---

75. Barth, "Theologische und philosophische Ethik 1930," p. 555.

76. Barth, "Theologische und philosophische Ethik 1930," pp. 552–3; pp. 553–6; pp. 556–9; also pp. 564–5. One again sees here Barth's rejection of Neo-Protestant and Catholic answers in dogmatics and the relationship of this rejection to matters of philosophy and ethics. In short, Barth frames the question of the relation of theology and philosophy along confessional lines.

77. Karl Barth, *Credo* (1935), (Eugene, OR: Wipf and Stock, 2005), p. 183; see pp. 183–6. Barth's summary of his principle of philosophical borrowing is succinctly given in a Pauline phrase and then elaborated: "All things are lawful for me, but nothing shall take me captive" (p. 183). Moreover, in attempting to speak the truth that has been heard in Scripture and in "making this witness my own, I am not free of all philosophy, but at the same time I am not bound to a definite philosophy" (p. 184). Such statements encapsulate Barth's own understanding of his differences from Bultmann and they perfectly summarize his position in their correspondence over the question of the relation of theology and philosophy. Such convictions only became more entrenched in time—see CD I/1: pp. 125 and 256; CD I/2: pp. 728–9; and Barth, *Evangelical Theology: An Introduction*, trans. Grover Foley (New York: Holt, Rinehart and Winston, 1963), pp. 90–2.

78. See Oakes, *Karl Barth on Theology and Philosophy*, pp. 159–60 and 161.

any particular interest in a systematic philosophical epistemology.⁷⁹ As Barth stated in 1929:

79. See Chalamet, *Dialectical Theologians*, p. 17. Chalamet asserts that "Barth had little interest for a 'critically realistic' epistemology" (p. 17). For a significant proposal for understanding Barth along such terms in the second *Romans* commentary but also beyond, see Bruce McCormack, *Karl Barth's Critically Realistic Dialectical Theology*, pp. 66-8; p. 159; pp. 207-9; pp. 225-6; p. 235; p. 328; pp. 354-67; p. 359; pp. 464-5. McCormack recognizes that Barth's philosophical standpoint evident in the second *Romans* commentary was largely unconscious and subordinate to theological concerns: "At no point during this phase did he give himself over to the task of sustained and rigorous *philosophical* reflection upon problems of epistemology. The shift which occurred in his philosophical *point of view*—it was never more than that—was the consequence of his concentration on the *theological* problem of the knowledge of God" (207). This is certainly true, and the only adjustment is to eliminate the opening phrase, "At no point during this phase," for Barth never dedicated himself to a "sustained and rigorous" examination of philosophical epistemology for its own sake, with the exception of his student days in reading Kant and Cohen. Nor did its questions much interest him. In this respect as well, attempts to describe Barth's theology in terms of idealism raise a number of problems, evident in the disagreements between those who interpret Barth on this score, and including the multiplication of definitions and lack of precision in the application of "idealism" to Barth's own thought. For a discussion of the complexity involved, see David Congdon, *The Mission of Demythologizing: Rudolf Bultmann's Dialectical Theology*, pp. 40-6. In truth, to use "idealism" without careful definition tells us nothing concrete about Barth's thought—idealism can be used to do at least the following: (a) designate the active function of mind in constructing knowledge, along with specifying the Kantian and/or Neo-Kantian elements of Barth's thought; (b) designate the centrality of personal versus propositional revelation and the focus upon divine subjectivity in Barth; (c) designate the precedence of law before gospel, rather than gospel before law, among Barth's contemporaries; (d) refer to Hegel's influence and import for Barth's thought; and (e) refer to post-Kantian theological positions such as those of Alois Biedermann in relation to Barth. On top of this, Congdon argues that there is an equivocation in McCormack's use of the term "critical" before "critical idealism" and "critical realism" and notes that Chalamet uses "critical idealism" and "idealism" simply interchangeably (see Congdon's discussion of Chalamet and McCormack, *The Mission of Demythologizing*, pp. 40-6). In spite of modifiers before "idealism" such as critical, speculative, dogmatic, Kantian, or Fichtean, such things remain elusive, evident in the fact that not only are such things difficult to pin down in relation to Barth's development, but also in regard to others such as Bultmann (see ibid., p. 45).

My concern here is in no way to sort out these matters (and, with regard to a precise historical genealogy of philosophical sources for Barth, I have long had my doubts that they can be sorted, doubts only reinforced by Webster's concerns in the first note above), but simply to propose the question of whether what Barth was about is best grasped by giving substantial weight to terms ("realism"; "idealism") which he used so idiosyncratically and casually rather than with any perceptible dedication to precision endemic to a specific philosophical school or tradition. For one attempt to transcend such questions by paying closer heed to Barth's biblical and theological reflections rather than such philosophical terminology, see Westerholm, *The Ordering of the Christian Mind*, pp. 34-59; esp. p. 37 and pp. 42-3.

The kinship between idealist and mystical thinking suggests that idealist theology does not necessarily originate from or point back to a philosophical system. Just as we avoided dismissing theological realism as a disguised philosophy, so we will now have to do the same justice to theological idealism. It is possible to be a theological realist or idealist without being tainted by the corresponding philosophy.[80]

Terms such as "realism" and "idealism" were baptized and taken up by Barth for theological purposes to argue against on the one hand a domestication of God in an identification of God with a general ontology of nature (realism) and on the other hand a projection of God as an element of thought produced by reason (idealism). They could indeed designate the general distinction between that which is known and the knowing subject and could also take up elements and questions of philosophical realism and idealism. But in their simplest forms, they served theological arguments against "demonology" (akin to idolatry) and "ideology" (akin to atheism), respectively. Both terms had for him no strictly defined philosophical content on their own, even if they did have some formal and even material similarities and overlapping uses with their philosophical backdrop.[81] This is not to say that theology and philosophy do not bump up against each other as each seeks to determine "truth" and "reality."[82] But theology is set apart

---

80. Barth, "Fate and Idea in Theology," p. 44. Barth's use of idealism here is idiosyncratic and serves simply to designate a critical element in theology, not as the representation of a defined concept belonging to a specific philosophical figure or school (p. 48). Moreover, it is difficult to make much headway in determining precisely what kind of idealism lies behind Barth's theology when he includes Plato, Augustine, Zwingli, and Calvin under its banner (pp. 43 and 48). As early as 1923 could speak of the "speculative idealism" of the Lutheran orthodox in comparison to the Reformed who wished to remain "critical idealists" in contrast to this (see Barth, *Theology of the Reformed Confessions*, p. 184). All of this holds true as well for his comments regarding "dogmatism," "self-criticism," and "dialectic" in "The Word of God as the Task of Theology 1922" in WGT, pp. 171-98; see esp. pp. 186-91. That Luther is mentioned as a practitioner of each of these types simply adds to the complexity. As already noted, any attempt to discern a clean and precise set of philosophical convictions behind Barth's theology and to designate these as strictly belonging to a specific school of idealism of any sort, Kantian or otherwise, is a Herculean errand and perhaps an impossible one. He simply did not care for nor intend such philosophical precision (whether for good or ill). Indeed, he seemed to oppose the human "will to system" (*Wille zum System*) categorically. See KD I/2: p. 971; ET: CD pp. 868-9; cf. Macken, *The Autonomy Theme in the* Church Dogmatics, pp. 35-6.

81. For an account of Barth's theological position along such lines, see Ingolf U. Dalferth, "Karl Barth's Eschatological Realism" in *Karl Barth: Centenary Essays*, ed. S. W. Sykes (Cambridge: Cambridge University Press), pp. 14-45 (see esp. p. 24); see also T. F. Torrance, "Introduction" in TC, pp. 7-54, esp. 36.

82. Barth, "Fate and Idea in Theology," pp. 51-2; cf. also Karl Barth, "Philosophy and Theology," (1960) in *The Way of Theology in Karl Barth*, pp. 79-95. Barth can in the latter speak of an "analogy of endeavors" between philosophy and theology and an "analogical equivalence of the words and concepts used on both sides" ("Philosophy and Theology," pp. 82 and 84).

from philosophy not, Barth insisted, by a separation from questions of "reality" or "truth" but the means and order of movement by which such are pursued, which for theology is "the primordial movement from above to below. The theologian stands and falls with this sequence, in fact, with its irreversibility."[83] Barth was in turn much more interested in Paul and Luther than any philosopher, and he did not think philosophy had much of substance to add to the theological task. At most, philosophy provides certain conceptual tools and resources that theology can borrow as it plunders the Egyptians to make its own temple furnishings.[84] He could even be quite dismissive of his own prior dependence upon specific philosophical systems and concepts, including his Platonic and Kantian ones. In 1935, when questioned as to his understanding of the relationship of theology and philosophy, he exhibited this dismissiveness with a remarkably frank and negative judgment upon his own borrowings during the period of the *Romans* commentary, noting that while some complained that he had abandoned the distinctive terminology of that period,

> On the contrary, you should be thankful that I no longer burden you with "void" (*Hohlraum*) and "death-line" (*Todeslinie*)! That served its day. To-day it would be confusing and wearisome if I were to continue with it. I profoundly hope that in five or ten years I shall be able to speak yet another language than I do to-day, and that then also I shall be *compelled* to speak it. I should therefore advise you to cease this lamentation. At that time my whole desire was really to elucidate Paul's Epistle to the Romans. That was done partly by means of a strange incrustation of Kantian-Platonic conceptions. I was *at liberty* then to use these conceptions, but if I were to be told to-day that I *had* to use them, I should say with decision, No. Further, it is forced down my throat that the Dogmatic theologian is under the obligation to "justify" himself in his utterances before philosophy. To that my answer is likewise, No. Dogmatics has to justify itself only before God in Jesus Christ; concretely, before Holy Scripture within the Church. Certainly it has also the responsibility of speaking so that it can be *understood*, but there is not the slightest chance that any philosophy could here step forth as norm. It is a misunderstanding to think that in the "Epistle to the Romans" I directed myself consciously in criticism against the thought of modern man. As a modern man

---

83. Barth, "Philosophy and Theology," pp. 84-5; cf. p. 87. To say that this order comes from above to below, from the Creator to the creature, is to recognize that theology is restricted to christology and not a general pursuit of truth: "For the path of Jesus Christ clearly leads from above to below and from there back towards the above, from the condescension of the Creator to the elevation of the creation and not the reverse" (ibid., p. 90; see pp. 88-90).

84. By 1960, Barth could propose that philosophy should conduct but two modest tasks: "to give therefore at best an analysis of its completed history and beyond that perhaps the drawing up of a formalized logic" ("Philosophy and Theology," p. 92). He recognized that this is an "impudent and intolerable demand" to make from a theologian to a philosopher (p. 92).

I attempted to submit myself to the word of Paul.—It cannot be otherwise than that Dogmatics runs counter to every philosophy no matter what form it may have assumed. In point of fact theology must oppose every kind of Realism and Idealism .... The question of the "proper" language of theology is *ultimately* to be answered only with prayer and the life of faith.[85]

This answer is, to put it mildly, not that of someone who is overly concerned with answering a philosophical problem or bowing before modern philosophical strictures or epistemological limitations.

Barth's stance toward the philosophy of his age never fundamentally changed from when this answer was given (and, as we have seen, it was already prefigured in the GD), but only became more radical in its implications. Reflecting upon his earlier theology in a letter to Bultmann in 1952, he re-expressed his philosophical indifference as well as recounted the historiography of his break with liberalism. Evident in his letter is not only his complicated relationship to philosophy, one that illustrates not only his move beyond the philosophical straightjackets of modernity, but also his position which rejected any real philosophical foundationalism altogether, such that his strongly non-ideological conviction is evident:

Look, after being a Kantian up to my ears in my young days, after having been tempted no less fully by Schleiermacher's romanticism, after being given later (when studying nineteenth-century theology) an unforgettable impression ... of the radiant certainty with which it was once thought that the first and last word about each and all "understanding" had been heard in Hegel—I am not an enemy of philosophy as such, but I have hopeless reservations about the claim to absoluteness of any philosophy, epistemology, or methodology. Occasionally I may cheerfully make use of existential categories—not without going back again sometimes to father Plato and others—but I simply do not summon up the ethical zeal to feel any consequent obligation to that philosophical approach. What do you want? Obviously I am no longer "existentially" (*existentiell*) captivated by it—as I was only too often earlier, but am now finally frightened off—just as I can no longer join any political party—I was once a Social Democrat.[86]

---

85. Barth, *Credo*, pp. 185–6. Already in 1919 Barth stated in his address "The Christian in Society" that "it would be wiser to speak quietly with the Bible than to speak loudly or even to shout about classical antiquity and German idealism" (WGT, pp. 31–69 [59]). This itself should mitigate any strong conceptions of his use of philosophy in either edition of the Romans commentary.

86. *Karl Barth-Rudolf Bultmann Letters 1922/1966*, pp. 105–6. That Barth, having thus embraced what can with justification be designated as particularism, pluralism, and fallibilism (as well as the conviction that the most significant categories of the mind were those socially constructed rather than innate such that no system of human thought could be basic and final) was thus moving in what might be broadly called a "postmodern" or "late modern" direction is evident already by the early 1930s. This did not entail that Barth

The extent of Barth's anti-ideological commitment is thus total. His position was that Christians could not embrace a single philosophical (or economic, or political) system without reservation for numerous reasons: (1) such would betray the eschatological nature of truth and deny the broken and provisional nature of the current world in its fallen state reflected in the individual; (2) it would allow a triumphalism of such a system to compel ideological enforcement and confuse the witness of the church with an alternative cultural, social, or political agenda; and (3) it would seek to achieve what even theology could not accomplish, which is to find a final, comprehensive, and static presentation of truth (e.g., worldview) that had no further need of revision.[87] In truth, Barth's commitment to Kantianism

---

replaced an absolute objectivism with relativism or gave up on the notion of discerning truth in human pursuits of knowledge. But it did provide him with a sense of epistemic humility regarding human intellectual achievements and an appreciation for both a delimited perspectivism and the provisionality of all human systems of thought, all accompanied by a strong opposition to ideology of any kind. For a discussion of this, see Bender, *Confessing Christ for Church and World*, pp. 315-51; cf. also CD I/2: pp. 733-4. This broad point is presented with the same connotation when Oakes concludes that "Barth tended to be more comfortable with philosophy as local knowledge or historical pursuit than he was with philosophy as a global venture" (*Karl Barth on Theology and Philosophy*, p. 160). Even here, however, Barth's concerns always remained theological, and it was theological convictions that shaped how he both embraced and rejected what might be termed modern positions and prefigured postmodern ones. So the provisionality of human systems was not simply based upon human finitude, but (and this should not be missed) the freedom of God to take up different systems of thought at different times in the service of his Word (see CD I/2: pp. 733-4). This is one reason why Barth's thought cannot be easily captured by the terminology, questions, or positions of a specific period, modern or otherwise. It also explains his lightly held commitments to philosophical schools and concepts, evident in a late conversation of 1968: "The respective philosophizings of a time are like my jacket—for when it gets hot, I take it off, right? And it *became* hot for me with Kant and Schleiermacher, and then I simply took it off. And you must [have] this freedom too, this is the 'glorious freedom of the children of God' [Rom. 8:21]." See Barth, *Barth in Conversation: Volume 3, 1964-1968*, p. 339; cf. Bender, *Confessing Christ for Church and World*, pp. 378-84, esp. p. 383 nt 53.

87. In this respect, Barth does share convictions with Schleiermacher. As Zachhuber writes, Schleiermacher was "deeply skeptical about the ability of the human mind to construct a system of thought capable of explaining reality in its fullness—hence his opposition to Hegel and Fichte" (*Theology as Science in Nineteenth-Century Germany*, p. 14). This was true of Barth as well, for he also refused all such philosophical ambitions. What in the end separated Barth from both Baur and Ritschl (as well as from both the older Ritschlians and the younger history of religions school) was, in the words of Zachhuber, his "abandonment of any attempt to integrate the specific truth claims of Christian theology into a general philosophical and historical framework" (ibid., p. 292).

was held no more tightly than his commitment to democratic socialism[88]—they could be provisional epistemological and economic systems, respectively, and they also might be judged superior to other alternatives (nothing said thus far should be taken to imply that Barth had no admiration or even proclivity for Kant's philosophy in the realm of its own jurisdiction, or that he gave up on the question of truth and the possibility of relative yet firm judgments). They might even be parabolic of the Kingdom of God and its truth. But they could not hold one's final or absolute allegiance. Such was at the heart of Barth's rejections of all meta-philosophies, worldviews, and ideologies, as well as his rejection of the *analogia entis*.[89]

Barth rejected meeting the challenges posed by philosophy (whether idealism in general, or that of Kant specifically) on its own ground, though, as seen above, this should not be taken to mean that he did not engage philosophical positions or think that they could be walled off through a kind of appeal to a separation of intellectual powers.[90] He had no pressing concern to address the post-Kantian problems of knowledge in any direct way, and certainly nothing akin to Schleiermacher's intentional acceptance of Kant's framework and dedication to both conform to and overcome it in the *Speeches*. What differentiates Barth not only from Schleiermacher but also Bultmann and Herrmann was his refusal to embrace Kant's limitations of

---

88. Even in the period of his socialist activity, Barth stated that the real task of the day was not to become socialists but new and right Christians. See Karl Barth, "Die Zunkunft des Christentums und der Sozialismus (1917)" in *Vorträge und kleinere Arbeiten 1914–1921*, ed. Hans-Anton Drewes (Zürich: Theologischer Verlag Zürich, 2012), pp. 390–407 (407); see also Karl Barth, *Final Testimonies*, ed. Eberhard Busch, trans. Geoffrey W. Bromiley (Grand Rapids: Eerdmans, 1977), pp. 37–9. To think that the "secret key" to understanding Barth can be found in a single non-theological conceptual scheme (whether absolutism, socialism, idealism, Kantianism, or, heaven forbid, totalitarianism) is a reflection in microcosm of a misplaced ambition of modernity to provide a universal Theory of Everything (see note 1, above), or a penchant in some forms of postmodernity to think that complexity can be reduced to simplicity by reading all of reality through a single grid of experience or power. Neither were ambitions Barth shared. Again, what so many such readings of Barth have in common is a refusal to take his self-description as a theologian of Scripture and the Reformation and his complexity as a person with real seriousness. See Holtmann, *Karl Barth als Theologe der Neuzeit*, p. 416; cf. p. 405; and, again, Jüngel, who sees such readings as at best abstractions of Barth's true concerns (*Karl Barth: A Theological Legacy*, p. 14). At worst, they engender distorted and narrow readings of Barth's work that even in their valid insights display a loss of proportion to the greater whole.

89. S. W. Sykes states: "What Barth feared in the *analogia entis* was a conceptual scheme, founded on the notion of being, which would link God and humanity in a single philosophical structure." See Sykes, "Introduction," in *The Way of Theology in Karl Barth*, ed. H. Martin Ruscheidt (Eugene, OR: Pickwick, 1986), pp. 1–24 (10). In truth, Barth feared more than this, but he did not fear less.

90. Oakes is particularly perceptive here when he asserts that such appeals to a complete separation of theology and philosophy could only in the end ignore "Barth's own warnings as to the wisdom of these apologetic settlements for a non-apologetic theology" (*Karl Barth on Theology and Philosophy*, p. 253).

religion to preclude theological knowledge and relegate it to the sphere of ethics or religious experience. This did not lead Barth to a positivism of revelation and infallible dogma, much less to a return to a simple orthodoxy or scholasticism of the past—he did have a critical element to his theology, albeit not one that was strictly Kantian in nature.[91] But it did lead him to insist that God joins himself to creaturely realities of historical particularity (such as the flesh of Christ, the words of Scripture, or the proclamation of the church) without being, as God, identified with or subsumed into such created realities. Thus God's event of revelation in this movement into history provides a true knowledge of God that can be expressed in doctrine. Such a view of course prefigures Barth's description of the three-fold form of the Word of God in the CD, though this view was firmly in place by 1924.[92]

Finally, in addressing the question of philosophy, Barth refused to prioritize reason to the exclusion of other human "capacities" as much of modernity had done. Certainly he acknowledged that revelation is a rational rather than irrational event.[93] Nevertheless, it was not only a rational event. However revelation encountered the human person, it did not simply overcome epistemological limitations as these might be construed over time and in any age but rather overcame unbelief and sin, and these were not limited to the cognitive aspects of human existence. For this reason, revelation does not address reason alone but grasps and addresses the human person in every aspect of his or her being: intellect and reason, but also will, conscience, and feeling, and anything else that might make up the person, such as the subconscious or intuition. In this refusal to wall these off from one another and turn revelation into a purely epistemological concern (as it was and is so often portrayed), or to locate religion in a delimited aspect of the human person (such as reason, conscience, or feeling), he was also swimming against a strong current of the modern age, as well as rejecting a timeless foundational anthropology of any kind.[94] Just as Christ in the incarnation

---

91. Barth could express his appreciation for the Protestant orthodox schools of the past, but he distanced himself from the rigidities of their thought, their certain metaphysical commitments, and their preoccupation with propping up arguments for revelation based on qualities of the creaturely medium of its manifestation—i.e., arguments for the verbal inerrancy of Scripture.

92. Barth, "Menschenwort und Gotteswort in der christlichen Predigt 1924," p. 441; cf. "Das Schriftprinzip der reformierten Kirche 1925" in *Vorträge und kleinere Arbeiten 1922–1925*, ed. Holger Finze (Zürich: Theologischer Verlag Zürich, 1990), pp. 500–44 (520).

93. CD I/1: p. 135.

94. "From different angles the determination of human existence by God's Word can be understood just as much as a determination of feeling, will, or intellect, and psychologically it may actually be more the one than the other in a given case. The decisive point materially, however, is that it is a determination of the whole self-determining man." See CD I/1: p. 204; cf. pp. 202–4. For a discussion of this passage along these lines, see Kimlyn Bender, *Reading Karl Barth for the Church: A Guide and Companion* (Grand Rapids: Eerdmans, 2019), pp. 86–8. That Barth refused to wall off these areas of human reality is mirrored in his refusal to separate ethics from dogmatics and in his incorporation of the former into the latter in the CD. See CD I/1: pp. 368 and 371.

has assumed whatever comprises the human person and has thereby healed all, so also revelation addresses whatever elements might comprise the human person and thus brings them into the realm of justification and sanctification. In this way, Barth was as patristic in his convictions as he was modern. In fact, he was pushing against modern elevations of reason (the Enlightenment) or feeling (Romanticism) as well as all such modern divisions of human life and the human person.

*Theology and the Modern Period*

Lastly, and most importantly for our purposes of historiography, not only was Barth generally uninterested in a definitive (modern) epistemology or philosophy, but he also did not think that modernity presented singular problems that were not present from the very beginning of the church. His rejection of Brunner's eristics, which Brunner believed necessary because he insisted that modernity's new and distinctive cultural and philosophical challenges had changed the game for theology, is clear on this point. He frankly refused to recognize any extraordinary character of the modern period. Certainly he was aware of and engaged its distinct questions and issues, as we have seen. Yet as he stated, "there is no theological foundation for the assumed difference between our own and earlier times."[95] He was focused upon a much longer timeline than many of his contemporaries like Brunner, and it was one that stretched back to the very beginning of the New Testament. The fundamental issue was not that of the knowledge of God threatened by newly discovered modern strictures upon human understanding, or the attendant rise of modern science or secularism or atheism and the need for the translation of the gospel into a new (existential) idiom, but the perennial problem of unbelief in view of the revelation of God, and an unbelief that should not be taken more seriously by the church than revelation itself.[96]

95. CD I/1: p. 28. "Has there ever been an age in which theology has not basically confronted a radical negation of the revelation believed in the Church?" (ibid., p. 28; cf. Barth, *The Knowledge of God and the Service of God According to the Teaching of the Reformation: Recalling the Scottish Confession of 1560*, trans. J. L. M. Haire and Ian Henderson [Eugene, OR: Wipf and Stock, 2005], p. 17). Berkhof, surveying the field of two hundred years' of theology, reaches the same conclusion, asserting that "the fundamental problematics of post-Enlightenment theology are, on closer scrutiny, essentially identical with the problematics in the Old and New Testaments and in earlier epochs of church history" (Berkhof, *Two Hundred Years of Theology*, p. 311). Correspondingly, Barth commented in a conversation late in his life: "I say 'modern man' in quotes, because I believe that the human has always remained the same." See Karl Barth, *Barth in Conversation: Volume 1, 1959–1962*, p. 137. He saw a fixation on defining such a modern person in Bultmann, Ernst Fuchs, and Gerhard Ebeling: "As if they knew who the modern person was!" (ibid., p. 273). In his estimation, they were, with their emphasis on subjectivity and soteriology without a doctrine of God, a throw-back to the nineteenth century (see ibid., p. 276).

96. CD I/1: pp. 28–30; see also Bender, *Confessing Christ for Church and World*, pp. 271–84, esp. 275–6.

In turn, Barth did not think that the most important problems of theology are those presented by modern philosophy or culture but those that arise from within the church itself.[97] It was not the challenges posed by the world, but the crises posed by a failure of the church to reach consensus on its internal confession, that were most important. Hence Barth's focus was not upon atheism or secularism (of which he could be quite dismissive), or upon philosophical or cultural developments and arguments, but upon heresy, which marked the prolegomena of the CD.[98] Theological prolegomena is not made necessary first because of the arguments posed by modernity which must be set forth and addressed before the dogmatic task can "get down to business"; it is necessary because of the Reformation and the division of the church that resulted from it.[99] This is why Barth oriented his entire prolegomena in the CD around defining the Evangelical Church (i.e., Reformational Protestant, specifically that constituted by the Lutheran and Reformed Churches stemming from the Reformation) in contrast to the Roman Catholic Church that required and requires reform but resisted and continues to resist it, and the tradition of Protestant modernism that betrayed the Reformation though it grew out of it. Such polemical exercises may be perceived as ill-advised or even off-putting today.[100] But to think that they are peripheral to Barth's project, thinking that it is really one founded upon answering modern challenges to the knowledge of God, betrays a misunderstanding of his prolegomena in the CD. It was the ecclesial

97. CD 1/1: p. 124; cf. Barth, *Theology of the Reformed Confessions*, p. 151. As Oakes states: "Barth seldom charges the pursuits of philosophy, history, anthropology, or higher criticism with the woes and distortions he sees in Christian theology" (*Karl Barth on Theology and Philosophy*, 165). Macken echoes this thought: "Barth found fault not with the evil world, but with the failure of the Church and of the theologians themselves" (*The Autonomy Theme in the* Church Dogmatics, 115; cf. 50).

98. "Faith does not stand only, or even in the first and most important sense, in conflict with unbelief. It stands in conflict with itself, i.e., with a form or forms of faith in which it recognizes itself in respect of form but not of content, in which it so seriously fails to do so in the latter respect that, although in them it must genuinely recognize faith, and even Christian faith, so far as form is concerned it can only understand this faith as another faith so far as concerns content.... The paradoxical fact to which we refer is that of heresy" (CD I/1: pp. 31–2).

99. CD I/1: pp. 34–5. The Reformation was "the first time that the Church learned what is meant by divergent faith. That is why there have had to be all types of dogmatic prolegomena from that day forward" (p. 35). Barth's only nod in the prolegomena to the CD to the specific problems of modernity that require special attention is briefly given: "We are now forbidden to take up the main content of dogmatics without express and explicit discussion of the problem of the way of knowledge" (CD I/1: p. 26). But he then turns not to discuss the modern challenges of Descartes, Locke, Lessing, or Kant, but those within the Evangelical tradition (i.e., the Protestant tradition of the Lutheran and Reformed faith), and its relation to the Roman Catholic and Protestant liberal traditions. It is also not incidental and peripheral but essential to his purposes there that the first volume of the CD is not consumed with Kant but with Luther (as we will see below).

100. Westerholm notes the limitations of Barth's doctrine of revelation in the first volume of the CD, asserting that Barth's doctrine of the Word of God is both "polemically and architectonically over-determined" (*The Ordering of the Christian Mind*, p. 29).

issues that framed the epistemological discussions in his mature prolegomena, even as the very existence of the church itself presupposed God's revelation.

Barth's theology thus became focused upon a timeline dominated by the NT and the Reformation and the aftermath of each. There were numerous theologians like Brunner who were consumed by the concerns of modernity in general and taking up the challenges Kant posed in particular. Herrmann was one of these, such as when he rested the Christian's consciousness of communion with God on "*two objective facts, the first of which is the historical fact of the Person of Jesus*," and the "*second objective ground . . . is that we hear within ourselves the demand of the moral law*."[101] Herrmann's commitment to grounding religion upon this second pillar and not only the first was one Barth rejected, as he did any attempt to ground religion in practical reason or to subsume it into morality.[102] He was not Kantian in this sense, nor was he especially modern if such immanentism, which was evident everywhere in the nineteenth and early twentieth centuries, is taken as a hallmark of modernity. This is not of course to deny that he was a person of his time and attuned to its issues. But his own interests and questions were remarkably wide-ranging across not only theological traditions but the church's past, as were the resources from which he drew for his theological project. In essence, it was the entire history of the church, rather than simply the age in which he lived, that dictated the terms of his theological engagement.[103]

---

101. Herrmann, *The Communion of the Christian with God*, pp. 102–3. Herrmann concluded: "There are no other objective grounds for the truth of the Christian religion" (ibid., p. 103; cf. pp. 108–9). It is unclear that Chalamet fully takes into account the weight of this second pillar, and thus Herrmann's immanentism. He writes: "Where does God reveal himself? Herrmann's answer is clear: in the power of Jesus Christ's inner life, in Jesus Christ who encounters us in our experience" (Chalamet, *Dialectical Theologians*, p. 55; cf. p. 107; also Oakes, *Karl Barth on Theology and Philosophy*, p. 57). In contrast, Herrmann speaks not only of this inner life of Christ but also of the universal "assumption that men know they are unconditionally bound to obey the law of duty" (Herrmann, *The Communion of the Christian with God*, p. 103). Herrmann's theology, at least here, displays a programmatic Kantian synthesis in its reference to a universal "law of duty" and of the individual's inner "sphere of conscience" (ibid., pp. 103 and 109). In light of this passage in Herrmann, the answer to the locus of revelation may be a bit more complicated, and this too bears upon the differences of Barth from his teacher, for Barth would abandon all appeals to a divine revelation in conscience or any element of the inner person.

102. This should not be taken to mean, however, that Herrmann wanted to reduce religion to ethics—far from it. Herrmann wanted to protect religion and faith from any form of moral or psychological reductionism. See Simon Fisher, *Revelatory Positivism?*, p. 143. The same was true of his rejection of historicism and positivism. Religion had its own integrity and irreducibility (*Selbständigkeit*) (see ibid., p. 143).

103. Referring to the early Barth prior to the Romans commentary, Simon Fisher states that "despite his readings of Kant, Cohen, and Natorp, Barth had no intention whatsoever of becoming a philosopher. He did, however, want to be a theologian and, indeed, a theologian who subscribed to the goals and methods of modern theology" (Fisher, *Revelatory Positivism?*, p. 185). Certainly the first part always was and remained true for Barth. He certainly saw himself as taken with theological, rather than philosophical, concerns throughout his life. But that he was bound to subscribe to the "goals and methods of modern theology" was something that, though broadly true, had an increasingly weakened hold upon him as his career progressed.

The conclusion that one can draw from all of these various observations over this long traversal is that Barth had no interest to belong to a philosophical school or in following one, had no proclivity to allow philosophy or culture to dictate theology's theme or questions, and therefore had no overriding preoccupation to construe revelation as an overcoming of a Kantian or any other epistemological problem, even if this was also not in principle excluded from his project. Barth, while unquestionably a modern person, and not unattuned to its challenges and drawing eclectically upon its resources, had no ultimate concern with being a modern theologian if this had any meaning beyond working with a sensitivity and awareness of the general challenges of historical consciousness and science in the modern period and responding to them with discretion and on theology's own terms, with an acknowledgment that any theology must speak to its age and its questions and not attempt a simple return to the past.[104]

Barth was therefore much more circumspect about the convictions of modernity and had an ambivalent and complex relation to it even as he could readily find elements to appreciate. But he did not fit neatly among the range of its central tenets. For instance, if "anti-supernaturalism," aka, a rejection of discrete divine miraculous acts, is a prerequisite of being modern (and of being "scientific," if D. F. Strauss was to be believed—and his influence was significant), then this makes little sense of one who held the virgin birth and the empty tomb as abiding signs and realities central to the church's witness, and held them against their ready dismissal even by his theological teachers like Harnack and his compatriots

---

104. One could perhaps add that Barth was anti-metaphysical (in the sense of anti-speculative, not in the sense of refusing to make metaphysical, i.e., ontological, claims about the Trinity or the incarnation), though he grounded even this concern in Luther and Calvin as much or more than Kant. One of the difficulties, which simply cannot be explored here in detail, is that to say that Barth is "anti-metaphysical" can mean so many different things—for instance, "anti-metaphysical" can mean at least the following: (1) anti-speculative (pertaining to a way of knowledge and the exclusivity of God's revelation in the Word); (2) a principled rejection of a foundational philosophical ontology that undergirds theology's claims, whether ancient or modern (e.g., Aristotelianism or existentialism); (3) a fundamental rejection of natural theology, including the value and/or validity of classical arguments for God's existence as proofs; (4) a specific rejection of a substantialist (ancient, Greek) metaphysics (often discussed in reference to Barth's actualism relating to his doctrine of God and his late christology); and (5) anti-ontological (a refusal to make any claims about ultimate reality). Barth did reject the first three, gives evidence, but also gives counter-evidence, of the fourth (counter-evidence including but not exhausted by his prior reference to Aristotle above and his enduring ability to speak of divine and human "essence" and "natures" even late—e.g., CD IV/2: 113); and certainly did not hold the fifth, for he could speak extensively of both Trinity and incarnation and certainly believed that the church could have and indeed did have true knowledge of God.

in other matters like Bultmann.[105] In this respect as well, Bultmann proved to be the more modern of the two.[106] Bultmann's objections to the miraculous were not only predicated upon a theological argument against objectification and a loss of divine hiddenness,[107] such that a miracle would sacrifice the latter and thus lose

---

105. For Barth on these signs (where he explicitly criticizes Brunner for his rejection of the virgin birth), see CD I/2: pp. 172-202; see also CD III/2: pp. 442-7; CD IV/2: pp. 142-3; cf. Bultmann, *Jesus Christ and Mythology*, pp. 16-17. Here, too, Herrmann was more constrained by the acceptance of modernity's constrictions, constrictions resulting from the law of natural cause and effect within a closed universe, constrictions also strongly upheld earlier by Schleiermacher. Sockness succinctly concludes on this point: "Herrmann wants to find a place for Luther's God in Kant's universe" (*Against False Apologetics*, p. 44). Fisher adds: "Although Herrmann never tired of proclaiming that God acts in the event of self-revelation, he could not ascribe any meaning whatsoever to the notion of God's acting in or upon the natural world," and God's activity is restricted to the "transcendental sphere of history" (*Revelatory Positivism?*, pp. 162-3). In truth, almost every modern theologian of the broadly liberal tradition was trying to find a place for God not only in Kant's universe but in Newton's, and such made miracles particularly problematic. This makes Barth's affirmation of the virgin birth all the more striking.

106. It is interesting that when asked for a brief description of Bultmann's work to be placed upon a public street sign named after him, three of his New Testament successors at Marburg (who presumably were well-acquainted with him and his work) came up with the following to encapsulate his theology: "Prof. D. Bultmann D. D. (1884-1976) sought to make the Christian message accountable to the modern consciousness of truth" (quoted in Hammann, *Rudolf Bultmann*, p. 533). This summation itself led to controversy (p. 533). Whatever the similarities of Barth and Bultmann, one would be hard pressed to find a line more suitable to encapsulate their differences.

107. Chalamet, *Dialectical Theologians*, pp. 269-70. His evaluation on this score is blunt: Like Herrmann, Bultmann "rejects the objective character of revelation" (p. 278). What might be said charitably is that Bultmann's consistent resistance to any identification of revelation with acts in history commendably was intended to resist the subsumption of God into creaturely realities. But what must also be said is that the radical nature of this separation entailed that Bultmann excluded God's action entirely out of the realm of public history, evident in his complete indifference to the details of Christ's life and ministry, and thus indifference to revelation as something that is tied to a narrated life, or to the details of that life of the years AD 1-30 as presented in the Gospels. The end result is that charges of the privatization of religion and subjectivism followed Bultmann to the end of his life, and, despite his resistance, his followers on the left called for a consistent and thus full demythologization of the kerygma itself such that it be shorn from the last remnant of historicity, the "thatness" ("das Daß") of Jesus, whether a historical figure or central conceptual element of authentic existence. To his credit, Bultmann refused to let go of this very thin strand of the scandal of particularity and christology. Barth of course held on to a much firmer and richer (christological and canonical) rope. In truth, his arguments with Bultmann over objectification and christology, as well as his fully mature positions on christology as thought of not only in terms of nature but of history, are already prefigured

the principle of *sola fide* and replace it by sight alone, but these objections were also rooted in a commitment to the scientific world-picture of modernity and its antisupernaturalism.[108] By way of contrast, Barth held to the legitimacy and importance of the virgin birth and the bodily resurrection of Christ as proper Christian doctrines, things Bultmann rejected for both of the reasons above.[109]

Other important recoveries of the past highlighted Barth's rejection of dominant forms of modern theological orthodoxies. He rediscovered patristic (Nicene and Chalcedonian) christology with appreciation and could hold and defend it against its dismissal by Schleiermacher and Tillich, and even in his mature christology its formal and regulative function as "guiding lines" were not simply sacrificed in the creativity of his thought.[110] He embraced a way of reading Scripture that

and present *in nuce* in his debate with Tillich in 1923: "For 'us' Christ is *the* salvation history, the salvation history *itself*." See Robinson, *The Beginnings of Dialectical Theology*, pp. 150-2 (150). With regard to Bultmann, this realization of the central issue of difference came to Barth in full force seemingly only in 1952 (see *Karl Barth-Rudolf Bultmann Letters 1922/1966*, pp. 106-8; also Chalamet, *Dialectical Theologians*, p. 278).

108. See Congdon, *The Mission of Demythologizing*, pp. 661-70. Bultmann was in favor of "finding a new formulation of the idea of God, because the theistic picture of God had become untenable in the modern world" (Hammann, *Rudolf Bultmann*, p. 470). This was of course intrinsic to Schleiermacher's program as well, for as much as he insisted that theology was predicated solely on theological and not metaphysical concerns, such concerns had no small part to play in shaping his view of what was and was not tenable to be held with regard to God's discrete action in the world with regard to the incarnation and the resurrection. See Bender, *Confessing Christ for Church and World*, pp. 253-84.

109. To read Barth on the narratives of the Gospels, including his accounts of the virgin birth and the empty tomb, and to read Bultmann's *Jesus Christ and Mythology*, is to read two minds that do not appear to be tracking the same or even reading the same book. The Bible for Barth is a witness (the authoritative witness as canon) to Jesus' person and rule calling forth faith and obedience not in spite of but through the narration of Christ's history. For Bultmann it is a source and compendium of myth awaiting clarification and interpretation characterized by little interest in this narration itself and read against its history. At the heart of Barth's disagreements with Bultmann on Scripture is that he felt that Bultmann treated the NT as a "historical source rather than as witness," as he expressed this in 1928 in a letter to Paul Althaus. Quoted in McCormack, *Karl Barth's Critically Realistic Dialectical Theology*, p. 394.

110. *The Beginnings of Dialectical Theology*, pp. 142-54 (151); CD IV/1: p. 127. From the GD onward, Barth completely broke with his earlier indifference to traditional christology (not to mention much of modernity's antithesis to it). For such early indifference, consider his statement during his time in Geneva as a young pastor when, commenting on the Chalcedonian definition, he stated: "If Jesus were like this, I would not be interested in him." See Eberhard Busch, *Karl Barth: His Life from Letters and Autobiographical Texts*, trans. John Bowden (Grand Rapids: Eerdmans, 1994), p. 54; cf. Fisher, *Revelatory Positivism?*, p. 213; pp. 279-80. Barth would look back with a critical eye upon his early theology as a student and young pastor. As earlier noted, Fisher's conclusion is that if Barth's later criticisms of Schleiermacher and his christology are accepted, then "Barth's own earlier

was more akin to Calvin than the historical critics of his day, even as he saw and embraced historical criticism as serving a propaedeutic function. He rejected a dominant modern preoccupation to determine an "essence of Christianity," acknowledging a center to the canon but no central "doctrine, concept or idea" that would be intended to serve as a key to unlock the whole but in truth would imperiously impose a foreign order upon it.[111] He had no time for theological positions that would pit theological concepts or central doctrines of the canon against the canon itself or that would allow pneumatology to be overshadowed by a historical-critical or hermeneutical program (and thus he gave no quarter to either the restrictions of Troeltsch's historical science or Bultmann's *Sachkritik*).[112] He had great faith in the adequacy of the Spirit to take up the particular words and

---

theology is susceptible to exactly the same objections" (ibid., p. 318). Fisher seems to see this as problematic; in fact, if Barth's estimation of his own early theology is taken with seriousness, he would no doubt agree. Fisher's central intention in his book is an argument for Neo-Kantian influence upon Barth's earliest theology; the success of this endeavor may be questioned. But what he has (unintentionally?) clearly demonstrated is not Barth's reliance on such schools of thought but rather how much his theology from the Romans commentary onward differed from and broke with his own earlier one.

111. CD I/2: pp. 861–6. See also S. W. Sykes, "Barth on the Centre of Theology" in *Karl Barth: Studies of His Theological Method*, ed. S. W. Sykes (Oxford: Clarendon Press, 1979), pp. 17–54 (25). Sykes in the end thinks that Barth did in fact have such a center in christology (ibid., p. 51). McCormack argues similarly, with election and christology, in reciprocal relation, possessing a determinative pride of place in Barth's theology—see McCormack, "Grace and Being: The Role of God's Gracious Election in Karl Barth's Theological Ontology" in *The Cambridge Companion to Karl Barth*, ed. John Webster (Cambridge: Cambridge University Press, 2000), pp. 92–110 (92–3). There is truth to both of these claims. Yet it must be emphasized that neither christology nor election as doctrines served as "deductive material principles" if such were taken to present a reductive theological or hermeneutical program that served a strict systematization of doctrine, and it must also be noted that Barth was inclined to speak of a "center" rather than a "material principle" of theology. He placed a divine act, rather than a concept, at the center of theology and understood this act of the covenant enacted in Christ as the heart of the canon. For a discussion of Barth on this score with reference to Sykes and McCormack, see Kimlyn J. Bender, *Karl Barth's Christological Ecclesiology* (Aldershot/Burlington: Ashgate, 2005), pp. 106–10.

112. Congdon states that Bultmann "identifies a more authentic form of myth—the kind found in the New Testament—that genuinely intends to speak about a transcendent divine reality but does so in an inadequate way" (*The Mission of Demythologizing*, p. 625). The solution for Bultmann to this inadequacy is hermeneutics. Barth resisted attributing inadequacy to the NT not because of the perfection of the text in its human character, but because of the authenticity, sufficiency, and perfection of its authoritative witness to Christ as this is actualized through the work of the Spirit, as well as its particular character as the divinely authorized witness to God's revelation. One cannot help but think that whereas Bultmann has a hermeneutical program, Barth has a pneumatology. Moreover, Congdon can state that myth in the NT is a "vehicle of a kerygmatic truth whose intercultural significance is revealed through demythologizing,"

witness of the canon and was little troubled by its cultural and temporal distance from persons in the modern world, a preoccupation of much of modern biblical, religious, and philosophical scholarship. In contrast, he was more concerned about the conceptualities we brought to the text than those in the text as hindrances to biblical understanding.[113]

Further examples could be given but they would but illustrate the general truth that Barth was not preoccupied with the boundaries or limitations of modernity as a discernible historical period, the exclusivity or uniqueness of its questions, or the maintenance of its orthodoxies. He roamed and quoted freely, almost casually, across the ages, drawing significantly from the entire range of the tradition, and from figures for whom he had deep esteem and from those of whom he had deep reservations—and sometimes he had both for the same figure, such as for Augustine, Luther, or Kierkegaard.[114] He engaged Anselm as intently as Ritschl and identified more with the former than the latter. He took the key task of

---

and that demythologizing "is the interpretive procedure that lets God come to speech *as God*" (ibid., p. 625; pp. 629–30). Whatever we make of such a claim, Barth would never agree to such sentences, first and foremost because there is no "procedure" that would be necessary to "let God" do something. Moreover, for Barth the first step to correcting the first of these two quotations would be to substitute the words "Holy Spirit" for "demythologizing." In truth, Bultmann and Barth had significant (formal) agreements on the nature of the Word that comes to us in proclamation *extra nos* and the necessity of the demythologization of ideologies of the world. But Barth's understanding of Christ and Spirit, as well as canon and tradition, was far removed from that of Bultmann when each of these terms is understood in all of its material richness.

113. CD I/2: p. 716.

114. Barth's concerns about Augustine are set forth in *The Holy Spirit and the Christian Life: The Theological Basis of Ethics*, trans. R. Birch Hoyle (Louisville, KY: Westminster/John Knox, 1993). For Barth's early ambivalence regarding Kierkegaard, see his essay "The Problem of Ethics Today," in WGT, pp. 131–69, esp. pp. 156 and 165; see also the chapter on Barth and Kierkegaard in this volume. For Barth's appreciative yet critical appraisal of Luther and Lutheranism during this early period, see "The Problem of Ethics Today," pp. 131–69, esp. pp. 160–3; also the 1923 essay "Luther's Doctrine of the Eucharist: Its Basis and Purpose," in TC, pp. 74–111; and *The Theology of the Reformed Confessions*, esp. pp. 1–37 and 153–206. Of these three figures, Barth's relation to Luther was particularly complex. Barth always esteemed Luther a theological paragon for his emphasis upon God's free grace and emphasis upon the Word of God that comes to us *extra nos* (as but one example, see Barth, "Need and Promise of Christian Proclamation," p. 125). Yet he could offer some trenchant criticisms as well. His general [Reformed] criticism of Luther and Lutheranism in the 1920s was that they often began theological reflection with the guilt of the sinner or the faith of the believer (these of course being for Luther two sides of one coin of Christian existence), rather than upon the revelation of God in Christ, and thus began with a theological anthropology rather than with christology (and thus, as Barth would later put this, with law rather than with gospel). With regard to Luther, however (though not, it seems, with later Lutheranism), this was not a uniform judgment—Barth could also find in Luther an emphasis upon revelation

and the divine initiative, as well as upon the faith that was believed rather than only the faith by which one believes, as when he appreciatively summarizes his own understanding of revelation by providing a citation from Luther in his ethics lecture: "I do not know or understand it, but I hear that it rings down from above, and echoes in my ears, what no human has ever thought" ("The Problem of Ethics Today," pp. 167–8).

Nevertheless, while Barth continued to revere both Luther and Calvin, he grew to distinguish them, and particularly their respective traditions, summarized well in his 1923 lecture "The Substance and Task of Reformed Doctrine": "The Reformed confessions [over against the Lutheran ones] did not lay the emphasis on the fact that the human is justified through *faith* instead of through *works*, but, rather, that it is *God* and not the *human* who completes this justification" (in WGT, pp. 199–237 [223; see also 231]). Barth's historical observation here in fact tracts with his personal judgment: that Lutheranism, following Luther, was overly concerned and began with the human subject, in terms of both his or her sinfulness and his or her faith.

Barth's specific criticism of Luther during this early period pertained not only to this penchant for starting with human subjectivity in relation to the experience of guilt and faith, but also that Luther and the tradition that followed in his name violated the dialectical relationship between God and the creaturely medium taken up by God for his self-manifestation. In other words, the indirect identity of revelation and the creaturely medium of revelation were flattened into a direct one such that the Creator and creature distinction was threatened. Therefore in reference to christology and sacraments, Barth wrote in his 1923 essay on Reformed doctrine: "The Lutherans went so far as to make a *direct*, miraculous, but earthly identity out of the indirect identity between the heavenly and earthly gifts that are only perfected in God himself, between the thing and the sign, between witness and revelation. Thus they made a direct mediation out of revelation, which, if it is real, is always a veiling. They constructed a religious 'givenness'" (Barth, "The Substance and Task of Reformed Doctrine," p. 227).

Barth's concerns with Lutheran theology can be summarized in light of this complicated relationship to Luther. First, he was concerned that in Luther and Lutheranism there was a *reversal* of the order of God and the human in theological reflection (beginning with the human person in terms of sin and faith rather than with divine revelation—in other words, with a grounding of theology in anthropology rather than christology); and second, he was troubled by a *confusion* of the divine and the human, such that the Word of revelation and the medium of its proclamation (in word and sign) became sacramentally confused, this confusion itself rooted in and given occasion by a christological one and a problematic understanding of the *communicatio idiomatum* (see "The Substance and Task of Reformed Doctrine," pp. 225–37). Barth's estimation is thus that Luther (and those who followed him) gave up a dialectical understanding of Word and sign with a direct identification of them (see Barth, "Luther's Doctrine of the Eucharist," p. 99; pp. 110–11). Later on, he would be worried about Luther's so-called two kingdoms doctrine and (in Barth's estimation) its worrisome effects for a rising German nationalism. But this goes beyond what can be explored here. Nevertheless, in the end, he thought Luther, despite his serious misgivings, a father of the church, and better in his teaching than his doubts—see Chapter 3 in this volume.

theology to be not translation but rediscovery, but never confused this with simple repristination which, in his words, was "nonsense."¹¹⁵ All of these positions he took would be criticized vigorously by others of his day and those that would follow, but where he stood on them is clear.

If Barth rejected an element of modernity above all, it was its historiography. He had a historiography that guided him, but it was not a triumphalism of the modern period with its notions of secular progress mirrored in the theological "coming of age" self-understanding of the broad liberal tradition. Nor did he accept the necessity of adopting modernity's imposed restrictions on theological knowledge or invitations to absolute freedom, autonomy, and an understanding of religion as immanent *anamnesis* (though he had defended these in his earlier theology).¹¹⁶ For all his sympathetic reading of theological figures of the immediate past (present even in his sternest reprimands, such as in his lectures on Schleiermacher), Barth nonetheless maintained that contemporary Protestantism and its theology were the end result of a two-century decline (a fall narrative?) in which the renewal of the Reformation had been quickly compromised by the problems of an orthodoxy that, in its failures, gave way to rationalism and

---

115. Barth, *Credo*, p. 182. Nor did Barth feel that one should simply mimic Calvin or strive to be a "Calvinist," a conviction he held from his first years as a professor to the end of his life. See Barth, *Theology of the Reformed Confessions*, p. 152; and Barth, *Fragments Grave and Gay*, ed. Martin Rumscheidt, trans. Eric Mosbacher (London: Collins, 1971), p. 110. He did not take over the thought of Luther and Calvin and the Reformation more generally without critical reflection and revision. Mere mimicry was something that he never found to be a true option for dogmatic work in the present. In this sense, he indeed did think one had to be a modern theologian—one could not live in or answer the questions of the past to the exclusion of present responsibility. See Georg Plasger, "Luther und Calvin" in *Barth Handbuch*, ed. Michael Beintker (Tübingen: Mohr Siebeck, 2016), pp. 37–42 (37); and Chapter 3 in this volume.

116. While Barth defended both individualism and autonomy in his early writings, in his mature theology he rejected any understanding of the human person as an autonomous agent (Kantian, Fichtean, or other) abstracted from humanity's theological identity. For a discussion of this theme in Barth's theology, see Macken, *The Autonomy Theme in the Church Dogmatics*; cf. Fisher, *Revelatory Positivism*, p. 178. Akin to Sonderegger's earlier observation, Westerholm incisively notes that Barth takes not Kant's autonomy but biblical obedience to be the foundation to proper reasoning in theology (*The Ordering of the Christian Mind*, pp. 14, 59, 151, 227–8). Barth's rejection of immanentism (and *anamnesis*) could range from repudiating Schleiermacher's religious feeling (*Gefühl*) to Rousseau's conscience to Kant's reason which served as a "God within ourselves." Such arguments were often framed in terms of Reformation convictions opposing modern ones centered upon the rejection of the particularity and exclusivity of Christian revelation—see Barth, *Protestant Theology in the Nineteenth Century*, pp. 457–73, esp. p. 458 on Schleiermacher; and pp. 281–6, esp. p. 284 on Kant; cf. also pp. 199, 221–2, 226–7, and 232–3 on Rousseau; pp. 156–7 on Christian Wolff; pp. 238, 241 and 246 on Lessing; and pp. 323–5 on Herder. Barth could also designate this *anamnesis* as "Cartesianism" and traced it back in Christian theology not to Descartes but Augustine, and rejected it regardless—see CD I/1: pp. 99–101.

pietism, with these in turn resulting in the anthropological theologies of the Enlightenment and Romanticism, respectively. The confluence of this movement of decline, and the person who stood both at the end of its development and at the beginning of its modern instantiation, was Schleiermacher. Insofar as Barth saw himself as a modern theologian, he ironically thought the proper task of being one was to provide a "counter-achievement" to Schleiermacher's own and to recover, though not simply return to, the achievements of the Reformation vision for a new articulation of them in the present against the modern theological trajectory. As he told his students in his course on Calvin at the beginning of his teaching career:

> We recall with shame and anger how 19th-century theologians sat at the feet of Kant in order that with the help of his critique of reason they might justify instead of challenge modern Christianity. Theologians have always been adept at ingeniously toying with the most radical and dangerous thoughts and feelings and then devaluing them in an attempt to justify and confirm contemporary religious thoughts and feelings.[117]

Regardless of criticisms of Barth's construal of such matters on any front, this broad historiography of modernity is everywhere evident in his writings from 1922 onward, and it deeply shaped his entire theological project and his own self-understanding.

## *Barth and the Reformation: The Center of Ecclesial and Theological Historiography*

While the modern period of course played a determinative role in Barth's development and theological vocation, the Reformation was distinctly formative for his mature theological identity. His own historiography gave pride of place to the Reformation as the deciding event of church history and theological importance. If he was ambivalent about modernity, he was settled in his understanding of the historiography of theology's demise, and what, in turn, was required.[118] In his lectures on Schleiermacher of 1923/24, he concluded by noting that considering Schleiermacher's achievement filled him with "*respect* and *admiration*" and averred that Schleiermacher was the greatest theologian since the Reformation. Yet Barth had deep misgivings about him and all that followed in his wake in a conclusion worth quoting at length:

---

117. Barth, *The Theology of Calvin*, p. 56.
118. Chalamet summarizes Barth's understanding: "The eighteenth and nineteenth century represented the beginnings of a long period of decline, and it was time to leave that period behind" (Chalamet, *Dialectical Theologians*, p. 168). In truth, Barth saw the seeds of decline as existing much earlier, as early as Beza (Barth, *Theology of the Reformed Confessions*, 151-2). As we have seen, he even had reservations about elements of Luther. He did not consider the Reformation to be a perfect age, but he did see it as setting forth the epitome of renewal and proper scriptural confession against which all later ages were judged.

Protestantism has not in fact had any greater theologian since the days of the reformers. But this theologian has led us all into this *dead end*! This is an oppressive and almost intolerable thought. How can it really be reconciled with confidence in Protestantism's power of truth? Or should we in fact say that this was and is the normal and legitimate continuation of the Reformation, the completion of the work of Luther and Calvin: this doctrine of the feeling of absolute dependence or of the universum and all that is connected with it? If it were, for me the right thing to do would be to become a Roman Catholic again. But at an even higher level, how can it be reconciled with the providence of God ruling over his church? Or should we reverently say that it is the inscrutable way of God on which we have been put and which we have to tread as children of our time? But disobedience to history has sometimes been better obedience to God's governance than obediently following a path that has been entered. Nevertheless, in view of the results of our study, these two questions, that of the truth of Protestantism and that of the divine guidance of the church, are very serious ones. And the more we ponder them, the more serious the situation becomes. If we reject the two suggestions above, if we cannot find in Schleiermacher a legitimate heir or successor of the reformers, if we cannot see in the indubitable domination of his thinking the gracious guidance of God but the very opposite, a wrathful judgment on Protestantism which invites it to repentance and conversion instead of continuation, then the only possibility that remains—and I do not see how one can avoid this—is obviously that of a *theological revolution*, a basic No to the whole of Schleiermacher's doctrine of religion and Christianity, and an attempted reconstruction at the *very* point which we have constantly seen him hurry past with astonishing stubbornness, skill, and audacity. The higher one values Schleiermacher's achievement in and for itself, and the better one sees with what historical necessity it had to come and how well—how only too well—it fitted the world spirit of Christianity in the 19th and 20th centuries, the more clearly one perceives how easy it is to say No in word but how hard it is to say it in deed, namely, with a positive counter-achievement. Schleiermacher undoubtedly did a good job. It is not enough to know that another job has to be done; what is needed is the ability to do it at least as well as he did his. This is the serious and humbling concern with which I take leave of Schleiermacher; and if you agree with my assessment, I hope you will share this concern. There is no occasion for triumphant superiority at this tomb, but there is occasion for fear and trembling at the seriousness of the moment and in face of our own inadequacy.[119]

---

119. Barth, *Theology of Schleiermacher*, pp. 259–60; cf. p. 205. The importance of the judgment Barth expresses here for understanding all of his later theology, and particularly the prolegomena of the CD, can scarcely be overestimated, for it is structured entirely along the lines of this passage. Barth's statement that Schleiermacher could only be answered with a corresponding oppositional "counter-achievement" was also iterated in his review of Brunner's *Die Mystik und das Wort* in 1924 and in his lectures on nineteenth-century Protestant theology. See Barth, "Brunner's Schleiermacherbuch 1924" in *Vorträge und kleinere Arbeiten 1922–1925*, ed. Holger Finze (Zürich: Theologischer Verlag Zürich, 1990), pp. 401–25 (424–5); see also

The ironic truth is that Barth simultaneously embraced his Reformed heritage and looked upon Protestantism since the Reformation with wistful sadness and consternation. His assessment of the theological decline since the Reformation was mirrored in his estimation of how the early church had, after the NT, lost the proper distinction of revelation and the church, resulting in time in problematic Roman Catholic doctrines of grace and ecclesiology. For Barth, the most pressing existential questions posed to Protestantism were not those regarding the need for the translation and modernization of its message and faith and their apologetic defense in light of cultural shifts and challenges. They were rather those that arose out of this internal decline and that pertained to how the decline itself might be reconciled with divine providence.[120] This disquiet was articulated in the conclusion

---

Hart, *Barth vs. Brunner*, pp. 49–53; and Barth, *Protestant Theology in the Nineteenth Century*, p. 427. His entire mature theological program was shaped by his conviction that what was required was not an answer to the external problems modern philosophy or culture might pose to the church, but a "counter-achievement" to the failure of modern Protestantism exemplified in Schleiermacher, a counter-achievement informed by a return to (though not simple repristination of) the central convictions of the Reformation.

Barth's remarkably ambitious theological project in the CD was nothing less than an attempt to produce as much. In this, it was not only a response to modern Protestantism but also an answer to the historic division of the church that came about from the Reformation, and thus an address to the challenge of Roman Catholicism. He took Catholicism, not liberalism, to be the only serious contender to an Evangelical Protestant (and thus Reformational) confessional Christianity, evident in his exchange with Georg Wobbermin, who accused him of abetting the conversions to Catholicism of Erik Peterson and Oskar Bauhofer. In response, Barth expressed what a burden it was to be a Protestant theologian and in what sad shape contemporary Protestantism existed as a "defeated army," noting that Catholicism was the only rival tradition that presented a truly serious alternative of Christian confession and existence. See Karl Barth, *Offene Briefe 1909–1935*, ed. Diether Koch (Zürich: Theologischer Verlag Zürich, 2001), pp. 227–8. That Barth thought Roman Catholicism a much more serious alternative to an Evangelical Protestantism than Neo-Protestantism was a sentiment he expressed on numerous occasions—for one example, see Barth, "Roman Catholicism: A Question to the Protestant Church," in TC, pp. 307–33 (314 nt.1). The irony is that Wobbermin's charges against Barth in an editorial of May 31, 1932, came at a time when Barth was intently focused upon a study of Luther for the development of his own Evangelical Protestant theology.

120. As Barth expressed such thoughts in a circular letter to Thurneysen and others discussing his lectures in 1924: "Things go no better with Schleiermacher but continually worse. The fact that it should be so with the chief figure of the nineteenth century is a serious problem for me (a) with regard to faith in the divine *Providence*, (b) with regard to the truth and mission of *Protestantism*. Do any of you know an explanation why that had to be as it was, and is it possible that the case of Schleiermacher is a slap in the face that resounds back into the sixteenth century in part?" See *Revolutionary Theology in the Making*, p. 175. Barth alluded to this sentiment regarding the failures of Protestantism and the problem of divine providence in both the conclusion to the Schleiermacher lectures (in the passage provided above), as well as in his review of Brunner's book on Schleiermacher—see Barth, "Brunner's Schleiermacherbuch 1924" p. 423.

to the Schleiermacher lectures quoted above, but it was common and frequent theme and conclusion to his historical work during his first professorate, as when he articulated the same thoughts in his lectures on the Reformed confessions of the same year:

> It is very different question as to how things now stand with us, the Reformed and also the non-Reformed children. If we look at our theology, then what we see first of all is a pile of ruins. Perhaps the best thing that can be done at this moment is to work on a historical orientation for what a real theology *would* look like. Beyond that, it is possible earnestly to *stand quietly* before the eternal questions and answers which once required of our fathers that they confess. We can do that, even if we are not able to utter their confessions with our lips. I am persuaded that we *must* do that even if we have only somewhat and only historically understood them. When that is done, more seriously perhaps by a *young* generation that knows better what real questions and answers are than do many older folks, then we need *not* be ultimately fearful about the future of theology and the church, in spite of all serious concerns about their present internal confusion.[121]

Such questions and judgments followed Barth throughout the 1920s and beyond. In reflecting on the Reformation in 1928, he stated that the history of Protestantism should give rise to serious reflection for all who "stand on its soil."[122] The venture of the original Reformers had, in truth, not been well-followed. The proof of their decision should have been evident in the continuation of faith among those who followed them, but, he conceded, it would be dishonest to celebrate the Reformation without recognizing that this proof was largely missing. The history of Protestantism, while not without real innovations and achievements, in truth reversed the Reformation's real intentions:

> We can no longer conceal the fact that today the venture to bind conscience to God alone has become the completely different venture to bind God to our human conscience alone, the venture of trusting in the free God [has become] the completely different venture of trusting in the free human person, and the venture with the Holy Spirit [has become] the completely different venture with one's own reason and strength, of which Luther wanted to know nothing.[123]

---

121. Barth, *Theology of the Reformed Confessions*, pp. 224–5. Barth maintained that certain Reformed resources were especially helpful in pointing a way forward, of which he held the Scots Confession in the highest regard (ibid., p. 133). It is therefore unsurprising that when he offered his Gifford lectures over a decade later, he chose the Scots Confession as his guide. See Barth, *The Knowledge of God and the Service of God According to the Teaching of the Reformation*.

122. Barth, "Das Wagnis des Glaubens 1928" in *Vorträge und kleinere Arbeiten 1925–1930*, ed. Hermann Schmidt (Zürich: Theologischer Verlag Zürich, 1994), pp. 296–302 (300).

123. Barth, "Das Wagnis des Glaubens 1928," p. 301.

If "the last word in the history of Protestantism is precisely this vulgar Protestantism represented by its most celebrated teachers" of the past two centuries, then it may indeed be better to return to Rome ["the inviting voice from beyond the mountains"] than to celebrate the Reformation, because at least in Catholicism it is still remembered that, despite its "strange disfigurement," Christianity is about God and not about human glory.[124] The question and task before the Protestant church today is precisely how it will come to terms with the meaning of its own history and with its own current witness which speaks to this history. That was indeed the question that shaped Barth's entire dogmatic project from his time in Göttingen onward. Schleiermacher marked a way for the church to take in modernity. But that way served as a warning, and Barth held to the conviction that both church and theology had to take "a radically different path" than that of Schleiermacher.[125]

What one sees, again and again in the decade of the 1920s, in the midst of all of the other debates and external questions that Barth faced, is an abiding disquiet about Protestantism in the modern period in the light of the Reformation. It is not simply a question about problematic individual figures (to whom Barth could be remarkably charitable, as seen in the introductory comments to his lectures on nineteenth-century Protestant theology), or even about liberalism itself, but about the entire culture and existence of theology and the Protestant church. His attacks are not only focused on his theological compatriots, but also aimed at church triumphalism of any kind. He thus appealed to the importance of the Reformation emphasis upon the crucified Christ and the accompanying distinction of Christ as the head of the church from the church as his body and entreated the church to embrace a life under the cross.[126] He wrestled with this deep crisis posed by the Reformation—both why it was needed in light of the developments of the church since the NT, but more acutely, why its convictions and commitments were so feebly embodied and then quickly betrayed by its own descendants.[127] For Barth, this was a crisis not only of history and the truth of Protestantism, but of the intelligibility of divine providence, and thus not simply a matter of human error or disobedience. Just like Augustine and the Anabaptists before him, he attempted to make sense of divine providence amid a history of human failure and the vicissitudes of history. The existential crisis he faced was not how faith might speak to the modern age or overcome its distinct philosophical challenges—at most, these were secondary concerns. Such was the crisis with which persons like Brunner and Bultmann and Tillich wrestled. Barth's was an

---

124. Barth, "Das Wagnis des Glaubens 1928," pp. 301–2. This seriousness about the Protestant condition and the consideration of the Roman alternative is the content of Barth's other 1928 essay, "Roman Catholicism: A Question to the Protestant Church," 307–33.

125. Barth, "Friedrich Schleiermacher: Zum 100. Todestag am 12. Februar 1934," p. 156.

126. Barth, "Die Not der evangelischen Kirche 1931" in *Vorträge und kleinere Arbeiten 1930–1933*, ed. Michael Beintker, Michael Hüttenhoff and Peter Zocher (Zürich: Theologischer Verlag Zürich, 2013), pp. 64–122 (79–80).

127. Barth, *The Theology of Calvin*, p. 74.

even deeper theological crisis, one constituted by a distinct set of questions: How had it become the case that the truths of the Reformation had appeared in history, and yet so quickly disappeared? And what did this say about the truth of Protestantism? More seriously still, what did this say about the divine providence of God in relation to the church? Such questions could be exacerbated by what he perceived as the solidity and confidence of Roman Catholicism in contrast to these Protestant anxieties and failures.[128]

While the mystery of divine providence could not be unraveled, the causes of theology's decline could be discerned from the side of human history, and this was the descriptive task Barth set before himself in delineating this historiography of decline, even as he simultaneously turned to the constructive task informed by a rich retrieval of Scripture and Reformational insights (along with the entire tradition of the church). Yet these tasks could not be divided. He was keenly aware that some might well conclude that modern Protestantism was, in the words of Harnack in debate with Erik Peterson, left with nothing but "the aroma of an empty bottle."[129] Yet while some persons, like Peterson, would follow this road to Rome in order to resolve the crisis, Barth would not. But this meant that for him there was but one alternative, for the way of Neo-Protestantism was for him a dead end.[130] In reflecting on this state of affairs, he set forth the only option he thought possible in a letter to Thurneysen in 1924: "But if that is so ... what a task it is then to make a fresh beginning once more with Protestantism (which the first time came out so wrongly!!)."[131]

---

128. This anxious judgment is incisively illustrated in Barth's 1922 lecture "The Need and Promise of Christian Proclamation": "How incomparably more securely, smoothly, and confidently the other church [Roman Catholicism] goes its way, having wisely left this dangerous principle of the Word undiscovered! And we have absolutely no reason to wrinkle our noses without further ado at this well-known Catholic certainty. What comes to mind is a story which was told to me by a Benedictine from Alsace about the time during the War. As the lead cantor of his cloister, he sang the Magnificat in harmony one evening with his fellow monks, and suddenly a French grenade crashed through the roof and exploded in the middle of the nave of the church. But the smoke dissipated and the Magnificat was continued. One may certainly ask, would the Protestant sermon have also been continued?" (WGT, p. 113). As earlier noted, a similar tone and dis-ease are evident in Barth's later essay directly addressing Roman Catholicism in 1928, "Roman Catholicism: A Question to the Protestant Church" (see nt. 124 above).

129. See Erik Peterson and Adolf von Harnack, "Erik Peterson's Correspondence with Adolf von Harnack," trans. Michale J. Hollerich, *Pro Ecclesia* II no. 3 (1993), pp. 333–44.

130. To follow on the line from "Schleiermacher by way of Ritschl to Herrmann" was the definition for Barth of this Protestant liberal tradition: "And in any conceivable continuation along this line I can see only the plain destruction of Protestant theology and the Protestant Church" (CD I/1: p. xiii).

131. *Revolutionary Theology in the Making*, p. 175; cf. pp. 167–8; see also Karl Barth, *Die Theologie Zwinglis 1922/1923*, ed. Matthias Freudenberg (Zürich: Theologischer Verlag Zürich, 2004), pp. 251–2.

Everything that would follow in Barth's life and work is shaped by this deeply engrained historiography. For what we have here, in essence, is a fall narrative, or in truth, a double fall.[132] Like many Protestant thinkers before him, he judged the church before the Reformation as one that required the deep-cutting revision that the Reformers provided, but what he added to this account was a view that their achievements were quickly distorted and that the Reformation legacy was compromised almost as soon as it occurred. He articulated numerous reasons for this, including the false starts of preserving the Reformation in orthodoxy and pietism, which, instead, ossified or spiritualized revelation (respectively) in the text or the self, both opening the door for all of the later problems of Enlightenment rationalism and Protestant modernism, and all the while all of them falling back into the errors of the Middle Ages and the council of Trent.[133] The betrayal of modern Protestantism came with a long genealogy of problems, which Barth could summarize as a line from "the Anabaptists to Pietism, Zinzendorf, and Schleiermacher, and from the Radicals to the Socinians, the Remonstrants, the Rationalists, and Schleiermacher again, and then from Schleiermacher to ourselves."[134] Thus the quintessential figure who displays the betrayal of the Reformation for Barth and embodies the confluence of these problematic developments was Schleiermacher, for he instantiated in his person and work the end result of rationalism and pietism in the form of romanticism, standing at the head of modern Protestantism and at the culmination of the Reformation's de-formation. Again, whether or not Barth is fair in all of his historical judgments in every respect with regard to these figures and movements, this was without question the historiography of Protestantism that shaped his entire project from the mid-1920s onward, one that caught up Schleiermacher, Ritschl, Herrmann, and Troeltsch, as well as figures as diverse as Karl Holl and Emanuel Hirsch and

---

132. In this historiography, Barth stands closer to Ritschl's understanding of a loss of NT vitality in later church history than to F. C. Baur's progressive view of religious history which saw that which was later in time always exceeding the earlier in excellence and sophistication (in a way reminiscent of Hegel). But he also stands against Ritschl in seeing the aftermath of the Reformation not as a history of progress but degeneration. For the contrast of Baur and Ritschl on this score, see Zachhuber, *Theology as Science in Nineteenth Century Germany*, pp. 171–4. Another way to understand Barth's historiography is to consider that he shared with Herrmann a higher view of the Reformation and its singular importance in comparison to Troeltsch, who considered the Reformation as still determined by and a part of the medieval world, but he had a much more critical view of the Enlightenment and modern theological developments than both of them—for a discussion of Herrmann and Troeltsch on this topic, see Sockness, *Against False Apologetics*, pp. 61–8.

133. For one such discussion, see Barth, *Protestant Theology in the Nineteenth Century*, pp. 97–9; cf. pp. 113–17 and 131–5.

134. Unterricht I, p. 257; ET: GD, p. 211. Barth could group orthodoxy, pietism, the Enlightenment, and Schleiermacher together as shorthand references to "the four cornerstones of the prison in which we all are stuck." See Barth, "The Substance and Task of Reformed Doctrine 1923" in WGT, p. 220.

Paul Althaus and Gogarten and Brunner and Bultmann in its judgment, and that singled out the Reformers in its commendation.[135] It shaped how he understood and contextualized the nationalistic theology ascending in the 1930s, and how he thought the church must respond.[136] At the center of this historiography was the Reformation which served as the singular and unique fixed point from which all of theological history was surveyed and understood:

> The Reformation was neither the last phase of medieval Christianity, as Troeltsch saw it, nor the first phase of modern Christianity, as popular modern theology sees it. Regardless of the traces of the medieval and the modern that cling to it, the Reformation stands over against both, at least in its core and its original intention, as something new and alien, a third entity. The young Luther does not fit neatly with either Dante or Goethe, Saint Thomas or Schleiermacher. He stands on his own, and in contrast to him the enormous contrasts between the medieval and modern approaches merge in a remarkable way into *one* front. Was he battling against the Middle Ages or modernity in his struggle with Erasmus? Should one not set aside this either/or and respond that, in Erasmus, both in their characteristic unity were positioned over against him? In his battle with the enthusiasts of his day, whom some justifiably see as the predecessors of modern Christianity, he used with instinctive certainty the same arguments that he used against the old church .... For him the papists were clandestine enthusiasts, as were the enthusiasts hidden papists.[137]

This was in fact not only the way Barth saw Luther specifically, or the Reformation more generally, but the way he understood himself and his own vocation. He saw his earlier theology not only as a liberal modern project that needed to be jettisoned, but that needed to be understood as actually *pre*-Reformational in character, for the theology against which Luther and Calvin had reacted had now reappeared in Protestant guise.[138] In this, his self-understanding of his break with liberalism was a reflection in his own life and work of Luther's break with the

---

135. See Barth, "Das erste Gebot also theologisches Axiom" in *Vorträge und kleinere Arbeiten 1930-1933*, pp. 209-41 (230-41); ET: Karl Barth, "The First Commandment as an Axiom in Theology," in *The Way of Theology in Karl Barth*, pp. 63-78 (72-8). Barth upholds Luther and Calvin as exemplars of obedience to the first commandment in contrast to Julius Wegscheider, Kant, Schleiermacher, Hegel, Ritschl, Troeltsch, Holl, Hirsch, Bultmann, Gogarten, and Brunner, as well as Roman Catholicism.

136. Barth, "Reformation als Entscheidung" in *Vorträge und kleinere Arbeiten 1930-1933*, pp. 516-50.

137. Barth, *Theology of the Reformed Confessions*, pp. 206-7; cf. *The Theology of Calvin*, pp. 17-21. Barth's basic decisions of the structure of the first volume of the CD, in which Evangelical Protestant faith and theology were set in contrast to two oppositional traditions that for all their differences were seen as deeply similar (i.e., liberal Protestantism and Roman Catholicism), were thus explicitly prefigured nearly a decade earlier.

138. Eberhard Busch, *Karl Barth*, p. 143.

Middle Ages. It was in his first professorate that he discovered Luther and Calvin anew, and it was there that, in is words, he "swung into line with the Reformation," even if not uncritically.[139]

The Reformation thus took a singularly important place in Barth's historiography, for it was not only a necessary development in the church's history in light of the Middle Ages and all that came before since the NT, but also the standard by which all later periods were evaluated. If there is an analogy in theological history to the "culmination of the ages" (1 Cor. 10:11) for Barth, a time in church history that served as a reflection of and unparalleled witness to the appearance of Christ and the time of the apostles, it is the Reformation. This does not entail—and this cannot be stressed enough—that he thought the Reformation to be a perfect age.[140] He was not romantic or pollyannaish in this regard, nor did he simply accept the teachings of the Reformers uncritically, for he did not think them to be infallible. Neither did he think that we in our time are called simply to recapitulate the words or teachings of the past (and hence "neo-orthodoxy" was never a description that he embraced or that fit him well).[141] As already noted, his view of straightforward repetition of the doctrinal formulations of the past was that it was nonsensical and impossible. Yet he saw the Reformation as a singular epoch in church history, the place where the church was renewed and definitively placed into crisis with a confrontation with Scripture such that division ensued from its accompanying polemical confessions regarding the church's true definition.[142] The Reformers, for him, were the quintessential witnesses to the apostolic witnesses whose testimony is recorded in the biblical canon. They therefore were the exemplary expositors of Scripture and in so doing set forth the conditions for a theology truly

---

139. Quoted in Busch, *Karl Barth*, p. 143. George Hunsinger comments: "Perhaps one way to appreciate the powerful impact on Barth of the primacy Luther assigned to God's Word would be to say that it led Barth, almost alone among modern theologians, to grant uncompromising precedence to the Reformation over modernity itself." See Hunsinger, *Disruptive Grace: Studies in the Theology of Karl Barth* (Grand Rapids: Eerdmans, 2000), p. 293.

140. Barth, *The Theology of Calvin*, pp. 49, 70, 73-5. In his discoveries of the Reformation, Barth appreciated Luther and Calvin especially but usually sided with the Reformed against the Lutheran position when they were in conflict even as he was also fully aware of the moral ambiguity of Calvin's emphasis on ethics and for a Christianity dedicated to action within the world (ibid., p. 344).

141. It is for the same reason not helpful to call Barth a "Neo-Reformationist" theologian, though that would be closer to the truth. He wanted to follow in the spirit of the Reformers but not simply mimic them, holding to their central convictions but extending them to their logical ends. As Hart concludes: Barth "built his theology on a radically christocentric, strongly actualist, thorough-going radicalizing of the Reformation *solas*" (see *Barth vs. Brunner*, p. 219; cf. pp. 215-16).

142. See Barth, *Dogmatics in Outline*, trans. G. T. Thomson (London: SCM, 1957), p. 145. There Barth states that when the Reformers appeared "the Roman Church remained behind the Reformed Church and separated from it."

centered upon Christ and the gospel.[143] And for these reasons they were the paradigmatic "church fathers" that he set forth in the first volume of the CD. The Reformation thus served as the pivot point of Barth's ecclesial and theological historiography, and an interpretive key to his own personal one. He identified its central achievement not as an esoteric or peripheral theological insight but a straightforward discovery of the heart of the biblical message and therefore the gospel:

> It made the discovery that theology has to do with *God*. It made the great and shattering discovery of the real theme of all theology. The secret was simply this, that it took this theme seriously in all its distinctiveness, that it names God God, that it lets God be God, the one object that by no bold human grasping or inquiry or approach can be simply one object among many others. God *is, He* lives. *He* judges and blesses. *He* slays and makes alive ... *He* is the Creator and Redeemer and Lord. The Reformation did not really engender any new thoughts about God. It did the simple thing of underlining the *He*. And that put an end to the Middle Ages.[144]

The Reformation therefore was not so much a period of church history as a way of Christian confession and existence that had to be rediscovered again and again. As Barth put this point in 1922: "Reformation is truly no less possible and necessary today than four hundred years ago."[145] At its core, he maintained, the Reformation was the rediscovery that God is God, along with its numerous unfolding entailments of God's lordship expressed in the inalienable and irreversible order of God's relation to the world, of Christ's relation to the church, and of the Spirit's relation to the sinner,

---

143. As Barth put this point: "Luther and Calvin did not need to aim at a 'christocentric' theology, like Schleiermacher and later A. Ritschl and his pupils, because their theology was christocentric from the very outset, and without the singular attempt to make or call it so. It did not need to become christocentric. And how can theology or piety or Church life become christocentric, if it is not so at the very outset? The strainings and the unhealthy zeal and historical and systematic devices by which the moderns have tried to become christocentric bear clear and eloquent testimony that they were not christocentric at the outset and therefore cannot be" (CD I/2: pp. 350–1). Nearly a decade earlier Barth stated that "Theology will really be theology ... when from beginning to end it is christology." See Barth, "Fate and Idea in Theology," p. 60; cf. CD I/1: p. 131. This conviction shaped his entire project in the CD: "A church dogmatics must, of course, be christologically determined as a whole and in all its parts, as surely as the revealed Word of God, attested by Holy Scripture and proclaimed by the Church, is its one and only criterion, and as surely as this revealed Word is identical with Jesus Christ. If dogmatics cannot regard itself and cause itself to be regarded as fundamentally Christology, it has assuredly succumbed to some alien sway and is already on the verge of losing its character as church dogmatics" (CD I/2: p. 123).

144. *The Theology of Calvin*, p. 39; see pp. 39–40.

145. Karl Barth, "The Need and Promise of Christian Proclamation," in WGT, p. 128. Barth continued: "Reformation occurs where reflection occurs" (p. 128).

a relation in which God alone was to receive the glory for the work of revelation as well as salvation, even as the sinner was in turn justified and sanctified for a life of obedience in the world. It was the restoration of "the immutable subjectivity of God, the freedom of God above all his instruments, the uniqueness of God's authority."[146] This authority of God in Christ through the Spirit was exercised through the Word of God in Scripture, which stood over both the church and its tradition. This confluence of the singularity of God's salvation enacted for God's glory and our good through Christ alone, by grace alone, received in faith alone, and authoritatively attested and proclaimed in Scripture alone—this, in sum, was the Protestant vision that defined all of Barth's theology. All epistemological, ecclesiological, and ethical questions were simply subthemes under this larger one of the "immutable subjectivity of God," and hence Barth's theology cannot be understood as primarily about one to the detriment of the others. God's lordship as God—in the realm of human knowledge in the light of divine revelation, of ecclesial action in the light of a finished divine reconciliation, of human obedience and gratitude in the light of a prevenient divine grace and command, in short, in every aspect of human social and individual life—this was the theme of Barth's theology that framed all other concerns and questions (and while such topics can be isolated for the sake of examination, his theology cannot be truly understood or appreciated by highlighting one of these to the exclusion or marginalization of the others). The centrality of this Reformation discovery is also why he could, however controversial it may be, judge the Middle Ages, and the modern period, equally against the standard of Scripture, and specifically against Scripture as recovered and read in the Reformation. And so not only would Augustine and Thomas be judged against its standard, but so would the two figures that perhaps typified the modern period more than any others for Barth—i.e., Lessing and Kant—along with all the theologians of the modern liberal tradition.[147] This is but one more reason that his theology cannot be easily delimited to the questions and concerns of any age, including his own modern one.

## Barth as the Last Protestant

The three-fold historiography now outlined over these many pages casts light upon a range of elements of Barth's theological existence—from how he attempted to determine what had gone wrong with the modern theological project, to his commitment to Scripture and its exegesis as the locus not only of theological reflection but renewal, to why he believed such renewal required a rediscovery of the Reformation and its central convictions, to his attempts to determine who had and who had not betrayed its central insights (witnessed in his early lists dividing theologians and Christian thinkers into two distinct camps, with some, like Kierkegaard, falling on both sides of the line depending upon the issue at hand); to his own discovery and determination of himself as a Reformed

---

146. Barth, "Roman Catholicism," pp. 324-5.
147. See note 116 above. One could add Goethe to this short list for Barth.

theologian before all other theological identities he might possess (dialectical, et al). This historiography illuminates his entire theological project from his first professorship onward, which was supremely centered upon setting forth the truth of God's revelation and salvation. But this ultimate goal could not be separated from the penultimate and accompanying one "to interpret the Reformation anew and to make it an actuality in the present."[148] A consideration of this historiography in turn provides an insight into the rationale for three realities of the prolegomena to the CD, which itself sets forth the intentions and aims of Barth's entire mature dogmatic undertaking.

The first insight is why Barth structures the first volume of the CD around an engagement with two rival traditions, setting forth his own program of an Evangelical Protestant dogmatics over against Roman Catholicism and Protestant modernism. The CD is set forth as an attempt to put the Protestant house in order, to articulate the original Reformation vision and to bring it to its full consistency, and to do so by providing an ecumenical and simultaneously polemical argument against both its only real rival (i.e., Roman Catholicism) and its own historical perversion (Neo-Protestantism).[149] Once this is understood, Barth's framework

---

148. Barth made this comment in a letter to Eberhar Bethge dated May 22, 1967. The German reads: "die Reformation neu zu interpretieren und aktuell zu machen." See Karl Barth, *Briefe 1961-1968*, ed. Jürgen Fangmeier and Hinrich Stoevesandt (Zürich: Theologischer Verlag Zürich, 1979), p. 404; cf. Eric Mosbacher's translation, which is close to the one I have (liberally) given: "to give a new interpretation of the Reformation and to make it an actuality" (Barth, *Fragments Grave and Gay*, p. 120). See also Matthias Freudenberg, *Karl Barth und die reformierte Theologie: Die Auseinaandersetzung mit Calvin, Zwingli und den reformierten Bekenntnisschriften währen seiner Göttinger Lehrtätigkeit* (Neukircher-Vluyn: Neukirchener Verlag, 1997), pp. 287-94, esp. pp. 287 and 294. Freudenberg states that for Barth the Reformation is not simply a historical period but a way of reflective theological existence: "Reformation is not only the description of a historical event in the sixteenth century but throughout the ages a sign of the being and nature of the church and theology" (p. 294).

149. Barth's project in the CD is a sustained explication of a confessional theological vision in which, by means of biblical exegesis, historical recovery, polemical argumentation, and constructive description, the Evangelical Protestant understanding of the "being of the Church" is set over against those understandings of the same within Roman Catholicism and Protestant modernism (CD I/1: pp. 6, 12; et al.). These serve as rival accounts of what constitutes this relation of Christ and the church and thus embodied ecclesial reality. Barth, throughout this extended project, attempts not only to engage these traditions on the discrete fronts of particular battles past and present, setting the Evangelical Protestant confession against the two traditions set in opposition to it. More importantly, he also attempts to provide a superior exposition of the whole and of the fundamental relation of Christ to the church which gives the church its identity. In so doing, it might be said that Barth prefigures a form of argumentation like that of Alasdair MacIntyre in his *Three Rival Versions of Moral Inquiry: Encyclopaedia, Genealogy, and Tradition* (Notre Dame: University of Notre Dame Press, 1990). In effect, both Barth and MacIntyre argue for the superiority of a

for the first volume of the CD is readily seen to be not simply a theological program to specify the knowledge of God in light of earlier modern failures, but a truly ecumenical and catholic project whose fulcrum is not the Enlightenment and its aftermath but the church divisions arising from the Reformation.[150] The key theme of the first volume is therefore not structured around the question of epistemology but the question of knowledge itself is taken up within the context of the central theme set forth at the beginning of the CD, one revolving not around a general God-world relation (as in the Romans commentary), but a very specific one: "Jesus Christ as the Lord of the Church."[151] The CD is therefore an explication

tradition (for Barth, confessional and theological; for MacIntyre, philosophical and ethical) not by appealing to a shared set of preliminary axioms, but by producing an explication of a consummate vision that is shown to be superior in its very explication while acknowledging the truth of the others even in their ultimate incommensurability to it. In short, Barth is, in the CD, attempting to produce the positive "counter-achievement" he stated was needed in order to respond to Schleiermacher. He is not arguing against Neo-Protestantism nor Roman Catholicism simply on the points of specific debates past or present, though that occurs as well. He is, rather, arguing by re-narrating the whole of Christian conviction via a "regular dogmatics." When this is understood, it becomes clear why Barth's CD was not only a massive project that consumed him for decades but also an unfinished one. It also displays why he may be a child of modernity but is intimating to a way beyond it (and its alternating foundationalism and relativism) in both argumentation and formal perspective. Moreover, it provides some indication as to why his theology has been taken to hold both great ecumenical promise and peril, as well as provides insight as to why Roman Catholic theologians were both some of Barth's greatest critics and admirers. For Barth's form of argumentation along the lines here given with an eye to similarities but also important differences from MacIntyre, see Bender, *Confessing Christ for Church and World*, pp. 315–51.

150. As time progressed (due to Vatican II), Barth emphasized more the catholic and ecumenical intent of the CD rather than its confessional and polemical nature, as in a conversation of 1964: "I claim, in all modesty, that my *Church Dogmatics* is neither a Lutheran nor a Reformed dogmatics. I don't want to boast—I actually wrote it as an ecumenical dogmatics." Karl Barth, *Barth in Conversation V. 3: 1964–1968*, ed. Darrell L Guder and Matthias Gockel, trans. Darrell Guder, Matthias Gockel et al. (Louisville, KY: Westminster John Knox, 2019), p. 9. The desire to put forth an ecumenical dogmatics was already stated at the very beginning of the CD, though there was and ever remained a tension between the evangelical, confessional, and polemical nature of Barth's dogmatics and its stated catholic and ecumenical objective. So on one hand Barth states: "Where dogmatics exists at all, it exists only with the will to be a Church dogmatics, a dogmatics of the ecumenical church" (CD I/2: p. 823). Yet on the other hand Barth asserts that the only church dogmatics that can truly make such a claim is an Evangelical Protestant one: "Church dogmatics is Evangelical dogmatics or it is not Church dogmatics" (CD I/2: p. 825; see Barth's discussion of the "confessional attitude" and its entailments for dogmatics, pp. 822–39). His attempt to reconcile this tension is revealed in his conclusion that "when the Church is the true Church it is the Evangelical Church" (CD I/2: p. 825). To say this is a contested notion is to but state the obvious.

151. CD I/1: p. 32.

of this lordship over all avenues of the church's life, and only then secondarily by means of extrapolation an explication of the general relation of God to the world. The question of knowledge of God is therefore framed within this theme, even as it is the presupposition for the theme itself.[152]

Barth's theology was a response to these two rivals of an Evangelical Protestant theology which he came to espouse and articulate. The first, Neo-Protestantism, was that which stood in the line of the Reformation but departed from its insights. The second, Roman Catholicism, was the tradition which rejected those insights when they appeared. Barth would link these two already in 1922, though the quintessential presentation of them as rivals to an Evangelical Protestant theology would occur a decade later in the first volume of the CD.[153] Barth was, in truth, much harder on the first than the second, even though his disagreements with Catholicism were significant. But it was modern Protestantism that did not have a good conscience and had no ground on which to stand in its oppositions to Catholicism, for whatever mistakes Catholicism may have made, liberalism made them in a much more egregious, clumsy, and inept fashion: "We find in it the forbidden immediacy, the direct manipulation of Christ and the Spirit, the underhand and hence not genuinely achieved contemporaneity, the abrogation of scripture as the independent Word of God in history, the conjuring away of the historical offense by the historicizing of revelation, the forgetting of a criterion that stands above the church."[154]

---

152. "Knowledge of the Word of God in this sense is the presupposition of the Church. We may and must also reverse the statement and say that the Church is the presupposition of knowledge of the Word of God" (CD I/1: p. 188). It is important to register that at no point does Barth speak of the possibility of the knowledge of God as a theoretical possibility. In contrast, he begins with the premise that the church has a knowledge of God and confesses it precisely because both the knowledge of God and the church exists, and the question of the conditions of the possibility of both knowledge God and the church's existence are only taken up in light of this recognized and presumed reality and are mutually implicating. Theological epistemology can therefore no more be extracted from ecclesiology than the mind can be extracted from the body—the question is not one of separation but of proper ordering. For Barth, the reality of God calls the church into existence in an irreversible order of revelation and the church, but without the church, there is no confession of the knowledge of the reality of God. The act of God's revelation is thus the very establishment of faith, both corporate and individual, which in turn is witnessed and confessed.

153. In the Calvin lectures Barth contrasted "Reformation and Protestant" theology with "medieval and modern theologies" in one breath, and averred that modern Protestants were closer to and would fare better with Thomas than Calvin (*The Theology of Calvin*, pp. 204–5). He also stated in 1925: "If one accepts Schleiermacher without blushing, then Thomas Aquinas is equally acceptable. Both are equally far from Luther and Calvin" (Barth, "Church and Theology 1925" in TC, pp. 286–306 [288]). He linked the theological problems of later antiquity and the medieval period with those of the modern period throughout his career—see, for example, CD IV/3.1: pp. 18–19.

154. Unterricht I, p. 257; ET: GD, p. 211; cf. Robinson, *The Beginnings of Dialectical Theology*, p. 152.

What Barth was seeking was not first of all the solution to a modern problem, whether of knowledge or action. Such epistemological and ethical questions were real but were set within a larger ecclesial and confessional one. What he was seeking, from at least 1924 onward, was a way to set forth the prevenience of God and the inalienability of his lordship in every area of divine and human encounter, and to do so by re-claiming a living and active evangelical theology for the good of the entire church. Barth was consumed by the question of restoring a viable Protestant theology, not in active contention with Rome (as he asserted, "we have had enough of that and more than enough") but in a straightforward way in light of the fact that "the most severe distress" has come upon the church not from without but within, when the church is uncertain and unclear as to its message. What he judged was needed was a return to a theology of Scripture as instantiated in an evangelical theology in the spirit of Luther, for this is how Protestantism began. "If in the long run it desired to continue on a different basis, it would have no right to exist."[155]

The second insight into the prolegoma of the CD that is illumined in light of this historiography follows from the first, namely, why Barth was so consumed with Luther (rather than with Lessing, Kant, Hegel, or any other modern figure) in the first volume of the CD, and especially the first part-volume. In brief, Barth's extensive quotations and numerous references to Luther display his implicit but easily discerned conviction that Luther must be rehabilitated and retrieved in light of his utilization by theological programs that would claim him for a theology of conscience, experience, or existential religion, whether it be that of Wilhelm Herrmann, Karl Holl, Georg Wobbermin, or that of Barth's own contemporaries Bultmann and Tillich.[156] Barth's frequent and extensive quotations from Luther serve not only to set forth the original intentions of the Reformation, but also to demonstrate that Luther (contrary to contemporary interpretations) was one who focused on the objectivity of the Word that comes to us *extra nos* and was not simply a precursor of an experiential and existential liberal theology, much less a Germanistic theology of National Socialism.[157] In brief, Barth was wrestling Luther

---

155. Barth, "Menschenwort und Gotteswort in der christlichen Predigt 1924," p. 452; cf. CD I/2: p. 460. Brunner, upon reading CD I/1, recognized Barth's Reformation program while rejecting it: "You are heading in the direction on the *theologia perennis*, which rejects the special feature of human questions for every time; you believe that, in the twentieth century, you must also answer the questions of the sixteenth century. I, on the other hand, have turned in the direction of the kind of dogmatics which sees its service as answering the questions asked by the modern person" (quoted in Hart, *Barth vs. Brunner*, p. 127).

156. For one example of Barth's reclamation project in such polemics, see CD I/1: pp. 232-6.

157. See Heinrich Assel, "Introduction: Luther Renaissance and Dialectical Theology—A tour d'horizon 1906-1935," in *Luther, Barth, and Movements of Theological Renewal (1918-1933)*, ed. Heinrich Assel and Bruce McCormack (Berlin/Boston: Walter de Gruyter, 2020), pp. 1-16. Assel writes: "Karl Barth's critique of contemporary Lutheran theology is, in my judgment, provoked by Hirsch's, [Werner] Elert's, and Gogarten's nationalistic political self-disclosure" (ibid., p. 9).

back from what he took to be a host of misreadings and wrongful annexations, whether they be those of Holl, Hirsh, or Herrmann, and thus he was attempting to drive a wedge between Luther and his later modern interpreters. Luther, despite his problematic elements that troubled Barth, was central for establishing a contemporary Evangelical Protestant theology, for it was he who stood between the errors of the Middle Ages and modernity and provided an answer to both, as seen above. The first part volume of the CD is thus in no small way an exegetical and theological reclamation of Luther, and thus a reclamation of a proper understanding of the origins of the Protestant tradition. If Luther's reforming movement was a recovery not only of Scripture but of Augustine, Barth's own reforming project was framed in no small part as a recovery not only of Scripture but of Luther.

Finally, the historiography here outlined provides insight into why Barth may have called his dogmatics a *church* dogmatics. In addition to his assertions about the misuse of the term "Christian" famously made in the preface to CD I/1, what must also be considered are his statements that dogmatics is an exercise conducted by and within the church.[158] By the time of the CD he had cast off all remnants of theology as an enterprise of modern individualism, and his dogmatics were entirely focused upon the ecclesial and confessional task of articulating the convictions of Evangelical Protestantism against its two ecclesial and theological rivals rather than the work and result of the individual theologian's creative achievements and discoveries. This has a number of further consequences for understanding the CD.

First, in this sense, the CD is the first truly *church* dogmatics Barth wrote. In the *Christliche Dogmatik* Barth could speak of the deep uncertainty of dogmatics and portray its task in terms of the work of the modern theologian facing the crisis of inner uncertainty.[159] But by the CD (KD) such anxiety had largely disappeared, as had the individualism behind it. No longer did Barth speak of the individual theologian as presenting his or her dogmatics as the result of a solitary struggle and achievement (even if informed by the Bible and the Reformation and the modern age), and no longer did he speak of theology as a task of presenting the Christian faith as a risk and responsibility of the individual theologian and his or her existence.[160] Regardless of how the CD follows in the wake of the ChrD and does build upon it, the voice, tone, and intention of the CD, as well as its framework, reveal that the CD truly is a *church* dogmatics where the primary agents are not theologians in dialogue and conflict, but the ecclesial traditions themselves. Barth's own voice, though of course always present, is more muted in the CD beyond anything found in the earlier prolegomena of the GD or ChrD. This is to be expected in light of his conviction that the CD is not so much a singular accomplishment of his own theological journey but a presentation of the task and teaching of the church, and specifically, that of the *Evangelische Kirche* in its confluence of the Lutheran and Reformed traditions. He was attempting not so much to set forth his theology

---

158. CD I/1: p. xiii. Barth adds: "The community in and for which I have written it is that of the Church and not a community of theological endeavour" (CD I/1: p. xv).

159. ChrD, pp. 19–24.

160. ChrD, pp. 22–4.

(though of course he could do nothing less), but a theology in faithfulness to the best insights and deepest convictions of the Reformation. These central convictions are consistent throughout the CD: Evangelical theology is a theology of the gospel, of Scripture, and of the Reformation.[161] It was also a christocentric theology, though not in a way that simplistically precluded the entire range of God's triune economic movement for the world's salvation.[162] It was christocentric because this was the manner in which theology had to be faithful to Scripture and to the deepest insights of the Reformation.

In carrying out such a project in the CD, Barth was the last stellar Protestant theologian to undertake his entire theological project under the conditions of the Reformation and Tridentine Catholicism and its aftermath. He would live to see Vatican II, and the thawing that followed would entail that the polemics of Barth's project (especially in CD I/1 and I/2) can now only appear, in their sharp edges, dated and belonging to a different age. In this respect, Barth truly can be esteemed to be the last major Protestant theologian in its truest sense, for his theology was centered upon answering a question of confessional protest articulated at the Diet of Speyer, a question that was determined by the conditions of a world created by the Reformation and the Council of Trent. That world, with its anathemas, would not exist in the same way with the changes brought by Vatican II and the modern thaw of ecclesial relations, though the division, of course, remains.

Barth's dogmatic program was the last and most ambitious Protestant theological achievement that occurred *before* this ecumenical détente. In this specific sense, he was the last Protestant, i.e., the last theologian of the tradition of protest against a Roman Catholicism that had declared it anathema and heretical, but which saw itself as the truest and most faithful church. That Barth saw himself in this light is evident throughout his writings. To recognize this is the only way to make sense of his charge in the CD that Roman Catholicism and Protestant liberalism were not only mistaken theological schools with which he engaged in an academic debate, but heresies:

> I would hazard the statement, therefore, that Roman Catholicism with its church principle and modern Protestantism are counterbalancing heresies, and if I had to choose between them I am not sure whether I would not have to prefer the classical heresy to the nonclassical one. At all events we have to realize that the Reformers' protest against the church principle applies above all to ourselves and leaves us in the air. For this reason I think it advisable to stop all inveighing against Rome, or to do it with tongue in cheek if the concrete situation so demands. For a long time we shall have our hands full putting our own house in order. Much later, perhaps, we can again think of protesting against what goes on elsewhere.[163]

---

161. These convictions of the CD are later summarized in Barth's lectures given in America. See Barth, *Evangelical Theology*, p. 5.

162. CD I/2, pp. 871–2. See also note 143 above. The specific shape of this christocentrism unquestionably developed over the course of the CD, most famously with Barth's rethinking of the doctrine of election in CD II/2.

163. Unterricht I, pp. 257–8; ET: GD, p. 211.

In short, Barth was not calling for a renewed polemical age, but for a renewed call to clarify and reform Protestantism and such could not entirely exclude a pointed engagement with its only real rival, as well as its wayward stepchild.

Amid all the studies of Barth and the sources that may or may not lie behind his theological construals, what should not be lost are the central themes that were determinative for his entire theological path from the 1920s onward. For him, so much of theological labor came down to rightly construing a historical narrative, and such a narrative was as integral to his constructive work as the conceptual borrowing which aided his dogmatic labors. His theology cannot be fully understood without an appreciation of its underlying yet powerful influence to shape his entire theological trajectory.

In light of this far-ranging examination, three final concluding remarks are offered. They follow from all that has come before, and they are here provided for future reflection and consideration.

First, readings of Barth that attempt to understand him through the limited questions of his relationship to such things as socialism or idealism or any such thing cannot help but be abstract and attenuated readings of his thought, perhaps insightful in places, but distorting if taken to be the overarching or even significant framework of his theological program and existence. The same holds true for attempts to read him primarily through the lens of the distinct period of modernity (or postmodernity) with its particular questions and concerns. In contrast to all such readings, he took up the riches of the patristic and Reformation heritages because he saw himself as situated in a modern stream of thought but one flowing into and from a larger river—the full history of the Christian church. He was as preoccupied with the questions and thought of Augustine, Aquinas, Anselm, Luther, and Calvin as he was of Schleiermacher—and he was certainly more dedicated to the Reformers than any figure of his time or the prior two centuries.

Moreover, to embrace, or dismiss, Barth due to his relationship to any modern thinker, whether Kant, Hegel, or any other, will invariably abstract him from larger more important questions and not treat him as he truly was—i.e., as an evangelical, ecclesial, ecumenical, and eclectic thinker whose theology does not hinge on the merits or viability of any single philosophical or theological figure or movement. It is especially important to remember that he was from first to last a theologian— dedicated to Scripture and its exposition (he lectured not on philosophers but on books of the Bible every semester at Göttingen); committed to the Reformed and larger Protestant tradition (turning to a central study of Zwingli, Calvin, and the Reformed confessions during his first professorate and indelibly impressed by his findings there); driven to an engagement with the world of Catholicism and the church's patristic and medieval traditions, with an intensive study of Anselm, of Aquinas, and of the Catholic thought of his age while in Münster and beyond, including intensive readings not only (famously) of Erich Przywara but (less famously, though as or perhaps even more importantly) of Matthias Joseph Scheeben, Johann Adam Möhler, and Karl Adam; and thus consumed by the dogmatic task in conversation with the full wealth of the church's history (a task he began in his first professorate, continued with a new start in his second, and took up anew in his third, a task that consumed nearly all of his remaining life). An appreciation of his historiography, intentions, and theological execution opens up for consideration that the most important question for the study of Barth going forward is not the production of an even more fine-grained timeline of his life and thought or an evermore sublime distillation of his background sources, however important these may be, but a serious consideration of the content, nature, purpose, and future of the ongoing witness of Protestantism and what part Barth might play for such a witness. This is truly the most expansive and important question with which Barth leaves us, and the one that most exercised him to the end of his life.

Second, the richness of Barth's theology will be best appreciated in light of a historiography that allows his work to be seen under the aegis of his own self-description, rather than read against it. As with Scripture, it is best to take up a hermeneutics of suspicion within a more encompassing hermeneutics of trust.[164] Certainly Barth may have misstated elements of his own past and work, but it is another thing entirely to think that he had no understanding of his own project (or intentionally masked his real motivations) and that it remains for us to discover its real nature by reading him against his own explicit repeated intentions evidenced in decades of work. Such proposals discount the predominant and frequent descriptions of his own personal and professional historiography and self-understanding; they are given to "de-coding" his life as something that to all appearances and explicit evidence it was not. Whatever merits of such readings in the details, they can only be distortive and at best lose a sense of proportion in the display of their subject. At worst, they lose all sense that his theology upholds the sovereign lordship of God the Creator in freedom not against but for the freedom of the creation. If Barth and his theology are to be rejected, then they at the very least should be rejected for what they were and are, rather than what they might be contrived to be in the pursuit of academic fashion.

And finally, and most importantly, to read Barth in light of this historiography is to read him again as an ecclesial theologian, one whose center of thought was the church (which he of course states clearly at the very beginning of the CD). There is a danger that the more he is portrayed as predominantly concerned with overcoming philosophical or cultural problems, the farther he is removed from speaking to the churches. And yet, if again he is to be believed according to his own self-description, he was much more driven and consumed by pastoral and exegetical than philosophical questions, and was more occupied with the church's witness than the condition of the larger culture.[165] To give Barth the courtesy

---

164. I owe this way of framing the issue to Richard Hays' work. See Richard B. Hays, *The Conversion of the Imagination: Paul as Interpreter of Israel's Scripture* (Grand Rapids: Eerdmans, 2005), pp. 190–201.

165. In his 1922 address "The Need and Promise of Christian Proclamation," he confessed to fellow pastors in the audience: "I have been pushed by various and sundry circumstances more and more strongly toward the specific *pastoral* problem of the *sermon*, and have tried to properly find my way, as you yourselves most certainly have as well, between the problematic of human living on the one side and the content of the Bible on

of such a reading that accords with his own self-understanding is to extend to him the conditions all theological figures would hope for themselves. This is true regardless of the judgments that time may make for or against him. It is to read him as he had hoped to be read—in a line from Luther and Calvin to the confession of the church today and even more importantly as a witness to its Lord and the subject matter of Scripture. It is to treat him as a member of a theological genealogy of witnesses.[166] And witnesses are best understood not as subjects in their own right, but as pointing beyond themselves, with all of their faults, to something, Someone, that precedes and supersedes them and their witness. For this reason, such witnesses can be assessed, but they can be neither canonized nor dismissed as if at the Last Judgment.[167]

If such a perspective is adopted, one in which historical investigation gives way to theological understanding, Barth will not simply be understood as an iconoclastic figure of European religious history, but as a teacher of the church at large. He is without question a modern one, both in placement, disposition, and, of course, in terms of a number of underlying philosophical, cultural, and political convictions and conceptions that marked his thought and existence. But he is first and foremost an evangelical theologian—one marked not only by a confessional Protestant (and specifically Reformed) heritage but by a deep commitment to the *evangel*, the gospel in all its shocking and extraordinary power as the divine Good News announced to the world. Moreover, he was a church theologian from first to last. This is how he wanted to be esteemed, for theology will only be alive if joined to the church, and the church will only be healthy if it takes the importance of its theology seriously.

Barth could bemoan the "unchurchliness" [*Unkirchlichkeit*] of modern theology's methods, but he could also turn this around and state that in the end every church gets the theology it deserves, and if the church gets clear on what it wants, theology will fall into line, for such ecclesial discernment is itself a theological exercise.[168] Theology stands or falls with the church, and both stand under the Word of God.

---

the other" (WGT, p. 106; cf. pp. 107–8; pp. 121–2). It is striking that the existential crisis that Luther felt at celebrating his first mass, an element illustrative of his own larger theological struggle, was one that Barth felt in the practice of preaching, which drove his own such struggle. For both this was a question of divine judgment, justification, and promise (see ibid., p. 128). This crisis of preaching was no small part why Barth's earliest dogmatics placed the question of proclamation at its center (see GD, p. 326).

166. This may be done regardless of whether one judges Barth a major, minor, or deeply problematic, member of such a line of witnesses in the history of the church.

167. See Barth, *Protestant Theology in the Nineteenth Century*, pp. 22–3. Here Barth provides a concise articulation of his understanding of how theological thinkers of the past are to be read; he emphasizes that whatever our judgments of such theological forebears may be, they cannot be "pronouncing canonizations or settling accounts and carrying out funerals" (ibid., p. 23).

168. Barth, "Menschenwort und Gotteswort in der christlichen Predigt 1924," p. 453.

Certainly, in light of the contemporary condition of both theology and the church in Europe and the United States, despondency and even the questioning of divine providence may creep back into our minds. Yet Barth did not succumb to despair. This did not preclude his acknowledgment and acceptance of divine judgment. But he continued to confess that despite all the church's failures, and at the end of all that it can do, at the very end of its prayer, "God stands and speaks his Word and professes himself in the service of the church, which truly is his church."[169] And for this reason, Barth was a church theologian precisely because he was an evangelical one.

---

169. Ibid., p. 456.

# Part II

ECUMENICAL CONVERSATIONS BETWEEN
DISTANT DESCENDANTS OF THE REFORMATION

## Chapter 5

## KARL BARTH, CONFESSIONALISM, AND A FREE CHURCH TRADITION

In his formative first years as a professor in Göttingen from 1921 to 1925, Karl Barth became the theologian he would be for the rest of his life. While he would of course continue to mature and grow in his following posts in Münster, Bonn, and finally Basel, the footings of his final, if unfinished, theological edifice were laid in the biblical and historical labors that he would undertake in the early 1920s with a sense of both personal inadequacy and professional as well as theological urgency. It was during those years that he set himself to acquire a knowledge of the Reformation tradition, and particularly, the Reformed heritage that he was called to teach in his chair as the Honorary Professor of Reformed Theology in Göttingen. Along with seminars in the theological exposition of particular biblical books, Barth spent his first years focused upon lecture courses on such renowned Reformed figures as Zwingli, Calvin, and the paragon of the nineteenth century, Friedrich Schleiermacher.[1] In the summer term of 1923, having a number of lecture series on the Heidelberg Catechism and both Zwingli and Calvin (as well as exegetical courses on Ephesians and James) behind him, he turned to his most ambitious project to date: a course on the Reformed confessions, surveying and engaging them in their dizzying array.

Barth's lectures on the Reformed confessions display all the marks of his distinctive theological acumen: a breathtaking facility to take in a staggering range of material quickly and adroitly; a careful attentiveness to the concerns of the partisans of the past that gives equal witness to intensive engagement and a commitment to

---

1. For Barth's time in Göttingen, see Matthias Freudenberg, *Karl Barth und die reformierte Theologie: Die Auseinandersetzung mit Calvin, Zwingli, und den reformierten Bekenntnisschriften während seiner Göttinger Lehrtätigkeit* (Neukirchener-Vluyn: Neukirchener Verlag, 1997); Eberhard Busch, *Die Anfänge des Theologen Karl Barth in seinen Göttinger Jahren* (Göttingen: Vandenhoeck & Ruprecht, 1987); John Webster, *Barth's Earlier Theology* (London/New York: T&T Clark, 2005); Bruce McCormack, *Karl Barth's Critically Realistic Dialectical Theology: Its Genesis and Development 1909-1936* (Oxford: Clarendon Press, 1995); and Busch, *Karl Barth: His Life from Letters and Autobiographical Texts*, trans. John Bowden (Grand Rapids: Eerdmans, 1994), pp. 126-98. For Barth's development regarding the question of confessions, see Georg Plasger, *Die relative Autorität des Bekenntnisses bei Karl Barth* (Neukirchen-Vluyn: Neukirchener Verlag, 2000).

evenhandedness, even empathy; and a burgeoning critical discrimination of both the accomplishments and shortcomings of his Reformed forebears. Driven by the recurrent deadlines of regular class presentations, Barth's lectures move at such a pace that they are not always protected against a loss of focus or an inordinate attention to incidental details, but they are, on the whole, a remarkable accomplishment. Here he was faced with the matter of the nature, endurance, and importance of confessions—indeed, of the act of *confessing* itself. Such issues introduced Barth to a range of interrelated and extended questions, and questions that could not be divorced from, but were in fact enmeshed with, his exegetical, and really dogmatic, understandings of Scripture. Indeed, it was his concurrent discovery during this period of the Scripture principle—that the Word of God is the basis and norm of all ecclesial confession and theological reflection and that this Word is found only in Holy Scripture—that lay at the heart of his understanding of confessions and the act of confessing itself, for to confess is nothing other than to acknowledge and witness to what has been heard in Holy Scripture.[2] In this light, confessions are the formal response of the church to declare what it has heard. And so in and beyond these early years of his theological development Barth's reflection upon both the nature of confessing and the historical confessions themselves was entangled in a web of related questions. Confession stood in a matrix of relations with other dogmatic subjects, and specifically, with revelation, with Holy Scripture, and with the doctrine of the church. A large part of Barth's theological work during this early period was to discern and determine the ordered relationships pertaining to these subjects. In this regard, he arrived upon the central conviction of the superiority of Scripture over the creeds and confessions of the church. This conviction was elucidated and balanced by the recognition of the proximate and real if relative authority of such ecclesial pronouncements and decisions. Barth understood confessions as ecclesial responses to a prior divine address, and this understanding arose from and was grounded in his initial reflections on the Reformed confessions.[3] He drew from the fruit borne of these course lectures on the Reformed confessions in a public address examining the nature of doctrine and the task of confessing for the contemporary Reformed context. His reflections there continue to have relevance for today.

2. Barth articulated this principle succinctly: "*The church recognizes the rule of its proclamation solely in the Word of God and finds the Word of God solely in Holy Scripture*"— see Barth, *The Theology of the Reformed Confessions*, trans. Darrell L. Guder and Judith J. Guder (Louisville: Westminster John Knox, 2002), p. 41. The doctrine of Scripture and the doctrinal understanding of confessions for Barth were intrinsically related. See Plasger, *Die relative Autorität*, p. 31. For Barth's discovery of the Scripture principle and its significance for his theology, see ibid., pp. 36–8; Webster, *Barth's Earlier Theology*, pp. 12–13; 46–9; 57–60; 69–71; and McCormack, *Karl Barth's Critically Realistic Dialectical Theology*, pp. 304–6; 317–18.

3. Plasger describes Barth's position as between (and rejecting both) a dogmatic confessionalism and a position that eschewed the authority of confessions altogether. He notes that confessions for Barth were understood as human responses to a prior divine address, and that this conviction lay at the heart of Barth's early discovery of confessionalism: "God himself addressed humanity before humanity could speak of God" (*Die relative Autorität des Bekenntnisses bei Karl Barth*, p. 9).

## Thinking through Reformed Identity

In the summer of 1923 while working through Reformed confessions for his course, Barth was invited to give a lecture to the Reformed Alliance, a gathering of Reformed congregations and individuals in Germany. Its assembly gathered biannually in various locations and was scheduled to meet in September of 1923 in Emden, Germany. Barth accepted the invitation and produced the lecture later published as "The Substance and Task of Reformed Doctrine."[4]

Barth began this lecture by quoting an earlier report from the Reformed World Alliance that had met not long before in Zurich. The quotation that Barth recorded states:

> Any observer who has been paying attention could not come away without seeing just how tiny a role *unfruitful theological discussion* plays these days. The conference was pervaded by a heartily spiritual streak, which seized and revived in as *untheological a manner as possible* the old truths of the Reformation in their religious meaning for today; with this turn back to the old and sacred legacy, the conference allowed itself to be led by a spirit of resolute decisiveness that presses *on* and wants to test out in practice these old truths through new relations. (204: ET 200–1)

Barth added emphasis to the phrases "*unfruitful theological discussion*" (*unfruchtbare theologische Erörterungen*) and "*untheological a manner as possible*" (*möglichst untheologisch*) in the quotation. And after providing this excerpt from the report, he stated that his own paper to be given, which was to address "doctrine, theology, preaching, and proclamation," could only be a thankless task if the sentiment expressed in this quotation really represented the majority opinion of the contemporary Reformed churches.

In the light of a modern reading, Barth's address is seen to be nothing short of a civil if nevertheless quite pointed attack upon this majority sentiment. He began by providing characterizations of and possible reasons for such a sentiment, and in so doing indicted its hostility to doctrine and theological matters. First, he charged, this sentiment marginalizes doctrine for the sake of pressing pragmatic concerns of "life" such as an emphasis upon concrete church practice and the anxieties that arise from modern secularization (204–5: ET 201). Moreover, matters of doctrine are ignored because they are not considered to be conducive to church unity but to threaten it, and thus are set aside for more readily achieved agreement over issues of ecclesial strategy and tactics. Yet, such a marginalization of doctrinal questions is in actuality symptomatic of an unspoken but real dilemma, in fact *the* dilemma of the modern Protestant churches, which is that there is in fact no doctrinal

---

4. Karl Barth, "Reformierte Lehre, ihr Wesen und ihre Aufgabe" (1923), in Barth, *Vorträge und kleinere Arbeiten 1922-1925*, ed. Holger Finze (Zürich: Theologischer Verlag Zürich, 1990), pp. 202–47; also found in English translation in WGT, pp. 199–237. All references to this work will be included parenthetically within the text, with the German pages followed by those of the English translation (ET).

center to confess at all. As he concluded: "The question about proper doctrine leads us directly to the vacuum at the *center* of our churches and Christendom" (206: ET 202–3).

For Barth, this vacuum at the center betrays a crisis of identity. It is this theme that haunts his address and gives unity to the plurality of matters that he examines in turn therein. The central question is, "What does it mean to be *Reformed*?" For Barth, *this* question lies at the heart of understanding the nature of Reformed doctrine and the task of confession, and his address is a sustained attempt to force attention upon this embarrassing and ignored wound at the center of the Reformed churches. No amount of pragmatic attention to practical matters can answer this fundamental question.[5] Barth thereby turns to the most popular answers given for what it means to be Reformed and thus used to cover this wound, and he identifies and investigates three specifically. While each is significant, he in the end dispatches them all, judging each inadequate. Insofar as these answers form the backdrop for his own answer, they merit significant attention.

The first answer to the question of Reformed identity that Barth considers is one of inheritance and tribal belonging. In sum, one is Reformed, and loves the Reformed church and its tradition, precisely because that is the inheritance one has received by one's birth and upbringing. As Barth writes: "This friend loves the church like he loves his people [*Volk*], his city, and the household tools of his forefathers. He loves them *more* than others because they are precisely *his* church, just as he loves the valley of his homeland more than other valleys" (210: ET 206). This is a piety, indeed a *pietas*, of the Reformed past that loves all things Reformed precisely because they are constitutive of the religious familial, literary, liturgical, cultural, institutional, and spiritual inheritance one has received and in which one "lives and moves and has one's being."

Barth does not underestimate this answer nor lightly dismiss it. Indeed, it is marked by a significant truth that must be acknowledged. All Christian faith *must* take a particular embodiment in a distinct place and time and in a distinct tradition that spans them, just as the individual Christian must and can live *only within* a spiritual community that exists not simply in the present but that is carried along in a long-running historical stream. Any attempt to take flight from history into an abstract and universal Christianity and to transcend historical contingency and confessional particularity is, for Barth, but an illusion (211: ET 206–7).

And yet, this first answer of tradition and historical inheritance will not suffice for the gravity of the question of Reformed identity. The Reformed church will not in the end be well served, Barth contends, simply by means of a sentimental (or unsentimental) antiquarianism committed to the preservation of past artifacts and the elongation of an esteemed historical tradition for its own sake (212: ET 207). Indeed, Barth's rejection of such traditionalism rests upon the acknowledgment of the uncomfortable fact that the original Reformed answer given to the question of

---

5. As Barth challenges his hearers: "Is the suggestion to 'press on' really so practical with this unsolved question at our backs?" ("The Substance and Task of Reformed Doctrine," p. 208: ET, p. 204).

its identity is at its root and in its founding one that radically calls into question all simple appeals to tradition of any kind, and in principle, even its own. And it is here, at this point, that the Reformed church set the Scripture principle as the antithesis against all warm-hearted and romantic, or even dogmatic, appeals to the centrality and normativity of tradition. Barth writes:

> From the beginning and standing everywhere in our church there is … a fundamental denial of the entire Christian tradition when it claims to possess religious meaning in itself, when it cannot justify itself before the spirits by the Scriptures which are witnessed to as truth by the Spirit. The "given" things in history that were laid before the feet of our forefathers were not the objects of a loving and devotional reverence but rather the objects of serious and critical examination. (212: ET 207)

These words do not constitute a denial by Barth that such a traditional heritage exists for the Reformed. Had he made such an argument, it could of course be readily and rightly dismissed. His point is subtler and significantly more paradoxical, which is that, at its heart, the Reformed standpoint relativizes tradition in a radical way such that even the Reformed tradition itself cannot be the determining center of its own identity. Such a relativization of traditional and confessional norms was a hallmark of the Reformed character from its inception, and this was true for the Reformed even more so than it was for their Reformation compatriots in Lutheranism, Barth avers, witnessed in the contrasting Lutheran emphasis upon the enduring normativity and authority of the Formula of Concord and the Augustana (212–13: ET 208).

And so, against the answer of received inheritance and beloved tradition, Barth sets the Scripture principle as the constitutive center of Reformed identity. It stands not only over the spiritual, pastoral, and liturgical life of the church, but even over its confessional and doctrinal heritage. Indeed, the Reformed confessions themselves, he notes, openly admit their own defectibility and their provisional nature with the admission of the possibility of better teaching in the future. He writes:

> The Reformed church does *not*, therefore, know of any "dogma" in the strict, sacerdotal sense [Ein Dogma im strengen hieratischen Sinn kennt die reformierte Kirche also gerade *nicht*]. The *authority* of doctrine in the Reformed church in no way lies in Christian history but rather in *Scripture* and the *Spirit*, *both* of which (even the Scripture!) stand on the other side of Christian history. Remaining true to the Fathers must mean, then, adhering precisely to history the way they themselves adhered to it: letting history speak but only as an indication beyond itself to revelation, not confusing age with originality, and not confusing the authority that is given to the Church with the authority by which the Church was founded. (213: ET 208)

With an allusion to the legend of William Tell, Barth argues that such a commitment to the sole authority of Scripture and the Spirit "does not bow down before any hat propped on a stick, even if it is the hat of Calvin himself" (213–14: ET 208–9). The real esteem the Reformed have for the past is therefore also relative and qualified, for both this past and the esteem for it are both open to a critical second look (214: ET 209).

Barth next turns to the second answer given to the question of why persons identify as Reformed. He summarizes this answer as that of "friends of a certain type of eclecticism when taking up characteristic ideas, tendencies, and institutions for the Reformed past and present" (214: ET 209). We might designate this answer as a kind of resonant idealism, an embrace of a tradition for the affinity one shares with its archetypical ideas, beliefs, convictions, and practices. Barth provides the example of one who embraces the relativization of all human ideals, such as justice, under the Reformed emphasis upon God's singular glory (214: ET 209). Or the opposite might be the case, providing an alternative example— one might embrace the historic Reformed emphasis upon human order and "a sharply pronounced individual and social ethos" (214: ET 209). Yet another example, different than each of these, might be an appreciation for the humanistic and intellectual achievements of the Reformed tradition, including an affinity for its harmonization with modernizing tendencies. Or maybe an embrace of the Reformed tradition is predicated upon nothing more than a simple affinity for its presbyterian polity or its austere liturgy. Such examples can of course be multiplied (see 214–16: ET 209–11).

Barth concedes that this second answer of principled resonance and idealism is a more sophisticated and indeed more worthy answer than the first, that of pure loyalty to one's religious inheritance. It displays a deeper appreciation of the question, for it is an embrace of the Reformed identity not "by birth but by conviction" (… so ein nicht nur geborenes, sondern überzeugtes Glied seiner Kirche zu werden) (216: ET 211). And as with the first answer, he does not lightly brush this second one aside but gives it its proper due. Certainly, there are many commendable achievements, ideals, and elements of the Reformed tradition that might provide and indeed warrant such an appreciation and embrace of its identity. Yet, the very plurality of such answers for claiming oneself as Reformed displays the weakness of such eclecticism, Barth contends. He presses the point:

> A church does not live from truths, even if they are numerous, profound, and alive. Rather, it lives from *the* one truth which cannot be conceived like any other teaching or conviction. Yet we *must* conceive of it, because this truth has *itself first* grasped the human and therefore has established the church. One can only 'be' Reformed for *this* reason and not for any other. (216: ET 211)

Once again, there may indeed be many compelling and commendable elements that have marked the Reformed tradition from its beginning, and the variety of these elements have been embraced by a variety of persons, all of whom may identify as Reformed though in reality do so for very different reasons. Such diversity reaches back to the differences between Zwingli and Calvin themselves, and it has been a constant accompaniment to the Reformed tradition through time. But while this may be a mark of the tradition, it again was not its *source*. Such a clear discrimination between characteristic and source, between trait and origin, as with Barth's earlier judgment of discernment between the authority that is given to the church and that which founds it, lies behind his incisive judgment regarding this second answer: "In any case, the Reformed church did *not* come into being in such a manner. Its beginning was not this pantheon of ideals but rather a site of the worship of the *one* God. Fire from *one* altar was originally the light of them all, in which one thought he saw the light here and then there" (217: ET 211).

What Barth is doing here should not be confused with a relegation of other doctrines to the periphery in light of a single central doctrine, such as in Lutheranism where justification served in this way.[6] What he is doing is again more understated and yet much more radical. It is the relativization of *all* doctrines in light of the object that grounds them all. More directly, he maintains that to be Reformed is to distinguish between the God that is revealed through his Word and Spirit and all things that witness to this God. It is precisely the commitment to making this distinction which stands at the heart of the Reformed faith and that then gives rise to all of the convictions and doctrines that in turn gesture toward this revelation which is itself not an idea, principle, or doctrine (217: ET 212). Against such eclecticism, he sets an answer of unity, and a unity very specifically defined.[7] At the center of Reformed identity is an inalienable commitment to distinguish *the* one thing that stands over and apart from all other things, no matter how good these things might be. The Reformed, Barth contends,

> do not set everything on the card of *one doctrine*, but rather in a theologically less elaborate and impressive manner they content themselves with the relationship of every doctrine to the one object, leaving it to God, not to their *thoughts about God*, but to God's *own* being, God *alone*, in God's proclaimed *Word* through the Scripture and Spirit, to be *the* truth. (217: ET 212)

---

6. This emphasis began with Luther himself. Bernhard Lohse states: "There is no doubt that the heart and soul of Luther's Reformation theology is the article on justification" (Lohse, *Martin Luther's Theology: Its Historical and Systematic Development*, trans. Roy A. Harrisville (Minneapolis: Fortress Press, 1999), p. 258. He continues later: "It was the first time in all of the history of theology and dogma that the decisive truth of Christian faith was concentrated in such fashion on one specific article" (ibid., p. 259). For a different reading of Luther's understanding of the doctrine of justification, see Gerhard Ebeling, *Luther: An Introduction to His Thought*, trans. R. A. Wilson (Philadelphia: Fortress, 1970), pp. 111–13. He states that Luther's emphasis upon justification was not a matter of preference for one doctrine but that which rightly gave a proper regard to all: "The proper function of the doctrine of justification is that of giving a true significance to all other doctrines" (ibid., 113). For an insightful discussion of the very notion of a doctrinal center in Barth's mature theology (as well as in Luther), see S. W. Sykes, "Barth on the Centre of Theology," in *Karl Barth: Studies in His Theological Method*, ed. S. W. Sykes (Oxford: Clarendon Press, 1979), pp. 17–54.

7. Barth notes that all of the conceptions may themselves become idols, even, he insists, the command "*Deo soli gloria*" ("The Substance and Task of Reformed Doctrine," p. 217: ET p. 212).

And then Barth drops a bombshell that no doubt must have puzzled his already shell-shocked audience: "It is God's Word, which, when necessary, stands *against* all our ideals" (218: ET 212).[8] Here Barth turns over all the Reformed apple carts of the second answer. To be Reformed, he argues, is not a commitment to various Reformed ideals, but rather a conviction that one cannot in fact define Reformed identity according to particular principles. This is so precisely because the heart of Reformed identity is not the freely chosen establishment of ideals but rather the acknowledgment that one is not free but bound to something higher than any ideal, and that all ideals must themselves stand under a higher judgment. The reformed confession is thereby not composed of a plurality of doctrines but rather rests upon a singular acknowledgment of an objectivity that has gripped us, a divine act of revelation that cannot be confused with, even as it establishes, all doctrines in its wake.

Barth's term for this objectivity is *Sachlichkeit*—a term that no English word can fully capture, yet one whose appreciation is absolutely central to capturing Barth's thought. It is this objectivity that stands over against us and to which all confessions and doctrines testify. The *ultimate* goal of Reformed doctrine is thus not simply accurate doctrinal description (as important as that may be), but the subordination of doctrine itself to an acknowledgment of this *one thing*. Perhaps better put, it is the acknowledgment of the one God who has spoken, and in turn submission to "the necessity of saying subsequently and humanly the one thing that has first been said to the human" (218: ET 213).

In sum, Barth's response to the second answer of plural eclecticism is an adamant avowal that what makes the Reformed what they are is *not* the embrace of many things, no matter how central or meritorious, but the acknowledgment of one thing—that they have heard a word from God that requires in turn its own human confession. Such thoughts had been germinating in Barth's mind for some time. Already in 1915 he could tell a Reformed Synod of the Aargau that the problem under which they suffered was that "we do not take God seriously" (wir nehmen *Gott* nicht ernst) and that "Our confession is a sham."[9] Now, however, Barth had accumulated richer dogmatic and historical resources from which to draw to give form and structure to such earlier inchoate thoughts, in effect critically judging the Reformed churches with their own inheritance. Such thoughts would find their richest expression in the *Church Dogmatics*.

Barth now turns to the third and final answer given for what it means to call oneself Reformed. This final answer is in his estimation the quintessentially modern one, and the one he takes to be the most prevalent in the current situation in which the Reformed find themselves. This third alternative might be described

---

8. This idea is set within a larger context within the original German: "Nicht das Wohlgefallen, das *wir* an gewissen Wahrheitsmomenten gefunden, sondern eine im *Objekt* und exklusiv *durch* das Objekt begründete Erkenntnis der *einen* Wahrheit, Gottes Wort wenn's not tut *gegen* alle unsre Ideale müßte uns zu Reformierten machen" (p. 218).

9. Karl Barth, "Antrag betreffend Abschaffung des Synodalgottesdienstes" (1915), in Barth, *Vorträge und kleinere Arbeiten 1914–1921*, ed. Friedrich-Wilhelm Marquardt and Hans-Anton Drewes (Zürich: Theologischer Verlag Zürich, 2012), pp. 164–76 (172).

as one of religious experience and of religious personalities—the answer, he declares, held by those whose "catchphrase is 'piety' [*Frömmigkeit*]" (218: ET 213). With this third answer, Barth turns from the prior two of sentimentalism and idealism, respectively, to one that reflects the heart of the religiosity of the nineteenth century. If this answer is less capable of careful or ready definition than the prior two, it is nonetheless the more relevant for understanding the persuasion of many in Barth's audience. Persons who are best described with this third answer are those who have embraced religion as a quality of piety and a particular kind of inner experience that finds its highest expression in the person of religious genius possessing a particularly subtle and refined religious sensitivity. In its less sophisticated though common form, this type of identification is simply a kind of hero worship, and for the Reformed, as Barth notes, such a form of affection is focused particularly on Calvin (see 218-19: ET 213).

While admitting the truly significant and even singular role such persons may play historically in understanding the Reformed heritage and identity, Barth nevertheless finds this third answer as problematic as those previously given. He begins by noting that it was the Lutherans who consistently invoked the name of their founder as an authority, but that this kind of appeal to an individual, no matter how revered as a founder, was not the way of the Reformed. Reformed church persons not only did not call upon the names of their founders in their confessions or appeal to their authority, but also even allowed Zwingli and Calvin to "disappear behind the matter [hinter der Sache]" (220: ET 214).[10] And so not only are the details of Calvin's conversion lost to history, but even his grave has fallen into oblivion. That the Reformed of today in Germany and Switzerland are resurrecting and celebrating a "Reformed cult of heroes" with such seriousness is

10. The German original states: "Es hat seinen Grund, daß die Bekenntnisschriften unsrer Kirchen in starkem Kontrast zur Konkordienformel von der Möglichkeit, sich auf Zwingli oder Calvin zu berufen, durchweg *keinen* Gebrauch machen, sondern auch diese Personen gänzlich verschwinden lassen hinter der Sache … " (p. 220). Like *Sachlichkeit*, *Sache* is a notoriously difficult term to translate, often done so with the phrase, "subject matter" or "object." For Barth's use of this term with particular reference to the theology of his commentary on Romans and this period under discussion, see Richard Burnett, *Karl Barth's Theological Exegesis: The Hermeneutical Principles of the* Römerbrief *Period* (Grand Rapids: Eerdmans, 2001), pp. 74-8. Recognizing that there is no English equivalent for this term, Burnett writes that "while it is clear that by using the term *Sache* to describe the Bible's content Barth wishes to indicate 'something' which is objectively real, it is also clear he is not referring to an empirical object, a *datum*. God is the 'object' of the Bible only to the extent that He is a Subject who must give himself to us as object if He is to be known. The *Sache* of the Bible is not therefore an object which gives itself to us without reservation or qualification such that it is ever 'at our disposal' as it were. He is an object which always remains Subject even as He gives Himself as object" (p. 75). He notes that Barth can also describe *die Sache* as "a dialectical relation between a specific, holy, transcendent God and a specific human creature" (p. 76). All of this theological freight is carried into the essay under discussion and lies in the background of Barth's use of such terms.

the ultimate irony, Barth asserts, for this is happening precisely at the time when they have become so unsure and "insecure about Reformed *substance* [*Sache*]" (220: ET 214).[11]

This shift in focus demonstrates just how different in mindset are the descendants from their ancestors. What would Calvin himself think of such attention, Barth asks with some sarcasm? In contrast, how *should* one truly revere such Reformed forebears? Here again Barth's answer to the question is not without high irony. One pays them the proper respect precisely by *not* revering them, but by revering what they in fact revered. What makes one a faithful disciple not only of Calvin but also of the Reformed tradition is not the adulation of Calvin (or anyone else) as a remarkable "religious personality," but the taking up of their mantle as a witness that points away from them and from ourselves to the God that is rightly revered. For the Reformed, Barth asserts, "The human does not come into consideration, not even as a prophet, never mind as a Christian hero but rather as a minister, as a *servant* of the divine Word" (221: ET 215). What makes one Reformed is therefore not a matter of piety or even religious genius but obedience, and again, this is a very *particular* obedience, namely, a service of indication that hears and sets forth the Word of God. The difference between a hero and a witness for Barth is here displayed as akin to and may in fact draw upon the difference that Kierkegaard delineated between a genius and an apostle.[12] There is, for the Reformed faith, no place for the emulation of heroes, which in fact leads to Barth's own highly ironic and dialectical emulation when he states:

> The greatness of the founders consisted precisely in the fact that they saw in the highest concreteness the barrier that lay in the way of all human greatness, especially their own; that they were so *little* occupied with themselves; that their confessions did not want to be presentations of what were nevertheless considerable inner experiences but rather something quite different, namely, 'conceptual testimonies of inner faith' [*testificationes conceptae intus fidei*]. (221-2: ET 215)

And it is this greatness of the *discovery*, and not of the discoverer himself or herself, that is to be revered. Barth concludes by putting forth a corrective and a way forward:

> Is there a better way to venerate and follow Calvin besides placing ourselves where he stood, namely, as those called to be obedient to the law? And if we no longer know the Christian meaning of obedience, calling, and law we ought

---

11. The double meaning of *Sache* in these sentences used both as the "subject matter" of revelation and as the "substance" of Reformed identity is of course lost in the English translation.

12. Søren Kierkegaard, "The Difference between a Genius and an Apostle," in Kierkegaard, *The Book on Adler*, ed. and trans. Howard V. Hong and Edna H. Hong (Princeton: Princeton University Press, 1998), pp. 173-88.

to continue asking until we know it again, without wasting time or energy in adoring or even imitating Calvin. (222: ET 216)[13]

In short, what we are to do, Barth tells his audience, is not to revere the Reformed founders or to try to return to their time. What we are to do is to become founders *ourselves* for our own time, in our time, by recovering and considering the astonished acknowledgment which they gave before an objectivity, a law, a concreteness that serves as a barrier against a focus upon their own personhood and greatness or that of ourselves. And if we were to confess that which they confessed, we would give them the honor of being the heroes that they can in fact never be as *personalities* but only as the *witnesses* that they were intended to be and in fact were, pointing ever away from themselves to the object of their astonishment:

> Then they would fulfill the mission which they will always have for us as individuals, as personalities, as heroes. If we were then thrown back onto ourselves from every historical role model, and if we would stand before the same barrier like the founders did—that which we would still risk confessing would then somehow ... be able to be called "Reformed doctrine." (222: ET 216)

Barth thus sets against a cult of personalities or religious piety a perspective that honors theological forebears as witnesses but not as ends in themselves, thus tracing the movement of their pointing arm to that of which they themselves stand in awe, that which transcends the self and all other selves, no matter how esteemed. As Barth challenges his listeners, to stand faithfully in the Reformed tradition is not to adore its founders but to adore what its founders adored and to serve what its founders served. Such service is nothing other than that service rendered as ministers of the Word of God who hear the voice of God in Scripture and confess it in turn in human speech. Such rapt attention to the Word of God does not negate such things as a distinctive Reformed piety, character, or mood, but it does place these in their rightful secondary place at the periphery of the

---

13. The original states: "Gibt es eine andere Verehrung und Nachfolge Calvins als die, die darin besteht, sich selbst dorthin zu stellen, wo Calvin stand: in den Gehorsam des Berufenen gegenüber dem Gesetz, und wenn wir etwa nicht mehr wissen sollten, was *Gehorsam, Berufung, Gesetz* christlich verstanden sein möchte, danach zu fragen, bis wir es auch wieder wissen, jedenfalls aber mit Calvinbewundern oder gar Calvinspielen keine Zeit und Kraft zu verlieren?" (p. 222). Barth's thoughts along these lines never wavered during the following decades of his life, witnessed in his similar comments upon the commemoration of the 400th anniversary of Calvin's death—Karl Barth, "Zum 400. Todestag Calvins," *Evangelische Theologie* 24 (1964), pp. 225–9; translated in English as "Thoughts on the 400th Anniversary of Calvin's Death," in Barth, *Fragments Grave and Gay*, ed. Martin Rumscheidt, trans. Eric Mosbacher (London: Collins, 1971), pp. 105–10. On such issues as the right and proper regard for the Reformers and the dangers of hero worship, these two pieces, separated by four decades, are entirely consonant.

question of identity. Such a view sees confessionalism not so much as a recovery or maintenance of the past confessions or even subscription to them, but as the recovery of their originating *act*.[14] In sum, what Barth sets against the adoration of historical heroes is the adoration of God alone, and this adoration takes concrete form in the obedience of faith that itself is fulfilled in the service of the Word of Holy Scripture.

As Barth construes this response and alternative to the third answer, the characterization of this faithfulness to the fathers once again finds its highest expression in the Scripture principle (223: ET 216–17). Scripture as the divinely appropriated medium of God's Word and instrument of his Spirit is thus the locus of God's revelation to the church and in turn the rule and norm of its faith and obedience. This acknowledgment, an acknowledgment that is not itself a particular dogma but in reality the source, foundation, and critical test of all dogmas, is, Barth contends, what is most properly called "Reformed doctrine" (223: ET 217). Such doctrine is nothing less than the crisis of those who have been addressed, judged, condemned, justified, refined, and purified by the Word of God in Holy Scripture. True, when they answer this Word and in turn confess it, their words are not a divine Word, but a human word. Yet because they have been so addressed, such human speech corresponds to the divine pronouncement and issues in proper doctrine and rightful confession. Such doctrine is a "legitimate, pure, 'predicate of the divine word'" (223: ET 217). It thus possesses a true and real, if relative, authority.[15]

Barth therefore has set three critical responses over against the most common proposals for understanding Reformed identity and has problematized them all. Behind the sentimentality and tribal identity of the past, the eclecticism of an idealism of concepts and principles personally embraced, and the religious experience of the self and of heroic personalities from long ago, lies not only something more fundamental, but something that fundamentally calls all of them into question. What he puts forward in their place is in essence but one answer. Behind all of the responses he has provided is a single theme, namely, that to be Reformed is to succumb to and render an acknowledgment that God has spoken a divine Word that has been heard in Scripture and a commitment to confess this revelation and to test all by it. Such is a doctrinal commitment that is not so much a doctrine but an act of confession and obedience, a standpoint that

---

14. Webster, commenting on Barth's lectures on the Reformed confessions, notes that according to Barth's reading the "unifying centre of the Reformed churches is not a public confession but the constant process of attending to Holy Scripture," a comment that illuminates the point that Barth is here making (*Barth's Earlier Theology*, p. 45).

15. "Barth steers a rather wary line, therefore, between a theology free from the church's confession and a theology which is slavishly confessional …. As Barth's work develops, however, he becomes increasingly convinced that to deny final authority to confessions does not mean that theology may float free from the confessing life of the community" (Webster, *Barth's Earlier Theology*, p. 61). See also note 3 above.

recognizes nothing on which to stand but the Word of God alone as it has come to us in Holy Scripture.[16]

Barth's conclusion is the same as his solution: the Reformed church needs to recover the original meaning of its name.[17] What Reformed doctrine needs, he asserts, is

> the knowledge of the Word of God from the Scripture and the Spirit, "born" with the natural violence of a volcanic outbreak, from the one-time unity of the Reformed church. Reformed "*through the Word of God*": This is the original and proper meaning of the name we carry. What does "a turn back to the old and sacred legacy" of the Reformation mean if in its reflection it does *not insist* on *this* sense of our name? (227–8: ET 220–1)

Without a recovery of this meaning, Barth asserts, all attempts to define what it means to be Reformed are ultimately insignificant. Without a recovery of this original genesis of the Reformed, all other attempts to speak of the doctrinal content of the Reformed church are evasive of that which is most basic and on which agreement must come before agreement on any other matter can be achieved (228: ET 221).

Barth's lecture ends addressing internecine quarrels with the Lutheran tradition. Such matters appear anticlimactic and somewhat betray the power of the lecture at its heart. Yet at the very end, Barth returns to the question of Reformed identity with the wistfulness of a churchman looking back to a tradition that somewhere had lost its center for matters on the periphery, one that had replaced its essential discovery for secondary and derivative matters that betrayed the founders and fathers even as it sought to honor them. Reformed doctrine will be for now, Barth sadly concludes in the end, "a torso–less–a silhouette [*Schemen*]" (247: ET 237). All that remains for us is to call upon the Spirit to reanimate the field of dry bones as it blows where it wills. It is in this cry for the Spirit where "we will meet up with the Fathers, whose legacy we have not yet earned fully enough to own" (247: ET 237).

---

16. Such calls to mind Barth's earlier related statement in 1922 that "when I look at it closely, what I might conceivably call 'my theology' consists of a single point, and not even a *standpoint*, which would be the minimum demanded of a proper theology, but rather only a *mathematical* point that one cannot stand upon. It is a mere *view*point. I have barely made a start with proper theology, and I don't know if I will ever get beyond it, indeed, if I even desire to get beyond it." See Barth, "The Need and Promise of Christian Proclamation," in WGT, pp. 101–29 (103). That Barth did in fact move beyond such minimalism was in no small way due to the fact that he became an ecclesial and confessional theologian.

17. "The question of 'Where to?' is finally identical to that of 'Where from'?" (Barth, "The Substance and Task of Reformed Doctrine," p. 228: ET p. 221).

## *From the Past to the Present, from One Confession to Another*

Apart from its historical interest as a window into Barth's theological development, his essay crosses the parameters of its original context and speaks into our own. While his concern was to examine the nature of an enduring Reformed substance under and beyond its more readily grasped qualities, the conclusions he reaches are not restricted within confessional boundaries, for the question of identity continues to haunt Protestants at large and all Reformation descendants. Baptists in particular have become consumed with such questions in recent decades. All three answers Barth addressed have in fact played a large role in Baptist discussion and have themselves been dominant Baptist responses to question of the irreducible and distinctive character of Baptist identity.[18]

For some, to be Baptist is ultimately a matter of antiquarian and sentimental loyalties, often tied to questions of familial and cultural legacy, regionalism, and an inheritance that shape a personal story or even temperament. To be Baptist is to embrace a heritage (or perhaps to exhibit a nonconformist bent). One should not underestimate the emotional force and real power of such a response. Yet such an answer can at best be a silhouette, or shadow, of what is needed. All of Barth's criticisms of such an answer directly translate from one confessional tradition to another, and thus to Baptist answers along such a line.[19]

Most often, the question of "Why I Am a Baptist" is answered with the resonance one feels for certain Baptist principles, axioms, tenets, or convictions.[20] This is, as Barth noted, a much more significant answer. Such convictions, which

---

18. This is particularly true for Baptists in North America, the focus of the following comments.

19. In words reminiscent of Barth and which have been echoed by many writers since, Walter Rauschenbusch noted that Baptists may begin as Baptists by birth (itself a questionable assumption) but must become in time Baptists by conviction—see Rauschenbusch, "Why I Am a Baptist" in *Christian Ethics Today* V.1.1 (April 1995), pp. 20–31 (20).

20. This second answer of Barth's essay predominates recent collections of responses to the question of Baptist identity, though the first and third of these answers are also prevalent. See, for instance, the essays in the collection edited by Cecil P. Staton, *Why I Am a Baptist: Reflections on Being Baptist in the 21st Century* (Macon: Smyth & Helwys, 1999). While one should not expect too much of such a format of personal responses, the essay by Brian Haymes is a marked exception to the others nevertheless. Instead of grounding the freedom of the soul in an inherent dignity or competency within the individual as so often witnessed in the other essays, Haymes grounds it as a corollary of the freedom and sovereignty of Christ, and thus in christology rather than anthropology: "If Jesus Christ is the one to whom absolute authority in heaven and on earth has been given, then all other claims to authority are relativized" (p. 68). Even freedom itself, so sacred to Baptists, is a secondary rather than primary conviction that Haymes refuses to idolize: "The gospel paradox to which Baptists have borne a sometimes costly witness is that only the sovereignty of the Christlike God can safeguard the freedom of the people …. I am glad of the Baptist stand for freedom, not as an absolute in itself but as the gift of the liberating God" (p. 68). Haymes article stands

can be multiplied not only by four but by forty or more, might include such things as soul freedom, the necessity of personal conversion, believer's baptism, congregational polity, church and state separation, or even the unique combination of them Baptists possess. All might be worthy of commitment and conviction, but again, such plurality, displayed in the eclecticism of their adoption and ranking, once again betrays the problematic reality that such things are often stood up

apart from the others in its keen understanding of the ordered relation between God and the creature as well as that between the singularity of the work of Christ and the church's witness to it. It exhibits a rare ability to transcend the weaknesses of the three answers Barth considers for a richer one such that ecclesiological distinctives are rooted in prior and more encompassing theological and christological convictions. Haymes also singularly displays a robust understanding of the purpose and nature of Baptist confessions and, like the author of the first epistle of John, refuses to pitch doctrinal and relational concerns, or matters of truth and experience, against one another in understanding the church, seeing both as necessary (see pp. 68-9). That Haymes was one of only two non-Americans included in this collection (and thus not defined by pitched Baptist battles North or South) may or may not be incidental but is an interesting fact regardless. At the very least, classical trinitarian, christological, and gospel-centered concerns rather than polemical ones drive his essay. In this regard, the collection of the same title edited by Tom J. Nettles and Russell Moore ironically suffers the same fate as the prior collection, though coming from a seemingly opposed standpoint—see *Why I Am a Baptist* (Nashville: Broadman & Holman, 2001). While aware of the problems noted above and intentionally attempting to overcome them with a more doctrinal emphasis in defining Baptist identity, the problem of eclecticism lingers. More seriously still, an undue accent upon such modern concerns as "inerrancy in the original autographs," itself obliquely and quietly undermined by the historic Baptist confessions and statements provided in the collection that show no such awareness (e.g., pp. 28 and 48), demonstrates a shift from the Scripture principle to a theory *about* Scripture. Such confusion in distinguishing between a confession regarding Scripture and a modern theory of bibliology in the end does not undergird but undermines the possibility of the distinction between the authority of Scripture and that of tradition and sets such tradition beyond the scope of critical examination. Such a failure to distinguish between a reverence before the Spirit's Word in Scripture whose truth is self-authenticated through the internal testimony of the same Spirit and a defense of the Bible and particularly of the qualities of texts now lost to history subtly if unintentionally shifts the grounds of faith from the Spirit's work to the results of textual criticism (p. 147). Thus confession gives way to apologetics in which the truth of Scripture is now a matter of human defense in a land of a thousand qualifications and strained harmonizations, and where unnuanced articulation of the divinity of the text *qua* text can in the end provide no clear reason why God is worshiped but Scripture itself is not. The conclusion to be drawn is that the answer to no confession is thus not bad confessionalism, nor is the answer to bad confessionalism no confessionalism at all. Both in the end confuse the periphery for the center, however differently they may do so, leading to heated battles, but poor alternatives.

like tin soldiers in a row with no sense of their intrinsic connection, and worse, no sense of their ordered relation to more central theological concerns such as theology proper, christology, pneumatology, and soteriology.[21] Avoiding such a thin eclecticism is the perennial challenge of a tradition that sees the centrality of its distinctiveness displayed in an ecclesiology rather than in a theological discovery. A rebuttal might be that Baptist theological convictions of God and Christ and Spirit are shared within the larger Christian and Protestant family and it is the particular emphases that give Baptists their identity and thus are so often highlighted. But an accent upon such particular principles can, it might be proffered in return, correspond to a neglect of the larger theological framework and provide the former principles with an importance and independence that lead to a loss of what is in fact central. It may also result in the faulty translation of such convictions into non-theological and thus foreign conceptual languages.

Therefore, it certainly must be admitted that the reason Baptists are a particular type of ecclesial people within the larger framework of those dedicated to the Scripture principle is in no small part due to specific secondary convictions regarding baptism, soul freedom, and so forth. But what must be recovered is that these are in fact secondary convictions that stand under one singular and primary one. When these convictions themselves become primary, we can only be left with an identity that is grounded upon general principles of ecclesial or social order and polity and those of individual competency, dignity, and protection from civil rule. Such principles, furthermore, are only further impoverished when

---

21. As but one example, the famous four "fragile freedoms" may be presented as apparently equal convictions of Baptist life. See Walter Shurden, *The Baptist Identity: Four Fragile Freedoms* (Macon: Smyth & Helwys, 1993). Shurden insightfully notes that the authority of Scripture cannot be separated from the authority of Christ. But what is not sufficiently clarified is that the latter three rely entirely upon the first and do not stand on the same plane, for it is the freedom of God, expressed through the particularity of God's revelation in Christ attested in Scripture, that is the ground, source, and that which in turn determines and defines human freedom. When this is forgotten, not only might the latter three be seen to stand independently of the first, but they may also take on a significance outside of their proportion and in turn become malformed. A rightful ordering of the latter three in light of both the formal and material determination of the first is decisive, for the first is the guard, and the only real guard, that stands at the door preventing freedom from devolving into pure license. Here again Barth was prophetic. When asked in an interview with *Newsweek* in 1962 regarding his thoughts regarding the malaise of contemporary Protestantism, he responded: "How shall I formulate it? The true thing in the original Protestantism was God's word to man, and then man's response to it. Modern Protestantism has lost its character as a response. If Protestantism is only a fight for individual liberties—freedom of the soul—then its cause is lost. Man is left alone with himself." See Barth, *Gespräche 1959–1962*, ed. Eberhard Busch, Anton Drewes, and Hinrich Stoevesandt (Zürich: Theologischer Verlag Zürich, 1995), pp. 446–7. The same of course could be said of ecclesial and religious freedom. For a further discussion of related themes, see Kimlyn J. Bender, *Confessing Christ for Church and World* (Downers Grove: IVP, 2014), pp. 243–69.

they are translated and articulated in the foreign speech of intrinsic rights and "private judgment."[22] In short, what remains are principles and axioms that are rooted in the human response rather than the divine initiative in the history of God's redemption, or worse, as intrinsic entitlements and capacities of the human person within the Enlightenment narrative of a natural theology and religion. Such are particularly open to perversion precisely due to their lack of setting, determination, and definition within a larger biblical and theological exposition of the divine economy of salvation and therefore the gospel. Freedom then comes to resemble little more than modern (Kantian) versions of autonomy and (Lockean) notions of religious independence from civil control, all expressed in the parlance of individual liberties expressed as rights.

It may appear strange but it is no less true that placing these Baptist distinctives in a much larger doctrinal tapestry in which they take a subordinate and peripheral place in relation to the theological center is in fact the best means for their preservation. They are thus protected precisely insofar as they are seen as secondary implications of the gospel rather than as primary doctrines, and it is in fact this placement that not only safeguards their rightful sense of order and proportion but also ensures their proper definition and integrity. Furthermore, they themselves may need to be reexamined, deconstructed, and re-articulated in light of Scripture and its theological implications.[23] In short, they may be rightly regarded and paradoxically retain their power as witnesses when they come to be not the focus, but the corollaries, of ecclesiology. And ecclesiology itself in turn must be the corollary rather than the focus of the church's task of proclamation and confession of the gospel of Jesus Christ, for the church does not proclaim itself, but Jesus Christ as Lord (2 Cor. 4:5).

22. John Webster, in noting the inadequacy of Charles Hodge's emphasis upon the "right of private judgement" as the proper explication of the clarity of Scripture (*claritas scripturae*) writes: "This is surely the wrong idiom for an account of the operations of Scripture. First, it assumes that office or tradition in the church are always instruments of suppression, and never act as guides; second, it thinks of the fellowship of the saints by analogy from the civil realm (as an aggregate of individual bundles of rights and judgements); third, 'judgement' is an odd description of the fear and trembling which the faithful have before the Word. And, most of all, the whole account is curiously deistic in its lack of language about the activity of God." See Webster, *Confessing God: Essays in Christian Dogmatics II* (London/New York: T&T Clark, 2005), pp. 53-4. The irony that the "right of private judgement" seems to be a central guiding principle for understanding the clarity of Scripture according to one of the fathers of a view of Scripture consonant with that of fundamentalism should not be lost, nor should the fact that what is often touted as a Baptist marker fits seamlessly into nineteenth-century Princeton Calvinism. Webster's critical questions to Hodge translate quite directly as challenges to Baptist conceptions of Scripture and its reception.

23. And this must hold for "soul competency" as well as for "inerrancy in the original autographs"—if, in truth, there are no sacerdotal dogmas in Baptist life. The Scripture principle is, without question, a refining fire that tests all and may purify all, but some dross will not survive.

We might take some comfort that Baptists have less often given the third answer. The Baptist cult of heroes is rather modest. Baptists tip their hats to the likes of John Smyth, John Clarke, Lottie Moon, Andrew Fuller, William Carey, and Roger Williams, among numerous others, but none with the reverence given by some in other traditions to a Luther or even a Calvin. And yet, Barth's response to this third answer might trouble us as much as the first two, for his questions seem to maintain their edge across years and confessional lines. A denominational tradition that does not have a theological center can only fall into forms of sentimentalism, eclecticism, or, in this third instance, into an admiration of past subjects. And it might be legitimately asked if Baptists are in fact protected from the latter simply because they do not bow down to any hat on a stick, whether it be Luther or Calvin or even Smyth or Bunyan, Fuller or Williams, when in reality they quietly and sometimes even proudly bow before the hat upon their own head.[24] One need not have a cult of heroes to fall prey secretly even if innocently and unconsciously to a cult of the individual whose salvation is secure and whose soul is competent.

Barth was aware that the crucial loss of the distinction between Scripture and church, a distinction that for him lay behind the entire Reformation discovery, could be lost not only in a Catholicism where Scripture was subsumed into the interpretation and tradition of the church under an infallible magisterium. It could also occur where tradition and interpretation, and the church itself, were subsumed into the solitary individual. Years after his address to the Reformed Alliance in 1923, when contrasting these views in the *Church Dogmatics*, he could relate that the loss of this crucial distinction between Scripture and church, and thus the distinction between the voice of the Lord and the voice of his servants, is even more clearly evidenced in such subjectivity than in the elevation of a papacy:

> Does it make any basic difference if this Christian thinker is not the pope and does not have a pope over him to decide authoritatively the extent of this perceiving and overcoming? Is not the nature of the basic view more clearly exposed, perhaps, if every man is called upon to be his own pope in virtue of the spirit that is alive within him as a member of the Christian community?[25]

Against such a religiosity and the domestication of the Word of God in these two forms Barth set forth a recovery of confessional practice grounded in a vigilant and attentive deference to Holy Scripture. Such confessionalism for Barth was not the attempt to recover the confessions for their own sake or to treat them as timeless and infallible—his was not a creedal fundamentalism. Such confessionalism

---

24. No person before or since has put this point as incisively and poignantly as Winthrop Hudson: "The practical effect of the stress upon 'soul competency' as the cardinal doctrine of Baptists was to make every man's hat his own church." See Hudson, "Shifting Patterns of Church Order," in *Baptist Concepts of the Church*, ed. Winthrop Hudson (Philadelphia: Judson Press, 1959), p. 216.

25. CD I/1: p. 258.

was not the slavish rigidity of adherence to past ecclesial statements or the "repristination of the steady certainties of orthodoxy."[26] It was, rather, a recovery of the truth that confession is but the public pronouncement of what has been heard in Holy Scripture. It was the recognition that confession is therefore a response to a Word spoken *extra nos* to the church and that its proper subject was the church first and the individual believer second. Confession is at its heart the acknowledgment that a barrier has been placed such that loyalty (no matter how noble), distinctives (no matter how admirable), or heroes (even if the heroic experience of ourselves) cannot lie at the heart of faith. What must reside there is the voice of Christ that is now acknowledged by acknowledging that his voice is heard for us in Holy Scripture. To recover this conviction requires a recovery of the basic disposition to listen anew to God and a deep commitment to the Scripture principle which, Barth contended, cannot function simply as a formula but must be a "living material principle in our churches" (228: ET 221).

Such confessionalism finds its concrete practice in a common confession of a church and churches in communion and association. It is therefore not acquiescence to a dogmatic and authoritarian subscriptionism from above but the only enduring basis for an associational connectionalism from below which is dependent upon a commitment to truth as well as to action and shared witness.[27] It provides a serious place to stand to consider larger ecumenical questions while refusing to see the singular answer to such questions in a catholic *ressourcement* that itself is susceptible to placing matters of the periphery at the center and that can in turn neglect evangelical Reformation discoveries, and indeed, its greatest one.[28] It also, as an acknowledgment of the Scripture principle, guards against a nebulous pneumatology in which God's Spirit and our own spirit or that of culture are perennially and hopelessly confused. It is not a form of romanticism

---

26. Webster, *Barth's Earlier Theology*, p. 60.

27. As Barth can elsewhere define such a confession in 1925: "A Reformed Creed [confession] is *the statement, spontaneously and publicly formulated by a Christian community within a geographically limited area, which until further action, defines its character to outsiders; and which until further action, gives guidance for its own doctrine and life; it is a formulation of the insight currently given to the whole Christian Church by the revelation of God in Jesus Christ, witnessed to by the Holy Scriptures alone.*" See Barth, "The Desirability and Possibility of a Universal Reformed Creed" in TC, pp. 112–35 (112). This essay, along with the lectures on the Reformed confessions of 1923 and the essay here under discussion of that same year, comprise the central texts displaying Barth's understanding of confessions during this early formative period.

28. Hence such confessionalism differs in significant ways from, even as it appreciates, recent attempts to define a Baptist catholicity as a project of *ressourcement* serving as an alternative to the problematic positions discussed above. For two notable recent examples of such a project, see Curtis Freeman, *Contesting Catholicity: Theology for Other Baptists* (Waco: Baylor University Press, 2014); and Steven Harmon, *Baptist Identity and the Ecumenical Future: Story, Tradition, and the Recovery of Community* (Waco: Baylor University Press, 2016).

but a return to a primitive acknowledgment that does not rest content in its historic articulations or embrace a rigid scholasticism. It is not a simplistic primitivism but strives to proclaim and confess the gospel in obedience to the demands placed upon the church in each age as it stands under the biblical canon that rules its faith and its life. Such confessionalism is, I would argue, the only viable resistance against succumbing to the problems of a seemingly inevitable and arbitrary eclecticism or, worse and more significantly, to the false alternatives of hierarchical authoritarianism or relativistic subjectivism. It eschews both the rigidity of narrow fundamentalism and the cultural captivity of nebulous progressivism.[29] It recognizes that the Lordship of Christ exercised in Scripture does not abolish but does relativize all other authorities, including the authority of the teaching church. Yet it also recognizes that the very same lordship of Christ also establishes the church's real if relative and proximate authority and thus the need to listen with deep respect and reverent attention to the church's past as one would honor one's own fathers and mothers in the faith. As Barth wisely noted, the first commandment does not undermine the fifth commandment though it does qualify it. It also provides it with its own qualified authority.[30] So also the confession of our fathers and mothers in faith must be revered and reverently consulted, but it cannot stand in for our own.[31]

The question of whether Baptists themselves must revisit what it might mean to be a confessional people—and not simply a denomination, a fellowship, much less a collection of singular priests—is pressing. The question points to the crisis of whether we have heard something, and therefore have something to confess, rather than simply glory in a heritage (or despair in it). This crisis is one we no doubt attempt to avoid in no small part through a celebration of our own distinctiveness and diversity. It may also lie behind the other self-inflicted maladies in Baptist life of our time of which authoritarianism and subjectivism are its principle

---

29. That Barth rejected both the positivism of creedalism and the relativism of a historicist view of creeds was due in no small part to his rejection of these alternatives advanced in the positions of Hermann Cremer and Adolf von Harnack in the battles over the Apostles' Creed (*Apostolikumsstreit*) in Germany that began in 1892. See Plasger, *Die relative Autorität des Bekenntnisses bei Karl Barth*, pp. 88–110; cf. p. 121. Barth had in fact been thinking of the difficulties posed by the seemingly sole alternatives of positivism and historicism, of dogmatism and liberalism, much earlier with regard to Scripture and would in fact reject them both. See Barth, "Zwinglis '67 Schlussreden' auf das erste Religionsgespräch zu Zürich 1523" (1906), in *Vorträge und kleinere Arbeiten 1905–1909* (Zürich: Theologischer Verlag Zürich, 1992), pp. 104–19 (113); cf. Barth, "Modern Theologie und Riechsgottesarbeit" (1909) in ibid., pp. 334–66 (341-7). In short, Barth was working through the deep tensions that would haunt Baptist battles in America decades before such battles were fought.

30. CD I/2: pp. 585–6; see also Bender, "Barth and Baptists," 255–61.

31. As Plasger states: "The Confession of fathers and mothers is not simply our confession, but rather reflects the knowledge of their time" (*Die relative Autorität des Bekenntnisses bei Karl Barth*, p. 110).

instantiations but are in fact symptoms of a still deeper disease. And yet there may be grace greater than our sin even here. It may be hoped that this is a crisis ultimately thrown upon us by a God from whom we have our life and whose Spirit may yet make perennially dead bones live. But we might begin for our part by confessing our helplessness and need instead of perennially boasting of our own competencies, rights, or resurgence (1 Cor. 1:31 and 2 Cor. 4:5).

## Chapter 6

## KARL BARTH AND PIETISM: TRACES OF A FAMILY RESEMBLANCE

In a letter to Rudolf Bultmann in 1952, Karl Barth compared Bultmann and himself to a whale and an elephant, two great beasts that are so different that communication is difficult if not impossible.[1] In Barth's assessment, Bultmann's emphasis upon the subjectivity of faith and his own emphasis upon the objectivity of God's revelation made any real understanding or affinity between them difficult if not impossible. Barth could not help but see Bultmann's theology as a continuation of the Protestant liberal tradition that he had resoundingly rejected, and if in his estimation Bultmann was the end product of the liberal tradition, Pietism was its forerunner. Barth understood Pietism in the history of Christian thought as a turn toward subjectivity that grounded faith in inner experience, and little could be more problematic for him than this emphasis upon inner religious subjectivity. Yet, as far removed as Pietism may appear to be from Barth at first blush, in this chapter I am going to try to bring the whale and the elephant into conversation.[2]

### *Reframing the Conversation*

It may seem strange to attempt a positive examination of Pietism in relation to Barth, for his open antipathy toward this movement is well known, and he could speak disparagingly of Pietism in his both early and later works.[3] Barth's

---

1. Karl Barth and Rudolf Bultmann, *Karl Barth-Rudolf Bultmann Letters*, ed. Bernd Jaspert, trans. Geoffrey W. Bromily (Edinburgh: T&T Clark, 1982), p. 105. Barth could use the same image for his relation to Emil Brunner elsewhere.

2. Because this chapter is focused on the specific movement of continental Pietism in the sixteenth century and its descendants, "Pietism" and "Pietist" will be capitalized here. The same will hold true for "Spiritualism" and "Protestant Orthodoxy" and "Puritanism" and "Romanticism" when used for distinct historical movements.

3. The classic study of Barth's early relationship to Pietism remains that of Eberhard Busch, *Karl Barth and the Pietists: The Young Karl Barth's Critique of Pietism & Its Response*, trans. Daniel W. Bloesch (Downers Grove: InterVarsity Press, 2004). For Barth's early negative assessment of Pietism's place in the history of theology and the church, see

relationship with Pietism was a complex and troubled one. While Barth grew within a familial and ecclesial climate amenable to Pietism, he could not be classified as belonging to this movement. His own very early sympathies for Pietism were in fact not due to an identification with it, but to the affinities he believed existed between the liberal theology he embraced as a student and Pietism's concerns. In his mind, both were marked by a religious individualism and the autonomy of religion, two elements fundamental for modern theology that he esteemed to be united in that Pietist of a higher order, Friedrich Schleiermacher. Barth thus perceived the merger of the concerns of Pietism and of Protestant liberalism expressed in the thought of his early teacher, Wilhelm Herrmann.[4]

When, however, Barth rejected the liberal theology of his youth, he turned on Pietism with a vengeance. The earlier coupling of Pietism and liberalism remained valid for Barth, but this relation was no longer seen in a positive fashion, for a break with liberalism now meant a rejection of Pietism itself. After his abandonment of the theology of his former teachers, Barth came to hold that Pietism turned from the revelation of God *extra nos* to an internal experiential religion, from a focus on the revealing God to the Christian subject, and thus stood as one source, along with medieval mysticism and Enlightenment rationalism, behind nineteenth-century Neo-Protestantism and its anthropological orientation.[5] Moreover, Barth could also link Pietism with the Romanticism of Schelling and Herder, Pietism and Romanticism being sibling sources behind the subjectivity and individualism of the Protestant liberalism he came to reject.[6] Pietism's turn to the subjectivity of faith and away from the objectivity of revelation was seen by Barth as its greatest failure.

Whether or not Barth's assessment of Pietism was fair will not be definitively adjudicated here, though it can be said that Barth treated it more as a type of theological failure than as a true historical movement in all of its complexity. Indeed, his early criticisms of Pietism in the first and second editions of the *Romans* commentary (and interestingly his criticisms seemed to differ between the first and the second editions) were made by defining its essence as a focus upon the inner religious subjectivity of the individual. While this may have been a generally

---

Karl Barth, *Protestant Thought in the Nineteenth Century* (Valley Forge: Judson Press, 1973), pp. 113–23. Barth's critical references to Pietism extend from the early to the late volumes of the CD; see, for example, his discussion of the devolution of hymnody through the influence of Pietism (CD I/2: pp. 250–7) and his late reference to Pietism in a similar vein with regard to hymnody as a companion to mysticism and romanticism and these as the precursors of Neo-Protestantism (CD IV/2: pp. 795–8).

4. Busch, *Karl Barth and the Pietists*, pp. 12, 14–17.

5. Barth, *Protestant Thought in the Nineteenth Century*, pp. 97–9; see also Barth's comments on "pietistic and rationalistic Modernism" in CD I/1: pp. 35–6; 251; cf. CD III/1: p. 17; CD IV/1: p. 757. For Barth, the subjectivism of Pietism was quintessentially evident in its hymnody (CD I/2: pp. 250–7). Barth could, however, classify Paul Gerhardt's hymns differently, placing him on the side of Luther, though he was an influence upon the later hymnody of Pietism (CD I/2: p. 255); cf., however, CD III/3: p. 32.

6. See CD III/3: p. 137.

fitting description of certain branches of Pietism, it did not adequately capture the complexity of other branches and their concerns.[7] Barth's early criticisms thus focused more upon the radical spiritualistic Pietists than church Pietists such as Philip Jacob Spener and August Hermann Franke.[8] Furthermore, Barth's criticism of Pietism on this score was itself ironically based upon discoveries for which he was indebted to other branches of Pietism which he appreciated, most notably, to figures such as J. A. Bengel and C. H. Rieger, as well as to those who had arisen from the Pietist tradition even if not remaining comfortably within it, most notably Christoph Blumhardt.[9] Barth thus saw classic church Pietism, with its retention of external means of revelation and grace in Scripture, sacrament, and doctrine, as "inconsistent" Pietism, but this was so only because Barth defined the essence of Pietism as religious individualism expressed in inner subjectivity, this essential definition in turn becoming the criterion by which all forms of Pietism were evaluated. Pietism for Barth was thereby treated as a pure type in turn used to judge its various instantiations under a common name.[10] Regardless of the perceptiveness of Barth's critique of the dangers inherent within the religious subjectivity of Pietism,

---

7. It should come as little surprise that Pietism is to this day a contested concept with disagreement as to its definition, with those who see it strictly as a historical movement of the seventeenth and eighteenth centuries begun by Philip Jacob Spener, and those who see it as extending beyond that period to all groups with similar tendencies to those of Spener and the early German Pietist movement. See Carter Lindberg, "Introduction," in *The Pietist Theologians*, ed. Carter Lindberg (Malden: Blackwell Publishing, 2005), pp. 1–20; also Martin Brecht and Carter Lindberg, "Pietism," in *The Encyclopedia of Christianity: Volume 4*, ed. Erwin Fahlbusch, Jan M. Lochman et al., trans. Geoffrey W. Bromiley (Grand Rapids: Eerdmans, 2005), pp. 218–24; as well as Roger Olson, "Pietism: Myths and Realities," in *The Pietist Impulse in Christianity*, ed. Christian T. Collins Winn, Christopher Gehrz et al. (Eugene: Pickwick Publications, 2011), pp. 3–16.

8. Busch, *Karl Barth and the Pietists*, p. 24; also pp. 61–2.

9. See Busch's discussion of Barth's dependence upon figures affiliated with Pietism in his criticism of Pietism itself in the first edition of the *Römerbrief* (*Karl Barth and the Pietists*, pp. 31, 36, 54, and esp. 62–4). While Barth's criticism of Pietism turned from focusing upon its individualism in the first *Romans* commentary to its religiosity in the second edition, Barth continued to quote certain Pietists such as Bengel approvingly, while still remaining critical of Pietism as a movement. For Barth's shift in his criticisms of Pietism between the first and second editions of the *Romans* commentary, see Busch, *Karl Barth and the Pietists*, pp. 91–130. Busch summarizes Barth's criticism in the second edition this way: "In Barth's view Pietism knows man is dependent on God's grace but does not know that man *remains* dependent on it, or does not know that grace *remains* free; instead it finally reestablishes a pious 'possession' of grace in the sight of God" (p. 97). Insofar as this is true, Barth's criticisms of Pietism foreshadow those he made of Protestant liberalism and Roman Catholicism in the following years.

10. This was certainly true for the early Barth of the first *Römerbrief* (see Busch, *Karl Barth and the Pietists*, p. 62), but I would add that this never really changes even in the later CD.

which is not in any way here called into doubt, such essentialism is nevertheless problematic and raises the question of Barth's fairness to the complexity of and diversity within Pietism as a whole.[11] So it should come as no surprise that Barth has been accused of reading all of Pietism through the eyes of its most spiritualistic figures.[12] Barth's criticisms of Pietism at times seem more akin to criticisms of mysticism and the Spiritualism movement, and while not entirely immune from Barth's criticisms of religious subjectivity, classical Pietism cannot be equated with Spiritualism, for Pietism's emphasis upon inner regeneration was always set against its emphasis upon Christ and the Bible as external means of revelation and grace, a fact that must in fairness be noted regardless of one's estimation of Barth's critique as a whole.[13] Even Barth conceded late in life that he had not given Pietism its fair due.[14]

Barth was aware of the ambiguity of Pietism much earlier. In his early student years, his liberal convictions led him to appreciate the religious subjectivity and interiorization of faith in Pietism and to criticize its inconsistency in maintaining external objective elements such as the Bible and orthodox doctrine as norms for faith and belief. Yet it was precisely after his break with liberalism that such inconsistency was understood in Barth's estimation as that which saved Pietism from total rejection.[15] There was always an external objectivity to faith in Pietism's

---

11. See Busch, *Karl Barth and the Pietists*, pp. 24-5.

12. F. Ernest Stoeffler thus states that Barth, with the exception of his appreciation for Zinzendorf, "consistently chose to subjectivize Pietism by making the spiritualistic element within the movement, typified by Tersteegen, the Pietistic norm .... This understanding of Pietism fitted in with Barth's thesis, of course, but it tends to do violence to the historian's sense of *was wirklich geschehen ist*." See Stoeffler, *German Pietism during the Eighteenth Century* (Leiden: E. J. Brill, 1973), p. 166nt. 1. Stoeffler also has questions with regard to Barth's appreciation and treatment of Zinzendorf. He emphasizes that Pietists like Spener in fact warned their followers against the dangers of subjectivism. See Stoeffler, *The Rise of Evangelical Pietism* (Leiden: E. J. Brill, 1965), p. 10.

13. This is not to say that Pietism and Spiritualism were entirely unrelated. One sees a movement into Spiritualism with some of the persons usually identified with Pietism, such as an early forerunner of Pietism, Johann Arndt, and some of his followers. As Johannes Wallmann states: "One may speak of a left wing of the Arndt school when Arndt's intention for orthodoxy is ignored and his intent to give the mystical and spiritualist traditions a proper home on the ground of Orthodox Lutheran ecclesiology is no longer maintained. The left wing of Arndt's followers inclined toward a church-critical Spiritualism that at times crossed into the camp of extra-ecclesial Spiritualism." See Wallmann, "Johann Arndt: 1555-1621," in *The Pietist Theologians: An Introduction to Theology in the Seventeenth and Eighteenth Centuries* (Oxford: Blackwell, 2005), pp. 21-37 (34). Nevertheless, to emphasize inner piety and godliness at the expense of the central place given to the Bible would be to misunderstand Pietism (see Lindberg, "Introduction," p. 4). For this reason, Barth's criticisms of Pietism seem more fitting for Spiritualists such as Jacob Boehme than for Spener.

14. Barth, *The Theology of Schleiermacher*, ed. Dietrich Ritschl, trans. Geoffrey W. Bromiley (Grand Rapids: Eerdmans, 1982), p. 262.

15. Busch, *Karl Barth and the Pietists*, p. 18 nt. 73.

emphasis upon Christ, the Bible, and the church (and indeed, in the confessionalism of many early Pietists, even though downplayed in relation to the Protestant scholastics). And when the actual elements of Pietism related to this external objectivity of revelation and faith are taken into consideration, there appear to be areas of overlap, like those in a Venn diagram, with Barth's own theological concerns and even convictions. For while Barth's rejection of religious subjectivity was consistently maintained after his turn from the liberalism of his teachers, his appreciation for Pietism could grow in time as he examined its understanding of the objective elements of faith.

In drawing attention to these similarities, I am not making a claim for a direct genetic relationship between the theological themes within Pietism and those found in Barth, though some may exist. While genetic studies of the influences upon Barth's early and mature thought have significant value, they also have real limitations.[16] There is no claim (nor denial) here for a direct influence of classical Pietist sources on Barth's own theology, for while he was certainly influenced by the Pietist heritage of his family and his early engagement with Pietist figures and their works, any evidence for his direct reliance upon classical Pietism for the development of his mature theology is spotty at best. While a direct influence of Barth's reading of classic sources of his Reformed heritage, for example, Calvin and the Reformed confessions, upon his early and later thought is quite readily confirmed in light of his early lectures upon these topics and their direct or indirect incorporation into his mature works,[17] his actual references to Pietist figures in the CD are sporadic and do not display an extensive reading or sustained interaction with their writings.[18] Even where a substantial interaction is more readily discerned,

---

16. For the limitations of genetic studies with relation to the search for sources in Barth's thought, see John Webster, *Barth's Early Theology* (London/New York: T&T Clark, 2005), pp. 7–8.

17. For these examples, see Barth, *The Theology of John Calvin*, trans. Geoffrey W. Bromiley (Grand Rapids: Eerdmans, 1995); and Barth, *The Theology of the Reformed Confessions*, trans. Darrell L. Guder and Judith J. Guder (Louisville: Westminster John Knox, 2002).

18. Barth's actual references to continental Pietists are quite sparse within the CD. He rarely references Francke or the oft-considered founder of Pietism itself, Spener, and does not discuss their writings in any engaged way. He can refer positively to and quote from the hymnody of Paul Gerhardt who, though not technically a Pietist, displayed pietistic themes (see CD IV/2: pp. 273, 613, 729; et al.—and in spite of his criticisms of Pietist hymnody), yet these references are brief and almost always made in passing. There is little or no mention of such Pietists and Pietist forerunners as Johann Arndt, Gottfried Arnold, Gerhard Tersteegen, or Friedrich Christoph Oetinger. The two most important Pietists for Barth's own thinking, excluding the later Blumhardts, are the biblical scholar Johann Albrecht Bengel, whom he can often cite with approval, and Nicholas Ludwig von Zinzendorf, who did not escape his criticisms but with whom he later expressed an affinity for his christological concentration (see CD IV/1: p. 683; cf. CD II/2: p. 568). This assessment does not, however, overlook the notable collection of Pietist works discovered in Barth's own personal library.

Barth took his own questions to the texts as much as he took things away from them. This problem of determining the nature of influence does not mean of course that there were no Pietist influences upon Barth's early or later development. One must immediately remember the important role played by Johann Christoph Blumhardt and his son Christoph Friedrich of the Württemberg Pietist tradition in Barth's development and even later work, though this admittance must be qualified by noting that he seemed to appreciate in the Blumhardts what he esteemed was most unpietistic about them, namely, their turn from inner subjectivity to history as the plane of spiritual conflict and God's in-breaking activity predicated upon an eschatological hope for the coming kingdom of God not only for the individual but for all.[19] Nor does a recognition of the sparseness of references to Pietists in the CD deny Barth's own later openness to Pietism's concerns and even an affinity for some of its classic fathers, most significantly, Nicholas Ludwig von Zinzendorf, though as with the Blumhardts, Barth was drawn to what he thought was most unpietistic in Zinzendorf's thought, namely, his emphasis upon the objectivity of Christ rather than the subjectivity of inner conversion and renewal of the individual.[20] Barth in his later years softened toward Zinzendorf, yet he did so by identifying Zinzendorf not as a Pietist but as an opponent of the Pietism of his own day.[21] This was precisely because Barth worked with a definition of Pietism as a pure type of religious subjectivity, and those persons and movements within Pietism that did not neatly fit within this definition but also focused upon external objectivity in revelation, such as Zinzendorf, were thus extolled not because of but in spite of their identification with Pietism. Hence Barth's late comment that Zinzendorf was not a Pietist but an opponent of Pietism (i.e., of Pietism as pure inner subjectivity).[22]

However strong or tenuous the historical influence of Pietism upon Barth's own writings may be, this study will now turn from historical questions to take a different path of exploration. Instead of attempting to draw a line from Pietism

---

19. For the deep and abiding impact of the Blumhardts upon Barth, see Christian T. Collins Winn, *"Jesus Is Victor!": The Significance of the Blumhardts for the Theology of Karl Barth* (Eugene: Pickwick Publications, 2009). That Barth was attracted to what he esteemed were the Blumhardt's departures from, rather than faithfulness to, Pietism, see Barth, *Protestant Thought in the Nineteenth Century,* pp. 643–53. Barth there writes of J. C. Blumhardt's discovery of Jesus as victorious redeemer: "For Blumhardt in the midst of Pietism this breakthrough represented a quite unpietistic discovery and recognition" (ibid., p. 644). In *"Jesus Is Victor,"* Winn himself shows the movement away from classical Pietism from father to son (pp. xv–xvi); he also notes the disagreement among those who debate whether the Blumhardts are within or without the bounds of Württemberg Pietism (pp. 68–76). Nevertheless, the elements that Barth thought most unpietistic in the Blumhardts themselves may have had precedents within Württemberg Pietism (pp. 72, 74).

20. CD IV/1: p. 756.

21. See Karl Barth, *Gespräche 1959–1962,* ed. Eberhard Busch (Zürich: Theologischer Verlag Zürich, 1995), p. 27. For later cordial discussions of Barth with Pietists, see ibid., pp. 13–41; 124–57.

22. Ibid., p. 27. See also CD IV/3.2: pp. 568–9.

to Barth in some kind of genetic fashion, I will instead take up the easier task of drawing attention to "family resemblances" (in the broadly Wittgenstinian sense) or common themes between Pietism and Barth with regard to their respective theological programs and specifically look at the early Pietists Spener and Zinzendorf. These similar themes need not be directly traced from Pietism to Barth, for they are more like overlapping areas of theological affinity than identical themes traced through a direct line of descent or essentially defined.[23] My hope is that this examination of similarities between the concerns of Pietism and the theology of Barth might shed light on how a further discussion between studies in Pietism and those of Barth might be conducted, and show that these similar concerns in Pietism and Barth might allow for a broader discussion in evangelicalism today pertaining to its own identity.

## Family Resemblances between Pietism and Barth

When one looks at the external objectivity of Christian revelation in Pietism and the theology of Barth with regard to Christ, Scripture, and church, one can discern among all the significant and very real differences a number of shared convictions and concerns. Such can be described as family resemblances rather than shared concepts essentially, analytically, and systematically defined or traced through history in a direct line from Pietism to Barth.

The first family resemblance between the theology of Pietism and that of Barth is a singular emphasis upon Jesus Christ as the center of theology and Christian life, witnessed in Barth's growing appreciation for Zinzendorf in particular. Such an emphasis upon the centrality of Christ took a different form for Barth than Zinzendorf, of course, for Barth emphasized the centrality of Christ not so much for a life of personal piety, as did Zinzendorf, but for the church's proclamation and confession and theology's center. Barth certainly had dogmatic theological interests and questions that Zinzendorf did not, most notably evident in a complex web of dialectical relationships between questions of election and christology, and certainly it would be remiss to treat Zinzendorf or his thought in systematic categories that misconstrued his own intentions and work.[24] Yet Barth could, nonetheless, see in Zinzendorf a kindred spirit. Hence his ability and willingness, in light of what he understood as a christocentric concentration in Zinzendorf, to say in a letter to Bultmann in 1952 that "I have become increasingly

---

23. Wittgenstein can say in the *Philosophical Investigations* in reference to family resemblances: "we see a complicated network of similarities overlapping and crisscrossing" (§66).

24. Indeed, Zinzendorf, of all the Pietists, was the one most opposed to systematic thinking, saying that "as soon as truth becomes a system, one does not possess it" (Stoeffler, *German Pietism*, p. 143). Certainly, Zinzendorf and Barth differ here, though Barth also did not think of the theological task as constructing a static and finished "system" that could capture the truth of revelation.

a Zinzendorfian to the extent that in the NT only the one central figure as such has begun to occupy me."[25] By this, Barth did not mean that he had become a Pietist. But he did not really consider Zinzendorf one either, at least according to his essentialist definition. Barth's numerous positive references to Zinzendorf later in life illustrate his own estimation of a common central concern between himself and this particular figure of Herrnhut Pietism.[26]

A second family resemblance between Pietism and Barth is found in their pneumatological emphasis upon Scripture as the Word of God that through the work of the Spirit speaks into the life of the church and the believer today. Barth, like the Pietists before him, places a more sustained emphasis in his theology upon the role of the Holy Spirit in the reading of Scripture in the present than upon the writing of Scripture in the past, especially if such writing is understood in light of elaborate theories of the inspiration and inerrancy of the text.[27] Barth shared with Pietism, against the progeny of the Protestant Orthodox scholastics of his time and theirs, an indifference to such theories. And while some may believe that the Pietists of the seventeenth century and even later *did* hold to a doctrine of the inerrancy of the text, there is no question that the focus of Pietism was not upon the text as a repository of inerrant information and even less upon formulating theories of inspiration or inerrancy, but upon seeing Scripture as the medium of God's self-revelation and communication to the believer through the work of the Spirit.[28] For both Barth and the earlier Pietists, the Bible was not seen as a collection of inerrant propositions but as the locus of the active revelation of God through the Spirit.[29] Both thus emphasized the illumination of Scripture in

---

25. Barth and Bultmann, *Karl Barth-Rudolf Bultmann Letters*, p. 107.
26. See note 18 above.
27. For Barth's understanding of Scripture, see esp. CD I/1: pp. 99-111 and CD I/2: pp. 457-538; also Bruce McCormack, "The Being of Holy Scripture Is in Becoming," in *Evangelicals & Scripture: Tradition, Authority and Hermeneutics*, ed. Vincent Bacote, Laura C. Miguélez, and Dennis L. Ockholm (Downers Grove: InterVarsity Press, 2004), pp. 55-75.
28. Whether Pietists did or did not adhere to a doctrine of inerrancy is a disputed question in contemporary evangelicalism. See Donald Dayton, "The Pietist Theological Critique of Biblical Inerrancy" in *Evangelicals & Scripture: Tradition, Authority and Hermeneutics*, pp. 76-89. For an attempt to argue that Bengel in particular held to the inerrancy of the biblical text, see Alan J. Thompson, "The Pietist Critique of Inerrancy? J. A. Bengel's *Gnomon* as a Test Case," in *Journal of the Evangelical Theological Society* 47, no. 1 (March 2004), pp. 71-88. Spener, however, does not seem to have held such a view; see K. James Stein, "Philipp Jakob Spener: 1635-1705," in *The Pietist Theologians: An Introduction to Theology in the Seventeenth and Eighteenth Centuries*, ed. Carter Lindberg (Oxford: Blackwell, 2005), pp. 84-99 (87-9); also Stein, *Philip Jakob Spener: Pietist Patriarch* (Chicago: Covenant Press, 1986), p. 151; and Stoeffler, *The Rise of Evangelical Pietism*, pp. 239-40.
29. So Spener could say that true faith is that which is "awakened through the Word of God, by the illumination, witness, and sealing of the Holy Spirit." See Spener, *Pia Desideria*, trans. and ed. Theodore G. Tappert (Philadelphia: Fortress Press, 1964), p. 46. For Barth on this point, see McCormack, "The Being of Holy Scripture is in Becoming," p. 62.

the present through the work of the Spirit with equal if not greater intensity than the inspiration of Scripture in its composition.[30] Barth, like the classical Pietists, understood the Bible as a book through which God spoke in a living and powerful way into the present life of the church and the believer, though again we should not flatten the differences between Barth and the Pietists, for Barth was more inclined to emphasize *God's action* in speaking to the believer in Scripture, whereas the Pietists could emphasize *the experience* in the life of the believer of God's action in Scripture.[31] Nevertheless, what we see in both Barth and Pietism (and here Spener specifically) is an emphasis upon the superiority and authority of Scripture in dynamic terms that relativizes creeds and confessions even as it recognizes their secondary and relative authority.[32]

There is a further similarity here with regard to the Bible, if of lesser import. Barth's own relation to the Bible expressed in his language for it displays affinities with Pietism's own devotional reading of and love for the Bible. Late in life, Barth could speak of the importance of daily Bible reading and meditation upon passages of Scripture not only for clergy and professional theologians, but as a source of joy for all believers (he did not like the word "laity"), evident when he asserted: "One must get used to living with the Bible" (*Man muß sich daran gewöhnen, mit der Bible zu leben*).[33] In this, we see that while the primary locus for the revelation of God in the present was for Barth the church gathered in community, he retained an important place for the reading of Scripture in the life of the believer. While Barth may have rejected religious individualism, he did not reject the reading of Scripture by the individual believer. Both Barth and the Pietists had a deep desire to see Scripture read and reflected upon not only by professional clergy, but by all members of the church. This leads to a third theme worthy of exploration.

---

30. Stein, "Philipp Jakob Spener: 1635–1705," p. 88. What is said of Spener by Tappert in his introduction to Spener's *Pia Desideria* with regard to the Scriptures could also be said of Barth with little qualification, namely, that he was "more interested in their content than in their form and in their effect than in their origin" (Tappert, p. 25).

31. Notice, for instance, Barth's reticence to speak of the experience of the Word of God (CD I/1: p. 110).

32. Barth's understanding of creeds and confessions in this way is already evident in his early lectures of *The Theology of the Reformed Confessions* (pp. 1–64). Spener stated with regard to creeds and confessions: "I do not oppose them, but hold fast to them with mouth and heart. However, my faith is not grounded upon the Nicene Creed or the Augsburg Confession but on the divine Word itself, from which all creeds have their authority" (quoted in Stein, "Philip Jakob Spener," p. 89). What Barth and Spener hold in common is a firm conviction of Scripture's superiority over the relative authority of creeds and confessions, a conviction they both emphasize against the orthodoxies of their own respective periods, and Lutheran scholasticism in particular.

33. Karl Barth, *Gespräche 1964–1968*, ed. Eberhard Busch (Zürich: Theologischer Verlag Zürich, 1997), p. 243. Barth could go on in this interview to speak of prayer in a way that also is reminiscent of Pietism (p. 244).

It is this third family resemblance between the theology of Pietism and Barth that I will explore in the most detail by examining the chief work of Spener, that is, the *Pia Desideria*, and the theology of Barth. This resemblance is the dedication of both Spener and Barth to an intentional church composed of serious members expressed in a strong commitment to the priesthood of all believers. Now it must be said that the emphasis upon personal moral concerns with regard to the church evinced in early Pietism, and in Spener in particular, would have had little appeal for Barth. Yet if one can look below the surface of Spener's worries over drunkenness and personal greed,[34] one can discern a deep conviction, shared by Barth, that the reformation of the church is an ongoing task not only in its doctrine but in its life, and that one sign of such ongoing reformation is that the church as a gathered body of believers takes its task of being the church seriously.

This seriousness is evident in Spener's concern for the church's renewal. In the *Pia Desideria*, Spener outlined a number of proposals for improving the condition of the churches. Spener's writing demonstrates a spirit of ecclesial dissatisfaction that calls for church reform yet also eschews separation from the church itself. Spener and the Pietists thus attempted to carry on the tradition of protest in Protestantism, and protest that was directed especially against "ecclesiasticism, theologism, and sacerdotalism," as well as against moral compromise and failure, or any easy accommodation of church and world.[35]

In the *Pia Desideria*, Spener begins his proposal to correct diagnosed problems with an appeal to the Word of God and a call for a renewed focus upon Scripture.[36] He writes that the Word of God, that is, Holy Scripture, is "the powerful means [to this end of reform], since faith must be enkindled through the gospel, and the law provides the rules for good works and many wonderful impulses to attain them. The more at home the Word of God is among us, the more we shall bring about faith and its fruits."[37] Spener may see Scripture more as a treasury of practical and personal moral instruction than Barth would, but both hold firm to the centrality of Scripture for the revelation of God to the church and for the renewal of its life in and for the world.

Part of the problem, Spener maintained, is that corporate worship did not expose Christian congregational members to enough of the Bible, but his answer was not simply more solitary home devotional reading. Rather, Spener espoused reading in community, first in the family (and for Spener, as a product of his time, this meant readings by the father of the house as the one responsible for its practice); second, in public readings of large portions of Scripture (without homiletical comment); and third, and most famously, in home meetings for the reading and discussion of Scripture, which Spener believed returned to a Corinthian pattern

---

34. Spener, *Pia Desideria*, pp. 58–9.
35. Stoeffler, *The Rise of Evangelical Pietism*, p. 2.
36. Spener, *Pia Desideria*, pp. 87–8.
37. Ibid., p. 87. Spener's words of Scripture being "at home" with the members of the church sound akin to Barth's words to "live with the Bible." See note 32 above.

of worship.[38] These home meetings became the famous (or infamous) *collegia pietatis*, or *ecclesiolae in ecclesia*, church groups within the state churches.

While Spener did see the ordained clergy as having an authority over such groups and in no way sought to undermine this authority, such reading was predicated upon a radical commitment to the common priesthood (today referred to most commonly as "the priesthood of all believers"). For Spener, it was the responsibility of all Christians to reflect upon Scripture and provide biblical instruction to others.[39] Appealing once again to Luther, Spener emphasized that not only ordained ministers but all members of churches are priests, and that they are responsible not only to study the Word of God but to "instruct, admonish, chastise, and comfort their neighbors."[40] He continued: "Every Christian is bound not only to offer himself and what he has, his prayer, thanksgiving, good works, alms, etc., but also industriously to study in the Word of the Lord, with the grace that is given him to teach others, especially those under his own roof."[41] What one sees in Spener is a serious attempt to address sacerdotalism, to break down absolute clergy and laity divisions while preserving their differentiation, and to deny any form of neo-clericalism that would limit the study, instruction, and theological reflection of Scripture only to a professional class of theologians and ministers.[42] For this reason, Stein can conclude that Spener was marked by a democratic principle and a desire to empower the laity to be the church, and he deems Spener "an unintentional democrat with a concern that the laity (including those of the peasant and laboring classes) be empowered and involved in the Church's mission."[43]

When one looks at Barth's understanding of the church, it is impossible not to see significant differences between his and Spener's theological and ecclesial positions, differences that cannot simply be dismissed by appeal to differing centuries and contexts. Yet while these cannot be minimized or dismissed, there

---

38. Ibid., pp. 88–90.
39. Ibid., pp. 89–92; see also Spener's treatise on the spiritual priesthood in *Pietism: Selected Writings*, ed Peter C. Erb (New York: Paulist Press, 1983), pp. 50–64; as well as Stoeffler, *The Rise of Evangelical Pietism*, p. 5; and the important discussion of Jonathan Strom, "The Common Priesthood and the Pietist Challenge for Ministry and Laity," in *The Pietist Impulse in Christianity*, ed. Christian T. Collins Winn et al. (Eugene: Pickwick, 2011), pp. 42–58.
40. Spener, *Pia Desideria*, p. 93.
41. Ibid., p. 94.
42. As Strom writes: "So while Spener preserves the clear distinction of laity and ministry and grants the ministry a certain priority, he nevertheless makes clergy and laity fundamentally interdependent" ("Common Priesthood," p. 49).
43. Stein, *Philipp Jakob Spener: Pietist Patriarch*, p. 5. This emphasis upon the spiritual priesthood recedes in later Pietism, even by the time of Franke, according to Strom ("Common Priesthood," pp. 51–4). For this reason, Strom argues that Spener is closer to Luther than Franke (or his Lutheran scholastic detractors). Spener thus stands against both a spiritual elitism of the clergy in later Pietism, and against the Orthodox conception of the authority of the clergy based purely on office (*Amtsgnade*).

are also noteworthy similarities as well, for while Barth did not advocate *ecclesiolae in ecclesia*, one would not be remiss to say that he advocated that the church itself be, from top to bottom, an intentional community of reform gathered around Scripture that embraced the seriousness of Spener's call for mission. What Spener hopes for the *ecclesiolae* Barth hopes for the *ecclesia* itself.[44]

This is seen in a number of areas. First, like Spener and some later Pietists, Barth has no place for strong clergy and laity distinctions. This rejection is evident already in his first cycle of dogmatics lectures, the *Göttingen Dogmatics*, where he readily rejects strong hierarchical distinctions between clergy and laity and displays ambivalence for strong conceptions of ecclesial office (one would be hard-pressed to find any appreciation for the term *laity* in all of Barth's corpus).[45] Later, Barth reiterated that such strong distinctions are mistaken, and that all members of the church, and not only professional clergy, are to live out a life and law of service. This service includes the interpretation of Scripture and the task of theology itself, which he states is not the precinct of a few, but of all members of the church.[46] Like Spener's picture of the conventicles, and even more radical than they, Barth conceives of the church not in institutional or sacerdotal terms but as a *Gemeinde* (i.e., community or fellowship) of persons who take responsibility for the study and teaching of Scripture and live this out in a life of obedience and service. His picture of the priesthood of all believers translates the intentional nature of the conventicle into the law of service of the church itself which pertains to all of its members.[47] There can be no hard demarcation beyond that of function between pastors and "ordinary" church members, for "the community is not divided by this ordering into an active part and a passive, a teaching Church and a listening, Christians who have office and those who have not."[48] Barth can thereby write with pietistic moral chastisement: "The statement: 'I am a mere layman and not a theologian,' is evidence not of humility but of indolence."[49] The church is a place for instruction in which every individual member need participate as a theologian among theologians, a member among members.[50] Indeed, Barth puts forth his

---

44. Barth did not outline a program for *ecclesiolae in ecclesia* (a solution he would have rejected), but instead described the church itself as a *Gemeinde*, a community. Barth thus looked past not only the establishment of the church, but its strong lines of institutionalization and the *corpus Christianum* itself. If this entailed that the church be smaller, so be it. He was thus indifferent and even opposed to polity that is universally ordained, to strong notions of office, and to views that see theology as pertaining only to professionals. He wanted the common priesthood of all believers to be the norm, and in this sense we can say that he embraced the spirit of Luther that survived in Pietism. For Barth's ecclesiology in this regard, see Kimlyn J. Bender, *Karl Barth's Christological Ecclesiology* (Aldershot: Ashgate, 2005).

45. Unterricht III: pp. 372–5.
46. CD IV/3.2: pp. 870–1; 882.
47. CD IV/2: pp. 692–5; also CD III/3: pp. 489–90.
48. CD III/4: p. 490.
49. CD IV/3.2, p. 871.
50. CD III/4: pp. 497–9.

own description for a place for catechetical instruction which is intended for the purposes of asking questions, providing answers, and the receiving of biblical and theological training that cannot be accommodated in formal worship. His description of this instruction is similar if not identical to Spener's description of his purposes for the small meetings and thus displays his own unique description of a *collegia pietatis*.[51] In sum, both Spener and Barth take the Reformation principle of the priesthood of all believers with radical seriousness and provide guidelines for an informed and intentional church gathered around Scripture in which all are responsible for its interpretation and teaching. They share this central and unwavering commitment to the priesthood of all believers that denies absolute distinctions between pastors and laity.[52]

This family resemblance between Spener's and Barth's ecclesial vision is not meant to deny very real differences between their ecclesiologies. Barth infamously divided Pietism from the church, stating that he would rather be with the church in hell than with the Pietists in heaven.[53] Yet this statement should not be given more weight than it merits. Barth certainly opposed any pietistic calls for separatism or perfectionism. But Spener opposed such separatism as well, and he was not deluded into expecting or believing that a personal or corporate perfectionism was possible.[54] Spener shared with Barth an abhorrence of separatism and could say: "I confess honestly that with all my heart I have a horror of separation and even consider it better to be in a corrupted church than in none at all."[55] In the end, is this exclamation really so different than Barth's earlier sentiment of wanting to be at home with the church in hell than in a heaven of the Pietists' own making? Here too, Spener does not seem to fit Barth's pietistic norm. Instead of a pure type in opposition to Barth, we have a family resemblance yet again. Moreover, even where the Pietists and Barth seem most divided, on the question of holiness and perfection, there are areas of overlap. For whereas Barth consistently rejected any

---

51. CD IV/3.2: pp. 870–2; cf. Spener, *Pia Desideria*, pp. 89–92.

52. Spener, *Pia Desideria*, pp. 92–5.

53. Karl Barth, *The Epistle to the Romans*, trans. Edwyn C. Hoskyns (Oxford: Oxford University Press, 1968), p. 337.

54. Spener, *Pia Desideria*, p. 80. Nevertheless, Spener did maintain that a type of perfection was to be striven for, and for those who failed to address sin, church discipline was an imperative (ibid., p. 81; see also p. 95). Yet here too, while Barth seems ambivalent and even acrimonious toward a personal drive to perfection, he could be just as hard on the complacency and cultural accommodation of the church in his own day, though for him, such failures were more theological and social than personal and moral.

55. Quoted in Stein, "Philipp Jakob Spener," p. 87. That Barth rejected separatism is evident in his *Romans* commentary (see *The Epistle to the Romans*, p. 371). Barth could write in a letter of 1925: "Naturally it dare not be a *new* church that we want but rather the *church* in distinction to sects or even to our own personal prophesying. Also our *protest* against the church, so far as it was valid, was intended as specifically *by the church*." See *Revolutionary Theology in the Making: Barth-Thurneysen Correspondence, 1914–1925*, trans. and ed. James D. Smart (Richmond: John Knox Press, 1964), p. 216.

hint of perfectionism which Spener may have denied but to which he believed all should aspire,[56] he nonetheless could speak in his first cycle of dogmatic lectures of the need for church discipline, so that while those in the church remain sinners, there is a need that justification be accompanied by sanctification and obedience.[57]

Where Barth's conception of the church is closest to that of Pietism is in the centrality of mission for its identity. The rediscovery of the church's mission mandate in the modern era was in no small part due to Pietism, and its theological rediscovery by Barth was in no small way due to his discovery of its advocacy in Pietism. It was precisely on this question that he was the most openly appreciative of Pietism, for it was among Pietists and other "sects," Barth stated, and not among the state churches of the magisterial Reformers, that the great truth of the indivisibility of church and mission, mission and church, was discovered and practiced.[58] Here Barth has his most positive if nonetheless qualified appraisal of Pietism, with Francke and the Pietism of Halle singled out for commendation, but none so praised as Zinzendorf and the Moravian community.[59] This last family resemblance in ecclesiology is therefore most noticeable in the centrality of mission for both Pietism and Barth with regard to understanding the church's calling, life, and very existence, a theme put into practice by Pietism throughout the world and thoroughly explored in the fourth volume of Barth's *CD*. So, in bringing full circle Barth's emphasis on mission with the commitment to an intentional community grounded upon the priesthood of all believers in a way that Pietists early and late could affirm, and thus bringing this section to a close, we end with Barth's own words: "We have to remember that every Christian is to be a missionary, a recruiting officer for new witnesses. If our congregations do not recognize this and act accordingly, they cannot be missionary congregations, and therefore they cannot be truly Christian."[60]

## Pietism and Barth in Retrospect and Prospect

The preceding investigation of family resemblances between the convictions of Pietism and those of Barth should moderate the stark antithesis that is often placed between them, in no small part due to Barth's own expressed early antipathy to

---

56. For one example of Barth's rejection of any attempt to purge the church of hypocrites, see Unterricht III, pp. 366-7.

57. Ibid., pp. 369-72.

58. For Pietism's emphasis upon mission as central to the church's calling and existence, see Stoeffler, *The Rise of Evangelical Pietism*, p. 2; and Richard V. Pierard, "German Pietism as a Major Factor in the Beginnings of Modern Protestant Missions" in *The Pietist Impulse in Christianity*, pp. 285-95. For Barth's discovery of the central place of Pietism and the left wing of the Reformation for the rediscovery of the church's missionary duty, see CD IV/3.1: pp. 25-38.

59. CD IV/3.1: p. 25.

60. CD III/4: p. 505.

Pietism, an antipathy in turn adopted by many, yet one that Barth himself set aside.[61] Pietism has been both lauded and chastised, identified as either "a narrow-minded moralistic, biblicistic flight from the world or as the most significant Christian movement in modern times."[62] It has in fact become the victim of a caricature of itself, portrayed as ascetic, world-denying, and purely introspective. In reality, Pietism could produce a tradition that, while often moralistic and subjective in the worst senses of those terms, could also turn from inner experience to a public communal life that channeled its moral intensity into programs that impacted culture, addressed social problems, and effected missions in unparalleled ways.[63]

If this study has demonstrated points of overlap between the concerns of Pietism and those of Barth, it has done so with modest intent. As stated, there is no attempt here to produce a strong relationship of influence between classical Pietists and Barth. Certainly the subjective emphasis in Pietism had little or no appeal for Barth, and he had no sympathy for an unmediated religiosity at all, whether of the Spiritualist or radical Pietist variety. He would reject all anti-ecclesial forms of religion, seeing the movements of mysticism, Spiritualism, and Pietism as problematic siblings of one family. He would do the same for social movements that abandoned the church as well, such as any form of socialism which grew out of an identification of the kingdom of God with the present age and sacrificed the eschatological character of Christian faith.[64] Nor would Barth have any time for the emphasis for "life" over "doctrine"—a view that he saw as fundamentally mistaken.[65]

Yet in spite of such significant differences, there are resemblances between ecclesial Pietism and Barth in the areas of Christ, Scripture, and church that mark out places of real if qualified agreement, for between Barth and Spener in particular there is a happy convergence of a commitment to a church centered on Christ, grounded upon Scripture, indebted to but not imprisoned by its confessions, intentional in its existence toward the world, and not tied or captive to cultural or civil respectability. Where Pietism displayed affinities to Spiritualism and to introspective religious subjectivity or privatization and cultural withdrawal, Barth opposed it. But it was also the case that where Pietism remained grounded in objectivity—with regard to the external Word of Scripture, the eschatological nature of God's relation to history, and the church and its practices, including social concern, action, and public witness—Barth had overlapping concerns with those of Pietism.

---

61. Barth, *Gespräche 1963*, ed. Eberhard Busch (Zürich: Theologischer Verlag Zürich, 2005), pp. 275–6. Barth stated in this conversation with young pastors that he had long ago made peace with Pietists (ibid., p. 276).

62. Brecht and Lindberg, "Pietism," p. 219.

63. See David Crowner and Gerald Christianson, "Introduction," in *The Spirituality of the German Awakening*, ed. and trans. David Crowner and Gerald Christianson (New York/Mahwah: Paulist Press, 2003), pp. 5–41 (7–10).

64. See Barth's discussion of this and his own complicated history with the Blumhardts and the socialist movement in CD II/1: pp. 633–8.

65. CD I/2: p. 254.

Most surprising of all, Barth could against all expectations even make a place for the introspection and self-examination so derided in Pietism. In the final volumes of the *Church Dogmatics*, Barth quoted August Tholuck, the nineteenth-century Pietist of the German Awakening, in a way that no doubt must have surprised many a reader:

> At every moment and in every situation we have to ask soberly and honestly: Who am I, and where do I stand, and what am I doing, and by what am I compelled? How is it with me? 'Brother, how is it with thine heart?' as the ageing Tholuck privately used to ask his students, rather penetratingly, but, rightly understood, very relevantly. And again: At any given moment and in any given situation in my life, how is it with my response to the grace and commandment of God?[66]

Barth could not have said this directly after his break with liberalism. But he could here. Just as he at the end of life could charitably look to the concerns of Schleiermacher, if not his solutions, so he could take up the concerns of Pietism, even if they themselves were taken up in a new key. Certainly they were in a new key, for he was ever careful that the subjective concerns of self-examination could never be divorced from and could only follow the larger context of christology and the centrality of Christ as the sanctified one, and in quoting Tholuck's question again in a different context later in the CD, this is quite clear.[67] Nevertheless, there is without question a concern and commitment to address these central themes of the Pietists in the later Barth, such that their questions are honored and respected, even if placed in a larger dogmatic framework. Whether or not all Pietists, historic or contemporary, would agree with his own answers to their questions is of course another matter. He both embraced and qualified his self-chosen moniker as a Zinzendorfian. But in light of his mature attempt to respect and answer these questions, perhaps Barth might be deemed to be a "Pietist of a higher order." This is not out of the question, for he could speak in ever-surprising ways. When he was late in years and reflecting upon the pace of life that kept contemporary theologians from spending time with the Bible, he came to his own unexpected conclusion: "What we need today," he said, "is almost a new Pietism."[68]

## Final Reflections

A nuanced evaluation of Barth's relation to Pietism might lead us to consider anew Barth's relation to evangelical Protestantism as well. There are two ramifications that we might draw in light of the conclusions made above.

First, any discussion of evangelicalism and Barth need not and should not restrict itself to areas of evangelicalism that are usually identified with its strictly

---

66. CD IV/1: p. 497.
67. CD IV/3.2: pp. 677–80.
68. Barth, *Gespräche 1964–1968*, p. 390.

confessional and more scholastic traditions. Barth's relationship to evangelicalism of this type could be rocky (e.g., the Westminster theology of Cornelius van Til). Yet, with regard to understandings of Scripture and confessions in particular, Barth may be more amenable to evangelicalism if seen in the light of its pietistic traditions and not solely in terms of those that espouse a more rigid subscriptionism as heirs of Protestant Orthodoxy, whether of the Lutheran or Reformed variety. The future of evangelicalism may thus find in Barth an ally, but not an ally that some might expect or even desire. Moreover, if such a nuanced estimation of Barth's relation to Pietism has validity, then comparisons between Barth and Pietism conducted by evangelicals need to be based upon an informed evaluation of the relation between a complex and subtle thinker and a complex and diverse tradition, not between a theologian dismissed through tired clichés and a concept essentially defined such that it is ruled dubious by its very definition, a tradition portrayed as a caricature of itself. Such things will not do. The simplistic caricatures (but not informed criticisms) of Pietism should now be laid to rest for good, and this should be done for Barth, too.[69]

The second ramification pertains not strictly to a comparison between Barth and evangelicalism, but to an understanding of evangelicalism itself. For evangelicalism, like Pietism, is also a contested concept, in no small way due to the confluence of various traditions that have formed it (English Puritanism and continental Pietism being two of the most important, and these themselves distinct but with their own areas of overlap).[70] If so, then the attempt to give essentialist definitions here, too, falls short. What we have in evangelicalism are various traditions not always directly related or derived from one another, but traditions able to recognize shared convictions and concerns between them. Such different traditions, both those primarily confessional and those primarily pietistic, bear family resemblances to one another. These traditions cannot be subsumed into one another but neither can they be entirely separated. Barth's essentialist

---

69. Estimations of Barth's criticisms of Pietism not only reflect how one views Pietism but how one views Barth's own concerns. Some might laud Barth as perceiving the deficiencies of anthropomorphic religion, seeing Pietism as the true forerunner of the turn from God to the human subject celebrated in Romanticism. Others might criticize Barth for a pneumatological deficiency or an underdeveloped theology of the third article for which Pietism is an answer. Whether these ways of thinking are really fair to either Pietism or Barth is itself a question of importance, but not one that can be taken up here.

70. That Puritanism and Pietism can no longer be seen as isolated traditions even if they can be distinguished is made evident not only in the scholarship of Stoeffler but also that of W. R. Ward—see his *Early Evangelicalism: A Global Intellectual History, 1670–1789* (Cambridge: Cambridge University Press, 2006). This conclusion is now generally accepted in historical scholarship—for example, Mark Noll, *The Rise of Evangelicalism: The Age of Edwards, Whitefield and the Wesleys* (Downers Grove: Intervarsity, 2003), esp. pp. 50–75. For Stoeffler's own comment on the pluriform influences behind American Christianity and both the virtues and vices of Pietism, see *Continental Pietism and Early American Christianity*, ed. F. Ernest Stoeffler (Grand Rapids: Eerdmans, 1976), pp. 266–71.

understanding of Pietism could not do justice to its complexity and diversity, but neither can an essentialist definition of evangelicalism that sees it solely as the product of Protestant Orthodoxy or Reformed confessionalism truly capture its diverse pedigree and character.

American evangelicalism is the product of a cross-fertilization of confessional and pietistic traditions. The cross-fertilization of English Puritanism (with its Reformed roots and doctrinal proclivities) and continental Pietism (with its Lutheran roots and experiential proclivities) produced seeds that blew across the Atlantic to germinate in the soil of America, producing the mixed harvest of New England Puritanism, but also the Great Awakening and later revivalism. This was a world of Whitefield and Wesley, Zinzendorf and Edwards, a world where the Puritan Cotton Mather could write and communicate appreciably with the Pietist Franke.[71] No longer can these traditions be seen as strictly isolated and neatly contained and circumscribed ones; they are not parallel lines that never touch, but strands crisscrossing in a tightly braided rope connecting the Old World and the New. A rope tightly woven cannot be neatly undone, nor can its identity, or even strength, be isolated to one strand, for as Wittgenstein relates, "the strength of the thread does not reside in the fact that some one fibre runs through its whole length, but in the overlapping of many fibres."[72]

Modern evangelicalism is indeed a multi-braided rope of many strands, its unity found not in a single narrative but in a weaving of various narratives recognized as similar through resemblances and common themes.[73] No wonder that some on both the Reformed and Wesleyan wings of this movement have thought that it is best to abandon the term "evangelicalism" altogether.[74] But that is only to move the question back a step, for "Reformed" is also a contested concept. Is Barth a Reformed theologian? Van Til might give one answer; G. C. Berkouwer may give another.

The future of a theological conversation is thus informed by historical narratives we tell ourselves—but it is and need not be strictly determined by them. This is as true for conversations pertaining to evangelicalism's evaluation and appropriation of Barth's theology as it is for conversations of the future (and meaningfulness) of

---

71. For the interconnections of all of these figures within the New World, see W. R. Ward, *The Protestant Evangelical Awakening* (Cambridge: Cambridge University Press, 1992).

72. *Philosophical Investigations*, §67. One is also reminded of Ecclesiastes 4:12. Wittgenstein intertwines the illustrations of family resemblances and those of a rope here in the *Investigations*, and so we may as well: while some may try to write the history of evangelicalism by excising pietistic influences, this is like someone cutting embarrassing cousins out of family photos. They remain part of the family. One can try to form a new family, and one need not invite the cousins to future family gatherings, but one cannot change the past—only try to re-write it.

73. Kenneth J. Collins, *The Evangelical Moment: The Promise of an American Religion* (Grand Rapids: Baker Academic, 2005), pp. 19–22.

74. There are of course other reasons one might abandon the term, but that is a story that cannot be told here.

evangelicalism's own identity. Typologies order experience, and thus they may be necessary, but neat and tidy typologies imposed upon history can classify traditions and schools and movements in ways that often distort as much as illumine the past. As with so many areas of historical investigation, in evangelicalism we are not left with clean lines of genetic descent, but crisscrossing and overlapping patterns of similarities. Perhaps the future of theology thus belongs more to Wittgenstein than to Plato. And in the face of increasing secularization without and dissolution within, some pause to evangelical infighting is opportune and need not betray doctrinal indifference. We should at least take time to ponder Ward's conclusion: "Whether either tradition [Pietist or Protestant Orthodox] can excogitate an effective approach to populations with no smoldering embers of faith to revive is doubtful."[75] The reason that we need not in the end despair over this prognosis is due to a promise that God himself upholds and one both Spener and Barth could claim, for both knew that it is no human hand that fans the flame.

---

75. Ward, *The Protestant Evangelical Awakening*, p. 355.

## Chapter 7

## KARL BARTH AND KIERKEGAARD: UNACKNOWLEDGED DEBTS TO A LUTHERAN EXISTENTIAL PIETIST

The relationship between the thought of Søren Kierkegaard and the theology of Karl Barth is one that, while receiving some consideration in the past, has in recent years begun to receive a deserved reexamination. In studies of Barth's theology, much more attention has been paid to the relationship of the nineteenth century's most famous theologian, Friedrich Schleiermacher, to Barth, and yet while Barth gleaned a number of important programmatic themes from Schleiermacher and the liberal tradition that is traced back to him, Barth rejected what he perceived to be the underlying anthropological starting point of Schleiermacher's work and the ensuing liberal tradition's theological program. In Barth's decisive break with Schleiermacher's legacy and Neo-Protestantism, he readily professed that he found an ally in Kierkegaard. Yet his appropriation of Kierkegaard was seemingly short-lived, for in time he came to consider Kierkegaard as part of the problem of the nineteenth-century heritage against which he was reacting, rather than as part of a solution to it.

In the following I set out to do three things. I aim, first, to trace the trajectory of Barth's reception of Kierkegaard's work; second, to delineate what Barth found increasingly problematic about Kierkegaard's thought and why he largely left it behind him; and third, to point briefly to areas where Barth, in spite of this open abandonment and criticism, nonetheless displayed in his work an ongoing debt to Kierkegaard. In other words, though Barth became more critical of Kierkegaard as time progressed, his appropriation of Kierkegaard's work in his early period incorporated themes that had an ongoing significance far beyond Barth's acknowledgment of them. As such, this relation deserves reconsideration by those who give attention to the development and content of Barth's theology.

### *Barth's Discovery of a Danish Ally*

Karl Barth was the product of German Neo-Protestantism and yet did more than anyone in his day to call it into question. Barth's break with the Neo-Protestant tradition, a tradition tracing itself through various tributaries that ran from Schleiermacher up through Albrecht Ritschl, Adolf von Harnack, and Wilhelm

Herrmann, and further on to Ernst Troeltsch and the *Religionsgeschichtliche Schule*, is well-rehearsed.¹ These figures could differ greatly in theological program—consider, for instance, the enduring debate between Herrmann and Troeltsch with regard to the relation between religious faith and historical science.² Yet what bound them together was that they all began the theological task with reflection upon human experience, whether Herrmann's description of the internal religiosity of the believer that was predicated upon and traced its source back to the inner consciousness and personality of Jesus, or the critical historicism of Troeltsch's comparative examination of Christian history carried out in order to find an essence of Christianity amid historical relativities, with Troeltsch himself becoming increasingly pessimistic of its very possibility.³ Barth came to spurn both of these pathways for theology as well as all forms of psychologism and historicism. He thus rejected both the immanentalism and positivism of nineteenth-century religion and alternatively began a new engagement with Scripture. Along the way he discovered new allies and resources for a theology that focused upon God's transcendent revelation that came from above (*extra nos*) and was set over against all cultural religiosity and its attendant domestication of divine revelation to serve personal, cultural, or national programs and purposes. One of the most important of these allies by Barth's own admission was Kierkegaard.⁴

Barth's discovery of Kierkegaard in the opening two decades of the twentieth century was not accidental. Looking back upon this period, Barth could in 1928 during a series of lectures in ethics make reference to a virtual "Kierkegaard-renaissance" of the previous decade.⁵ While it is difficult to discern what exactly

---

1. For Barth's early education, development, and eventual break with Neo-Protestantism, see Eberhard Busch, *Karl Barth: His Life from Letters and Autobiographical Texts*, trans. John Bowden (Grand Rapids: Eerdmans, 1994), pp. 33–125; Gary Dorrien, *The Barthian Revolt in Modern Theology* (Louisville, KY: Westminster John Knox, 2000), pp. 14–80; and Bruce L. McCormack, *Karl Barth's Critically Realistic Dialectical Theology: Its Genesis and Development 1909-1936* (Oxford: Clarendon Press, 1995), pp. 31–125.

2. Brent Sockness, *Against False Apologetics: Wilhelm Herrmann and Ernst Troeltsch in Conflict* (Tübingen: J. C. B. Mohr, 1998); Hendrikus Berkhof, *Two Hundred Years of Theology: Report of a Personal Journey*, trans. John Vriend (Grand Rapids: Eerdmans, 1989), pp. 143–62; and George Rupp, *Culture-Protestantism: German Liberal Theology at the Turn of the Twentieth Century* (Missoula, MT: Scholar's Press, 1977).

3. Berkhof, *Two Hundred Years*, pp. 156–9.

4. Nels F. S. Ferré, "Contemporary Theology in the Light of 100 Years," *Theology Today* 15 (1958), pp. 366–76 (371); see also Hans Urs von Balthasar, *The Theology of Karl Barth*, trans. Edward T. Oakes (San Francisco: Ignatius Press, 1992), p. 69.

5. Karl Barth, *Ethik I 1928*, ed. Dietrich Braun (Zürich: Theologischer Verlag Zürich, 1973), p. 10; ET: *Ethics*, ed. Dietrich Braun, trans. Geoffrey W. Bromiley (New York: Seabury Press, 1981), p. 8. Barth would reflect upon his own place in that renaissance years later upon his reception of the Sonning Prize in 1963—see Karl Barth, "A Thank-You and a Bow—Kierkegaard's Reveille," in *Fragments Grave and Gay*, ed. Martin Rumscheidt, trans. Eric Mosbacher (London: Collins/Fontana, 1971), pp. 95–101 (98); originally published in *Evangelische Theologie* 23 (1963), pp. 337–42.

Barth was reading leading up to and following the writing of his second edition of the *Romans* commentary in 1922, itself a significant milestone in his break with the liberal tradition, Philip Ziegler has stated that it is safe to say that Kierkegaard was mediated to Barth in three ways during this time.[6] First, Barth himself read Kierkegaard during this early period. He read at the very least Kierkegaard's *Practice in Christianity* and *The Instant*, along with selections from Kierkegaard's journals and diaries, at some point during 1920 and 1921.[7] Second, Barth became familiar with Kierkegaard's thought through his close friend and colleague Eduard Thurneysen, who also introduced him to Dostoevsky. Finally, Barth became acquainted with Kierkegaard through his encounters with Emmanuel Hirsch, his colleague in Göttingen who joined the theological faculty there at the same time as Barth in 1921.[8] These influences were not of a piece, however. While Barth welcomed Thurneysen's recommendations as his close colleague and collaborator, Barth chafed at the German nationalism that surfaced as Hirsch rather ignored Kierkegaard's later theological works and appropriated Kierkegaard for a German nationalist agenda.[9] Kierkegaard's impact upon Barth's development thus came in the midst of a general Kierkegaard renaissance, but one made up of various and competing voices.

---

6. Philip Ziegler, "Barth's Criticisms of Kierkegaard—A Striking out at Phantoms?," *International Journal of Systematic Theology* 9 (2007), pp. 434–51 (435–7); cf. Lee C. Barrett, "Karl Barth: The Dialectic of Attraction and Repulsion," in *Kierkegaard's Influence on Theology: Tome I: German Protestant Theology*, ed. Jon Stewart (Aldershot: Ashgate, 2012), pp. 1–42 (7–19).

7. Ziegler maintains that Barth also read the *Philosophical Fragments* during this same span of years evidenced by references to it in Barth's dogmatics lectures of 1924. That there are affinities between the *Fragments* and Barth's first dogmatics lectures will be addressed below. Heiko Shultz states that Barth did indeed read the *Fragments* as well as *Practice in Christianity*, along with Kierkegaard's journals and other works, by the time of the second edition of the Romans commentary. See Heiko Shultz, "A Modest Head Start: The German Reception of Kierkegaard," in *Kierkegaard's International Reception: Tome I: Northern and Western Europe*, ed. Jon Stewart (Surrey/Burlington: Ashgate, 2009), pp. 307–419 (336); cf. Barrett, "Karl Barth," pp. 11–12.

8. Added to Ziegler's list of influences might be another person of great impact upon Barth's early thought, Leonhard Ragaz, who was the first in Switzerland to delve deeply into Kierkegaard. In a phrase pregnant with Barthian reverberations that could have been written by Barth himself to reflect his own development, Ragaz reflected upon his early years: "If Kierkegaard meant the great No in my life, Blumhardt meant the great Yes." See Leonhard Ragaz, *Mein Weg: V. 1* (Zurich: Diana Verlag, 1952), p. 114; quoted in James D. Smart, *The Divided Mind of Modern Theology: Karl Barth and Rudolf Bultmann, 1908–1933* (Philadelphia: Westminster Press, 1967), p. 64. The same indirect influence may also have come to Barth through J. T. Beck, for whom Kierkegaard was "the only distinguished theologian of the time of whom Beck had a good opinion." See Karl Barth, *Protestant Theology in the Nineteenth Century* (Valley Forge: Judson Press, 1973), p. 618. Balthasar attributes this influence of Kierkegaard also indirectly to Barth's own teacher Wilhelm Herrmann (Balthasar, *The Theology of Karl Barth*, p. 34).

9. Ziegler, "Barth's Criticisms of Kierkegaard," pp. 436–7.

Kierkegaard's impact on Barth could at times be seen in subtle ways during this period. For instance, Barth borrowed Kierkegaard's title "Training in Christianity" for his last two confirmation classes in Safenwil in 1920/21 and 1921/22.[10] As one pastor to another, he could write to Thurneysen in June of 1920 that in his preparation for his work in 2 Corinthians he often began with Kierkegaard: "The composition frequently begins with a little private morning devotion [*einer kleinen privaten Morgenandacht*] from Kierkegaard."[11] Indeed, Barth's letters to Thurneysen from the opening years of the 1920s contain numerous passing references to Kierkegaard.

The most important reference to Kierkegaard during this period, however, and the high point of Barth's open and appreciative dependence upon Kierkegaard's work, occurred in the second edition of Barth's famous *Romans* commentary published in 1922. In its preface, Barth listed a number of influences upon his thought that shaped the changes that were made from the first to the second edition, a list headed by the Apostle Paul himself, but including an assortment of persons such as the critic of religion Franz Overbeck, the philosophers Plato and Kant, and the works of Dostoevsky and Kierkegaard.[12] It was of the last that Barth famously wrote in response to charges by reviewers of the first edition that he had imposed his own "system" upon the Pauline text: "My reply is that, if I have a system, it is limited to a recognition of what Kierkegaard called the 'infinite qualitative distinction' between time and eternity, and to my regarding this as possessing negative as well as positive significance: 'God is in heaven, and thou art on earth.'"[13] References to Kierkegaard are widespread throughout Barth's commentary, and it is characteristically deemed to be the highpoint of Kierkegaard's influence upon Barth's thought, witnessed not only in its frequent use of and allusion to paradox, but also Barth's utilization of a highly dialectical method of presentation.[14]

---

10. Karl Barth, *Konfirmandenunterricht 1909–1921*, ed. J. Fangmeier (Zurich: Theologischer Verlag Zürich, 1987), pp. 263 and 405.

11. Letter of June 7, 1920 in *Barth-Thurneysen Briefwechsel 1913–1921*, ed. Eduard Thurneysen (Zürich: Theologischer Verlag Zürich, 1973), p. 395; ET: *Revolutionary Theology in the Making: Barth-Thurneysen Correspondence, 1914–1925*, trans. James D. Smart (Richmond: John Knox Press, 1964), p. 51.

12. Karl Barth, *Der Römerbrief* (Zollikon-Zürich: Evangelischer Verlag, 1940), p. 7; ET: *The Epistle to the Romans*, trans Edwyn C. Hoskyns (Oxford: Oxford University Press, 1933), pp. 3–4. Barth would reiterate this list years later in his Sonning Prize address (Barth, "A Thank-You and a Bow," pp. 97–8).

13. Barth, *Der Römerbrief*, p. 13; ET: p. 10. An essay of 1922 entitled "The Word of God as the Task of Theology" also makes reference to this "infinite qualitative distinction" as the "infinite distance between Creator and creature" (WGT, pp. 171–98 [189]). For instances of this phrase in Kierkegaard's own work, see Søren Kierkegaard, *Practice in Christianity*, ed. and trans. Howard V. Hong and Edna H. Hong (Princeton: Princeton University Press, 1991), pp. 127–8 and 140; also Søren Kierkegaard, *Sickness unto Death*, ed. and trans. Howard V. Hong and Edna H. Hong (Princeton: Princeton University Press, 1980), p. 126; cf. pp. 99 and 121.

14. For a list of references to Kierkegaard in the second edition of Barth's commentary, see Barth, "The Word of God as the Task of Theology," p. 189 n. 57; for a (partial) index of Barth's references to Kierkegaard throughout his corpus, see Barrett, "Karl Barth," pp. 35–6.

Kierkegaard was being read not only by Barth and his friend and collaborator Thurneysen, however, but also by numerous persons who, with Barth, would form the so-called dialectical school of theology centered around the journal *Zwischen den Zeiten*, persons such as Rudolf Bultmann, Friedrich Gogarten, Paul Tillich, and Emil Brunner.[15] If we appreciate the significance of this fact, we may be on our way to understanding why Barth in time distanced himself from Kierkegaard.

## Barth Reveres the Ally, but Now with (More) Reservations

Barth's relationship to Kierkegaard was never simple. Even in the period of Barth's most open appreciation for Kierkegaard, his approval was never without some equivocation, such as his reference to the poison of Kierkegaard's intense pietism even in the *Romans* commentary (*der giftige Überpietismus, den Kierkegaard*).[16] Perhaps not too much should be made of this allusion, however, for even though this judgment foreshadows Barth's estimation of Kierkegaard as the years went by as witnessed below, Barth could in the very same passage here referenced equally criticize the religiosity of other important and named shapers of his thought, including the "hysterical world-fatigue" or "inner conflict" (*die hysterische Zerrisenheit*) of Dostoevsky and the "far too easy complacency" (*die allzu große Gemütlichkeit*) of the elder and younger Blumhardts.[17] Nevertheless, Barth's references to Kierkegaard in the immediate period following the composition of the second *Romans* commentary were markedly even if not uniformly positive. In a lecture given in June of 1922 entitled "The Need and Promise of Christian Proclamation," Barth could compare his own theology to the "pinch of spice" that was Kierkegaard's, a phrase famously made by Kierkegaard in reference to his own thought.[18] Barth saw himself and Kierkegaard as kindred spirits and prophets in arms who provided a dialectical and polemical criticism of mistaken theological positions and the Christendom of their respective times, but neither as providing a truly new school of thought. In this, Barth saw Kierkegaard not only as an ally but a forerunner of his own task, the most esteemed and bold of "knights on a chessboard," an open allusion to Kierkegaard's "knight of faith."[19]

---

15. See the essays on these figures, as well as those on Hirsch and Overbeck, in Stewart, ed., *Kierkegaard's Influence on Theology: Tome I: German Protestant Theology*; also Niels Thustrup and M. Mikulová, eds., *The Legacy and Interpretation of Kierkegaard* (Copenhagen: C A. Reitzels Boghandel, 1981), pp. 68–83 and 224–42.

16. Barth, *Der Römerbrief*, p. 259; ET: p. 276.

17. Barth, *Der Römerbrief*, p. 259; ET: p. 276. At the very least, such a reference cannot be used to argue against Kierkegaard's importance to Barth during this period without also extending such an argument against the importance of the Blumhardts.

18. Søren Kierkegaard, *Buch des Richters. Seines Tagebücher 1833–1855*, ed. and trans. Hermann Gottsched (Jena and Leipzig: Diederichs, 1905), pp. 99–100; Barth, "The Need and Promise of Christian Proclamation" in WGT, pp. 101–29 (104; cf. 128).

19. Ibid., pp. 103–5.

This positive estimation of Kierkegaard during this period is perhaps nowhere as evident as in a lecture given in October of the same year. There Barth placed Kierkegaard in a genealogy of august forebears to which, Barth insisted, theology must be oriented for the future. In that lecture entitled "The Word of God as the Task of Theology," later published, Barth stated:

> I would like to conclude this discussion with a historical footnote. If my reflections here are decisive in any way, then the line of ancestors upon which we have to orient ourselves runs through *Kierkegaard* to *Luther* and *Calvin*, to *Paul* to *Jeremiah*. Many are used to calling upon these familiar names.

Barth emphasized that this line of theological ancestry did not include but stood over against another one from Erasmus to Hans Lassen Martensen, the Lutheran bishop of Denmark whose funeral sermon given at the burial of his predecessor Jakob Peter Mynster led Kierkegaard to take up a strident attack against the church of his day.[20] Most notably missing from the approved genealogy, Barth emphasized, is Schleiermacher. What is important to note here is how Kierkegaard is placed firmly in a list of Barth's theological heroes—Jeremiah, Paul, and the Reformers Luther and Calvin—and correspondingly how Schleiermacher is placed within a line that may not unwarrantedly be termed "theological traitors." In the following year during a series of lectures on Schleiermacher, Barth could in like manner place Kierkegaard in a more contemporary list of theological and intellectual stalwarts such as J. C. Blumhardt and his son Christoph, Franz Overbeck, J. T. Beck, and Hermann Kutter (among others), and stated that "it would be well worth giving a series of lectures on these seven thousand who did not bow the knee to Baal [cf. 1 Kings 19:18]."[21]

While Barth could continue to make positive reference to Kierkegaard in these immediate years following the writing of the second edition of the *Romans* commentary, this positive appraisal and citation nevertheless always coincided with an ambiguity regarding Kierkegaard's thought. Even in 1922 there are hints of a more reserved and critical estimation of Kierkegaard. In his very same October lecture, after listing Kierkegaard in his esteemed genealogy of heroes previously mentioned, Barth nevertheless went on to state that Kierkegaard cannot provide the last word for theological reflection, for even with his incisive criticism of the human situation, "we do not get beyond the violent sharpening of the question as a question." He continued:

> What this means, then, is that when the human is called into question, we must show—properly show—the place where the speaking of God can happen. But even this is not yet speaking of God. It is not yet it. Even Luther's and

---

20. Barth, "The Word of God as the Task of Theology," pp. 182–4; for Martensen, see p. 182 n. 45.
21. Karl Barth, *The Theology of Schleiermacher: Lectures at Göttingen, Winter Semester of 1923/24*, ed. Dietrich Ritschl, trans. Geoffrey W. Bromiley (Grand Rapids: Eerdmans, 1982), p. xv; cf. however p. 230.

Kierkegaard's attacks upon Christendom were not it! The cross is erected, but the resurrection has not yet been proclaimed. And ultimately, it is not the cross of Christ that is being erected here, but some other kind of cross. The cross of Christ certainly does not need to be erected by *us* first! The question has not yet received an answer here. *God* has not yet become human. But now more than ever, the *human* has again become human. And that is not a salvific event. More than ever now, the human's subjectivity towers like a glorious, broken column toward heaven. There is speaking of God only where *God* becomes human (in that objectivity which orthodoxy knows so much about!); only where he enters into our emptiness with his *fullness*, into our 'No' with his 'Yes.' The mystics, and we with them, do not speak about this God.[22]

What is particularly noteworthy is that a number of Barth's later criticisms of Kierkegaard are already present here in nascent form in 1922: first, that Kierkegaard focuses upon anthropological analysis and begins with human subjectivity rather than with God's revelation and objectivity for his understanding of God and the human person; and second, that there is a dourness in Kierkegaard's thought that betrays an implicit legalism and emphasis upon divine judgment, cross, and discipleship that in turn overlooks the transcending message of divine grace, resurrection, and finished divine accomplishment. Moreover, one also sees that Barth's critical estimation of Kierkegaard rides in tandem with his increasingly wary estimation of Luther, for whom Barth had nonetheless an ongoing and inestimable appreciation and respect.[23] In brief, Barth was concerned that in Luther and Lutheranism there was a *reversal* of the order of God and the human in theological reflection (beginning with the human person in terms of sin and faith rather than with divine revelation, thus grounding theology in anthropology), as

---

22. Barth, "The Word of God as the Task of Theology," p. 190. Barth placed Kierkegaard not in the dialectical way of theology that Barth was proffering, but as an example of the way of self-criticism (also called the way of mysticism or idealism—itself set over against the way of dogmatism). For Barth, the questioning of the human does not reach or constitute revelation. It is, rather, simply the diagnosis of a disease and thus remains very much a human word (p. 190). Interestingly, Barth's layered estimation of Luther (see the following note) is mirrored in the fact that he finds Luther's own thought as presenting examples of all three of these ways—those of dogmatism, self-criticism, and dialectic (p. 186).

23. Barth could also link Luther and Kierkegaard in an ambivalent way in his 1922 lecture "The Problem of Ethics Today" (see WGT, pp. 131-70 [156]), but alternate this with a more positive assessment of them (p. 165; cf. pp. 167-8). For Barth's appreciative yet critical appraisal of Luther (and Lutheranism) during this period, see "The Problem of Ethics Today," pp. 131-69, esp. 160-3; also the 1923 essay "Luther's Doctrine of the Eucharist: Its Basis and Purpose," in TC, pp. 74-111; and his 1923 lectures published as *The Theology of the Reformed Confessions*, trans. Darrell L. Guder and Judith J. Guder (Louisville: Westminster John Knox Press, 2002), pp. 1-37 and 153-206.

well as a *confusion* of the divine and the human, such that the Word of revelation and the medium of its proclamation (in word and sign) become identified.[24]

Nevertheless, these newly articulated criticisms did not preclude Barth from continuing to make positive references to Kierkegaard's theological contribution in the ensuing years and indeed for years to come. In a public and published debate with Paul Tillich in 1923, Barth could compare Tillich's "positive paradox" to the loss of the dialectical relation of God and world, such that Tillich's understanding of God and the world resembled for Barth no longer the God of Luther and Kierkegaard but that of Schleiermacher and Hegel.[25] Moreover, Tillich runs the risk of "letting the justified polemic against the '*man-god*,' once waged by Kierkegaard and Dostoevsky, be converted into its opposite, the polemic against the *God-man*."[26] There is no doubt here which side Barth himself endorses.

After 1923, however, the scales begin to tip in Kierkegaard's disfavor, as Barth's positive references to Kierkegaard become more infrequent and his critical comments increase. In his response to Erich Peterson in 1925, Barth can still speak of Kierkegaard's polemical project as necessary in some regard, but now Barth seems equally mindful of the deficiencies of Kierkegaard's despondency and of his individualism, a third and enduring criticism of Kierkegaard that Barth now adds to the two given earlier: a dour legalism and an anthropological starting point in human subjectivity.[27] This ambiguity regarding Kierkegaard's individualism is in evidence in Barth's first dogmatic lectures of 1924–6, lectures marked by Barth's characteristic mixture of appreciation and criticism of Kierkegaard. Two prominent examples of his criticism of Kierkegaard's individualism mark this new theme in Barth's work and are related to one another. First, Barth stated that Kierkegaard's individualism cannot do justice to the place and identity of the preacher within the church: "The Christian preacher is not only the 'Individual,' as Kierkegaard

---

24. Barth judged this sacramental confusion to be rooted in a christological one and a problematic understanding of the *communicatio idiomatum*. See Karl Barth, "The Substance and Task of Reformed Doctrine" in WGT, pp. 199–237 (225–37).

25. Karl Barth, "Von der Paradoxie des 'positiven Paradoxes.' Antworten und Fragen an Paul Tillich, 1923," in *Vorträge und kleinere Arbeiten 1922–1925*, ed. Holger Finze (Zürich: Theologischer Verlag Zürich, 1990), pp. 349–80 (369); ET: James M. Robinson, ed., *The Beginnings of Dialectic Theology*, trans. Keith R. Crim and Louis De Gratzia (Richmond: John Knox Press, 1968), pp. 133–58 (149). In this debate, Barth turns Kierkegaardian themes (such as paradox and indirectness) against Tillich, but also notably contrasts Tillich and Luther. Yet as earlier noted, Barth could at times criticize Luther for the same reason as he could Tillich, that is, for sacrificing the indirect nature of the relationship between God and the world. Where Barth decisively differed from Tillich (as well as from Bultmann and Herrmann) was in his strict reversal of their law-gospel distinction with its focus upon soteriology and subjectivity, a reversal culminating in his own gospel-law concept as rooted in christology and his emphasis upon the objectivity of revelation. Here he also differed from Kierkegaard—see Barrett, "Karl Barth," p. 32.

26. Barth, "Von der Paradoxie des 'positiven Paradoxes,'" pp. 370–3; ET "The Paradoxical Nature of the 'Positive Paradox,'" p. 151.

27. Karl Barth, "Church and Theology" in TC, pp. 286–306 (306).

described him" (*Der christliche Prediger is nicht nur der "Einzelne", wie Kierkegaard ihn geschildert hat*). He is this, and must be this, but he is not only this, for he is set within the wider context of the history of those others who have spoken about God within the church.[28] Here Barth's more positive ecclesiology begins to sharpen his criticism of individualism and its nineteenth-century emphasis.

The other side of this criticism of Kierkegaard's individualism is therefore Barth's estimation that Kierkegaard has not taken the church with sufficient seriousness. Barth can express thankfulness for Kierkegaard's trenchant criticism of the church's sinfulness and failure and even acknowledge the necessity of a prophetic polemic against its triumphalism (a polemic Barth could share), but he also states that the invisible church in the visible, the church believed in faith that exists in spite of such sinfulness because of God's divine activity in and through it, cannot lose its righteousness or the Holy Spirit. This is so not because of an intrinsic quality within the church, but because of God's own faithfulness and action: "The body of Christ can be sick, but it cannot die." Persons must take great care, Barth warns, that when they criticize the church, they do not overstep the boundary and criticize Christ. Kierkegaard has overstepped this boundary, Barth charges, and for this reason should not be followed in this regard.[29]

Thus by 1926 Barth's three essential criticisms of Kierkegaard that he would later summarize in his famous Sonning prize address in 1963 are already in place and made explicit. For Barth, Kierkegaard's thought began with reflection upon human subjectivity (rather than the objectivity of revelation), betrayed a moralistic seriousness that verged on legalism, and was marked by an individualism that failed to take seriously the church as Christ's body in the world.[30] Such subjectivity, moralism, and individualism marked Kierkegaard as not the solution to, but an exemplar of, the nineteenth-century theology that Barth had rejected.[31]

In light of these criticisms, Barth began to distance himself from Kierkegaard's thought. This distancing was entwined with and even to some degree due to Barth's more circumspect attitude to Luther and Lutheranism, but this was not the most important reason. The primary reason Barth seems to have distanced himself from Kierkegaard was his own negative estimation of Kierkegaard's emphasis upon human subjectivity that he saw mirrored in and influencing the anthropological and existential theologies of the other dialectical theologians that he had earlier esteemed kindred spirits but now held to be still mired in the liberal theological way of the nineteenth century—particularly Bultmann, Tillich, Gogarten, and, though to a lesser degree, Brunner. Barth's growing negative assessment of Kierkegaard was tied to Kierkegaard's

28. Unterricht I, p. 63; ET: GD, p. 53.
29. Unterricht III, pp. 355–6. Barth brings these criticisms together in CD IV/1: p. 689; cf. Karl Barth, *The Christian Life*, trans. Geoffrey W. Bromiley (Grand Rapids: Eerdmans, 1981), pp. 83–4 and 189.
30. See Barth, "A Thank-You and a Bow," pp. 99–101. These three criticisms are well explored and evaluated by Ziegler, "Barth's Criticisms of Kierkegaard," pp. 434–51.
31. As Barth would make this point in 1963: "To sum up, Kierkegaard was bound more closely to the nineteenth century than we were willing to believe at that time" ("A Thank-You and a Bow," p. 100).

emphasis upon exegeting human experience and subjectivity as the precondition for religious faith. This emphasis upon an examination of human subjectivity was, in Barth's estimation, echoed in and indeed furthered by the existential starting points and projects of Bultmann, Tillich, and Gogarten. These were paths Barth simply came to reject. Barth decisively broke up the dialectical school in light of these insurmountable disagreements between himself and these others because he came to see these colleagues as retaining and continuing the fixation on human subjectivity endemic to the nineteenth century with its attendant individualism, moralism, and religious inwardness. They were, in Barth's judgment, simply continuing in new form a mistaken liberal tradition. To reject them meant he had to renounce one of their significant theological and philosophical forebearers, namely Kierkegaard.[32] The division between Barth and his colleagues included a decision by Barth to concede Kierkegaard, at least on questions of theological method, to their side of the ledger.

That Barth thought precisely along such lines is readily witnessed in his correspondence from this time. We have already examined Barth's debate with Tillich, so we turn to his distancing from Bultmann during this same period, which displays a darkening appraisal of Kierkegaard. That Barth and Bultmann began as allies is unquestioned, but this was always an uneasy alliance.[33] By 1925, this alliance was significantly fractured. In a letter to Thurneysen in February of that year, Barth recounted how Bultmann visited him in Göttingen, and, while they stood united in public, in private conversation they chided one another and argued their differences. Barth wrote:

> He [Bultmann] reproaches me that I have no 'clean' concepts (concerning which there is really something to be said) and I him that he seems to me too anthropological-Kierkegaardian-Lutheran (+Gogartenian) ('To speak of God means to speak of man'), deals with the Bible after Luther's example with a shocking eclecticism, also has not yet got free of the historical eggshells.[34]

32. Barrett, "Karl Barth," p. 16.
33. See Barth's Preface to the third edition of his *Romans* commentary and his response therein to Bultmann's review of the second edition (Barth, *Der Römerbrief*, pp. 19–23; ET: pp. 15–20). For Barth's complex relationship to Bultmann and the dialectical school, see Christophe Chalamet, *Dialectical Theologians: Wilhelm Herrmann, Karl Barth and Rudolf Bultmann* (Zürich: Theologischer Verlag Zürich, 2005); and Konrad Hammann, *Rudolf Bultmann: A Biography*, trans. Philip E. Devenish (Salem, OR: Polebridge Press, 2013), pp. 139–53, 205–6, 216, 233–9 and 337.
34. Letter of February 15, 1925 in *Barth-Thurneysen Briefwechsel 1921–1930*, ed. Eduard Thurneysen (Zürich: Theologischer Verlag Zürich, 1974), pp. 306–7; ET: *Revolutionary Theology in the Making*, p. 206. McCormack notes that Barth's break with Bultmann and Gogarten was bound up with his Reformed standpoint that he believed conflicted with their Lutheranism (*Karl Barth's Theology*, p. 392; cf. Chalamet, *Dialectical Theologians*, pp. 196–7). It is noteworthy and telling that Bultmann disagreed with Barth's exclusion of Schleiermacher from his list of theological paragons: "I myself put Schleiermacher in the sequence from Jeremiah to Kierkegaard. Yes, I do." See *Karl Barth – Rudolf Bultmann Letters 1922–1966*, ed. Bernd Jaspert, trans. Geoffrey W. Bromiley (Grand Rapids: Eerdmans, 1982), p. 6; see also pp. 49–50, 57–9 and 63–5.

Here Barth displays a number of striking shifts from his earlier thought. First, Barth, as before, aligns Luther and Kierkegaard together. But now they belong to a more problematic pedigree, not simply a straightforwardly positive one, for Barth's comparison of Bultmann to Luther and Kierkegaard, not to mention Gogarten, is here not a compliment to any of them. It is, rather, an indictment of a theological tradition that (in its problematic elements, such as those found in certain aspects of Luther's thought, and in programmatic approach, as witnessed in Kierkegaard and Bultmann) had in Barth's judgment given itself to human subjectivity as the starting point for theological reflection. Barth seems, in regard to the question of theological method, to have here shifted Luther and Kierkegaard from the hero to the, if not traitor, then at least mistaken or problematic, side of the theological ledger.[35]

Barth certainly would not abandon Luther to that side of the ledger, though that is a complex topic unto itself, as witnessed earlier. He would also not abandon Kierkegaard to it entirely. Barth's vacillations in his evaluations of Kierkegaard (like those of Luther) demonstrate how difficult it was for Barth to draw up his own theological ancestry and how uncertain he was as to which side of the "naughty or nice" list Kierkegaard should be placed. Even in his next cycle of dogmatic lectures, published as the *Christliche Dogmatik* in 1927 two years after his debate with Bultmann, Barth would reiterate that Kierkegaard stood in the path of those who had "not walked on the main road of more recent theology," that is, not in the liberal tradition of the nineteenth century, and he provided a list of recent theological paragons (which included Kierkegaard) not unlike that given in his Schleiermacher lectures earlier noted.[36] Yet he could also reflect years later that in this second dogmatic cycle he had to move beyond Kierkegaard and his earlier dogmatic lectures in Göttingen:

> I simply could not hold to the theoretical and practical *diastasis* between God and man on which I had insisted at the time of *Romans*, without sacrificing it ... I had to understand Jesus Christ and bring him from the periphery of my thought into the centre. Because I cannot regard subjectivity as being the truth, after a brief encounter I have had to move away from Kierkegaard again.[37]

This quotation itself must be read in light of the still later comment where Barth criticized his own failure to leave anthropology entirely behind even in the *Christliche Dogmatik*.[38]

---

35. In other words, Barth is re-writing his theological family tree on the fly, and whereas some persons seem relatively fixed in this line, Kierkegaard's place (as Luther's) is more tenuous. Indeed, their place shifts depending on the topic under discussion as witnessed earlier (see note 23 above). Later Barth would designate Kierkegaard as the forerunner of a much more problematic group of persons—see CD IV/1: p. 609.

36. Karl Barth, ChrD, vi. Cited in Busch, *Karl Barth*, p. 173.

37. Quoted in Busch, *Karl Barth*, p. 173.

38. CD III/4: p. xii; cf. CD I/1: pp. xi–xvi.

And so these concerns of theological method, of an emphasis upon human subjectivity and existence, and of Kierkegaard's relation to Bultmann, all come together in Barth's *Ethics* lectures of 1928. By then, his criticisms of his contemporaries, whether Emanuel Hirsch on his right, or Bultmann on his left, were tied together by the common thread that each was dependent upon Kierkegaard and the existentialism he fathered.[39] Barth writes:

> For dogmatics, at any rate, it cannot be a matter of indifference that here in the concern of ethics as its own proper concern it comes up against the question of human existence. It is not at all true—I cannot approve of this intrusion of Kierkegaard into theology as it may be seen, if I am right, in Bultmann—that the question of human existence is as much the theme of theology and dogmatics too. The theme of theology and dogmatics is the Word of God, nothing else, but the Word of God is not merely the answer to the question of human existence but also its origin.[40]

Barth's own intentional movement away from Kierkegaard would not be lost on Bultmann in the following decade. In a letter of 1935, he wrote to Barth: "I might also say that the Kierkegaardian element that once influenced you and Thurneysen so strongly has now disappeared."[41]

Bultmann was within his rights to make such a judgment, even if Kierkegaard did not disappear from Barth's work entirely. For Barth came not only to distance himself from Kierkegaard in light of his own estimation of Kierkegaard's influence upon his estranged contemporaries whose way he rejected, but Barth in turn began to downplay Kierkegaard's influence even upon his own prior development. In a 1926 letter to Pastor Harald Wellejus in Denmark, who had asked as to Kierkegaard's influence upon him, Barth stated that while he knew of Kierkegaard for a long time, he did not know him well, and for that reason had no systematic or final position (*systematische und abgeschlossene Stellung*) regarding him. Moreover, Barth averred, he had the impression that others overestimated Kierkegaard's influence upon him. What he owed to Kierkegaard, Barth maintained, were certain individual important suggestions (*einzelne wichtige Anregungen*) that could be easily discovered in the second edition of his *Romans* commentary. But Kierkegaard remained foreign to him. And if, Barth added, it is the case that Kierkegaard is a Pietist, then that would be all the more terrible (*Denn sofern er Pietist ist, ist er mir schrecklich*). Yet he also admitted that he did

---

39. Barth, *Ethik I*, p. 10; ET: p. 8. That Barth discussed Kierkegaard with Hirsch with some intensity is evident from his letters to Thurneysen—see *Barth-Thurneysen Briefwechsel 1921–1930*, pp. 171–2.

40. Barth, *Ethik I*, pp. 25–6; ET: p. 17. Barth had in fact spoken more positively of Kierkegaardian subjectivity only a few years before in 1924/25. See *Unterricht I*, p. 168; ET: GD, pp. 137–8.

41. *Karl Barth—Rudolf Bultmann Letters 1922–1966*, p. 83; see also p. 98.

not know Kierkegaard well enough to make a judgment on this.[42] This did not, it seems, keep Barth from making just such a charge in his 1922 commentary. Despite twists and turns, Barth's general estimation of Kierkegaard was nevertheless for all intents and purposes determined by 1926, regardless of his later positive (and negative) comments referring to him, or any later interaction with his writings (which was rare). To see how far Kierkegaard had fallen in Barth's estimation, one should consider not only what Barth writes about him but also what he does not—Kierkegaard is not even addressed in Barth's lecture cycles on nineteenth-century Protestant theology.[43]

So while Barth could quote Kierkegaard appreciatively during the course of the *Church Dogmatics*, and thus throughout the remainder of his life, it must be admitted that from the mid-to-late 1920s onward Kierkegaard was more and more a peripheral figure whose influence was sporadically witnessed and whose support was drawn upon in a passing and ad hoc manner without exhibiting sustained and deep engagement.[44] With a few minor exceptions that space does not allow us to examine here, there is no serious interaction with Kierkegaard's corpus in Barth's later work. Moreover, the criticisms he has in place in the mid-1920s are simply repeated decades later. This is true not only in the famous Sonning Prize address, Barth's best-known commentary upon Kierkegaard in his later years, but in other lesser-known remarks of that final decade of his life. He had traveled through Kierkegaard, Barth could remark in 1966, like one who traveled through a tunnel that he had entered but out of which he had also passed. Every theologian had to allow oneself to be frightened by Kierkegaard and to take heed of his warnings—but the train needs to keep moving, and Barth was pleased to move on to Luther and Calvin. He had not forgotten Kierkegaard, but he could not simply remain with him, either. To remain simply a Kierkegaard follower (*einfach*

---

42. Karl Barth, *Offene Briefe, 1909–1935*, ed. Diether Koch (Zürich: Theologischer Verlag Zürich, 2001), pp. 107–9. Barth came increasingly to see Kierkegaard through this pietist lens, witnessed in the following comments tracing the genealogy of nineteenth-century liberalism: "The anthropologising of theology was complete. And it is a serious question whether the same is not to be said of the existential element which is demanded to-day from theological thinking and utterance under the influence of Kierkegaard, but supremely if sometimes unconsciously in continuation of the Pietist tradition" (CD I/1: p. 20). He could also state late in life that "Kierkegaard at once appeared to me to be a super-Pietist." See Karl Barth, *Gespräche 1964–1968*, ed. Eberhard Busch (Zürich: Theologischer Verlag Zürich, 1996), p. 294; also Barth, "A Thank-You and a Bow," p. 100; and Karl Barth, "Kierkegaard and the Theologians," in *Fragments Grave and Gay*, pp. 102–4. Hence his criticism ends where it began in 1922—with the association of Kierkegaard with a kind of *Überpietismus* (see note 16 above). For Kierkegaard's background in Pietism and complex relation with it, see Christopher Barnett, *Kierkegaard, Pietism and Holiness* (Surrey/Burlington: Ashgate, 2011), esp. p. 201.

43. These lectures exist in English translation as *Protestant Theology in the Nineteenth Century* (see note 8 above).

44. For an instance of such positive reference, see CD I/1: p. 172.

*als Kierkegaardianer*) is to remain angry. Yes, anger is needed at times, but one cannot maintain such a stance.[45]

A year before his death, Barth echoed these earlier comments and gave his final word on Kierkegaard, and his estimation of him remained ambiguous and mixed to the very end. Barth made peace with Kierkegaard, but it was not a particularly secure one. In a letter to Martin Rumscheidt in November of 1967, Barth wrote:

> Regarding your translation of the essay comparing Kierkegaard and me, perhaps you had best approach Eberhard Busch, as proposed. But I can at least tell you that I am as little an opponent of Kierkegaard now as I was earlier. On the other hand, not even in *Romans* was I a real friend of Kierkegaard, let alone a Kierkegaard enthusiast. I have seriously let his words be *spoken* to me—and let him who wants to be a theologian see to it that he does not miss him. But I have also let his words *be* spoken to me and then gone merrily on my theological way—for I still think that he who meets him and stays with him must take care that the gospel does not become for him an irksome and legalistic thing.[46]

In the end, it may not have been Kierkegaard's fixation on subjectivity, his existentialism, his individualism, his moralism, or even his pietism, that bothered Barth the most. If Barth's last word is any indication, it may have been Kierkegaard's melancholy and dour disposition that Barth felt could not serve well as a witness to the Good News of Jesus Christ, the gospel of grace, God's "Yes" to the world.[47]

Yet there is a notable exception to these late judgments, too. In the final volume of the *Church Dogmatics* on the doctrine of reconciliation, Barth could write that Kierkegaard's focus on human subjectivity did indeed point to an important truth. As Barth came to a realization that an emphasis upon a diastasis between God and man, upon a "wholly other" God, was not a sufficient word but had to be taken up into a fuller understanding of the humanity of God, he could now acknowledge and even embrace the anthropological concerns and even focus upon the individual (if not individualism) found not only in Kierkegaard but in the liberal tradition that he had earlier spurned. He could also therefore take up and appropriate similar themes in Luther and even in Pietism that he had before found so troubling.[48] In commenting on human subjectivity, but now as seen through a firm christological

---

45. Barth, *Gespräche 1964–1968*, p. 294; cf. Barth, "Kierkegaard and the Theologians," pp. 102–4.

46. Barth, *Letters 1961–1968*, ed. Jürgen Fangmeier and Hinrich Stoevesandt, and trans. Geoffrey Bromiley (Grand Rapids: Eerdmans, 1981), p. 273.

47. Kierkegaard may well have recognized this problem of melancholy in himself: "Christianity is not at all closer to heavy-mindedness [*Tungsind*] than to light-mindedness; they are both equally worldliness, equally far away, and both have just as much need of conversion" (*Practice in Christianity*, p. 154).

48. See Karl Barth, *The Humanity of God*, trans. Thomas Wieser and John N. Thomas (Richmond, VA: John Knox Press, 1960) pp. 45–6.

prism and ecclesiological lens, Barth could write that indeed "Jesus Christ is *pro me*," though never in the abstract, and always as "enclosed by the communal *pro nobis* and the even wider *propter nos homines*." He continued:

> In saying this we have made the statement or statements which bring us to the high-water mark of our serious agreement with one line of Luther's thinking, with that of Pietism old and new, with that of Kierkegaard, with that of a theology like W. Herrmann's, and with that of the theological existentialism of our own day (so far as it can be seriously regarded as theological). In this respect they all were and are right: that the question of the individual Christian subject has to be put, and that it has to be answered with the *pro me* of faith. Without the *pro me* of the individual Christian there is no legitimate *pro nobis* of the faith of the Christian community and no legitimate *propter nos homines* of its representative faith for the non-believing world. The being and activity of Jesus Christ has essentially and necessarily the form in which He addresses Himself, not only also, but just to the individual man, to thee and to me, to this man and that man, in which He makes common cause with the individual in his very isolation, in which His Holy Spirit speaks just to his spirit.[49]

In short, Barth could take up the concerns of a line he had spurned, but concerns that had now been transformed and determined by christology (the human person determined by a relation to Christ, rather than an abstract subjectivity per se); by ecclesiology (the communal *pro nobis* and *propter nos homines*, rather than individualism *in se*); and by an unmistakable key of grace and fulfillment *extra nos* (rather than legalism or moralism of any kind).

## *An Inconclusive and Unscientific Postscript*

The preceding depiction of Barth's relationship to Kierkegaard might reinforce a commonly held notion that Kierkegaard's influence on Barth was minimal and that Barth's dismissive judgments of Kierkegaard put this matter to rest, but that would be unfortunate, for the portrait painted above gestures toward a much more intricate and multifaceted reality. First, this picture should give one pause regarding Barth's mature dismissal of Kierkegaard. Barth's distancing of himself from Kierkegaard cannot be separated from his own growing concerns with Luther (and Lutheranism), his negative appraisal of Pietism, and his renunciation of the residual liberalism he esteemed in his own contemporaries, a liberalism now in an existentialist key, but in Barth's estimation a liberalism nonetheless. In time, Barth associated Kierkegaard with all three—Lutheranism, Pietism, and existentialism—and this did not bode well for Barth's estimation of him, especially when he in

---

49. CD IV/1: p. 755.

turn could relate each to Schleiermacher's theology.[50] It should be recognized and acknowledged, however, that Barth's negative evaluation of Kierkegaard in the later 1920s and beyond was due not to an increasing engagement with his actual authorship but through a rapidly changing web of allegiances and alliances, as well as a judgment of Kierkegaard by means of guilt by association.

Second, while Barth's criticisms of Kierkegaard must be seen as relatively consistent from the 1920s onward, with all three of his general criticisms included in the Sonning Prize address already articulated by 1926, such consistency does not necessarily entail complete accuracy. Whether these criticisms are entirely fair to Kierkegaard in every respect is disputable. Ziegler has convincingly shown that Barth's criticisms, while not entirely wide of the mark, are nevertheless selective, characterized by broad stereotype, and do not take into account and overlook important themes in Kierkegaard's actual corpus. While Barth's criticisms of Kierkegaard's individualism and neglect of ecclesiology can be readily defended (though also not without some qualification), his censures of Kierkegaard's subjectivity and legalism, while not indefensible or unwarranted, are nonetheless to a large degree quite broad and unnuanced. At the very least, they overlook Kierkegaard's own important emphasis in some of his works upon christology and a revelation that calls forth, but is not determined by, faith and human decision.[51] Indeed, Kierkegaard could stress the objective reality that made faith possible (incarnation and christology), as well as the divine action required for faith to take its rise (in an at best implicit pneumatology).[52] In other words, Barth failed to acknowledge Kierkegaard's commitment to an objectivity that in point of fact undergirded his emphasis upon subjectivity, even though the latter often

---

50. See Barth, *Theology of Schleiermacher*, p. 271; also CD II/2: p. 308; CD III/2: pp. 21 and 113; CD IV/1: pp. 149-50; and CD IV/3.2: p. 498. Barth in his Sonning Prize address stated that "a theology oriented decisively towards and subsisting essentially on Kierkegaard was possible only where Schleiermacher had not been read with sufficient care and one had not been warned definitely against a continuation of his programme, including an existential one" ("A Thank-You and a Bow," p. 100).

51. Ziegler, "Barth's Criticisms of Kierkegaard," pp. 438-51. For Kierkegaard's christological reflection, see especially his *Philosophical Fragments*, trans. Howard V. Hong and Edna H. Hong (Princeton: Princeton University Press, 1985), esp. pp. 9-36; and *Practice in Christianity*, esp. pp. 123-44.

52. Kierkegaard's discussion of how belief must begin by an act of divine self-disclosure in a creaturely medium (rather than through an act of inner recollection or awareness), a self-disclosure that, to be recognized, itself requires a divine act, is found in the *Philosophical Fragments*—see pp. 23-36; cf. pp. 14-15, 46-7, 55-71, 100 and 104. This act of divine self-disclosure is portrayed by Kierkegaard as an act of self-humiliation for the sake of love for the creature. Both Kierkegaard's christology and pneumatology are underdeveloped in the *Fragments* due to the nature of the thought-experiment he is conducting via Climacus.

overshadowed and at times arguably even undermined the former.[53] Yet most ironic is that Barth's own early christological thought borrowed a number of significant themes from Kierkegaard, as will be seen below.

With these observations in mind, it might be opportune to reconsider Kierkegaard's influence on Barth's thought, and in particular his influence during the period when Barth was actually reading and most open to Kierkegaard's work. Certainly this includes the second edition of the Romans commentary, though this ground is well traveled.[54] Of more interest might be how Kierkegaard's influence extends beyond that work. We have already seen how Kierkegaardian themes permeated Barth's response to Tillich in 1923. But Barth's other famous debate of 1923, that with Adolf von Harnack, also displays Kierkegaard's influence, particularly in arguments against historicism that echo Kierkegaard's thought.[55] The shape of Barth's arguments against historicism there displays at the very least an affinity, if not outright dependence, upon Kierkegaard's thought that cannot simply be explained (away) by the opposition against historicism that Barth inherited from Herrmann.

In turn, when one reads *Practice in Christianity*, as well as *Philosophical Fragments* (granted, pseudonymous writings of Kierkegaard), one is struck not so much by Kierkegaard's emphasis upon subjectivity and human experience, themes so prevalent in many of his other writings, but by his emphasis in these works upon the person of Christ as God's presence indirectly revealed in history behind a veil of human suffering. Christ is thus the incarnate God who stands as the paradox and sign of contradiction, a sign that can be apprehended not by historical investigation or speculative reason, but only in faith, and a faith made possible only by the one who reveals it. In other words, we are confronted with Kierkegaard's focus upon the *objectivity* (and indeed *particularity*) of revelation that precedes, determines, and sets the boundaries for the subjectivity of faith.[56] *Practice in Christianity* (and the *Fragments* as well), along with other more brief

---

53. Ziegler, "Barth's Criticisms of Kierkegaard," p. 439. For a discussion of Kierkegaard's christology, see Murray Rae, *Kierkegaard and Theology* (New York: T&T Clark, 2010), pp. 58–82; also David R. Law, *Kierkegaard's Kenotic Christology* (Oxford: Oxford University Press, 2013), pp. 154–266. That Barth may also have overlooked Kierkegaard's emphasis upon grace as that which framed his understanding of radical obedience is argued by Rae, *Kierkegaard and Theology*, pp. 104–8. For a mitigating discussion of his individualism, see pp. 133–4.

54. See Barrett, "Karl Barth," pp. 7–19.

55. This exchange between Barth and Harnack may be found in Karl Barth, *Offene Briefe 1909–1935*, pp. 55–88; ET: *The Beginnings of Dialectical Theology*, pp. 165–87. Barth's arguments against historicism closely resemble those of Kierkegaard, especially as witnessed in *Practice in Christianity*, pp. 23–30 and 123–44; cf. *Philosophical Fragments*, pp. 55–71, 89–110.

56. Alisdair McKinnon highlights this focus upon the incarnation in Kierkegaard and states that for Kierkegaard "it is the responsibility and duty of the serious Christian to reshape his conceptions of God and man in light of this event." See McKinnon, "Søren Kierkegaard," in *Nineteenth Century Religious Thought in the West*, V. 1, ed., Ninian Smart, John Clayton et al. (Cambridge: Cambridge University Press, 1985), pp. 181–214

writings such as "The Difference between a Genius and an Apostle," were read by Barth in this early period, and their influence on Barth may be greater than he himself acknowledged, a possibility especially intriguing when Barth's early reflections on revelation, christology, and canon in the *Göttingen Dogmatics* are read in their light.[57] Such themes as the divine concealment behind a creaturely veil, the divine incognito, and the indirectness of divine communication understood christologically, leading to the confrontation of Christ as an offense, are all readily witnessed in *Practice in Christianity* and the *Fragments*, but they find their counterparts throughout Barth's first set of dogmatic lectures.[58] They are, in fact, particularly concentrated in Barth's reflections on the incarnation.[59] As but one example, Barth writes: "Now God's revelation in any case means God's revelation in his concealment. It means the radical dedivinization of the world and nature and history, the complete divine *incognito*, God's dealings with us exclusively by *indirect communication*, revelation by law and limit, by distance and judgment."[60]

At the heart of this understanding is that "God takes on concealment in his revelation," and one can ask if there is any direct precedent that provides a context

(199 and 200). Similarly, Hugh Pyper notes: "The common error is to suppose that the Kierkegaardian subject has some form of true existence prior to the fact of God's coming in Christ … Truth is subjective because truth constitutes the subject. This differs crucially from the existentialist misapprehension that it is choice itself that constitutes the subject." See "Søren Kierkegaard," in *The Oxford Companion to Christian Thought*, ed. Adrian Hastings et al. (Oxford: Oxford University Press, 2000), pp. 368-70 (368). Rae argues that Kierkegaard's anthropology is in fact "thoroughly Christological. Christ is the criterion for what it is to be human" (*Kierkegaard and Theology*, p. 98). He draws a direct line from Kierkegaard to Barth on this very point.

57. See note 7 above.

58. For the divine incognito and hiddenness of God, see Kierkegaard, *Practice in Christianity*, pp. 23-6 and 127-33; cf. Kierkegaard, *Philosophical Fragments*, pp. 23-36 and 64; for indirect communication in its christological form, see *Practice in Christianity*, pp. 123-44; cf. *Philosophical Fragments*, pp. 87 and 93; for Christ as an offense, see *Practice in Christianity*, pp. 23-40; cf. *Philosophical Fragments*, pp. 49-54, 93, 94; for Christ as paradox, see *Practice in Christianity*, pp. 25, 30, 63, 82, and 123; for contemporaneity with Christ, see pp. 62-6, 81-3, 94-102. These themes permeate Barth's first dogmatics lectures, the *Göttingen Dogmatics*—for the divine incognito, see GD, pp. 138, 144, 333 and 446-8; cf. p. 178 where it takes on different connotations. It is an absence of this concept that condemns Schleiermacher's theology, p. 184; for a similar appraisal of Roman Catholicism by Barth, see p. 211. For the theme of indirect communication, see pp. 144, 151-2, 178; for Christ as offense, see pp. 131, 157-8, 211, 214, and 334; for Barth's particular take on contemporaneity [*Gleichzeitigkeit*] as pertaining not only to Christ but canon and proclamation, see pp. 142-52, 201-11 and 267-8. For a further comparison of these themes, see Chapter 4 in this volume, above.

59. See particularly Unterricht I, pp. 160-206; ET: GD, pp. 131-67.

60. GD, p. 144 (emphasis added); cf. pp. 138, 152-3, 329-31, 392 and 446.

for such an idea better than Kierkegaard's notion of God's self-revelation precisely through the act of self-disguise, as a king who hides himself in a commoner's apparel to win a maiden. Moreover, even if the general theme of the hiddenness of God can be found in Barth's teacher Herrmann, this christological conception did not belong to the inheritance he left to Barth.[61] It is also the case that Barth in fact juxtaposes Kierkegaard's terminology with his own when he describes the medium of the revelation in Christ as "the *veil*, the *incognito*, in which the divine subjective, I am who I am, the living God, conceals himself and wills to be known, in this way giving himself to be known."[62] And Barth, following Kierkegaard's lead, depicts the great decision prompted by a consideration of Jesus Christ's identity not as one between faith and historical skepticism or doubt (the overriding alternatives as presented in much of modern theology), but rather presents Jesus as the occasion for *offense*, with faith and offense the only two options possible.[63]

This Kierkegaardian influence lessens but nevertheless extends into the *Church Dogmatics*, where Barth draws heavily upon themes such as paradox, contemporaneity, and indirect revelation (communication) in the divine veiling and unveiling. This act of veiling and unveiling takes place by God taking up an inalienable secularity, a form of contradiction intrinsic to the divine act of revelation. All of these Kierkegaardian concepts are readily discerned in Barth's discussion of "The Word of God as the Speech of God," "The Speech of God as the Act of God," and "The Speech of God as the Mystery of God."[64] To acknowledge this debt does not entail that we overlook the fact that Barth did not simply take these concepts over but appropriated and reformulated them for his own distinctive purposes, as he had already done in the *Göttingen Dogmatics* (and earlier in the Romans commentary), often replacing their Kierkegaardian setting in matters of Christian discipleship and subjectivity for one in which they now serve the purposes of illuminating and explicating the divine Self-disclosure in the objectivity of revelation. Nevertheless, in light of such appropriation, it is overly simple and indeed misleading to claim that Kierkegaard served only as a critical and not as a constructive resource for Barth's theology.

Moreover, Kierkegaard's influence may extend even beyond the opening volumes of the *Church Dogmatics*, and a further comparison can reveal surprising

---

61. GD, p. 331; see also p. 446; cf. Kierkegaard's *Philosophical Fragments*, p. 23–36. Kierkegaard can thus state: "If Christ is true God, then he also must be unrecognizable, attired in unrecognizability, which is the denial of all straightforwardness" (*Practice in Christianity*, p. 36). Both Kierkegaard and Barth are clear in their contemplations on divine concealment that these deliberations are best understood not as examinations of *a priori* conditions for the possibility of the incarnation, but as *a posteriori* reflections upon the reality of God's incarnational revelation. See Kierkegaard, *Philosophical Fragments*, pp. 35–6; cf. p. 40; and GD, p. 141.

62. GD, p. 333 (emphasis added); cf. pp. 446–9.

63. See note 58 above.

64. CD I/1: pp. 132–86.

affinities. For Barth in time travels a path Kierkegaard also traveled as he comes to see not only the scandal of the radical particularity of revelation in which God enters the world, but also the particular scandal and offense of the divine abasement and humiliation, and yet one rooted in the eternal decision of God. Barth came to see the proper theological task as the narration and explication of this particular divine movement as a history. Kierkegaard (by means of Climacus) could narrate this movement as a thought experiment in a new poetic key, but saw this poetic translation in the end not as an act of artistic creativity, but a readily acknowledged act of plagiarism of the one divine story divinely revealed.[65] In this respect, Barth and Kierkegaard are not so much set against each other as working from two directions toward the same christological question, and one that was largely framed for both by Paul's own poetic reflections on this movement of divine condescension in the second chapter of Philippians. Both were thinking through the meaning and ramifications of the fact that the way of God was one traveled to a far country through an act of supreme humiliation for the sake of sinners, though Barth developed this theme in a way far beyond what Kierkegaard's brief aphoristic and poetic discussions intimated. Yet it was Kierkegaard who intimated the theme in the direction Barth would develop it.[66]

These observations and comparisons should at the very least caution against a simple acceptance of Barth's downplaying of Kierkegaard's influence upon his own work. Kierkegaard's influence upon Barth certainly did not rival that of Paul or of the Reformation heritage, but it was not insubstantial and left lasting impressions.[67]

---

65. Barth writes: "The atonement is, noetically, the history about Jesus Christ, and ontically, Jesus Christ's own history" (CD IV/1: p. 158). Kierkegaard hides this history behind a retelling only in order to recapture its offense for his time. But it is a lightly veiled retelling, which, as he admits, anyone can see is but an act of plagiarism of the divine story. See Kierkegaard, *Philosophical Fragments*, pp. 35–6.

66. Thus Kierkegaard foreshadows Barth's significant use of the parable of the loving father and lost son of Luke 15 (following those of the lost sheep and the lost coin) as a description of the incarnation of God in Christ: "He walks—but no, he has walked, but infinitely farther than any shepherd and any woman.—Indeed, he walked the infinitely long way from being God to becoming man; he walked that way in order to seek sinners!" (Kierkegaard, *Practice in Christianity*, p. 20). And so also Barth: "The particularity of the man Jesus in proceeding from the one elect people of Israel, as the confirmation of its election, means decisively that the reconciliation of sinful and lost man has, above all, the character of a divine condescension, that it takes place as God goes into the far country" (CD IV/1: p. 168; cf. pp. 157, 158–9). For the divine condescension in this movement, see Kierkegaard, *Practice in Christianity*, p. 40; cf. CD IV/1: pp. 130–2. Thus Barth's christological use of the parable of the loving father may be another lingering debt to Kierkegaard. At the very least, the fact that both use the parable in this idiosyncratic yet programmatic way is striking.

67. Beyond the influences already mentioned, though unable to be explored here, are the notions of revelation as *self*-revelation and of God as ever subject, never object, both themes evident in Kierkegaard's writings and central to Barth's theology.

This claim is not in any way meant to overemphasize this influence. Nor does it overlook the obvious fact that Kierkegaard's focus in much of his writing upon human subjectivity and human decision, upon an analysis of human existence, and upon a tendency to give precedence to law before (and in places over and independent from) gospel were themes Barth could not embrace.[68] Certainly at the very least he had different preoccupations.[69]

Nevertheless, Barth's relationship to Kierkegaard is not best thought of as a light borrowing of philosophical terms that can be easily stripped away. The borrowing was more significant than this, for if ever there was a relationship that might be described as paradoxical and dialectical, it was Barth's to Kierkegaard.[70] Recognizing this fact might be enough justification to revisit this relationship, if for no other reason than to discern if there are more affinities between Kierkegaard

---

68. Dividing Barth from Kierkegaard remains the fact that, for Kierkegaard, the objectivity of revelation is almost always framed within the subjective question of faith and becoming a Christian (*fides qua creditor*), whereas for Barth the subjective appropriation of faith is always framed within the objectivity of the revelation that constitutes it (*fides quae creditor*). So Kierkegaard could summarize his life as that of a religious author whose "whole authorship pertains to Christianity, to the issue: becoming a Christian, with direct and indirect polemical aim at that enormous illusion, Christendom." See Søren Kierkegaard, *The Point of View of My Work as an Author*, ed. and trans. Howard V. Hong and Edna H. Hong (Princeton: Princeton University Press, 1998), p. 23. For Barth's approach, see his comments in CD IV/1: pp. 149–50; and CD I/1: pp. 227–47. Barrett concludes: "Kierkegaard remained soteriocentric while Barth became radically Christocentric. For Kierkegaard, Christianity is the drama of the individual's transition from a worldly, prudential, and self-gratifying way of life to a life of extravagant love for God and neighbor. Of course the whole existential drama is sustained by God upon whom the individual must rely. Of course the individual will fail to adequately instantiate that love and must have recourse to God's forgiveness. But the whole saga is governed by the drama of the individual's struggle to instantiate an ideal. For Barth, on the other hand, the essence of the Christian message is the triumph of God's reconciling grace in Jesus Christ, a triumph that eclipses the significance of the individual's struggle to respond appropriately to God's love" (Barrett, "Karl Barth," p. 33).

69. As Sylvia Walsh notes: "Kierkegaard was not interested in expounding the doctrines of the incarnation and atonement as such but in clarifying their meaning for the single individual who encounters Christ and must decide whether to believe or to be offended at him." See Walsh, *Kierkegaard: Thinking Christianly in an Existential Mode* (Oxford: Oxford University Press, 2009), p. 111. Rae concurs: "Kierkegaard's overriding interest in what it means *to be* a Christian means that we do not find in him anything remotely resembling a systematic presentation of Christian doctrine" (*Kierkegaard and Theology*, p. 3). Yet Kierkegaard could state that his work "presupposes dogmatics." See Søren Kierkegaard, *The Concept of Anxiety* (Princeton: Princeton University Press, 1980), pp. 20–4.

70. Pyper writes that Kierkegaard "is claimed as the hero or villain, depending on one's point of view" ("Søren Kierkegaard," p. 370). All the more remarkable is that with Barth these different points of view could exist within the same person.

and Barth that may exist.[71] Stated more provocatively, Kierkegaard deserves to be given the same serious attention that others like Kant and his progeny have been given in understanding Barth's early development. Barth may in fact provide the best rationale for this (possibly controversial) conclusion, for he asserts that it is God's revelation that establishes God's otherness from us, and that the confession of this is not a conclusion drawn from a philosophical epistemology, Kantian or any other, but from the revelation of God as a hidden God even in his Self-giving.[72] And it is Kierkegaard and his language and concepts of paradox, of contemporaneity, of offense, and especially of indirect communication, that shape Barth's own early reflection on revelation and christology. Moreover, their presence lies closer to the surface, and they are in turn more readily discerned, than the evidence for the philosophical inheritance of Kant and Hegel. They are in fact materially and christologically formative for Barth's early theology in ways that transcend the philosophical and epistemological concerns of the latter two.[73]

In the end, regardless of weak or strong genetic ties between Kierkegaard's corpus and Barth's own development, of more importance are questions of theological compatriotism. For here one comes upon the crux of the matter, the true reason for a reconsideration of their relationship. Kierkegaard's radical emphasis upon the *particularity* of God's revelation in Christ framed as a movement from God to us—rather than as the realization of a perfect religious consciousness in a human ideal (à la Schleiermacher), or of a moralistic essence of Christianity distilled by means of historical science (à la Ritschl and later Harnack, with debts to Kant, who in truth had little time for such particularity or historical contingency), or of a historical instantiation, and thus really illustration, of a more general unity of God and world (à la Hegel)—is something that sets Kierkegaard apart from many in the century in which he lived and yet puts him very close to Barth in the next.[74] This is a kinship of far more significance than that

---

71. For an insightful survey of recent studies examining this relationship, see Barrett, "Karl Barth," pp. 19-26.

72. See GD, pp. 134-5.

73. If Bruce McCormack is correct that the "heartbeat of Barth's conception of revelation in the *Göttingen Dogmatics* is the notion of indirectness," then that provides yet one more reason to give consideration to the conceptions of Kierkegaard (whether directly or indirectly obtained) and not only those of Kant. See McCormack, *Orthodox and Modern: Studies in the Theology of Karl Barth* (Grand Rapids: Baker Academic, 2008), p. 81. For a measured and astute assessment of Kierkegaard's lasting impact upon Barth's theology, see Chalamet, *Dialectical Theologians*, pp. 136-8. He writes: "Kierkegaard's influence may have been restricted to a few intuitions, but some of these intuitions would remain important to Barth for the rest of his life" (p. 137).

74. Arguments against such romanticism, historicism, moral essentialism, (Hegelian) rationalism, idealism, and general immediacy of revelation run throughout Kierkegaard's *Philosophical Fragments* and *Practice in Christianity*. See also Murray Rae, *Kierkegaard's Vision of the Incarnation: By Faith Transformed* (Oxford: Oxford University Press, 1997), pp. 41-6.

of a shared criticism of cultural and ecclesial triumphalism and complacency, or even a joint commitment to an "infinite qualitative difference" between God and the world. This is so not least because it is founded upon a shared conviction, a recognition, that psychologism, historicism, and speculative rationalism do not help us discover Christ but are the means by which a confrontation with his true identity is evaded and his offense averted.[75] These approaches may leave us with admirers of Christ, but not disciples or witnesses.[76] On these points, Kierkegaard may stand closer to Barth than nearly any other major theological figure of the nineteenth century. Barth certainly had no nineteenth-century ancestor so united with him in his embrace of the gospel's radical and scandalous particularity and his mature rejection of that century's understanding of religion as *anamnesis*, though whether Kierkegaard's rejection of immanentalism was consistently maintained throughout his work is not as clear.[77] At the very least, its rejection arose from his own distinct convictions and concerns.

## *Epilogue*

In the end, there can be no easy synthesis of Barth and Kierkegaard, nor should such be attempted. Stark differences remain and many can be conceptually clarified, though some are not given to such analysis and are better attributed to differing Christian vocational (self-)understandings and even to striking disparities of personal disposition. Other differences might be illumined by considering the distinct images that dominated the respective imaginations of both of these figures.

For Kierkegaard, the image that captured and constrained his thought was Thorvaldsen's depiction of Jesus Christ as the great Inviter above the altar of the

---

75. To argue this claim here would lead to another study. Yet it is not a groundless assertion. For whatever one may say of the Christ of Kant, of Schleiermacher, or of Hegel, theirs is not a Christ who causes *offense*. For a description of Kierkegaard in contrast to such figures, see Rae, *Kierkegaard and Theology*, pp. 106-7; see also Robert C. Roberts, *Faith, Reason, and History: Rethinking Kierkegaard's* Philosophical Fragments (Macon: Mercer University Press, 1986), pp. 30-7.

76. And as Kierkegaard famously asserted, such admiration and veneration of Christ were "not worth a pickled herring" (*Practice in Christianity*, p. 40).

77. Kierkegaard's attack on Hegel via Socrates at the beginning of the *Philosophical Fragments* is his classic text; see also *Practice in Christianity*, pp. 125-2. For Barth, see CD 1/1: pp. 99-101. That Kierkegaard *did* hold to a qualified if "direct or intuitive awareness of God" within the human person is argued by C. Stephen Evans in *Subjectivity & Religious Belief* (Washington, DC: Christian University Press, 1978), 107-8. If true, how this immanent awareness of the divine is to be reconciled with Kierkegaard's other convictions of God as wholly other, the radical nature of human sinfulness, and the necessity of revelation and reconciliation in Christ that come *extra nos*, and thus with his christology, is not readily apparent (see *Philosophical Fragments*, pp. 13-22). It would, however, vindicate Barth's judgment that Kierkegaard had not escaped the nineteenth century unscathed.

cathedral in Copenhagen, Christ with outstretched and open arms who beckoned all to rest, yet also paradoxically evoked restiveness. This image, rendered in stone, was set upon a base with the simple chiseled words, "Come to Me," words that Kierkegaard read as both comfort and command (Matt. 11:28; cf. Mt. 19:21), a call to discipleship that shaped his Christian imagination and consumed his life.

For Barth, the dominant image of his life and work was that of Jesus Christ as the crucified Lord depicted at the center of Grünwald's Isenheim altarpiece, an image of Jesus Christ which overwhelmed yet called forth a witness by one in its shadow, a figure (i.e., John the Baptist) whose meaning and life could only be found within the larger frame and who was subservient to the Lord at its center. This witness who prefigured all later ones could but point with a long bony finger away from himself as a "single individual" to Christ on the cross, the "Lamb of God who takes away the sins of the world" (Jn. 1:29; cf. 3:30).

These works of stone and paint depict dissimilar images. Yet what cannot be forgotten is that they are nonetheless images of the same Christ.

# Part III

## CHURCH AND ACADEMY EVER REFORMING

## Chapter 8

## THE ASCENSION OF CHRIST AND THE PILGRIM CHURCH

In John Bunyan's *Pilgrim's Progress*, we see the travels of a journeyer from one life to the next. Bunyan's classic work presents us with a picture of the Christian way as marked by distress and trial, all displayed with the vivid description of internal anguish accompanied by external danger at every hand. Indeed, it is this combination of internal spiritual affliction and external trials and temptations (all of these caught up in Luther's *Anfechtung*, perhaps the perfect though untranslatable German term by which to capture much that is at the heart of this stolidly English text) that provides Bunyan's allegory with such acute force.[1] Yet despite its serious and sober tone, it also displays the help that can come for the beset pilgrim from fellow travelers like Faithful and well-placed and well-tempered spiritual guides like Evangelist. The protagonist Christian does not, therefore, travel all alone.

Yet despite such moments of companionship amid confraternity, it must be admitted that the pilgrim imagery of Bunyan's text is focused upon the sole Christian as both allegorical character and the one that in our world such allegory signifies. This story of the singular traveler concerned with escaping a coming wrath, enduring various ordeals, and reaching a final destination of peace and rest provides the work with an acute existential potency, no doubt part of its universal and timeless appeal. But the power of this portrayal of the Christian also seems to hinge somewhat upon paying a requisite price of abstracting the individual Christian journey from the communal aspect of Christian existence as one set within the rich shared life of God's people who, as Christ's body of brothers and sisters, walk together through this world. This journey is one where they not only pass through but also dwell within the world and share a common life with its citizens, even as they are set apart from and exist for the sake of the world as a distinctive fellowship not only of kindred minds but also more importantly of the Holy Spirit. Bunyan provides us with a brilliant travel narrative, but one where the traveler is largely excised from Christian *societas* and where worldly

---

1. For a survey of the rich connotations of this term in Luther's thought, see David P. Scaer, "The Concept of *Anfechtung* in Luther's Thought," *Concordia Theological Quarterly* 47, no. 1 (1983), pp. 15-30.

encounters are overwhelmingly negative in character. In other words, Bunyan's narrative centers around Christian existential concerns more than ecclesiological ones, and ones that display a markedly pessimistic view of the world. Yet if such puritan perspectives have found their balance in recent years in an increasing emphasis upon the church and its mission to the world, the question that now confronts our time is whether ecclesiology itself may also fall prone to its own form of abstraction, and one not remedied simply by a dialectical (or reactionary) return to more individual (existential) matters from communal (ecclesiological) ones. The question merits attention.

This essay is an examination of ecclesiology as a theological (i.e., dogmatic) area of investigation through the aperture of a single image. This image arises from Scripture and in turn takes on constructive significance as one that can allow us to understand the church within the larger frame of reference of God's mighty work of salvation. It can thereby also provide a standpoint from which to discern the entailments of that situated location within the history of redemption. Before introducing that image, something might be said about the current state of ecclesiological reflection in general. For the direction of the argument in this paper will run against the grain of much of contemporary ecclesiological convention.

There can be no doubt that ecclesiology has assumed a significant role in recent theological work within the past fifty years and its preeminence has only increased in the last two decades. From the Roman Catholic side, such attention of course precedes the recent half-decade and flows from the birth of modern Roman Catholic ecclesiology in the work of Johann Adam Möhler and the Tübingen school to the important labor by the theologians of *ressourcement* prefiguring the Second Vatican Council.[2] Most important of course are that Council's documents themselves, with none so significant as *Lumen Gentium*, documents that have given impetus to a wealth of ecclesiological literature and debate as to their meaning, coherence, implications, and continuity with past Catholic teaching.[3] More recently, ecclesiology has become the touchstone for much work in Protestant theology as well, particularly among those affiliated with what have come to be known, however broadly or imprecisely, as a high-church form of Lutheranism and Anglicanism designated as evangelical catholic, as well as within that ill-defined school known as postliberalism. One can think here of the ecclesial focus

---

2. For Möhler and the Tübingen school, see Michael J. Himes, *Ongoing Incarnation: Johann Adam Möhler and the Beginnings of Modern Ecclesiology* (New York: Herder & Herder, 1997). For the theologians of *ressourcement*, see especially the works of Yves Congar and Henri de Lubac.

3. For the Second Vatican Council Documents, see Austin Flannery, ed., *Vatican Council II: Constitutions and Declarations* (Northport, NY: Costello, 1996). Such ecclesiological reflection was renewed in Orthodox theology as well, seen in the most seminal work of John Zizioulas, *Being in Communion: Studies in Personhood and the Church* (New York: St. Vladimir's Seminary Press/Athens Printing, 1985).

of such persons as Robert Jenson and Carl Braaten as representatives of the former movement, and George Lindbeck and Stanley Hauerwas as representatives of the latter one.[4]

More pertinent than these examples taken singly, however, is the fact that in much of contemporary Protestant theology the topic of ecclesiology has extended beyond its traditional and relatively bounded range of questions and in turn has swallowed up much of the dogmatic corpus, growing thus into a kind of meta-doctrine. In light of such developments, Kevin Vanhoozer has described the theological landscape as one in which ecclesiology has become for many "first theology." As he writes: "The doctrine of the church has, in the last decade or so, moved to the forefront of theological research and writing, primarily among non-evangelicals—so much so that ecclesiology has effectively displaced the doctrine of revelation as 'first theology.'"[5] Indeed, one could argue that the epistemological concerns reaching back behind Descartes to the post-Reformation period, concerns which in time prioritized and problematized the doctrine of revelation and its attendant questions of authority, Scripture, and magisterium, have in more recent decades given way to linguistic, sociological, and now ethnographic concerns resulting in the rise of a theology which takes its primary task to be the thick description and examination of the narratives, rituals, and practices of the church. One might be forgiven for summarizing this shift as one from a predominance of concern with the questions of Descartes and Kant to the questions of Wittgenstein and MacIntyre.

Yet whatever gains may have accrued in such a shift, and they are real and need to be acknowledged, a lingering question remains. Does replacing a doctrine made foundational due to an epistemological crisis of authority with one of Christian communal self-description necessarily entail a revitalization of theology itself? A movement from modern to postmodern sensibilities (broadly defined) may alleviate the tensions of the first but introduce new ones, and though foundationalism can rightly be set aside, one can ask if communitarianism is an

---

4. For representative works of the evangelical catholic position, see the essays in Carl E. Braaten and Robert W. Jenson, eds., *The Catholicity of the Reformation* (Grand Rapids: Eerdmans, 1996); also Braaten and Jenson, eds., *Marks of the Body of Christ* (Grand Rapids: Eerdmans, 1999); and Braaten, *Mother Church: Ecclesiology and Ecumenism* (Minneapolis: Fortress, 1998). For representative works of postliberalism with pertinence to ecclesiology, see especially George Lindbeck, *The Nature of Doctrine: Religion and Theology in a Postliberal Age* (Philadelphia: Westminster, 1984); also Lindbeck, *The Church in a Postliberal Age* (Grand Rapids: Eerdmans, 2003). From Hauerwas' vast corpus of work, see especially Hauerwas, *A Community of Character: Toward a Constructive Christian Social Ethic* (Notre Dame: University of Notre Dame Press, 1981); Hauerwas, *The Hauerwas Reader*, ed. John Berkman and Michael Cartwright (Durham: Duke University Press, 2001); and Stanley Hauerwas and William H. Willimon, *Resident Aliens* (Nashville: Abingdon, 1989).

5. Kevin Vanhoozer, "Evangelicalism and the Church: The Company of the Gospel," in *The Futures of Evangelicalism: Issues and Prospects*, ed. Craig Bartholomew, Robin Perry, and Andrew West (Grand Rapids: Kregel, 2004), p. 63.

adequate replacement as the linchpin and fulcrum for theological work. One need not deny that placing revelation as a self-standing and preliminary doctrine at the head of, rather than embedded within, the task of dogmatic description created numerous excrescences particularly witnessed in certain discussions of Scripture (for Protestants) and the teaching office (for Roman Catholics).[6] Nor need one deny that the attempt by Schleiermacher to ground theology in the religious consciousness of the subject or community was an even greater mistake and in time degenerated from his brilliant if flawed confessional program of mediation to the ensuing problems of individualism and unconstrained subjectivity shorn from all confessional guidance, accompanied by the evisceration of doctrinal substance and content characterizing his lesser successors. Yet one wonders if an adequate cure has been found for such a disease simply by trading the community for the individual as the focus and starting point of theological explication, or more circumspectly, whether the malaise can be dealt with by an ever more dialectical ordering of individual and community on this horizontal axis (however necessary). Nevertheless, it is safe to say that in recent years the doctrine of the church has overtaken discussions of revelation on one side and religious subjectivity on the other as the center of the theological enterprise for many.

As already intimated, this substitution may introduce its own problems. Indeed, it may be a sign that the dogmatic ship has righted an epistemological lilt with an ecclesial overcorrection and still remains precariously out of kilter. Warnings of such dangerous lurching have indeed been sounded. Paul Zahl has stated that in his judgment "any period of Christian history for which ecclesiology and polity are the driving issues is decadent by definition."[7] Less provocative but no less forceful is Vanhoozer's own conclusive judgment: "Ecclesiology cannot be first theology because the church enjoys only the first fruits of its salvation. As an eschatological reality, it is indeed already in union with Christ, but not yet completely so. The visible unity of the church is something for which we work and hope."[8] In this essay I want to

---

6. With respect to Scripture, one can witness such foundationalist outgrowths in the inerrancy theories of Charles Hodge and the Princeton school, preceded in certain arguments of Protestant orthodoxy, and simplified and echoed in populist if unnuanced apologetics and polemics of fundamentalism. With regard to Roman Catholicism, one can think of the development of claims to the authority of the magisterium culminating in the papal infallibility doctrine of Vatican I declared in 1870.

7. Paul Zahl, "The Bishop-Led Church: The Episcopal or Anglican Polity Affirmed, Weighed, and Defended," in *Perspectives on Church Government: Five View of Church Polity*, ed. Chad Own Brand, R. Stanton Norman, and Daniel Akin et al. (Nashville: B&H Academic, 2004), p. 210.

8. Kevin J. Vanhoozer, *The Drama of Doctrine: A Canonical Linguistic Approach to Christian Doctrine* (Louisville: Westminster John Knox Press, 2005), p. 163. For a further assessment of why ecclesiology cannot become "first theology," see John Webster, *Confessing God: Essays in Christian Dogmatics II* (London: T&T Clark, 2005), p. 155. He writes with regard to such attempts: "Ecclesiology can so fill the horizon that it obscures the miracle of grace which is fundamental to the church's life and activity."

examine these themes that Vanhoozer introduces—the church as an eschatological reality which he states is united with Christ, but, in his words, "not yet completely so." Moreover, I want to reflect upon why ecclesiology can only be misshapen when it becomes the center of the dogmatic corpus, and I want to give some encouragement to right the ship and strive for a more even keel. What is provided here is but an appeal for a change of direction, a proposal for rethinking ecclesiological reflection by thinking through the implications of starting with the simple admission that the church is a pilgrim community, a description that finds precedence in all strands of Western Christianity—Roman Catholic, magisterial Protestant, and the Free Church—and thus may itself hold some ecumenical promise.

To state that the church is a pilgrim people should be seen as in alignment with a well-attested theme in the biblical witness but should not be understood simply or even primarily under the rubrics of image or metaphor, nor even of model or type. Certainly the image of pilgrimage from one land to another permeates the canonical witness. Abraham is called from his home to a new one, and his descendants inherit that call as they are led from Egypt to the promised land. Their descendants are marked by a movement to an exiled existence and then in time a return to their Judean home. The New Testament witnesses can appeal to this imagery in explicating the church's earthly existence as the fulfillment of these Old Testament precedents and types, and the author of Hebrews provides the quintessential summation of this transitory identity when he writes that as pilgrims, the Old Testament predecessors of faith were "strangers and foreigners on the earth" seeking a "homeland," a "better country" (Heb 11:13-14). Remarkable here is that the movement is no longer seen as that from one place to another upon the earth, but is now portrayed as one from earth to heaven. They are exiles not in Babylon awaiting a return to Jerusalem, but exiles upon the earth looking for a heavenly city. Their memory is evoked by the writer of Hebrews for the purpose of spurring on the church, so that its members, being "surrounded by so great a cloud of witnesses," might as pilgrims themselves in this world "lay aside every weight and the sin that clings so closely," and "run with perseverance the race that is set before us" as they look to Jesus, "the pioneer and perfecter of our faith" (Heb 12:1-2). This is, quite simply, a pilgrimage of a different order entirely from those portrayed in the Old Testament. The author of 1 Peter can echo this theme of the church when he identifies the recipients of his letter as those who are "aliens and exiles in the world" (1 Pet 2:11). Thus the church is a *communio viatorum*, a church on the way.

One might take this image of the church as a pilgrim people simply as metaphor, and certainly such would appear appropriate at first glance. Metaphors speak of similarity in difference and are less nailed down than analogies while more evocative in nature. Yet to use the language of metaphor cannot exhaust what is truly being asserted when the church is described as a pilgrim people. Nor, however, can such a description be understood as one more model for the church.[9] Indeed, to provide models for the church is in itself of limited value. Not only

---

9. The quintessential typology of ecclesiological models in recent decades is that provided by Avery Dulles. See Dulles, *Models of the Church* (New York: Image, 1991).

are such models purely idealized abstractions, and thus prone to the limitations of any typology, but for this very reason the actual churches of every branch of Christianity do not see themselves as being rightly represented by any one model. The issue is more problematic still, for a typology of models intrinsically focuses upon an implicit if reductive institutionalism, functionalism, or essentialism that treats the church simply as the embodiment of a particular form (such as the church as hierarchy), as the locus of a particular practice or activity (such as proclamation in the model of herald), or as a reality captured by an essential if somewhat abstract concept (such as sacramental mystery). There is of course no little truth to the importance of such activities and conceptions, and thus the relative hermeneutic benefit of such models. Yet such abstract functionalism and essentialism can be more distorting than illuminating in understanding the church, and for the following reasons.

A typology of function and essence addresses the church primarily in terms of a self-contained institution or people, but in both cases as an independent entity that can be grasped simply by means of a comparative ecclesiology. A comparison of models thereby abstracts ecclesiology from its placement in the larger backdrop of the entire range of God's salvific action as well as the corresponding larger dogmatic fabric, particularly one that is trinitarian, christological, pneumatological, and eschatological in its determinations. With this in mind, ecclesiology must be located in a surrounding matrix of theological topics in order to be rightly balanced. In effect, the church must be understood not primarily in terms of models of institutions, functions, or essences, nor even of polity and practices. Before these ecclesiological questions are (necessarily) addressed, the church must first be understood in regard to its placement within the divine economy of salvation, and for this to be so, its curious eschatological location and its specific and ordered relation to and distinction from Christ who is its head and the Spirit who calls it into existence must be apprehended and appreciated. Behind both relations lies the fundamental distinction between God and his creature.[10] In sum, all ecclesiology must begin with attention to the particular temporal location of the church in the light of God's eschatological kingdom, as well as the relations of the church to God's action for the world's salvation through Christ and the Spirit who moves to inaugurate and bring to completion that kingdom. In short, the church must find its identity within the matrix of God's marvelous work of salvation, and most immediately his work to reconcile the world to himself and bring it to its glorious redemption.

---

10. Webster, *Confessing God*, p. 163. He writes: "The ontological rule in ecclesiology is therefore that whatever conjunction there may be between God and his saints, it is comprehended within an ever-greater dissimilarity" (p. 171). For an argument akin to that which I am making here, see ibid., pp. 153–93. Elsewhere Webster can state: "The distinction between uncreated and created being is ecclesiologically foundational" (Webster, *The Domain of the Word: Scripture and Theological Reason* (London/New York: Bloomsbury T&T Clark, 2012), p. 24.

To say that the church is a pilgrim people is therefore not to propose yet one more biblical image as the preeminent one, nor even less one more model for the church or "blueprint ecclesiology," to borrow the term of Nicholas Healy.[11] It is, rather, to draw attention to the *placement* of the church within the time of God's salvific action, and its *location* within a set of relations of that action, first to God, Christ, and Spirit, and then in turn to the world. To determine this location rightly is to go a far way toward understanding the church's own proper identity, activity, and end.[12] Yet what must be said above all is that to determine this location within God's economy of salvation cannot be separated but indeed is intertwined with, even as it presupposes, a clear vision of the relation between God and his created and redeemed people, which itself is reflected in the relation between Christ and his earthly body, and the Holy Spirit and his spiritual fellowship and temple. It is indeed only then that the relation of the church and the world can be taken up and rightly understood and an evaluation of its form of life undertaken. In short, the horizontal relationship of church and world can only be properly understood and their identities demarcated when the vertical relationship of God and his people, Christ and his earthly body, and the Spirit and his saints is accurately grasped and depicted.

To focus upon the church as a pilgrim people is therefore on this account not simply a cursory reflection upon a collection of pertinent biblical references to pilgrim imagery. It requires, rather, the explication of the church as a journeying people in its placement in the economy of God's salvific time and in relation to that God who calls, sends, accompanies, and beckons this people. A large part of rightly understanding the church is composed of determining its special temporal and ontological location, namely, in terms of eschatology and the ordering of its relations, and specifically that pertaining to the reality and activity of the triune God.

That the church is best judged in terms of this location and these relations leads to a number of important corollaries which can be unpacked when the pilgrim status of the church is taken with real seriousness and understood as fundamental to its life. The following theses and their exposition attempt to delineate the nature of the church in terms of its unique time and location.

1. **To speak of the church as a pilgrim people is to recognize its temporal location as that between Christ's first and second advents. This time is rightly spoken of in the first and primary instance as the time of Christ's ascended lordship, and secondly and derivatively as the time of the church's witness.**

---

11. Nicholas M. Healy, *Church, World and the Christian Life: Practical-Prophetic Ecclesiology* (Cambridge: Cambridge University Press, 2000), pp. 25-51.

12. These three are inseparable in actuality but can be somewhat conceptually distinguished for the purpose of teasing out different aspects of the church's reality.

To see the church as existing between Christ's first and second advents signifies that it lives between the time of Christ's ascension and that of his return. As such, it lives as it has been called into existence through the power of the promised Holy Spirit at Pentecost, and as it continues to be called together, constituted, and commissioned by its Lord through his Spirit. The church's pilgrimage is neither initiated nor ended by its own determination, for it inaugurates neither Pentecost nor parousia. The destination is therefore, like the outset, not self-enacted, enabled, or achieved—the end of the pilgrim journey is marked not by a triumphal arrival by the church but the return of Christ in the clouds just as he departed (Acts 1:11; cf. 1 Thess. 4:13-18; 1 Cor 1:7). That the church lives in this time between the times means that the time of the church is not an era of glorious fulfillment but of promise as the church lives between memory and expectation. Thus the relation of the church and the kingdom of God is not one of absolute contradiction nor of coterminous identity but of promise to fulfillment, wherein the church is a sign of the kingdom but not its completion.

To understand this temporal location between its divinely effected beginning and its divinely appointed end is to recognize that the church exists not as a continuation of Christ's ministry nor as a subsequent economy of salvation following upon his own, but in, with, and under Christ's continuing lordship which he now exercises at the right hand of God. That Christ is seated at the Father's right hand is both the sign and reality of the completion of his atoning work, but is not to be taken as a state of passivity, as if at the ascension a baton had been passed to an active church that now extends and completes his ministry because it has also assumed his authority.[13] Nor is it to be thought of simply as a time of Christ's absence, for Christ remains active and present to the church though in a way that must also acknowledge an ascended departure. Yet this time of the church does not mark the end of Christ's own. That Christ continues to instruct, intercede for, and rule over the church and indeed the world with the singular and supreme authority given to him entails that the church's own life and activity be articulated in the categories of reverent attention, receptive commemoration, and humble service. These dispositions and activities take their particular form *precisely because* they are a response to a wholly prevenient and perfect and thus completed and finished work, and one of an entirely different order and efficacy.[14] It is only in this light that the church can then in its own appointed area and in its own circumscribed way, and indeed with its own qualified authority and liberating freedom, take up its divinely commissioned and corresponding task as a teaching

---

13. As Karl Barth wrote: "Christ's bestowal of his power on his Church cannot be reasonably understood to mean that he had partially relinquished his own power, that in relation to the Church he had ceased to be wholly God." Barth, "Church and Theology," TC, pp. 286–306 (293).

14. Such a three-fold ministry of the church corresponds to, but does not mirror, supplement, or complete Christ's own inimitable and singular three-fold prophetic, priestly, and kingly ministry. Here the distinction of the Lord and his servants is irreversible and irrevocable.

church that intercedes for the world and that orders its own disciplined and indeed exemplary and ethical life. All of these tasks are themselves framed and shaped by the church's prior act of response in praise and thanksgiving for the grace and gospel that grounds it, which is nothing more or less than its worship of the God who creates and saves, the One who made all things and makes all things new.

To rightly recognize the church's placement in this particular time of Christ's ministry is inseparable from the church acknowledging its Lord and its relation to him. Christ is the head of the church, ascended on high, yet joined to the church through the Holy Spirit. As such, Christ graciously joins the church to himself, but his activity is not dependent upon or exhausted by the church's life. Such is not to denigrate the church but to remind it that his relation to it is one of freedom and lordship, while that of the church to him is one of obedience and service. Karl Barth articulates this state of affairs succinctly:

> The ascension means not only ... the transfer of a delegated, secondary power to the Church, but also the departure of the actual, primary holder of that power. It means that the eschatological limit set for the Church becomes visible. The exaltation of the Head really means for the body a lowering, its demotion to a position of humility and waiting, and a definite limitation of the miracle of Pentecost.[15]

For the church to truly know itself as existing in a state of such humility and waiting is nothing other than to understand its pilgrim existence.

2. **To speak of the church as a pilgrim people entails that ecclesiology be understood as an exercise in the church's proper self-understanding by means of a rightful appreciation and conception of the implications of both Christ's presence and absence during this time of his ascended lordship.**

As already introduced, the church's self-understanding is intricately interwoven and follows from a proper understanding not only of Christ's cross and resurrection, but also the oft neglected matter of Christ's ascension. That Christ is not only raised in body but ascended in body entails that it is mistaken to see his subjectivity and agency as raised and assumed without remainder into the church and its life, or his authority passed from him to the church as if his time and the church's own were two consecutive eras marked by two differing authorities and salvific economies.[16]

---

15. Barth, "Church and Theology," p. 294.
16. Such a view of the time of Christ and the time of the church as two different ages, with the ascension marking Christ's absence from the latter, was due in no small part to the influence in biblical studies of Hans Conzelmann and his reading of the book of Acts. See Conzelmann, *The Theology of St. Luke*, trans. Geoffrey Buswell (London: Faber & Faber, 1960), pp. 184–5; 204; 207–9; 224. I owe this insight to Beverly Gaventa.

Christ remains Lord even in his resurrection and ascension.[17] He thereby remains over against the church and is not extended by nor subsumed into its life. That he is Lord entails that his agency and subjectivity, his life and activity, his rule and reign, cannot be raised into and thus dissolved into the subjectivity of the church, its kerygmatic proclamation, its sacramental realities, its missional and ethical activity, or its own story.[18] Christ is raised *into* nothing else or other than his own singularly glorious and incomparable and inalienable and exalted life. And in that life, bearing the marks of his passion and sacrifice, he is raised first from death to life in Easter wonder and then to the glory of the Father's right hand. In his state of ascension, there is no doubt that Christ fulfills his promise always to be with the church—it is indeed Christ's very presence that prevents the church as serving as

---

17. The importance of Christ's bodily ascension (and not only his resurrection) has been argued most incisively in recent years by Douglas Farrow, *Ascension and Ecclesia: On the Significance of the Doctrine of the Ascension for Ecclesiology and Christian Cosmology* (Grand Rapids: Eerdmans, 1999). One need not entirely follow Farrow's own sacramental line of reasoning to appreciate the overarching cogency of his larger argument of the ascension's neglected, yet central, place for Christ's identity and ministry.

18. This particularity not only of incarnation and revelation, but also of resurrection and ascension, marks the dividing line between the church's historic confession and the demythologization, and thus relativization, of Christ's unique identity and agency in modernity, though one can find such moves predating the modern period. Nor should it surprise us that it is during this period that the bodily resurrection of Christ in his unique identity set over against the church fades into the far horizon until it disappears. That Christ is neither raised nor subsumed into the church and its consciousness (Schleiermacher), its authentic existence or "new being" (Tillich), its proclamation or faith (Bultmann), its sacramental life (Robert Jenson), or its mission, ethical or otherwise (Ritschl and his modern day liberal descendants) is at the heart of *evangelical* faith, for such faith and its confession simply extend the *solus Christus* from cross to resurrection to ascension. Christ, and he alone, *reigns*, even as he alone saves. That this confession also rules out a more general union of God and the world of which the incarnation is but an illustration or instantiation (Hegel and Strauss) should go without saying. But the divinization of the world in the modern period is in the end no large surprise once the divinization of the church is granted. It is simply to extend an error from the inner to the outer circle of Christ's reign, from its center to its periphery. But both moves in fact arise from the same transgression, and it should not surprise us that if this is true of the church the world in turn follows suit. In short, if Christ is not raised in his unique particularity and agency but rather into the life of the church, and once this barrier is crossed, then how is one to prevent a further step, which is that Christ is raised into the world? To reject the first scandal of particularity simply is mirrored in the second, and both for reasons of inclusive immanence. There is not so far a line from the first to the second, from certain Christian confusions to their Hegelian and other mystical and pantheistic extensions. It is thus best remembered right at this point that "judgment must begin with the household of God" (1 Pet 4:17).

a kind of ecclesial vicariate or *alter Christus*.[19] But there also can be no question that this promise to the church can be fulfilled only because Christ stands *over*, and *over against*, it.[20]

Yet it is precisely this over-againstness that entails not only the comfort but also the crisis of the church, and such must be acknowledged without despair or embarrassment. Here in the church's cry of "*Maranatha!*," the tension between Christ's bodily absence and his promised and real presence must be felt with full force (1 Cor 16:22; cf. Matt 28:20). The very fact that Christ is not raised into the church's life, nor the Spirit given as a *possession* of the church, entails that the church must live in constant consciousness of both a real absence and a promised and no less real presence. Nothing tempts the church so much as the ever-constant desire to eliminate this tension, either into a moralism which makes Christ simply an exemplar from its past, or into an ecclesial sacramental objectification in which Christ is a constant presence guaranteed by the church's life understood as an extension of his own incarnate life. As such his heavenly and earthly bodies are collapsed into one and the hypostatic union's uniqueness and singularity are threatened with a doctrine of the church as an ethical savior or mystical body. Both such moralism and such ecclesial mysticism in the end, however, sacrifice Christ's lordship over the church and replace Christ with the church itself, the first by sacrificing Christ's promised presence to his absence, the second by denying his real absence by subsuming his life into the church to secure his constant presence. The problem of such a presence, however, is that if Christ is present everywhere, then Jesus as a distinctive subject and particular person is nowhere, a question not so much about physical location as the preservation of Christ's unique agency and identify. The church assures itself of his presence only by dissolving his personhood and particularity, and thus in turn his lordship.[21] Moreover, the Spirit also is subsumed into the life of the church, for the Spirit no longer is that which joins the ascended Christ to his earthly body since the distinction of Christ and

---

19. As Luther noted, however polemically: "See how different Christ is from his successors, although they all would wish to be his vicars. I fear that most of them have been too literally his vicars. A man is a vicar only when his superior is absent.... How much more properly did the apostles call themselves servants of the present Christ and not vicars of an absent Christ?" See LW 31: p. 342.

20. Such entails a rejection of all forms of christological objectification or subsumption into ecclesial or sacramental realities such that Christ becomes an object of, rather than an inalienable subject and agent in relation to, the church's activity.

21. Farrow, *Ascension and Ecclesia*, pp. 12–13. For such a view, Farrow writes, the "ascension means, not the consummation, but simply the *end* of Jesus-history" (p. 13). Such again recalls the comments of notes 16 and 18 above.

church is now collapsed.[22] The net effect is that the Spirit's own work and that of the church are directly identified.[23]

Therefore in neither understanding of the relation of Christ and church does Christ remain a free Lord, and thus in neither can Christ be both recognized in his ascended bodily absence and particular life and in his faithful presence through the work of the Holy Spirit who joins Christ with his earthly body. To lose this tension is to sacrifice in christology what must also be held in tension in eschatology, namely, the "already and not yet" nature of the kingdom, which in christology is translated as the presence and absence of Christ. Neither of these relations is identical with, yet both are intricately joined to, the unity-in-distinction of Christ and his church. All are dialectical in nature, and the last is so as it maintains the proper distinctions and irreversible order between its terms. Farrow succinctly puts the matter of distinction: "It is the divergence of Jesus-history from our own that gives to the ecclesia its character and its name."[24] Yet it would be wrong, once again, to see these as only divergent histories or contiguous salvific eras. For the history of the church is not an extension of Christ's own, but neither is it an autonomous one. It is, rather, best identified by the principles of annexation and inclusion. In short, Christ's history takes up the history of the church into his own as the time of his ascended lordship and earthly witnesses, just as he calls and forms and commissions a people through whom he pronounces his own presence to the world in the time of his bodily absence (as witnessed across the NT, such as in Matt 28:18-20; Luke 24:48-9; and Acts 1:8). He does so such that these histories are distinct even in their unity, and with the church's history dependent upon his own with no hint of symmetry or equality between them. Jesus Christ is Lord, and the church is the witness, herald, and servant of that lordship. In the time of Christ's bodily absence, the church exists in the expectation of his return even as it journeys with his promised presence through his Spirit. To understand this unique journey between memory and expectation is nothing less than for the church to understand herself as a pilgrim people.

**3. To say that the church is a pilgrim people thus entails that it is both being led and comforted but also commanded and ruled by the free voice of Christ in the present.**

22. It is thus curious that criticisms of a christocentric ecclesiology fail to appreciate exactly this point. It is precisely because Christ remains distinct from the church and its life that the Spirit's joining of them is irreplaceably necessary. Should one wonder where the Spirit is, the Spirit is precisely here. The Spirit is the divine empowering presence that joins Christ with his earthly body and communicates his presence and thus his benefits to his community. The irony of an exaltation of the church as an extension of Christ is that the fellowship between them is lost, for there can be no fellowship where there is no demarcation between subjects (for a similar point, see Webster, *Confessing God*, pp. 166–7).

23. For all of the problems accompanying such understandings, see Kimlyn J. Bender, *Confessing Christ for Church and World: Studies in Modern Theology* (Downers Grove: InterVarsity, 2014), pp. 91–123. One might also remember Barth's warning that the danger of an over-realized eschatology is an ever-present one. See Barth, CD III/2: pp. 510–11.

24. Farrow, *Ascension and Ecclesia*, p. 10.

That Christ continues to guide and lead his church in his ascended state of exaltation through the power of the Holy Spirit entails that the site of his address to the church be acknowledged. If Christ remains a Lord who *speaks*, the question must remain where his address to the church occurs, where he remains the Subject and agent of his own communication, where he commands so that the church might obey. This is the place of demarcation between the direct and absolute authority of Christ and the commissioned and relative authority of the church, "the cardinal point at which the subordination of the Church under its Lord comes to view."[25] The church has recognized this point as Holy Scripture.[26] In it the church acknowledges not only the location of this address, but the correspondent rule for its own faith and life. For Scripture is Christ's self-appointed witness in the works of prophets and apostles which in turn becomes the means of his own pronouncement to the church and the medium of his own presence and present rule.[27] It is the locus from which faith is called forth and from which arises the divine command that requires human obedience. From another angle, Holy Scripture is the medium produced, inspired, taken up, and illumined by the Spirit for the mediation of Christ's own pronouncement to the church as the very revelation of God. Calvin thus stated what was at the heart of not only his own but Luther's discovery, and one that long predated them both, when he declared that it is the preaching of the gospel as found within Scripture that is "the scepter by which the heavenly King rules His people."[28]

---

25. Barth, "Church and Theology," p. 295.

26. Here traditions have moved in two directions. For some, the bridge between these two histories requires a link in sacramental reality. Yet if the question is framed not in terms first of *provision* but of *lordship*, then the question can be articulated in this way: "Where is the point at which Jesus Christ's rule becomes concrete and evident in the church's life?" And the answer that the church has given in its history, and particularly in its evangelical form, is that of Holy Scripture. Here too traditions can converge, for the answer that has been given by some in the Western church to the question of this site has been that of Peter's personal successor and the office of the magisterium. Whether, as Barth asked, such a view can truly preserve the *over-againstness* of Christ to his church, and thus the rightful distinction of a Lord who commands and a church that obeys, is a matter of ongoing dispute. See Barth, CD I/1: pp. 102-4.

27. "It is therefore true that Holy Scripture is the Word of God for the Church, that it is Jesus Christ for us, as He Himself was for the prophets and apostles during the forty days" (Barth, *CD* I/2: p. 544).

28. John C. Olin, ed., *John Calvin and Jacopo Sadoleto: A Reformation Debate* (Grand Rapids: Baker, 1976), p. 60. Here again a division becomes evident. When Henri de Lubac states, "Thus if one thing is certain in this world, it is that, for us, the Church precedes the Gospel," the rift seems to widen, particularly when it is remembered that the gospel is grounded in the singular work of Christ. See Henri de Lubac, *The Motherhood of the Church*, trans. Sergia Englund (San Francisco: Ignatius Press, 1971), p. 8. The issue at hand is not best approached under the topics of soteriological extrinsicism and ecclesial inclusion and mediation, but first must be articulated in terms of Christ's uniqueness, antecedence, and lordship. When this is understood, the mist departs and the one thing that must be confessed for certain is that Christ precedes the church. At issue is of course how that precedence is preserved, exercised, and expressed during the time of his ascension.

Christ's rule is thus made real and effective as the Holy Spirit empowers Holy Scripture to be the voice of Christ to the church through the voices of his witnesses in the prophets and the apostles. That Christ alone exercises his rule entails not only that he alone is Lord, but also that he remains the one true shepherd with all others who are commissioned to feed his sheep—his shepherds not by proxy but by their being conscripted for the purpose of serving the pronouncement of his one true Word and the provision and care for his people. Thus if Calvin described Holy Scripture as the scepter by which Christ rules his church, it might also be portrayed as the rod and staff that give comfort yet also provide necessary correction and direction to the church as his flock.

That Holy Scripture serves as the *canon*, even as it exists as such, entails that it is not simply a product of a people's desire for help on a journey or even ecclesial expediency, much less something the church gives to itself, but the result of a recognition that there is a Shepherd who not only accompanies the travelers on their way but stands ahead of them and rules over them. Their conversation is therefore not only a community dialogue among journeyers but also the response to a Lord who has spoken and still speaks. In Scripture the church confesses that it hears the true voice of its Shepherd and in turn renounces the voices of strangers. In Scripture the church and its members acknowledge that it is God who calls them and God who sends them and God who leads them as he speaks through his Word by the power of his Spirit. In short, they live not by bread alone but by every word that proceeds from the mouth of God (Deut 8:3; Matt 4:4). Insofar as the church acknowledges that it can live only in response to this Word given to it, it acknowledges that it lives by faith and not by sight (2 Cor 5:7). To acknowledge this existence of faith and hope is nothing other than for the church to recognize that it is a society of pilgrims gathered around Holy Scripture with the awe and expectation of Moses before the bush that burned but was not consumed.

4. **To say that the church is a pilgrim people entails that its existence is provisional and its authority and activity are relative and stand under the absolute authority and activity of Christ.**

If the history and existence of the church are assumed by Christ's history rather than seen as an extension, continuation, or completion of it, and if it exists both in union and distinction from Christ's own, then the church finds the dignity, integrity, and purpose of its life and history in taking up its proper role of creaturely witness and service in freedom and joy. This is indeed its own glory. As a human response and witness to the Word of its Lord, the church's confession and life, its doctrine and practice, possess a real and true, though qualified and derivative, authority. As Christ is both joined to yet ever distinct from his earthly body, and as the Holy Spirit empowers but is never assumed into his fellowship, so also must the appointed witness of Holy Scripture ever be seen as precedent not only in time but also in rank over all later confession and practice by the church. The particularity and finality of God's revelation in Christ entail and find their reflection and echo in the particularity and finality of the canon. Failures to demarcate between Christ and his earthly body, between the work of the Holy Spirit and that of the church, are thus themselves echoed in a corresponding failure to recognize the demarcation of Scripture and later tradition, of canon and confession, of absolute and relative authority.[29]

All such errors of demarcation are of one type, namely, a failure to retain the distinction, the asymmetry and the irreversibility of the relation, such that each relation is improperly ordered or reversed. The words of Christ from the cross announcing the completion of the divine self-giving and atonement for sin, consummated and manifested in his glorious resurrection, are words before which the church can only stand in awe and in turn attest but not call into question by the self-attribution of language of incarnational extension and salvific continuation.[30] This is at the very heart of saying that the church is a pilgrim, rather than pioneer, community, and that it stands both after and before the finished and eschatological work of Christ. This recognition is not a denigration of the church, but the very means of the preservation of its own *creaturely* glory.

If the church's confession and practice are thus framed within the category of response to the work of Christ and the Spirit, and if they are framed within the larger relation of the Creator to his creature, then all such confession and practice, as well as liturgy and law, must themselves be seen as possessing a real though circumscribed authority, as provisional not only due to the church's belonging to the category of creature but also as standing within a timeframe where sin has not disappeared even from its own life. The church's journey is a following after Jesus in the midst of confusion and uncertainty, and such are not only extrinsic to its walls. Its words and actions are to be faithful but can imply no ultimate finality. It is for this reason that attention to its own faithfulness in its worship and its common and uncommon life, as reflected in the truthfulness of its confession and the fidelity of its action, is indeed right and necessary. Perhaps most overlooked is that nowhere in Scripture is the church as close to its Lord as in the sharing of

---

29. That the canon was first the product of an *acknowledgment* of the church rather than a matter of its *establishment* was well understood and argued by Barth and is now well-attested by New Testament scholarship—see Bender, *Confessing Christ for Church and World*, pp. 172; 221. As James D. G. Dunn has stated: "In short, the New Testament canon was not so much decreed as *acknowledged*" (cited in ibid., p. 221).

30. Such a sober assessment is not a denigration of ecumenical achievement but the first step toward its very possibility. It does, however, entail the serious consequence that ecclesiological differences may go deeper than differences of polity or even soteriology. They are sometimes, at their root, differences of christology itself. Douglas Farrow is thus correct in stating: "However it is asked, the question about Jesus underlies the question about the church" (*Ascension and Ecclesia*, p. ix).

his cross, though here too these are not the same.³¹ It is thus true that the time of Christ's ascended reign is also the time of the martyrs. And because the Lord who has ascended is the Lord who still bears the marks and form of his crucifixion and servanthood, the church called to bear his own likeness can never ascribe glory to itself.³² To recognize the provisional nature of its teaching and life, to admit that it "sees through a glass darkly," to confess that it must live by daily graces given as it travels on a journey to a destination at which it has not yet arrived, and to acknowledge that it will necessarily suffer on this way—these are nothing less than the first steps for the church to accept the call and costs of what it means to live as a pilgrim people.

**5. To say that the church is a pilgrim people entails that it lives not only apart from but within the world and is not unaffected by it even as it resists its assimilative power.**

The distinction between the church and the world, as that between Christ and the church, is also of a dialectical ordering. But the absolute distinction between the ascended Lord and the church is not replicated in that between the pilgrim people

---

31. As Barth writes: "The special fellowship of the Christian with Christ involves participation in the passion of His cross" (CD IV/2: p. 604). Yet he also later adds: "Between Christ and the Christian, His cross and ours, it is a matter of similarity in great dissimilarity" (ibid., p. 605). Once again we are faced with the necessity of a proper ordering but not a choice, and in this case that between a substitutionary and an exemplarist christology, with the first firmly restricting but also establishing the second. It is in fact the high christology of the former that grants weight and urgency to the latter. Moreover, that the cross of the disciple as witness (*martyr*) is not Christ's cross of atonement does not in any way lessen the authority of the call that it be carried or the weight of its own cost. But it does allow us to reconcile Christ's words from the cross as to the finality of his work (echoed and expanded upon by the author of Hebrews) and those of Paul that commend his own sufferings as "completing what is lacking in Christ's afflictions for the sake of his body, that is, the church" (Col 1:24). Careful readers of Paul (or any Pauline author) could never accuse him of collapsing these distinctions or confusing the message of the cross of Christ with his own self-commendation. Here everything hangs on defining what is truly "lacking."

32. This point was possibly most fully appreciated in the modern world by Søren Kierkegaard. For Kierkegaard's understanding of the lowliness of Christ even in his ascended and exalted state and the ramifications of this for the church and the Christian, see Kierkegaard, *Practice in Christianity*, ed. and trans. Howard V. Hong and Edna H. Hong (Princeton: Princeton University Press, 1991), pp. 24–5; 167–79; also David R. Law, *Kierkegaard's Kenotic Christology* (Oxford: Oxford University Press, 2013), pp. 260–1; 263–5; 280–1. For Kierkegaard (via Anti-Climacus), the exalted Christ continues even in his ascension to address the church in the form of a humble servant depicted in the canonical gospels. Law writes: "This means that human beings are presented with a *task*, namely that of following the suffering Christ and, like him, learning obedience to the Father" (*Kierkegaard's Kenotic Christology*, p. 281).

and the world, for the relation between church and world is such that no ethical absolutism between them can be maintained that overlooks the church's sharing in the world's own history and misery. The church journeys in and among the peoples of the nations and is called to be a light in the midst of a common life with them, and a life marked not in the first or last instance by opposition but enclosed within the recognition that "God so loved the world" (John 3:16). The second great temptation of the church in this horizontal sphere is an echo of that in the vertical one. It is to eliminate the ramifications of the tension of Christ's presence and absence in this time between Pentecost and parousia by eliminating the tension it faces with the world through either withdrawal or assimilation.

That the church's own life is called into existence by the Holy Spirit and is to be fashioned according to Christ's own, that it lives not only within this world but as a sign pointing to a kingdom beyond it, does grant to the church a unique role as an exemplary community.[33] Yet its true reality cannot be fully grasped by an appeal to its ordinary visibility or by a summation of its traditions and practices no matter how distinctive. That the church is in but not of the world means that it must be spoken of as both invisible and visible. The first is not a flight from its responsibility to embody the rule of Christ in its concrete life, but rather the acknowledgment that the ultimate power of that life lies not in the forms and practices that give it its visible concreteness.[34] To say that the church is in but not of the world is not first of all an ethical distinction (though it does entail such) but an acknowledgment of the spiritual power that gives the church life, and a life which precedes even as it calls forth the particular liturgical, confessional, and ethical form of life it takes. Yet it is precisely because of the uniqueness of the Spirit of holiness who constitutes it and the Lord who rules it that the church is to be a community that lives not only within but also as set apart from the world. As Farrow succinctly states this point: "Now the church is only really itself when it accepts and embraces this situation of radical continuity, and equally radical discontinuity, with the world."[35]

That the shape of what this life should look like is the cause of internecine arguments taken up within the church as it journeys through various times and

---

33. This entails not only, positively, that the church sets forth another way of life than that of the world, but negatively, that there are things of the world in which the church cannot participate. There is thus a real and proper necessity to speaking of the "otherness" of the church. Such "otherness" cannot be abstracted from, but is a necessary implication of, the very act of the church's confessing its faith. This truth is appreciated when the church resists relegating Daniel and Revelation to the far neglected margins of the canon, a temptation for the church in every age that seeks the accreditation and legitimation of its existence from the culture that surrounds it. It is also a temptation for the church which fears the strangeness and embarrassment, and not least self-conviction, such apocalyptic books offer.

34. Both its divine origin and its creaturely reality are evident in Webster's definition of the church: "The church is the form of common human life and action which is generated by the gospel to bear witness to the perfect word and work of the triune God" (*Confessing God*, p. 175).

35. Farrow, *Ascension and Ecclesia*, p. 11.

places should not be surprising (one can think of the first church council in Jerusalem, or the heated confrontation of Peter by Paul over the ramifications of Gentile inclusion in the new community, as well as the perennial debate of whether force can ever be taken up by Christians in the pursuit of justice or to defend the weak). That in this time between the times the church exists between these poles entails that it is not, will not be, and has never been a static entity of absolutely fixed forms or practices. It is a people that exists in movement, and its existence is not only marked but also constituted by this movement. As such, its life is one of navigation marked by necessary, recurrent, yet provisional judgments within the circumstances of an ever-changing journey with all the promise and dangers the translation of its message in new contexts entails. Faithfulness on the journey requires constant vigilance, creative imagination, resolute perseverance, and even the negotiation of firmly held internal standpoints as to what such faithfulness requires and what form it takes in the face of external challenges. To appreciate this fact is itself for the church to understand that it is a people who are strangers in a strange land and yet also sharers in that strangeness. It is to embrace the particular existence of pilgrims who are called not in spite of but in and through these challenges to live for Christ and for the good of the lands in which they find themselves.

## Conclusion

Let us circle back around to the beginning to reach our end. The way forward may be not without some irony a coordination of two errors that leads to a resolution of their missteps. A doctrine of revelation cannot, as has often happened, decontextualize Scripture by removing it from its ecclesial setting in which it exists and over which it serves as Christ's own appointed means of his self-presentation and communication, which in reality is Scripture's larger context of meaning and significance.[36] But ecclesiology can suffer its own form of decontextualization and abstraction. When rightly understood in the light of its unique temporal location and its subordinate place in relation to the triune God and God's revelatory, reconciling, and redemptive activity, the church's identity and task begin to come into sharper focus and can be seen in their true proportion. Ecclesiology is shown to be a secondary doctrine, one that is seen as the corollary, and not the source, of the prior divine work of salvation as set forth in theology proper as well as in a rich and developed christology accompanied by an attendant pneumatology. The church must therefore be understood not only as the setting of the reception of Christ's self-communication, but also as the penultimate goal of God's work. It is the representative people reflecting in this given time the final summation of the kingdom, a people who are called to exist "for the praise of his glory" (Eph 1:12) and for the sake of witness to the world.

36. Webster writes that "Scripture is an ecclesial reality because the place of Scripture is in the economy of salvation, and the economy of salvation concerns the divine work of restoring fellowship through the gathering of the *sanctorum communio*" (*Confessing God*, p. 53).

Granted, what has been provided here in placing the church in its unique time between Christ's ascension and parousia itself requires some attention to the difficult question of this time's own relation to pretemporality and indeed supratemporality, just as the work of God's salvation that provides for the ordering of the relation of God to his people, of Christ to his earthly body, and of the Holy Spirit to his fellowship requires seeing this work as grounded in God's own inner life and eternal election. But that exceeds what can here be done and perhaps what can be done. Regardless, it need not be undertaken for the more delimited investigation here made. For the mystery of God's will has been revealed in time (Col 1:25-29). And in the revelation of Christ crucified, risen, and ascended to the right hand of the Father from where he now reigns through the Spirit's power and from where he will return to judge the living and the dead, we find the proper understanding of the church's place in this time of the ascension. It is the time of Christ's self-mediated presence, though he is Lord and agent of this act of self-pronouncement and address now in heaven as he was on earth, and both then and now no one can confess him as Lord apart from the act of the Spirit (1 Cor 12:3). Such mediation is thus properly ascribed to the Holy Spirit and not those who are the recipients of the Spirit's revelatory and reconciliatory benefits. Insofar as this is so, the church lives as it is joined to Christ through the Spirit who enlivens, empowers, and equips it for its own proper task as a light to the nations to the glory of the Father.

Ecclesiology is in this light best served not by its neglect but by recognizing its proper situatedness and location in the dogmatic corpus that in turn pays tribute to the church's own proper context within the larger areas of God's work of salvation in Christ by the Spirit. A way to translate this claim is to confess that salvation comes from God alone, through Christ alone, by the Spirit alone, but all for our good and in order to establish fellowship with the triune God. The church is invited and indeed commissioned not only to participate in but also to proclaim this fellowship to the world. The work of God thus precedes, frames, and establishes the real and proper work of the church. When this is understood, a proper distinction between questions of revelation and ecclesiology, and in turn the distinction between Scripture and tradition, and both reflecting the fundamental unity-in-distinction of Christ and the church, can be maintained. Here again, the way forward is not predicated on a matter of choice between two terms but of their right and proper ordering that preserves their intricate union but without sacrificing their distinction and proper rank.

The righting of the dogmatic ship is in this light not achieved by a neglect of ecclesiology, but a placing of it within its theological context and the church within its own proper sphere of operations, which is that of the divine self-giving as mediated through Christ and the Spirit.[37] What we might discover, amid such

---

37. "The task is not that of putting the church in its place so much as recognizing the place which is prior to the doctrine of the church in an orderly unfolding of the mighty works of God" (Webster, *Confessing God*, p. 156).

work, is not only the distinctive calling and shape of our discipleship, but also the evangelical convictions that must precede and undergird them. We may discover that such an ecclesiology is an *evangelical* ecclesiology for an evangelical church—humble in tone, responsive in posture, confident in a hope that originates outside itself, rejoicing in rather than resenting its creatureliness, urgent yet not despairing in its witness, and grounded in the gospel of Christ. Not least, the church will be marked by prayer first and last because it recognizes God's prevenience and provenience as the basis of both its redeemed and created existence, announcing and displaying God's mercy in the Word made flesh as its proper form of life. That the church might be characterized as a creature of the Word of God will then be seen not so much as an evangelical distinctive but as its true and proper catholic description.

## Chapter 9

## THE CONFESSIONAL TASK OF THE CHRISTIAN UNIVERSITY

For well over twenty years, Christian scholars and educators of various disciplines have been engaged in an examination of the nature of Christian and secular higher education. Much of that reflection with regard to the North American context in particular has turned on one of two types of examinations. The first type is defined by a positive assessment of Christian higher education and its specific goals and achievements as these are embodied and witnessed in self-identified Christian colleges and universities. The second and arguably more dominant type is marked by a sober appraisal of the loss of Christian influence and identity in the sphere of higher education in general over the past two centuries. The argument offered here differs from both of these types of contributions and is, instead, a theological account of the university, and specifically of the Christian rather than the secular one, though that task has its own place and integrity.[1]

1. Persons such as Mike Higton, James Wm. McClendon, Jr., and John Webster have provided recent reflections upon theology's task and relation to the university and theology's place within it. See Mike Higton, *A Theology of Higher Education* (Oxford: Oxford University Press, 2012); James Wm. McClendon Jr., *Witness: Systematic Theology* (Nashville: Abingdon, 2000), pp. 387–420; John Webster, "Theological Theology," in *Confessing God* (London: T&T Clark 2005), pp. 11–31; John Webster, "*Regina Artium*: Theology and the Humanities," in *The Domain of the Word: Scripture and Theological Reason* (London: Bloomsbury T&T Clark, 2012), pp. 171–92; and John Webster, "God, Theology, Universities," in *Indicative of Grace—Imperative of Freedom: Essays in Honour of Eberhard Jüngel in His 80th Year*, ed. R. David Nelson (London: Bloomsbury T&T Clark, 2014), pp. 241–54. Stanley Hauerwas stands closer to my task in giving attention to the identity of a distinctively Christian university—see Hauerwas, *Christian Existence Today: Essays on Church, World and Living in Between* (Durham: Labyrinth Press, 1988), pp. 221–35; see also pp. 237–52. For Hauerwas, a university is Christian "if it receives its financial and moral support from the church" (*Christian Existence Today*, p. 223). Without denying the important issues raised by such a characterization and the compelling arguments in its favor, such is an insufficient definition in that some colleges may continue to receive both of these but have in reality very little of Christian substance remaining within them. A Christian university requires a more robust and theological definition than such a pragmatic one provides, whatever its merits.

Mike Higton, in his recent book, *A Theology of Higher Education*, attempts to mediate between explicitly Christian aims and ends as embodied in the church's doctrinal, moral, and liturgical life and those aims and ends of the secular university. He seeks to draw lines of coordination between a specifically Christian theology of the university and the secular university's own self-understanding, practices, and activities.[2] Other projects attempt to display the inherent appropriateness of including theology as a discipline within the secular university context. Such studies often are particularly European in flavor due to the historic placement of ecclesial centers of training and divinity schools within national research universities, but James McClendon has made a related case for including a department of theology composed of various religious traditions within secular American universities.[3] The task I undertake here differs from these in that it is a theological description of the Christian university, attempting to render its unique position within the economy of God's work in creation and redemption and its placement in relation to the church and the world.

To begin, we might articulate how such a theological account will differ from the two types of examinations of Christian faith and the university earlier noted. On one side, much reflection upon Christian higher education has been rooted in

---

Interacting with Hauerwas' later work, and giving his own argument for what a distinctively Roman Catholic university might entail, is Gavin D'Costa, "On Theology, the Humanities, and the University," in *Theology, University, Humanities: Initium Sapientiae Timor Domini*, ed. Christopher C. Brittain and Francesca A. Murphy (Eugene: Cascade, 2011), pp. 194–212; and Gavin D'Costa, *Theology in the Public Square: Church, Academy, and Nation* (Malden: Blackwell, 2005). The present essay resonates with much in D'Costa's important work but in its particular approach presents the commitments of a Christian university more indebted to Reformation convictions. I am nevertheless addressing the Christian university in the broadest sense while not overlooking, though not here addressing, the question of a university's ecclesial and denominational identity.

2. Higton finds such mediation particularly surrounding the themes of intellectual virtue and the negotiation between Christian and classical virtues. See Higton, *A Theology of Higher Education*, pp. 175–81.

3. McClendon, *Witness*, 387–420. For a related discussion of such a department made up of confessional theologians of different religious traditions, see Robert L. Wilken, *Remembering the Christian Past* (Grand Rapids: Eerdmans, 1995), pp. 1–24. For the distinctive development of modern European universities in relation to questions of theology, see Thomas Albert Howard, *Protestant Theology and the Making of the Modern German University* (Oxford: Oxford University Press, 2006); Zachary Purvis, *Theology and the University in Nineteenth Century Germany* (Oxford: Oxford University Press, 2016); Johannes Zachhuber, *Theology as Science in Nineteenth-Century Germany: From F. C. Baur to Ernst Troeltsch* (Oxford: Oxford University Press, 2013); and Higton, *A Theology of Higher Education*. For the influence of such universities upon those in North America, see Hermann Röhrs, *The Classical German Concept of the University and Its Influence on Higher Education in the United States* (Frankfurt am Main: Peter Lang, 1995).

a celebration of its distinctive goals and achievements. Such reflection has been primarily historical, genealogical, and ethnographic in its description of the rise and flourishing of Christian colleges and universities and their future prospects.[4] Alternatively, other such works have focused upon the distinctive virtues, habits, and practices that Christian scholarship and education embody and strive to display and instill, while others entail theoretical, disciplinary, and pedagogical discussions of how such confluences of faith and learning can be understood and achieved.[5] While such studies are numerous and significant, the most well-known investigations of the relation of Christian faith and higher education have been of a different second type, ones quite pessimistic in tone. James Burtchaell's *The Dying of the Light: The Disengagement of Colleges and Universities from Their Christian Churches* and George Marsden's *The Soul of the American University: From Protestant Establishment to Established Nonbelief* reveal their dark conclusions in

---

4. See William C. Ringenberg, *The Christian College: A History of Protestant Higher Education in America*, 2nd ed. (Grand Rapids: Baker, 2006); Robert Benne, *Quality With Soul: How Six Premier Colleges and Universities Keep Faith with Their Religious Traditions* (Grand Rapids: Eerdmans, 2001); Philip Gleason, *Contending with Modernity: Catholic Higher Education in the Twentieth Century* (New York/Oxford: Oxford University Press, 1995); and Paul J. Dovre, ed., *The Future of Religious Colleges* (Grand Rapids: Eerdmans, 2002).

5. See Douglas V. Henry and Michael D. Beaty, *The Schooled Heart: Moral Formation in American Higher Education* (Waco: Baylor University Press, 2007); Perry L Glanzer and Todd C. Ream, *Christianity and Moral Identity in Higher Education* (New York: Palgrave Macmillan, 2009); and Cary Balzer and Rod Reed, eds., *Building a Culture of Faith: University-Wide Partnerships for Spiritual Formation* (Abilene: ACU Press, 2012). The study by Todd C. Ream and Perry L. Glanzer entitled *The Idea of a Christian College: A Reexamination for Today's University* (Eugene, OR: Cascade, 2013) pushes beyond such subject-centered approaches to ask regarding the identity of the Christian university in terms of "God's story," but does so primarily through an examination of the character to be formed in its members and thus falls back into this latter category as well. So also does James K. A. Smith's *Desiring the Kingdom: Worship, Worldview, and Cultural Formation* (Grand Rapids: Baker, 2009). For all of its attempts to reframe the question in terms of liturgical rather than moral categories, Smith's work still begins with the fundamental concepts of habits and practices and thus with a "philosophical anthropology," though with the human person now framed as a religious animal rather than fundamentally a moral or rational one. It thus, too, can be placed here. For notable examples of philosophical and pedagogical essays on the relation of faith and reason in college, culture, curriculum, and classroom, see Nicholas Wolterstorff, *Educating for Shalom: Essays on Christian Higher Education*, ed. Clarence W. Joldersma and Gloria Goris Stronks (Grand Rapids: Eerdmans, 2004); and David I. Smith and James K. A. Smith, eds., *Teaching and Christian Practices: Reshaping Faith & Learning* (Grand Rapids: Eerdmans, 2011). See also Michael L. Budde and John Wesley Wright, eds., *Conflicting Allegiances: The Church-Based University in a Liberal Democratic Society* (Grand Rapids: Brazos, 2004).

their very titles.⁶ These two may be the classic texts of this genre, but they do not stand alone. Numerous theologians, philosophers, and educators have decried the wilting phenomenon of Christian scholarship and the demise of the moral coherence of the modern research university as two sides of an unforgiving narrative.⁷ My purpose here is not to add another pessimistic account of the future of Christian higher education or decry the current state of the modern secular university. Nor is it my intent to provide an alternative optimism, but rather to ask a prior question: What *is* a Christian university, and how might it be theologically understood? Moreover, where is its location within the field of God's activity of redemption and creation, or more sharply, within the economy of God's salvific, sanctifying, and sustaining work?⁸

---

6. James Burtchaell, *The Dying of the Light: The Disengagement of Colleges and Universities from Their Christian Churches* (Grand Rapids: Eerdmans, 1998); and George Marsden, *The Soul of the American University: From Protestant Establishment to Established Nonbelief* (Oxford: Oxford University Press, 1996). See also Jon H. Roberts and James Turner, *The Sacred and the Secular University* (Princeton: Princeton University Press, 2000); Douglas Sloan, *Faith and Knowledge: Mainline Protestantism and American Higher Education* (Louisville: Westminster John Knox, 1994); and Perry L. Glanzer, Nathan F. Alleman, and Todd C. Ream, *Restoring the Soul of the University: Unifying Christian Higher Education in a Fragmented Age* (Downers Grove: IVP Academic, 2017). For a work that warns of a similar future looming on the Catholic horizon, see Melanie M. Morey and John J. Piderit, S. J., *Catholic Higher Education: A Culture in Crisis* (Oxford/New York: Oxford University Press, 2006); D'Costa contends that it is a present reality—see *Theology in the Public Square*, pp. 38-76.

7. See Stanley Hauerwas, *The State of the University: Academic Knowledges and the Knowledge of God* (Malden/Oxford/Carlton: Blackwell, 2007); for a related though different perspective, see C. John Sommerville, *The Decline of the Secular University* (Oxford: Oxford University Press, 2006). Sommerville argues that it is the secular university that is becoming increasingly marginal to American society and that this is, ironically, on account of its secularism and failure to take theological and religious thought with any seriousness (p. 4).

8. In asking the question in this way, I seek to provide a truly theological, rather than historical, sociological, or religious account of the university. For an excellent work in regard to the latter categories, see Glanzer, Alleman, and Ream, *Restoring the Soul of the University*. They provide an illuminating historical account of the university, including the specifically Christian university, as well as an *apologia* for theology as required for rightly ordering its ends and practices and a diagnosis of the problems that arise when theology is neglected. This avenue of description and argument is impressively executed and indeed necessary, but such is not, of course, a theological account of the university itself. Nor is the worthy placement of the university within the history of its development the same as situating it within the economy of salvation or coordinating its identity within the field of God's action in Christ and in relation to the church. This distinction is of course the difference between discussing the relation of the university to the discipline of theology and discussing the university in light of the subject matter of theology itself. Hence, the university is in the present work situated not only in relation to culture but to the covenant that stands at the center of God's relation to his creation. I therefore seek to provide a decidedly *theological* account of the university, rather than a historical, sociological, or

It should be noted from the outset that the very idea of a Christian university has been questioned even by those one might expect to be sympathetic to its cause. James McClendon has stated that the secular university simply *is* the university as it currently exists as a social institution and that one cannot even provide a meaningful definition of what a Christian university would be.[9] McClendon's point should not be lightly dismissed, for it gestures to a larger more general question of what makes something outside of the church itself "Christian" at all. Karl Barth designated his constructive dogmatics the *Christliche Dogmatik* (*Christian Dogmatics*), but he rethought this title when making a new start at writing it in view of his own self-perceived false starts. When he began again to compose what would become his definitive work of systematic theology, and one that would occupy him for the next three decades of his life, he renamed it the *Kirchliche Dogmatik*, or *Church Dogmatics*. Barth stated that he had become wary of the overuse of the title "Christian," and this concern pertained not only to his own constructive theology.[10] Barth rejected the attachment of the adjective Christian to other projects as well, and especially, to the state or any political organizations within it—he renounced all talk of a "Christian" nation and frowned upon the establishment of "Christian" political parties. He moreover criticized the attachment of the label to other social and political causes by which the church defends its own rights and furthers its own ends in ways that can only appear to the world as self-serving and even indulgent.[11] In short, Barth's rejection of the adjective "Christian" for such descriptions was a perceptive judgment of the danger of domesticating the gospel for other ends while claiming their legitimation by christening institutions, movements, and programs that serve such ends as "Christian."

In light of such a warning, it might be responsibly questioned whether the adjective "Christian" should be attached to any university (or college) at all.[12] My

religious one. While the latter types in fact dominate the literature, such horizontal descriptions cannot neglect the vertical unless faith itself give way to a purely historical and sociological account, or the theological be sacrificed to the pragmatic. This neglect is itself a symptom (and more than that) of the disease all these works seek to address, for the problems to be faced are much deeper than pedagogical, administrative, or even cultural ones.

9. McClendon, Jr., *Witness: Systematic Theology*, pp. 388-9.

10. Karl Barth, CD I/1: pp. xii–xiii.

11. Karl Barth, "The Christian Community and the Civil Community," in *Community, State, and Church: Three Essays* (Gloucester: Peter Smith, 1968), pp. 149-89; see esp. pp. 182-4. He noted: "The secret contempt which a Church fighting for its own interests with political weapons usually incurs even when it achieves a certain amount of success is well deserved" (ibid., p. 165).

12. Thus Hauerwas writes: "Please note I am not trying to argue for something called the Christian University. Sam Wells has pointed out to me when 'Christian' is used as an adjective you can be confident that you are reproducing the habits of Constantinianism. Rather I am pressing the question of the difference church practices might make for the very shape of knowledge in the university" (*The State of the University*, p. 7).

tentative and provisional conclusion is that this may in fact be done, but only because the university, like the hospital of today, was in fact a gift of the church to culture at large, and thus it grows out of, and at best exists in conformity with, rather than in contradiction to, the unique task of the church.[13] It is to this relation of church and university that we now turn.

The relation of the church and the Christian university is one of a particular complementarity, never one of identity. The university does not and should not seek to replicate the church or its distinctive witness. Yet it is nevertheless the case that as the ancient church advanced in history and geography, schools were formed, culminating in the rise of the medieval universities, and such schools were seen as institutional implications of the spread of the gospel, rather than intrinsically inimical to it. While such history provides an initial justification for considering the coherence of the notion of a Christian university, I also want to explicate why the adjective "Christian" cannot and should not cease to be a contentious one when attached to a university. This is so precisely because of the unique and perpetually precarious place that Christian universities inhabit between what Barth designated the Christian community (i.e., the church) and the civil community (i.e., the state—or in the usage of this essay, society more broadly conceived as composed of its political, social, economic, and cultural realities).

Much will thereby turn upon what it means to designate a university "Christian." This designation cannot be fully captured in categories of ethics or even doctrine. It is not enough to say that a university is Christian because it has a Christian heritage or even a doctrinal statement (since such a statement might be ignored or quietly set aside as years pass, or even marginalized in times when lip service is paid to it). Nor is it enough to say that a university is Christian because it focuses upon certain forms of moral or even spiritual formation, since such forms might remain in a later pluralistic environment when the specifically Christian content, convictions, and practices of a university have been left behind—consider, for example, moral leadership programs and resident chaplaincies and religious studies departments that are included within the university but peripheral to its heart and life and devoid of any specifically Christian commitments.

It is also not enough to see the Christian character of a university as captured in its endeavors to instill intellectual or moral virtues within its constituent members by

---

13. See McClendon, *Witness*, pp. 389-97. Reflecting upon such Christian beginnings to the university, Higton writes: "One of the storylines that weaves through the emergence of the University of Paris, therefore, is the story of the nurturing by some university practitioners of what they saw as the new form of spiritual discipline: a contemplative and purificatory *meditatio* outside the monasteries, ordered towards the establishment of well-ordered individual and public life before God" (Higton, p. 36; also pp. 39-41). I do not here explore, however, whether already in the establishment of the university of Paris the seeds were sown for the insulation of theology from the other disciplines of the university and in turn their inevitable secularization. See Oliver Crisp, Gavin D'Costa, Mervyn Davies, and Peter Hampson, eds., *Christianity and the Disciplines: The Transformation of the University* (London: T&T Clark, 2012), p. 2; and D'Costa, *Theology in the Public Square*, pp. 10-11.

means of the emulation of mentors or exposure to classic texts. Even such worthy things might be constructed along the lines of purely classical (Aristotelian?) models, and even if more specifically Christian ones are in view, such a focus upon the character of the subjects of teaching and learning can lead to an abstraction of such personal goals from the other disciplinary and institutional ones that mark the university's intrinsic ends. In other words, the Christian university is rightly seen as not less than a school of virtue, and truly a school of virtue, but it is nevertheless more than a school of virtue (and even such a claim requires some careful attention in light of problematic conceptions of virtue themselves, though these difficulties exceed the immediate purview of this essay).[14] To designate a university as Christian therefore cannot be equated with specifying the components of its institutional life, whether academic, moral, or even spiritual, even though these are necessary for its historical embodiment and Christian identity. So a Christian university may incorporate an office of spiritual life and a chaplaincy, but their presence by themselves does not make a university Christian in the full sense here considered. Nor is it Christian, obviously, by the mere fact that classes are opened with prayer, though this may be a good start to what I will argue.

In the end, there must be a more substantive meaning to the adjective "Christian" when placed before the noun "university" to render it coherent and significant. To designate a university Christian comprises the recognition that a university is marked by a confessional task, and one indeed larger than a commitment to the intellectual and moral and even spiritual formation of its individual members. The confessional task of the Christian university is to see itself in relation to God's act of creative, sustaining, and salvific activity in Jesus Christ through the Spirit heralded by the church for the sake of the world, to see all aspects of the created and social order in this light, and to see the university's own existence as set within the realm of human obedience and in correspondence to, though not as a replication of, its ecclesial parentage.[15] This realm of human obedience and vocation takes its rise from and is comprised by the creature's all-embracing response to the Creator's gracious divine prevenience and salvation. The form this obedience takes with specific regard to the vocation of learning and investigation embodied in the institution of the university is a dedication to see all areas of exploration in light of that divine activity and as a response to it, setting not only such central practices of

---

14. For a perceptive presentation of the relation of a university's required intellectual and moral practices, between the "public law of studies" and the "private law of persons," see Jaroslav Pelikan, *The Idea of the University: A Reexamination* (New Haven: Yale University Press, 1992), pp. 44-56. What Pelikan does not provide is a theological examination of the problems, as well as benefits, of such accounts of the virtues themselves.

15. Such a university will recognize not only its historic but its continuing relationship to the church and the churches, and it will in humility seek the freedom of exploration unhindered by narrow ecclesial concerns but also recognize that it serves the larger purposes of the church as a herald of the gospel even in its real though relative independence, for when seen in the scope of God's redemptive purposes and action, the Christian university is at most a reflection of the church, not the church of the university. When the order of this relation is forgotten, the university cannot help but become tempted by forms of idolatry.

the university but all peripheral ones—artistic, athletic, and administrative—into a rightful ordering in light of that vision and for its furtherance. Such requires an obedience of the intellect as well as the will, and thus of the entire person and of the entire community of scholarship in which such persons find themselves.

It is the perennial struggle to bring these complex practices into alignment with that confession that leads to the knife edge on which the Christian university balances, a struggle that cannot be underestimated in light of the particular pressures placed upon this task by the number, variety, strength, and seductiveness of the temptations that press against the university. The Christian university is not the church, but neither is it simply the world in the Johannine sense of ignorance or opposition to God's will and activity.[16] Augustine's binary distinction between the City of God and the Earthly City, however brilliant in its execution, will not serve adequately as a typology for the understanding and placement of the Christian university which stands, in the order of its being, between the church and the world.[17]

Such is an intrinsically paradoxical and precarious placement. On one side, the Christian university does not seek to embody in its life a commitment to a confession that rivals or duplicates the church's own in either its distinctive commission or task. The Christian university is not, it must be adamantly re-stated, the church, and it stands as an entity distinct from it.[18] But from the vantage of the other side, and in taking up its particular confessional task in correspondence and

---

16. 1 John 2:15-17.

17. The Christian university therefore accepts the ambiguity of creation and history in its current state but also its own ambiguity in the economy of redemption. The university is not a neutral place from which to stand and view a fallen creation but a participant in that creation even if, as a Christian university, it attempts to view it from the stance of reason renewed by grace and brought under the purview of reconciliation. What is required is not a stark dualism, but an ordered relation, between church and the Christian university, and of the Christian university and the world. In effect, the Christian university is situated within a precarious concentric circle inserted between that of the church and that of the world, participating in the realities of both. It thus exists between the Christian and civil communities, in Barth's parlance. The church therefore may in fact exist "at the heart of the Christian university" in its ideal existence, as D'Costa hopes for a truly Catholic university (*Theology in the Public Square*, p. 218; cf. p. 51). But the university itself also exists within the boundaries of the world.

18. It is not confessional in the same sense as the church is, for the Christian university is not a church and is not divinely entrusted as the herald of God's redemption. But it does display, in its own correspondent way to the confession of the church, a disposition to unite its tasks in light of a recognition of God's works in the economy for the world's creation, preservation, and redemption. It thus sees the world through the prism of a doctrine of creation rather than considering it as a purposeless realm of nature, and a creation reconciled and awaiting redemption. It sees sin as a fundamental category for the understanding of Christian reason and knowing, and thus understands the particular temptations of the university that include, but exceed beyond, the intellectual vices of pride and an undisciplined curiosity. That curiosity can betray rather than reflect the call of the gospel is argued by John Webster in *The Domain of the Word*, pp. 193–202.

analogy to the confessional task of the church in its proclamation of God's action for the salvation of the created order, the Christian university stands over against the world, and specifically the secular university, as a place committed to present in an intentional way a parable and indeed embodiment of the life of obedience to the gospel in the distinct vocation of intellectual endeavor.[19] In this time of Christ's ascension between the times of his first and second advents, its goal is not, however, so much the achievement of a synoptic vision of all things, but the disposition to embrace by faith that such a united vision is to be had, even should it in the end be beyond our comprehension in light of its infinite mystery and our fallen confusion. In this sense, the Christian university confesses, in analogy to the church's confession of the unity of the Scriptural canon amid all of its diversity, the unity of the created world as a universe despite all of its wondrous and rich plurality.[20] It seeks something the achievement of which it knows is always ahead of it, and which will not be completed in the course of history but only at its end, and even then perhaps never comprehensible to us in its full grandeur. Yet its very name as a *university* displays the nature of its confession to a singular truth that lies behind all truths, to a sovereign Creator that stands behind the disparity of all the manifold witnesses in creation and the inscrutable contingencies of history.

So in analogy to the church's confession that one Lord stands behind the diversity of the canon, the Christian university confesses in both its words and deeds that the universe in both its natural and social history stands under the sovereignty of a single Lord who has called the world into existence "from that which was not" (Heb. 11:3) for the purpose of establishing a covenant of fellowship with it "before the foundation of the world."[21] This Lord has acted salvifically "in the fullness of time" to bring such to completion.[22] The Christian university makes this confession despite the necessary plurality of the constitutive disciplines within it that, as John Henry Cardinal Newman knew, were indispensable intensifications and restrictions in the scope of an examination of creation and history in order to focus upon an aspect of a larger reality that none of them alone could fully perceive or comprehend.[23] The Christian university thereby embraces a task to bring every thought under the rubric of God's activity in creation and redemption

---

19. "But in the long run, Christian schools and universities are the way in which churches take responsibility for the process of education so that knowledge, wonder, love and service may once more be united" (Crisp, D'Costa, Davies, and Hampson, *Christianity and the Disciplines*, p. 4).

20. For the unity of the canon amid arguments of its diversity, see Barth's insistence upon this point in debate with Adolf von Harnack, a debate examined in Kimlyn J. Bender, *Confessing Christ for Church and World* (Downers Grove: InterVarsity Press, 2014), pp. 179–205. For the centrality of christology for understanding creation, see ibid., pp. 287–314.

21. 1 Peter 1:20; cf. also Rev. 13:8; John 17:24; Ephesians 1:4.

22. Galatians 4:4; cf. Eph. 1:10.

23. John Henry Newman, *The Idea of a University* (London: Longmans, Green, and Co, 1896), pp. 46–7; cf. pp. 43–70.

even in the midst of its diverse departments, disciplines, and practices, but to do so with no pretensions of achieving an ultimate conceptual or philosophical synthesis or sacrifice of disciplinary integrity.[24] It dedicates itself to see the world as a created and good reality that, despite its complexity and even fallen disorder, stands under the sovereign care of a good and wise God who has acted to reconcile it to himself through the cross of Christ and whose end is not dissolution into non-existence but a promised hope of redemption by the Holy Spirit.[25]

This singular and distinctive placement of the Christian university between the church and society at large, a placement set forth and indeed established in its unique confession, requires constant vigilance by such a university against the perversion of its own identity. The reason that the Christian university as an institution rarely endures as a distinctly Christian project is in large part due precisely to its peculiar and vertiginous placement. The force of the world's gravity upon the Christian university cannot be overestimated. Its unchecked result is that the Christian university is pulled entirely into the world's orbit such that its identity is compromised in reality if not in name. Moreover, the greatest temptation of the Christian university is, ironically, to see itself as *intrinsically* and *essentially* Christian, namely, to take its adjectival description as designating the possession of a state of sanctification rather than an intentional act of confession that is never completed but unending, and one that is a confession not only of God's reign over all creation and human endeavors, but also a confession of the university's failure to live up to its own aspirations to embody that prior profession in all of its life. The self-delusion of the moniker Christian comes when we think of this as an adjective signifying a permanent and settled state of affairs such that the "lordless powers" (in the language of Barth) are understood as purely external rather than also internal to the university, a threat outside rather than within the university

---

24. In this, the Christian university stands closer to the humility of Schleiermacher (whatever his other problematic legacies to the university) than to the pretensions of Hegel. As Zachhuber writes, Schleiermacher was "deeply skeptical about the ability of the human mind to construct a system of thought capable of explaining reality in its fullness—hence his opposition to Hegel and Fichte" (*Theology as Science in Nineteenth-Century Germany*, p. 14). Correspondingly, any philosophy mediating the disciplines to themselves (or, in some cases, mediating between them and theology) must itself be one pursued with both commitment yet also a humble fallibilism—and this pertains to any school, whether existential, phenomenological, Thomist, or other. It may be helpful to consider that Gödel's incompleteness theorem reflects an eschatological truth that extends beyond mathematics to all systems of thought (while not absolutizing the theorem itself).

25. Romans 8:18-25. While the fruits of the Christian university's labor gleaned from teaching and research should be shared with other universities and the world at large, it is this confession of humility and hope that is the greatest gift that the Christian university holds before the world. This truthful confession is a particular kind of reflection of Christ's own illumination of the world in its state of sin and promised salvation, a bulwark against succumbing to either (modern) triumphalism or (postmodern) nihilism.

itself.[26] Such delusion comes not so much by forgetting that the university is not the church, but that it is placed so firmly in the world.

Intrinsic to a Christian university therefore must be the recognition of an eschatological reservation and corresponding humility regarding its own achievements. To treat its adjectival identity as one of essence rather than as lived existence, as being rather than as act, is in turn the very source for the means of self-deception by which it underestimates its real temptations and overlooks the real failures of its own practice. To think of its description as Christian as an achievement rather than an aspiration, as a possession rather than an orientation toward obedient action, is precisely the construction of the canopy under which it willingly or unwillingly, consciously or unconsciously, justifies its less than sanctified ideals rather than confesses its own need for justification and forgiveness. In this construction, a Christian worldview becomes an ideology, a cloak of invisibility hiding other ideological commitments, a mantle shielding them from critical scrutiny. The result is a university's particular failure of receiving and exercising diagnostic examination and discernment. It is in the end the confusion of the result with the ground of the university's existence, so that the university esteems that what makes it Christian is best captured by its intrinsic character rather than its witness to a gospel external to its own life that calls it in every new generation to a perpetual and unfinished task of obedience and witness in the specific realm of human intellectual effort.

To note as much is not a naïve call for moral perfectionism nor the misapplication of the personal to the institutional—just the opposite, in fact— though it is a call for intellectual and moral vigilance and intensive ongoing theological reflection that cannot be limited to a specific and necessary department under that name in practice or effect. A Christian university recognizes the need for grace and repentance in order to resist the commodification and indeed idolatry of knowledge that arises when the production of knowledge is valued above wisdom and the gospel. Such an admonition is not a call to sloth, but to a particular form of diligence that guards against the singular temptations that not only are brought by numerical or financial success, but that see these as the primary indicators of a mission fulfilled. The Christian university, by means of its own confession, can never confuse the ultimate execution of its mission with these quantitative indicators of success, however important or necessary they may be. In short, a Christian university cannot be Christian by abstracting its identity from the larger economy of God's action and correspondent realm of human obedience without succumbing to thinking of its own success in purely immanent terms, such as

---

26. For the "lordless powers," see Karl Barth, *The Christian Life: Church Dogmatics IV/4 Lecture Fragments*, trans. Geoffrey W. Bromiley (Grand Rapids: Eerdmans, 1981), pp. 213–33. That Barth discusses such "powers" as government, mammon, and ideology, along with such things as entertainment, technology, and sport, should be enough to commend this as required reading for not only all university administrators and trustees, but its faculty and staff as well.

quantities of research produced, moneys secured, students enrolled, or even wins accumulated. Such things take on disproportionate or even singular importance when the intrinsic confessional identity of the university is marginalized from the center of the university's own self-reflection and mission.[27] For this reason, the most important ongoing task of the Christian university must be to remember and discover anew the nature of the adjective that describes it.[28] A Christian university is as such not a permanent and enduring achievement but a command heard and task embodied afresh by Christians in every new generation. Such is not a denial of historical continuity and existence, nor the rejection of rightful forms of tradition and authority, but the recognition that a university cannot live simply off the faith of its founders or consider past obedience as a loan that can be redeemed and cashed in the present.

27. Such marginalization results in a state of affairs where arenas of university life begin to take on ends that are devoid of this particular confessional determination, such that the adjective Christian applies not to the whole but only to a limited range of the university's constituent areas. Thus money, power, and success measured in specific quantifiable achievements become the final ends of the sub-disciplines that exist in relative autonomy. This is true not only of academic departments, but of all auxiliary and secondary areas, including the arts and athletics. Such is the road to the dissolution not only of the university's Christian identity, but of the university as a *uni-versity*. In this sense, in truth to its historic form, only a confessional university can be a university at all.

28. A Christian university thus wears its moniker lightly but holds it with more tenacity than other institutions of human affairs. Nevertheless, its Christian status cannot be seen as a possession of a particular and enduring nature. Such may seem to be the case in light of the institutional structures of buildings, names, and charters that provide the identity to a particular institution, but even a cursory perusal of the history of American universities displays how ephemeral such things can truly be. To think of a university as Christian can refer only in the end to a particular confession of the university in the present and not solely rest upon the embracing of a past heritage. It is to confess anew and repeatedly that all disciplines, departments, and practices of the university are undertaken for the sake of and shaped by the recognition of the larger narrative of the gospel that calls them into being. Such is not to impose simplistic religious perspectives upon the disciplines, nor to ignore the nature of their own integrity and subject matter. But it is to see them as part of a single whole in correspondence to the confession of a single Lord who has called the natural and social world from nothingness into existence for the purpose of a covenantal end. It entails that the disciplines cannot either fall into line with overarching ideologies that contravene the gospel, or exist as hopelessly competitive areas of investigation and discourse that are unrelated in a multiversity. The Christian university must equally portray an eschatological reservation that staves off triumphalism, and an eschatological hope that someday the many will be seen in their unity. It therefore must, ironically, oppose premature synthesis as much as seek it, and recognize that the ultimate knowledge of all things is an eschatological hope rather than solely the product of rightly exercised reason (1 Cor. 13:12). This alone protects the university from falling under captivity to ideologies of any stripe—or at least gives it the freedom and ability to name them.

The primary task of the Christian university as a whole is therefore the testing of its practice and speech against its own confessional identity. No small part of this is, as here attempted, the placement of the Christian university within the wider field of God's activity directed toward the redemption of human life and its unique placement between church and world. An appreciation of this placement is necessary and worthwhile if only because it reveals why the perennially pessimistic understandings of Christian scholarship are not so much to be rued but to be expected. The Christian university, like the Christian hospital, both gifts of Christianity to culture at large, is shaped by a resonance for the gospel but also predicated upon certain practices that are easily and unavoidably influenced by the increasing bureaucratic, regulatory, and managerial demands of the state and of consumer wishes. Such demands are in turn shaped by market forces that provide a constant torrent of pressure upon the university's ends and goals and which in turn begin to affect them, as consumerist and materialistic forces apply unending pressure upon institutional decision-making. Unresisted, such pressure can result in an exchange of bureaucratic efficiency and assessment for a university's proper ends, in effect reducing the examination of a mission's goals to the language of numerical indicators and quantifiable data of enrollment and revenue. Added to all of this is the increasing anti-intellectualism and coarseness of a growing segment of the culture at large, one marked by a populism and pragmatism gone to seed. The Christian university cannot retain its soul for long should it gain a solid and peaceful place in such a world. In light of this reality, the Christian university is not an achievement to be celebrated, but the proposal of a perennial argument for an intellectual and indeed moral endeavor and vocation shaped by a very different faith, a communal and institutional life determined by and for gospel-shaped ends. For a university to embrace the adjective Christian is not so much for the purpose of self-description as for the purpose of adopting an intention and aspiration to discipline all of intellectual endeavor in light of gospel truth. It is the pronouncement and embrace of a never-ending discipleship of the mind, an *intellegentia viatorum*, not the celebration of a synoptic vision achieved. It is the vocation and labor of the intellect shaped by, in Luther's parlance, a theology of the cross rather than one of glory.

In the end, it must be admitted that the existence of Christian universities is not an undisputed good. If such universities exist (and this is not here a given, nor taken for granted), they find their justification finally and only in their service as a witness to learning that is brought under the discipline of the gospel. They should not be seen as private enclaves but as public visible institutions that in turn display not only their own winsome witness to a form of intellectual and moral life shaped by the good news of God's salvation, but also in so doing witness to the fact that the secular liberal university is not free of its own theological convictions and ideological captivities. The Christian university pronounces that an alternative to such a secular ordering and plural disorder exists. Christian universities therefore can be places of sustained and contested agreement and harmonious disagreement because they live under the aegis of a conviction that it is not the research published, moneys received, or arguments won that provide the intrinsic value to the persons who undertake them.[29] Such universities are not to serve first as the location of polemical argumentation against rivals but as a form of corporate lived obedience guarded by a Christian confession that opposes the instrumentalization of the world and the loss of its superfluous wonder that exceeds human comprehension or utility. This confession rejects both old and new forms of reductionism that sacrifice the true mystery of the cosmos and of persons as objects of God's creating and saving action. It also staves off a curiosity that lacks discipline and a form of investigation that lacks a corresponding vocation of service to others and moral character of the self. It opposes captivating ideologies as well as historiographies of both triumph and grievance that make repentance and reconciliation impossible and that deny the tragic yet divinely sustained nature of human history and its political, cultural, and social arrangements. And it provides alternative models of artistic expression that are clear-sighted yet not narrowly defined by indulgent and nihilistic trends that revel in darkness, license, and indentured degradation. In the end, Christian universities should be places that are the freest in their avenues of possible exploration and the most humanistic of all human institutions. They can be such precisely because truth, rather than power, must ultimately order their ends, and because both freedom and humanism are reconstituted along gospel lines, and thus redeemed. And they can be such because they are called in their own way to reflect and correspond to the divine beneficence shown to the world. Such service to the world in the area of human learning concretely serves human knowledge, wellness, and flourishing. The university can trust that this service might be given because the Lord of the Christian university is also the Lord of the world. It can likewise be confident that the command to love one's neighbor holds even in this arena of human life.

An honest evaluation of how far Christian universities actually fail to fulfill such a task leads to a sober assessment. It would be easy to give in to cynicism in light of such a reality. Christian universities stand every moment between the line of correspondence to the confessional task of the church and the movement

---

29. This conception of the university draws upon the work of Alasdair MacIntyre in his *Three Rival Versions of Moral Inquiry: Encyclopaedia, Genealogy, and Tradition* (Notre Dame: University of Notre Dame Press, 1990). Reflecting upon a Christian theology of scholarship, Mike Higton concludes: "It turns out that the picture of learning suggested is not one of competitive achievement, where the knowledge that Christians secure stands over against, and trumps, the knowledge secured by others. It is not one in which it makes sense for a Christian to lord his or her knowledge over others, nor to delight in the demonstration that their learning is nothing and that only Christian learning reaps the truth. It is, rather, a form of learning understood as the reception of a gift; it is a form of learning that involves travelling humbly the way of the cross; and it is a form of learning that inherently involves participation in a certain kind of gracious and open community" (*A Theology of Higher Education*, p. 151). This is a description of the learning of the church, and one that Higton wants to translate to secular learning, but it is not inimical to that of the Christian university and in fact well describes it.

of slipping into a post-confessional and thus post-Christian identity. We are seemingly left again with a quite pessimistic prognostication. Indeed, we may wonder if Christian universities as here described exist. But in conclusion we might remember two things.

First, such real failures should not be equated with the fate of the university and a loss of its identity—the Christian university, like the Christian, is always a paradox of sin and obedience. Such an observation does entail, however, that it might be impossible fully to designate whether a university is actually faithful and obedient in a specific point in time—here is the tension between a formal identity and a material reality, and a tension that points to a judgment, and justification, that cannot be determined ultimately from the human side. It is not certain, in fact, if the question of a university's Christian identity can truly be humanly answered. Its appropriateness may be reserved not only to the judgment of future generations, but to the One who stands beyond such generations themselves.

And this leads to the second and final point—if it is remembered that the Christian university is not so much an achievement but a task it will also be recognized that it is not so much a gift self-produced but itself dependent upon the good grace of God, for all human forms of devotion and obedience have their divine prerequisite. Certainly the university cannot overreach and claim promises that Christ has made not to it but to the church. Nevertheless, God's faithfulness to the church is that same faithfulness that calls forth a response on the part of the Christian as reconciled creature in all areas of creaturely vocation. Even here, the creature is not left alone to his or her own devices and vices. Indeed, insofar as divine faithfulness remains, as the divine light still shines, there is yet hope that the light of the Christian university may not die or be extinguished.

> "For with you is the fountain of life; in your light we see light."
> Psalm 36:9

# Part IV

POSTSCRIPT

## Chapter 10

## THE AMERICAN EXPERIENCE OF A DARKENING AND RECEDING PROVIDENCE: THE CIVIL WAR AND THE UNMAKING OF AN AMERICAN RELIGIOUS SYNTHESIS

One hundred and fifty years ago, America was deeply divided and engaged in a great Civil War. That war, which has shaped so much of American life ever since, is the subject of great curiosity, horror, and fascination, a nationalistic calamity from which we cannot, collectively, look away. The strategy and tragedy of its military engagements have been studied and reenacted, its political ramifications and justifications discerned and debated, its generals idolized and vilified, its central character reviled by a few but revered by many, an enigma apotheosized as a national martyr whose leadership in life was disputed, but whose reputation since his death has grown to overshadow that of any other American president before or since. The Civil War has been the subject of more books in the history of the United States than any other single topic; their number is well on the way to, if not surpassing, one hundred thousand. The Civil War has been the focal piece of one of the greatest documentaries America has produced[1] and is itself nothing less than the central fulcrum of America's history, such that before the war it was said, in Shelby Foote's words, "The United States *are* ..., " whereas after it was said, "The United States *is* ...." This full and final realization of the motto *E pluribus unum* was achieved not through the memorial words of politicians alone but at a staggering cost of life. Here an American civil religion was born out of the ashes of destruction and the bloodshed "on the altar of a nation,"[2] history literally bleeding into mythology.

What has received less attention than the political and military aspects of the Civil War is the religious life of the Americans who lived through it. One of the most important works to rectify this neglect was *Religion and the American Civil War*, a collection of essays published in 1998.[3] One could argue, however,

---

1. Ken Burns, *The Civil War* (PBS (DIRECT), 2011).
2. Harry S. Stout, *Upon the Altar of the Nation: A Moral History of the Civil War* (New York: Penguin Books, 2007). Along with a national civil religion, a sectional religion with its own mythology was also born for the postwar South (see note 22 below). For the history of civil religion in America, see Catherine L. Albanese, *America: Religions and Religion* (Belmont: Wadsworth Publishing, 1981), pp. 283-309.
3. Randall M. Miller, Harry S. Stout, and Charles Reagan Wilson, eds., *Religion and the American Civil War* (Oxford: Oxford University Press, 1998).

that the most important single-author book to appear on the topic to date is George C. Rable's *God's Almost Chosen Peoples: A Religious History of the American Civil War*.[4]

Rable's book is an exhaustive examination of the religion of those in the North and the South during the Civil War period. It is encyclopedic in its scope, a masterful display of the full and concentrated surplus of sincere if at times strikingly simplistic religious devotion and conviction among Americans during this time. Rable narrates the common pieties of soldiers and civilians, as well as what most modern American readers, Christian or otherwise, would consider the uncommon, naïve, and unadoptable practice of drawing a direct line from particular battlefield victories and defeats to divine blessing and judgment.

Rable's work traces the myriad elements of religious belief entangled in the lives of those in the North and the South, not least the defense of slavery as a divinely ordained institution by some even while it was decried as a national sin by others.[5] Yet amid all of the pieties of common persons and soldiers, through all of the personal animosity expressed against enemies by devout souls, if there is an overarching theme in this work, it is that a deeply ingrained providential outlook on life marked Americans both of the North and of the South. Events on the battlefield were interpreted without remainder, nuance, or doubt by a remarkable number of Americans as the direct outworking of a divine providence, a view of divine sovereignty, as Rable notes, "firmly rooted in the Protestant Reformation, English Puritanism, and the Great Awakening."[6] Such a view of cosmic and historical providence, shared not only by Calvinists but also by Episcopalians and Methodists and others, was oftentimes linked to personal as well as corporate and national piety and devotion. As one Civil War historian has put this, "Americans believed that God was on the side of those who were right with Him."[7] Such belief was succinctly articulated by an Illinois Presbyterian minister during the war: "The law of retribution pertains to nations as well as individuals. God's providence is against the people that do iniquity as truly as against the individual transgressor of his holy commandments."[8] With such statements, the Civil War became an event in the nation's history where growing cultural and secularizing forces in nineteenth-century Europe that excluded God from explanations of nature and history were still held at bay by and directly contrasted with distinctively American popular conceptions of divine providence and action, conceptions in which divine foreordination was invoked as the direct and ultimate cause of all events. Rable reflects upon the America of this time, "In what remained a largely pre-Darwinian

---

4. George C. Rable, *God's Almost Chosen Peoples: A Religious History of the American Civil War* (Chapel Hill: The University of North Carolina Press, 2010).

5. Ibid., pp. 155, 190.

6. Ibid., pp. 1–2.

7. See also a similar sentiment in Stout, *Upon the Altar of a Nation*, p. 51.

8. Quoted in Rable, *God's Almost Chosen Peoples*, p. 43. Such favor could be restored through collective acts of contrition, such as fast days commonly declared in both North and South during the war.

world, countless Americans would have agreed that the Lord's will governed all operations in the universe."[9]

What is striking in considering the religious convictions of this period is not only the widespread adherence to this view of both general and special providence, wherein history as a whole and in every part was considered to be the direct outworking of divine purposes writ large and small, but the unquestioned conviction and supreme confidence that both those of the North and the South held as to knowing whose side God was on, and whom and what God had chosen for his providential blessing. History was thus believed to be a book open and clear to the discerning reader, but the irony was that the readers did not agree as to its meaning. Hermeneutical disputes over Scripture and the divine ordination or opprobrium of slavery that were irresolvable before and during the war were mirrored in a hermeneutics of history in which God's purposes were exegeted to be either the preservation of the Union or Southern independence, with both interpretations put forward with unquestioned vigor, yet diametrically opposed, and largely ignoring the actual embodied plight of those enslaved.[10] Two sides read the same Bible and observed the same historic events, but read God's purposes very differently in both. Thus, the war set against each other not only two sides of a national house divided but two views of divine will, purpose, and favor in irreconcilable tension within an America that was, at the start of the war, the world's most Christian nation.

So, two readings of history and of Scripture went to war. With a self-assurance rivalling that of medieval Crusaders, Northern and Southern troops marched against one another as armies viewing each other as a threat not only to liberty and freedom but to a divinely sanctioned moral order, each side looking to God for victory and meaning.[11] The North had "In God We Trust" placed on its currency; the Confederacy, "Deo Vindice" upon its seal. Each side appropriated Scripture for a nationalistic typology in which both the Union and the Confederacy were deemed "the new Israel," and the biblical invectives against Old Testament enemies were applied to those across the Mason-Dixon line. In their flags of battle unfurled,

---

9. Ibid., 2. Such direct attribution can be seen in a Charleston sermon preached by Thomas Smyth after the fall of Fort Sumter in 1861: "Extraordinary providences are instinctive warnings of great importance in God's government of the world, and to be solemnly considered. The voice of the Lord crieth out unto the city and the men of wisdom shall see his name …. In the events connected with the occupation, siege and fall of Fort Sumter, and the unconditional surrender of its garrison, we have a signal display of the powerful providence of God" (quoted in Stout, *Upon the Altar of a Nation*, p. 44).

10. For the debate over Scripture and slavery, see Mark Noll, "The Bible and Slavery," in Miller, Stout, and Wilson, *Religion and the American Civil War*, pp. 43–73; also Noll, *The Civil War as a Theological Crisis* (Chapel Hill: The University of North Carolina Press, 2006), pp. 31–50. For a perspective on how the African American experience was neglected in the antebellum evaluation of the war's meaning, see David W. Blight, *Frederick Douglass' Civil War: Keeping Faith in Jubilee* (Baton Rouge: Louisiana State University Press, 1989).

11. Miller, Stout, and Wilson, *Religion and the American Civil War*, pp. 4–5.

the poet Julia Ward Howe could see "the glory of the coming of the Lord," as well as the loosing of "the fateful lightning of His terrible swift sword," a "fiery gospel writ in burnished rows of steel ... "[12] As Rable perceptively notes, "The relentless, often careless application of biblical typologies to national problems, the ransacking of scripture for parallels between ancient and modern events, produced a nationalistic theology at once bizarre, inspiring, and dangerous. Favorite scripture passages offered meaning and hope to a people in the darkest hours and, at the same time, justified remorseless bloodshed."[13] Such hermeneutical and rhetorical inventions were the product of and justified by preachers like James Henry Thornwell of South Carolina, who declared that the battle was between "atheists, socialists, communists, red republicans, jacobins, on the one side, and friends of order and regulated freedom on the other .... Christianity and Atheism the combatants; and the progress of humanity at stake."[14] Such vitriol could be matched by Northern preachers, who, like their Southern counterparts, again in Lincoln's words, read the same Bible and prayed to the same God.[15]

Yet the deep and abiding question, raised by few, was whether religious convictions were shaping political convictions, or whether it was the other way around.[16] As one Northern Methodist bishop proclaimed, "We will take our glorious flag ... and nail it *just* below the cross!" As Rable comments, "His words reportedly had an 'electrical' effect on his audience, which may well have preferred placing the flag above the cross." It would take not a preacher but a New York editor to provide some semblance of caution in remarking, "Those of us who profess and call ourselves Christians ... used but lately to place the cross of Christ above every thing else."[17] Yet such voices of temperance and theological caution were drowned out by other voices, one Methodist bishop in the North proclaiming that he would "fire into them [the Confederates] most benevolently," another Methodist preacher in the South in turn confessing that "it is doing God service

---

12. Julia Ward Howe, "The Battle Hymn of the Republic" (lyrics).
13. Rable, *God's Almost Chosen Peoples*, p. 4; see also pp. 223-4. "The divisions and strains in the churches occurred despite the fact that northerners and southerners had shared a common religious language. A pervasive belief in providence, a firm conviction that God punished nations for their sins, a penchant for drawing comparisons to ancient Israel, and a persistent millennialism remained powerful features of northern and southern religious identity" (ibid., p. 62).
14. Quoted in ibid., p. 13. Such convictions were held widely, and perhaps without exception, in the South: "The belief that God was on the side of the Confederacy was universal south of the Potomac." See Thomas L. Connelly and Barbara L. Bellows, *God and General Longstreet: The Lost Cause and the Southern Mind* (Baton Rouge: Louisiana State University Press, 1982), p. 12.
15. For similar Northern religious sentiment during the war, see James H. Moorhead, *American Apocalypse: Yankee Protestants and the Civil War 1860-1869* (New Haven: Yale University Press, 1978).
16. Rable, *God's Almost Chosen Peoples*, p. 49.
17. Ibid., p. 65.

to kill the diabolical wretches [Federals] on the battlefield."[18] Yet both sides were spectacularly incapable of placing themselves empathetically into the thought of the other or of imagining them capable of holding sincerely to convictions they felt equally right. As one mother from Tennessee wondered, "Have Christian mothers North laid their sons with the same loyalty of feeling upon their country's altar that we mothers of the South have done .... I feel it can hardly be possible."[19]

Whatever was lacking in sympathetic understanding and empathetic imagination, however, was made up for in prophetic fervor and creative historical and theological re-narration, each side effortlessly able to see military victories as transparent signs of divine favor and to render military defeats, though they were often disheartening and less open to straightforward interpretation, as temporary setbacks, taking them up into larger frameworks of meaning and an ever greater "narrative of suffering." Thus defined, they were not signs of an ultimate divine judgment upon the national cause itself but chastisement for lesser sins and a cleansing and preparation for a greater victory and glory yet to come.[20] So at the beginning of the war, the famous Northern preacher Horace Bushnell in a sermon transformed the federal defeat at Bull Run from a confusing event that gave rise to initial national misgivings about divine approval of the Northern cause into a penultimate instance of God's needful chastisement and humbling that would ultimately lead to blessing, and which thus actually proved, rather than questioned, divine favor for the preservation of the Union.[21] In like vein, even with utter Southern destruction inevitable, and even after its actual realization in Southern defeat, many in the South refused to face it as divine judgment upon the rightness of the Confederate cause but rather viewed it as a providential mystery, which would lead, if not to Southern political independence, nevertheless to some yet unrealized future Southern glory and cultural victory. Such views were the seeds that would germinate into the South's own sectional and romantic religion of the Lost Cause as a means of reconciling divine providence with national defeat.[22]

---

18. As quoted in ibid., pp. 67 and 68 respectively.

19. Quoted in ibid., p. 73.

20. Ibid., pp. 75, 346. Stout writes the following with reference to the South, but it is also true of the North: "Each victory would be interpreted as God's work, a gracious favor just short of the miraculous that signified a triumph of divine justice. A defeat, however, was never a sign that the cause was not righteous, or that God had deserted His chosen people, but rather that God was purifying His people through the fires of adversity so that they would come to depend only on Him. At that point, victory would be granted" (*Upon the Altar of a Nation*, p. 52).

21. Rable, *God's Almost Chosen Peoples*, p. 79.

22. See Charles Reagan Wilson, *Baptized in Blood: The Religion of the Lost Cause, 1865-1920*, 2nd ed. (Athens: University of Georgia Press, 2009); Connelly and Bellows, *God and General Longstreet*; and W. Scott Poole, *Never Surrender: Confederate Memory and Conservatism in the South Carolina Upcountry* (Athens: University of Georgia Press, 2004), esp. pp. 53-6.

Behind such firm assurances to the rightness of the Northern and Southern causes stood always a deep belief in a providential ordering of history, a divine determination of every event, "predestination with a vengeance."[23] Thus Christian zeal in action became wedded to a stoic resignation of outcome. As Rable concludes, "Believers' powerful and sustained faith in divine providence could at times become a fatalistic attitude toward both ordinary and extraordinary events."[24] Such an attitude could lead to confidence in action that was little troubled by moral reflection or misgivings, since all things in the end were defined as the result of the divine will. Thus it could lead to moral quietism in the North with regard to the question of slavery. It could also take the form, in both North and South, of an imperturbable sense of resignation wedded to a profound sense of duty and honor. In particular instances, such firm conviction could be displayed by a pious Calvinism that could border on stoic fatalism.

With a firm belief that God's providence ordained Southern independence, Thomas "Stonewall" Jackson, a devout Presbyterian, displayed an unusually intense and focused but not uncommon trust that all events of life were divinely ordained and predetermined.[25] Having maintained extraordinary and eerie equanimity in the heat of battle, Jackson was asked by a Confederate captain three days after First Manassas as to the secret of his insensibility to danger and cool demeanor as bullets and shells rained around him. Jackson replied, "Captain ... my religious belief teaches me to feel as safe in battle as in bed. God has fixed the time for my death. I do not concern myself about that, but to be always ready, no matter when it may overtake me." Looking the captain square in the face, he then said, "That is the way all men should live, and then all would be equally brave."[26]

Such conviction in a particular providence could provide comfort in life and in death, yet death itself could throw such a conviction into question. As Rable writes, "Battlefield victories lost their luster for families whose view of the war

---

23. Rable, *God's Almost Chosen Peoples*, p. 173.

24. Ibid., p. 24. And elsewhere: "Believers had searched their Bibles for historical analogies and lessons but, as the Deep South states left the Union, could agree only on the fact that all things remained in the hands of providence. That could just as easily spawn a dangerous fatalism; it could also harden into a conviction that God's views on these questions coincided with one's own" (ibid., p. 50; see also pp. 54, 142, 171). "Christian assurance and stoic resignation thus blended together" (ibid., p. 142).

25. Peter Cozzens, *Shenandoah 1862: Stonewall Jackson's Valley Campaign* (Chapel Hill: The University of North Carolina Press, 2008), p. 8.

26. Quoted in ibid., pp. 13-14. As the war progressed, Robert E. Lee, like Jackson, could articulate similar convictions: "We do not know what is best for us. I believe a kind God has ordered all things for our good" (quoted in Connelly and Bellows, *God and General Longstreet*, p. 14). Northern soldiers could reason likewise. Lieutenant Colonel William Franklin Draper could write his wife, "I am getting to be a believer in pre-destination ... It is the most comfortable belief a soldier can have" (as quoted in Rable, *God's Almost Chosen Peoples*, p. 160).

had largely come down to one particular soldier," a son lost.[27] Jackson's own death by friendly fire was the preeminent example of such a crisis in the South during the war.[28] Some held firm to strict Calvinist convictions on providence. The Presbyterian Robert Lewis Dabney eulogized Jackson while offering unwavering confidence in providential oversight even of so apparently tragic a death: "God's special providence is over all his creatures, and all their actions; it is them that fear Him; for their good only. By that almighty and omniscient providence, all events are either produced; or at least permitted, limited, and overruled."[29] But for others less stern of heart, Jackson's death, as much as any other event during the war, created a crisis not only of hope for the South's future in the war but of divine meaning and purpose in relation to such particular and seemingly meaningless and purposeless events that could not easily be reconciled with belief in a good and benevolent providence. Yet while many were too shaken to make providential sense of Jackson's death, such an existential crisis required resolution if the will to war was to remain firm. The means of such reconciliation was again achieved by an appeal to a moral failure chastised in order to bring about a more devout and perfect obedience, itself to be rewarded in future victory and vindication. Thus Jackson's death was given a sensible meaning by the conclusion that it was indeed the widespread idolization of Jackson by Southerners that led God to remove him from them, for, as one Episcopal clergyman articulated this sentiment, Southerners had "trusted too much in *him* and too little in *God*." The sister of Jackson's first wife was even more direct: "The people made an idol of him, and God has rebuked them."[30]

As jarring and foreign as such judgments might sound to modern ears, they were common sentiments of the time, and they allowed for meaning to be found in seemingly meaningless events in a way that great defeats might be recontextualized within ever-larger frameworks of purpose that preserved the hope of victory and a confidence in the divine blessing of an ultimate cause. For Southerners, this narration of meaning meant that, despite the jarring tragedy of his death, Jackson alone was lost and not the cause for independence and freedom, a cause still under the sun, though greatly beclouded, of divine favor.[31] The only things that stood in the way of the realization of this final blessing were the sins of pride and idolatry. Not without some dark irony, Jackson's own life was full of such fear of idolatry that could lead to divine punishment. Writing his wife after receiving word on the birth of his daughter in 1862, Jackson warned, "Do not set your affections upon her, except as a gift from God. If she absorbs too much of our hearts, God may remove her from us."[32] And in time, this was the exact reason given by many Southerners for Jackson's own death. Jackson himself had warned

27. Rable, *God's Almost Chosen Peoples*, p. 181.
28. Daniel W. Stowell, "Stonewall Jackson and the Providence of God," in *Religion and the American Civil War*, ed. Miller, Stout, and Wilson, pp. 187–207.
29. Quoted in Rable, *God's Almost Chosen Peoples*, p. 2.
30. Quoted by Stowell, "Stonewall Jackson and the Providence of God," p. 192.
31. Ibid., p. 191.
32. Quoted in Rable, *God's Almost Chosen Peoples*, p. 138.

that to place trust in generals and arms rather than God would lead to defeat. In a letter to his pastor, Dr. William S. White, Jackson, uncomfortable with his new fame upon military successes, wrote, "I am afraid that our people are looking to the wrong source for help, and ascribing our success to those to whom they are not due. If we fail to trust in God and give Him all the glory, our cause is ruined."[33] Such a judgment was common. When two adored colonels were lost in a Texas cavalry regiment, a Presbyterian chaplain drew "the orthodox conclusion: 'God has come and taken our idols from us in that we may not rely too much upon the arm of flesh, but trust more in Him.'"[34] Such judgments were echoed in the North after Lincoln's own tragic death.[35]

For those in the North, the ending of the war confirmed their convictions of providence, and it was of course easier for them than for those in a vanquished South to see God's hand in the outcome. Charles Hodge of Princeton Seminary wrote, "Never before have there been such frequent, open, devout recognition of the authority of God as the ruler of nations, and of Jesus Christ, his son, as the Saviour of the world by our public men."[36] Yet such celebrations of patriotic virtue ironically lessened the ability to provide prophetic critique of public life or warn of providential judgment, as evangelical Christianity was thus wedded to America's power and destiny. Such prophetic judgment upon war's patriotic fervor thus had to fall to those less conventional in their religious convictions and more circumspect in their views of providence.[37]

Lincoln is the preeminent example of a steadfast refusal to see God on one's side and to identify the meaning and purpose of immediate events with the eternal will of God in a direct way. This did not mean, however, that Lincoln did not find providential meaning in history, for while he rejected the simplistic Calvinism of his youth, he never could fully leave its providential understandings of history behind, and it seemed to grow as the war progressed. Yet, neither a crude biblical literalism nor an unsophisticated theological historicism had any appeal for him. When one preacher expressed hope that "the Lord was on our side," Lincoln

---

33. Quoted in Cozzens, *Shenandoah 1862*, p. 513.

34. Robert Franklin Bunting, *Our Trust Is in the God of Battles: The Civil War Letters of Robert Franklin Bunting, Chaplain, Terry's Texas Rangers, C.S.A.*, ed. Thomas W. Cutrer (Knoxville: University of Tennessee Press, 2006), quoted in Rable, *God's Almost Chosen Peoples*, p. 147.

35. Rable, *God's Almost Chosen Peoples*, p. 378.

36. Hodge, "President Lincoln," *Biblical Repository and Princeton Review* 37 (July 1865): 443, quoted in George M. Fredrickson, "The Coming of the Lord: The Northern Protestant Clergy and the Civil War Crisis," in *Religion and the American Civil War*, ed. Miller, Stout, and Wilson (Oxford: Oxford University Press, 1998), pp. 110-30 (123).

37. Fredrickson, "The Coming of the Lord," p. 124. The wedding of the destiny of the church and the state was matched in the South. The clergy had achieved such a synthesis at a loss of prophetic distance. As Stout writes, "Having already sacrificed a prophetic voice of their own to the sacred cause, their fortunes were linked inextricably with their government's" (*On the Altar of a Nation*, p. 409).

reportedly replied, "The Lord is always on the side of the right … But it is my constant anxiety and prayer that I and this nation should be on the Lord's side."[38] He came to read both Scripture and history with an eye toward broad and more ambiguous themes rather than particular and literal meanings easily discerned and unabashedly pronounced. Yet for Lincoln, such tropes could be found. In a much more refined, reflective, and chastened way than most of his day, Lincoln remained a reader of both Scripture and history, placing each in conversation, and could hold that history followed a divine providential ordering that could be expressed in the imagery of Scripture, though one not at all as transparent, nationalistic, or directly typological as those of his fellow countrymen. Lincoln had attempted to articulate his understanding of the war privately in a document that came to be called his "Meditation on the Divine Will," but Lincoln's highest public expression of his conviction on the matter was of course the Second Inaugural Address, and this, along with his Gettysburg Address, became the sacred scripture of America's nascent civil religion. His death would lead to questions in the victorious North as Jackson's had in the South, and he would be beatified in death as Jackson was in the South. As some in the South had done of Jackson, others in the North surmised that it was Lincoln's idolization in life that was in turn the cause of his divinely ordained removal. Jackson and Lincoln thus came to be viewed as the quintessential martyrs the Civil War produced for the South and the North, respectively. Their deaths would become atoning martyrdoms of the civil religion of the nation and the sectional religion of the antebellum South. Lincoln's death was given all the more meaning as martyrdom by its occurrence upon Good Friday.

## The Aftermath

At the end of the conflict, however, what the war revealed for many was not so much the rightness of one side in clear and decisive victory over against the other but the ambiguity of a war in which staggering losses came to both sides, even if one was, in the end, victorious. While providential understandings of sectional destiny survived the war to become translated into a larger understanding of America's Manifest Destiny (or the South's Lost Cause), and while this national destiny was often narrated by means of a sacralization of that destiny rendered through the blood sacrifice of the thousands who laid their lives "on the altar of a nation," there

---

38. Quoted in Rable, *God's Almost Chosen Peoples*, p. 187; see also pp. 193–4, 370–87. For Lincoln's religious views on such matters and their expression, see also Ronald C. White Jr, "Lincoln's Sermon on the Mount: The Second Inaugural," in *Religion and the American Civil War*, ed. Miller, Stout, and Wilson (Oxford: Oxford University Press, 1998), pp. 208–25; Noll, *The Civil War as a Theological Crisis*, pp. 88–90, 94; and Noll, *America's God: From Jonathan Edwards to Abraham Lincoln* (Oxford: Oxford University Press, 2002), pp. 426–38. Stout comments that Lincoln "had a growing sense of Providence, but without the self-righteous evangelical piety that went along with so much patriotism in the North and South" (*On the Altar of a Nation*, p. 145; see also p. 146).

were some in both North and South who could no longer embrace a providential and teleological understanding of history, having witnessed the senselessness and brutality of war. For a few of these, the Civil War led them to abandon not only a providential understanding of history but a belief in God entirely, though this was rare, particularly in the South.[39] Nevertheless, while a great number of white Southern evangelicals, though shaken to the core in defeat, came to accept the war's outcome as a severe mercy but looked to a future Southern rehabilitation and glory, others could not reconcile a belief in God's providence with the defeat of the Confederacy and the devastation of their homeland. For them, the ultimate idol that was thrown down was the Confederacy itself.[40] A few gave up on such a providential framework altogether.

Some in the victorious North did the same and moved to leave traditional Christian faith behind them. The poet Emily Dickinson had begun to write poetry, but she could not write poetry like that of Julia Ward Howe. Dickinson could not see so many deaths as part of any providential plan, and rejected not only a theological view of the war but any theological viewpoint altogether.[41] She was not alone. One Wisconsin captain found it incomprehensible that people "argued and upheld stubbornly that a mercifull, All-wise, Allmighty God ordains and conducts wars to obtain his ends." Such a defense of war, which was but "cruelty and barbarism on a large scale," was a kind of blasphemy.[42] And if General Jackson displayed an unshakable conviction in divine foreordination of all earthly affairs, his coarser counterpart in the North, William Tecumseh Sherman, was unburdened by any such conviction. For Sherman, war unfolded according to a natural, nearly mathematical, order, and thus God had little if anything to do

---

39. For Lost Cause advocates, rather than giving up on providence or their cause, a "catastrophe did not prove lack of merit, but only demonstrated God's providence at work. Thus success proved nothing about right and wrong. After all, if Christ had his Gethsemane, Lee endured Appomattox" (Connelly and Bellows, *God and General Longstreet*, p. 29).

40. Rable, *God's Almost Chosen Peoples*, p. 394. As Connelly and Bellows write, "Reading through the political and patriotic rhetoric of postwar military apologies or historical justifications for secession, one views something far deeper than the literary polemics of men who were confused, angry, and frustrated by defeat. In essence, the South was spiritually unprepared for Appomattox" (*God and General Longstreet*, p. 14). Greater than the economic and social devastation was the view that Southern defeat pointed toward "a far greater calamity, that of *estrangement* from their Creator …. Beneath the realities of poverty, social disruption, and political readjustment, there was something far more difficult to reconcile. This was the awful prospect that God had turned His back upon the Confederacy" (ibid., p. 16).

41. Rable, *God's Almost Chosen Peoples*, p. 182.

42. Quoted in ibid., p. 339. As Phillip Paludan writes, "To see 620,000 dead and recognize the limited victories of Reconstruction, to link these to the knowable purposes of God and be able to say, 'So that's what God wanted,' is to acknowledge something not easily thinkable about God" ("Religion and the American Civil War," in *Religion and the American Civil War*, ed. Miller, Stout, and Wilson," pp. 21–41 (37).

with it at all. Providence was, as Sherman admitted, "inscrutable to me."[43] And Sherman, in the end, won more than his war over Jackson. The future of much of the country belonged to Sherman's view.

The Civil War marked a turning point in American history, perhaps imperceptible among common American Christians who for years after the war continued to appeal to a providential ordering of history, and who linked divine providence now no longer solely to sectional interests but to the national one of American exceptionalism and Manifest Destiny. But as Dickinson could not hold to such a theological and teleological view of history, neither could others in a small but growing and influential group of religion's cultured despisers. The distinctive American storyteller who undermined American conceptions of race in *Huckleberry Finn* was also alienated from religion on numerous fronts, not least because of his own personal tragedy of the loss of a number of his own children. But he was also disillusioned and jaded because of the loss of countless sons in the Civil War. Overlooked in the life of Mark Twain were his sensitivity, underneath a comic exterior, to the religious hypocrisy of war and his deep skepticism of divine benevolence and providence. To the countless prayers of the war offered in churches, he added his own "War Prayer":

> O Lord Our God, help us to tear [enemy] soldiers to bloody shreds with our shells; help us to cover their smiling fields with the pale forms of their patriot dead; help us to drown the thunder of the guns with the shrieks of their wounded writhing in pain; help us to lay waste their humble homes with a hurricane of fire; help us to wring the hearts of their unoffending widows with unavailing grief; help us to turn them out roofless with their little children to wander unfriended the wastes of their desolated land in rags and hunger and thirst .... We ask it in the spirit of love, of him who is the Source of Love, and who is the ever-faithful refuge and friend of all that are sore beset and seek His aid with humble and contrite hearts.[44]

Twain was atypical of Southerners in his cynicism and agnosticism, but he was not alone in the nation. Others were awoken from their patriotic slumbers by the sheer brutality of the age and abandoned not only a triumphal patriotism but also religious faith. Some persons could of course object to the killing while remaining within a

---

43. Rable, *God's Almost Chosen Peoples*, p. 351. For Sherman's disconnect between God's providence and the outworking of the war, see Stout, *On the Altar of a Nation*, p. 371. Stout writes, "Almost alone among Civil War generals, Sherman forsook God as well as the rules of war, and, to all appearance, never entertained the possibility that Providence would make him pay" (p. 401).

44. Quoted in Paludan, "Religion and the American Civil War," p. 36. Twain's skepticism was furthered by his own personal tragedies of loss. Twain looked to God, in the words of one biographer, "less like a coldhearted nonbeliever than like a jilted lover. His torment was Job's torment, the transitory agony of one driven from the comforts of orthodox faith, who seeks a new faith system to fill the void." See Ron Powers, *Mark Twain: A Life* (New York: Free Press, 2006), p. 31.

Christian framework. As sadly incisive as it was rare, the statement of an Indiana soldier revealed the problem of war for Christians: "Read all Christ's teaching, then tell me whether *one engaged in maiming and butchering men*—made in the express image of God himself—*can be saved* under the gospel."[45] Such questions ran deeper than the moral failure of killing. They called out to make sense of the violence itself and how it could be reconciled with the ways and means of a benevolent God. "How inhuman and wicked this thing called War. It utilizes men and crushes out Christian feeling," one Iowa volunteer bitterly mused.[46] Yes, Twain would agree, and so much the worse for Christian feeling. The Civil War marked a turning point in America's religious history, a move to a more visible and influential rejection of a providential ordering of things altogether, even while such providential understandings continued to remain widespread among the general populace for some time after.

Twain's Southern jocular cynicism was matched by the sober analysis of his Northern counterpart, Oliver Wendell Holmes. Having volunteered for the war effort of the North while in college as Twain had volunteered for the South (Twain serving all of two weeks), Holmes was wounded a number of times in various battles and, according to Louis Menand, came out of the war a changed man. Before the war, Holmes was already quite far from traditional Christian faith, but after the war his views were radicalized. He had, according to Menand, lost not so much belief in God as his "belief in beliefs."[47] It also made him lose his faith in any notion of a benevolent providence, or of providence at all.[48]

This is not to say that Holmes could not appeal to fate in his life, but he could equally appeal to fortune, and for Holmes, they are not easily distinguished. Fate depends on a roll of the dice, a consistent theme in his thought.[49] The meaning of history was not found in discerning the ways of God within it. The meaning of history was not discovered at all, but created, imposed on history rather than revealed within it. In a Memorial Day address of 1884 in which he reflected as a veteran upon the war, Holmes disclosed a belief in a glory in war not because of its wedding of divine and national purpose but because of its being a celebration of human faith in a self-chosen cause, a tribute to human action and commitment. Memorial Day "embodies in the most impressive form our belief that to act with enthusiasm and faith is the condition of acting greatly."[50] In a universe inscrutable in meaning, all that a person can do in a situation and "the only success which it is his to command is to bring to his work a mighty heart."[51] This passage of

---

45. Quoted in Rable, *God's Almost Chosen Peoples*, p. 145.
46. Quoted in ibid., p. 179.
47. Louis Menand, *The Metaphysical Club: A Story of Ideas in America* (Farrar, Straus and Giroux, 2002), p. 4; cf. pp. 37-8. Menand writes, "The lesson Holmes took from the war can be put in a sentence. It is that certitude leads to violence" (ibid., p. 61).
48. Moreover, Menand writes that Holmes had "an intense dislike of people who presented themselves as instruments of some higher power" (ibid., p. 62).
49. Oliver Wendell Holmes, *The Mind and Faith of Justice Holmes: His Speeches, Essays, Letters and Judicial Opinions*, ed. Max Lerner (Boston: Little, Brown and Co., 1946), p. 5.
50. Ibid., p. 10.
51. Ibid., p. 16.

youth, this fire of the heart in a cause chosen, *is* the only purpose in history. The turn is now complete, a turn from divine providence to human passion, from a predestination of God to a mortal determination of events and their significance. It is not God that gives meaning to the mysteries of war, but it is we ourselves who impose a meaning upon the madness.

In another Memorial Day address more than a decade later in 1895 entitled "A Soldier's Faith," Holmes retracted none of these themes but expanded them. Time had buttressed Holmes' views with the shaking of religion's foundations by science, so that "the rainbow flush of cathedral windows, which once to enraptured eyes appeared the very smile of God, fades slowly out into the pale irony of the void."[52] Yet Holmes expressed no remorse for a changed world but a new humanistic faith in the glory of struggle itself: "For my own part, I believe that the struggle for life is the order of the world, at which it is vain to repine. I can imagine that burden changed in the way in which it is to be borne, but I cannot imagine that it ever will be lifted from men's backs."[53] The purpose in life is thus not to discover a divine will but to impose a will upon history as we choose the world as we want it to be and struggle to bring this world to pass. This is itself the honor and duty of the soldier, an honor not so much imposed by God or country but self-selected. Though Holmes had no hope for a transcendent revelation of history's meaning, he also had no place for a dismissive and trivial cynicism or nihilism. For those who have experienced the glorious horror of war, the one thing that is certain is that "man has in him that unspeakable somewhat which makes him capable of miracle, able to lift himself by the might of his own soul, unaided, able to face annihilation for a blind belief."[54] Menand claims that Holmes hated the war, and this may have been true while he was in it, but to read this Memorial Day address thirty years after the war's completion is to see almost a worship of war's glory for what it can bring out in a person.[55] Holmes seemed to realize as much: "War, when you are at it, is horrible and dull. It is only when time has passed that you see that its message was divine."[56] In a moment of complete self-transparency and philosophical summation, Holmes revealed his guiding life convictions:

> I do not know what is true. I do not know the meaning of the universe. But in the midst of doubt, in the collapse of creeds, there is one thing I do not doubt, that no man who lives in the same world with most of us can doubt, and that is that the faith is true and adorable which leads a soldier to throw away his life in obedience to a blindly accepted duty, in a cause which he little understands, in a plan of campaign of which he has no notion, under tactics of which he does not see the use.

---

52. Ibid., p. 19.
53. Ibid.
54. Ibid., p. 21.
55. See Menand, *The Metaphysical Club*, p. 3.
56. Holmes, *The Mind and Faith of Justice Holmes*, p. 23. These words bring to mind Lee's own upon the slaughter of federal troops at Fredericksburg: "It is good that war is so terrible. We should grow too fond of it."

So what are the final lessons taken from the war by Holmes?

> That the joy of life is living, is to put out all one's powers as far as they will go; that the measure of power is obstacles overcome; to ride boldly at what is in front of you, be it fence or enemy, to pray, not for comfort, but for combat; to keep the soldier's faith against the doubts of civil life, more besetting and harder to overcome than all the misgivings of the battle-field, and to remember that duty is not to be proved in the evil day, but then to be obeyed unquestioning; to love glory more than the temptations of wallowing ease, but to know that *one's final judge and only rival is oneself*.[57]

With Kierkegaard, yet so very differently from him, Holmes concluded that "faith is a passion." But this passion is not in the service of a providential God but a human, so very human, faith. It is a return to the glories of duty and honor shorn of transcendent meaning, an articulation of Achilles' own faith in the *Iliad* were the gods not to exist. It causes one to wonder if it is not the faint vaporous swirls of Nietzsche, rather than those of Kierkegaard, that have reached across the ocean to American shores, an existentialist faith dressed in the garb of American pragmatism.

If Twain is the voice of American humor and cynicism, the voice of a lover jilted who takes up the part of religion's jester, Holmes is the quieter but in the end perhaps more influential American voice. For after the war, the world to Holmes "never seemed quite right again."[58] It had changed, and so had he. In Holmes we see a providential view of history recede into the distance and a rising pragmatism take its place. And the impact of such a pragmatic understanding, skeptical of large truth claims and agnostic and practical in its implications, with science rather than theology as its *lingua franca*, would become in time the dominant philosophy, indeed theology, of much of America, a philosophy in whose shadow the American churches continue to live.[59] Rable is no doubt correct when, with regard to the war's immediate religious aftermath, he remarks: "Disillusioned intellectuals often had interesting things to say but hardly spoke for countless

---

57. Ibid., p. 24 (emphasis added).

58. Menand, *The Metaphysical Club*, p. 69.

59. With regard to philosophical pragmatism, Menand perceptively writes, "Pragmatism's appeal in these circumstances is not hard to understand. Everything James and Dewey wrote as pragmatists boils down to a single claim: people are the agents of their own destinies. They dispelled the fatalism that haunts almost every nineteenth-century system of thought—the mechanical or materialist determinism of writers like Laplace, Malthus, Darwin, Spencer, Huxley, and Marx, and the providential or absolutist determinism of writers like Hegel, Agassiz, Morris, and the Pierces" (*The Metaphysical Club*, pp. 371-2). The pragmatists "put an end to the idea ... that beyond the mundane business of making our way as best we can in a world shot through with contingency, there exists some order, invisible to us, whose logic we transgress at our peril" (ibid., p. 439). Finally, pragmatism's influence may wax and wane (such as during its own receding during the Cold War), but it never has disappeared, nor has postmodernism replaced it. Pragmatism and postmodernism are, rather, complementary.

fellow citizens who still embraced quite conventional and orthodox religious views."[60] But this is to fail to acknowledge the turning of the tide. Never again in American history would temporal events be so directly and easily identified as the outworking of a perceptible providence. It was not immediate, but the change was irreversible with the passing of the war. It may indeed have come regardless, for things that would challenge traditional providential understandings of history were already underway before the war's occurrence. But such an observation does not nullify the importance of the Civil War as the central catalyst for such change.[61] As Rable notes, the ultimate irony is that historians of the Civil War today eschew providential and teleological understandings of history though they were central to those who participated in the war itself.[62] Here Sherman again seems to have come out as victor, and George Pickett could in time follow Sherman's charge. When asked after the war to what he attributed the Confederate loss at Gettysburg, he appealed neither to Confederate failures nor to a divine will but is said to have retorted, "I think principally to the Yankees."[63] Sherman would have smiled at this.

## A Divine Providence, Stripped of Christ

Ronald Numbers has said, "Nothing has come to characterize modern science more than its rejection of appeals to God in explaining the workings of nature."[64] The death of a simplified providential view of life is in fact often attributed to the rise of this view in science, in which an acceptance of evolution as a scientific theory was seen as the precursor of a social Darwinism in which history is stripped of purpose and meaning, of teleology and moral values. Certainly there is no small truth to this, and Holmes could appeal in his Memorial Day address to a changed state of religious affairs in the culture no doubt moved along by Darwin's publications. But the truth is more complex than usually taken, and if the story told above has merit,

---

60. Rable, *God's Almost Chosen Peoples*, p. 395.
61. "Urbanization, industrialism, pluralism, and the various modes of scientific thought had unleashed their power against traditional dogmas before Sumter" (Moorhead, *American Apocalypse*, p. 243, cf. pp. 242-4). See also Noll, *The Civil War as a Theological Crisis*, pp. 90-4. Noll writes that after the war, intellectual progressives such as Holmes and Dewey "had no use for the confident trust in divine providence that was everywhere on display in the war years" (p. 92). Noll concludes, "One of the most important reasons for this change of convictions over time was the hallowness of providential reasoning that was everywhere on display in the War between the States" (p. 92). One wonders if Noll meant "hollowness."
62. Rable, *God's Almost Chosen Peoples*, p. 396.
63. Ibid., p. 397.
64. Ronald Numbers, "Science without God: Natural Laws and Christian Beliefs," in *When Science and Christianity Meet*, ed. David Lindberg and Ronald Numbers (Chicago: University of Chicago Press, 2003), pp. 265-85 (265).

the reverse was also true.⁶⁵ The loss of faith in human history and divine purposes within it was followed by, and not simply caused by, the revolution in the sciences in America. What came together in America was not solely a loss of faith due to a scientific theory but the softening of the ground for the theory because of a general loss of faith in a special providence in history.

The Civil War revealed the problem of what the doctrine of providence had become. Providence was shorn of its origin in a doctrine of divine *provision* and became simply an explanation for what was, and thus a justification for outcomes devoid of moral reflection, a doctrine flattened out into fatalism and resignation. As Stout ably puts this,

> When Providence explains everything in absolute categories, it explains nothing at all in particular. If victories and defeats, life and death, good times and bad times are all caused equally and decisively by divine Providence, then nothing can explain particular events or experiences. Fate takes the place of a biased deity—*my* prayers or *my* failure to pray. Whether I live or die is "in the cards."⁶⁶

Stout may overstate this—many in the Civil War did place their hope in the ability of their religious devotion and moral obedience to affect divine action. Nevertheless, what was truly missing was any circumspection whether the entire affair of the war or particular actions within it were moral and divinely approved or to be easily impressed with a divine imprimatur. Stout grasps this when he draws the conclusion that,

> [O]n a commonsense level, fatalism became ingrained so that nothing was unacceptable; it just *was*. No destruction could be too great because God, not man, was orchestrating affairs. All one could do was mouth the proper rituals, beat the drum of patriotism, and keep fighting, confident in the right and ultimate vindication.⁶⁷

---

65. Hodge came to see Darwinism as atheism outright, but such was not the conclusion of his predecessor at Princeton, Benjamin Warfield. Nor was it the conclusion of an American scientist like Asa Gray, who espoused in the nineteenth century both a commitment to the explanation of natural law and God's superintendence of nature. See Livingstone, "Re-placing Darwinism and Christianity," in *When Science and Christianity Meet*, ed. Lindberg and Numbers, pp. 183-202; also John Hedley Brooke, *Science and Religion: Some Historical Perspectives* (Cambridge: Cambridge University Press, 1991), pp. 275-320; and Jon H. Roberts, *Darwinism and the Divine in America: Protestant Intellectuals and Organic Evolution, 1859-1900* (Madison: University of Wisconsin Press, 1988).

66. Stout, *On the Altar of a Nation*, p. 93.

67. Ibid., p. 93. Noll writes the following in relation to Hodge, but it is true for a preponderance of theological thought at the time: "With a simplistic trust in immediate divine causation, it was no longer necessary to sweat over what one should do, and one was no longer required to think hard about what was happening and why it happened" (*The Civil War as a Theological Crisis*, p. 93).

America had enshrined a separation of the church and the state in the Constitution, but such separation was never absolutely applied to reflections upon its actual history, and in the Civil War, the wall of separation was completely broken down. At its worst, what one sees in Civil War America was the complete abandonment of anything like Augustine's circumspection regarding the relation of the City of God and the City of Man and the full embrace of Eusebius' wedding of *evangelium* and *imperium*.[68]

For a number of reflective persons, the Civil War brought to a head the impossibility of attributing all historical events to the direct work of God. The doctrine of providence would continue, but as time progressed, those who drew direct lines from natural or historical tragedy to the hand of God were increasingly seen not as perceptive prophets at the center of America's religious and cultural life but as misguided relics of a bygone age. Arguments for the divine purpose of historical events and their direct evidence of providential design proved as tenuous as arguments for design in the created order. A theology predicated on acts read off of the surface of history proved as problematic as a theology predicated on apparent design in nature, whether the human eye of Paley or the spider's web of Jonathan Edwards.[69] Increasing numbers of persons in the latter nineteenth century came to set aside nature *and* history as divine narrations. In both the natural world and the social world, God was seen by the likes of persons such as Twain and Holmes as receding behind an impenetrable veil of tragic and incomprehensible events. In the end, it was not only Scripture but also history and nature that awaited a second naiveté.

Yet one cannot help but conclude that American Christians of the Civil War period were themselves complicit in all of this. If America was a nation with the soul of a church, that soul was remarkably devoid of theological and christological circumspection or profundity.[70] Few outside or inside the church pondered that perhaps God's ways are hidden and can only be discerned in the particular revelation in Christ, rather than in the wheels of history, the circles of

---

68. See Brenda Deen Schildgen, *Divine Providence: A History—The Bible, Virgil, Orosius, Augustine, and Dante* (London: Continuum, 2012).

69. For the problems posed by natural theology and its inherent weaknesses as developed in the Enlightenment period, see Brooke, *Science and Religion*, pp. 192-225. With regard to Edwards' appeal to the web of a spider, Brooke notes, "A spider's web was, however, a fragile thing on which to suspend proof of God's providence" (p. 196).

70. This conundrum has been most incisively explored by Noll in *The Civil War as a Theological Crisis*. He dryly concludes, "Despite the absence of serious historical investigation, however, we can surmise that lack of attention to theological profundity in the Civil War is almost certainly related to the fact that there simply existed so little theological profundity" (p. 16). Time exposed this lack of profundity's costs, for the defense of slavery by many Christians of the era now appears to be nothing less than a betrayal of the gospel and its entailments and little more than a defense for inhuman (racial) injustice and economic self-interest.

the planets, or the cycles of victory and defeat in battles. During the Civil War, rather, Americans were driven by a nationalistic stoicism baptized by an appeal to a general and particular yet abstract providence readily appropriated to national and sectional concerns, all interpreted through confident and brash historical hermeneutics. In all of this, Christ was curiously absent. The tragedy is not so much that this was the theology of a nation. The tragedy is that so few churches had any other.

## *An Epilogue*

"God did not grant a Reformation to American Christendom. He gave strong revivalist preachers, men of the church, and theologians, but no reformation of the church of Jesus Christ from the word of God .... American theology and the churches as a whole have never really understood what 'critique' by God's word means in its entirety. That God's 'critique' is also meant for religion, for the churches' Christianity, even the sanctification of Christians, all that is ultimately not understood. One sign of this is the general insistence on natural theology. Christendom in American theology is essentially still religion and ethics. Hence, the person and work of Jesus Christ recedes into the background for theology and remains ultimately not understood, because the sole foundation for God's radical judgment and radical grace is at this point not recognized. The decisive task today is the conversation between the Protestantism without Reformation and the churches of the Reformation."

Dietrich Bonhoeffer
*Essay about Protestantism in the United States of America*—August 1939[*]

---

[*] Dietrich Bonhoeffer, *Dietrich Bonhoeffer Works, Volume 15: Theological Education Underground 1937-1940*, ed. Victoria J. Barnett, trans. Victoria J. Barnett, Claudia D. Bergmann, Peter Frick, and Scott A. Moore (Minneapolis: Fortress, 2012), pp. 438–62 (461–2).

# NAME INDEX

Abraham 33, 229
Achilles 276
Adam, Karl 150
Agassiz, Louis 276 nt. 59
Althaus, Paul 140
Anselm of Canterbury 112 nt. 65, 130, 150
Aquinas, Thomas 107, 109, 140, 143, 146 nt. 153, 150
Aristotle 114 nt. 72, 126 nt. 104
Arndt, Johann 182 nt. 13, 183 nt. 18
Arnold, Gottfried 183 nt. 18
Augustine 7, 25 nt. 52, 26, 37, 38 nt. 31, 43 nt. 56, 79 nt. 4, 81 nt. 7, 107, 117 nt. 80, 130, 132 nt. 116, 137, 143, 148, 150, 252, 279

Balthasar, Hans Urs von 201 nt. 8
Barrett, Lee C. 105 nt. 50, 219 nt. 68
Barth, Heinrich 100 nt. 40
Barth, Karl 3–4, 25 nt. 49, 35 nt. 24, 38, 41 nt. 48, 47 nt. 66–7, 52 nt. 75, 232 nt. 13, 233, 236 nt. 23, 237 nt. 25–7, 239 nt. 29, 240 nt. 31, 249–50, 252 nt. 17, 253 nt. 20, 254, 255 nt. 26
Bauhofer, Oskar 135 nt. 119
Baur, F. C. 85, 95, 120 nt. 87, 139 nt. 132
Bayer, Oswald 17 nt. 33, 33 nt. 19, 42 nt. 49
Beck, J. T. 57, 96 nt. 34, 201 nt. 8, 204
Bellows, Barbara L 272 nt. 40
Bengel, Johann Albrecht 181, 183 nt. 18, 186 nt. 28
Berkhof, Hendrikus 93 nt. 28, 101 nt. 44, 114 nt. 72, 123 nt. 95
Berkouwer, G. C. 196
Bethge, Eberhar 144 nt. 148
Beza, Theodore 133 nt. 118
Biedermann, Alois 116 nt. 79
Blumhardt, Christoph 181, 184, 193 nt. 64, 203–4
Blumhardt, Johann Christoph 184, 193 nt. 64, 203–4
Boehme, Jacob 182 nt. 13

Bonhoeffer, Dietrich 48, 280
Braaten, Carl E. 227
Brooke, John Hedley 279 nt. 69
Brunner, Emil 80 nt. 5, 81 nt. 5, 87 nt. 18, 106 nt. 51, 107 nt. 53, 110, 113 nt. 71, 123, 125, 127 nt. 105, 134 nt. 119, 135 nt. 120, 137, 140, 147 nt. 155, 179 nt. 1, 203, 207
Bultmann, Rudolph 80 nt. 5, 86 nt. 18, 88, 89 nt. 21, 90 nt. 21, 94–5, 96 nt. 33, 101, 103 nt. 47, 113, 114 nt. 72, 115 nt. 77, 116 nt. 79, 119, 121, 123 nt. 95, 127–30, 137, 140, 147, 179, 185, 203, 206 nt. 25, 207–10, 234 nt. 18
Bunyan, John 174, 225–6
Burnett, Richard E. 165 nt. 10
Busch, Eberhard 181 nt. 9, 212
Bushnell, Horace 267

Cajetan, Thomas 7, 12 nt. 16
Calvin, John 7, 8 nt. 2, 10, 19 nt. 38, 20–2, 37, 44 nt. 59, 49 nt. 70, 82–4, 93 nt. 29, 94 nt. 30, 117 nt. 80, 126 nt. 104, 129, 131 nt. 114, 132 nt. 115, 133–2, 140–3, 146 nt. 153, 150, 152, 157, 162, 165–7, 174, 183, 204, 211, 237, 238
Carey, William 174
Chalamet, Christoph 80 nt. 5, 87 nt. 19, 92 nt. 25, 93 nt. 28, 106 nt. 51, 116 nt. 79, 125 nt. 101, 127 nt. 27, 133 nt. 118, 220 nt. 73
Clarke, John 174
Cohen, Hermann 116 nt. 79, 125 nt. 102
Congdon, David 103 nt. 47, 116 nt. 79, 129 nt. 112
Connelly, Thomas L. 272 nt. 40
Conzelmann, Hans 233 nt. 16
Copernicus 39 nt. 40
Cremer, Hermann 176 nt. 29

Dabney, Robert Lewis 269
Dante 140

Darwin, Charles 276 nt. 59, 277
D'Costa, Gavin 246 nt. 1, 248 nt. 6, 252 nt. 17
de Beauvoir, Simone 99 nt. 38
de Lubac, Henri 24, 237 nt. 28
Descartes, René 81 nt. 7, 97, 124 nt. 99, 132 nt. 116, 227
Dewey, John 276 nt. 59, 277 nt. 61
Dickinson, Emily 272–3
Dostoevsky, Fyodor 57, 201–3, 206
Draper, William Franklin 268 nt. 26
Dulles, Avery 229 nt. 9
Dunn, James D. G. 239 nt. 29

Ebeling, Gerhard 60 nt. 16, 123 nt. 95, 163 nt. 6
Eck, Johann 7
Edwards, Jonathan 196, 279
Elijah (prophet) 64 nt. 34
Erasmus, Desiderius 43 nt. 56, 140, 204
Eusebius 279

Farrow, Douglas 234 nt. 17, 235 nt. 21, 236, 239 nt. 30, 241
Ferré, Nels F. S. 200 nt. 4
Feuerbach, Ludwig 35 nt. 24, 60 nt. 17, 98, 111 nt. 64
Fichte, Johann Gottlieb 86 nt. 17, 120 nt. 87, 254 nt. 24
Fisher, Simon 81 nt. 7, 125 nt. 103, 127 nt. 105, 128 nt. 110
Foote, Shelby 263
Francke, August Hermann 181, 183 nt. 18, 188 nt. 43, 192, 196
Freudenberg, Matthias 144 nt. 148
Fuchs, Ernst 123 nt. 95
Führer, Werner 42 nt. 53, 43 nt. 54
Fuller, Andrew 174

Gaventa, Beverly 233 nt. 16
Gerhardt, Paul 180 nt. 5, 183 nt. 18
Glanzer, Perry L. 248 nt. 8
Gödel, Kurt 254 nt. 24
Godet, Frédéric Louis 57
Goethe, J. W. von 140, 143 nt. 147
Gogarten, Friedrich 80 nt. 5, 87 nt. 18, 111 nt. 64, 140, 203, 207–9
Goldsworthy, Graeme 52 nt. 75
Gonzalez, Justo 13 nt. 21
Gray, Asa 278 nt. 65

Hagar 36
Hammann, Konrad 87 nt. 18
Harnack, Adolf von 80, 81 nt. 6, 85 nt. 16, 89 nt. 20, 91 nt. 23, 93 nt. 29, 94, 95, 96 nt. 33, 99 nt. 38, 126, 138, 176 nt. 29, 199, 215, 220, 253 nt. 20
Hart, John W. 106 nt. 51, 107 nt. 53, 141 nt. 141
Hauerwas, Stanley 227, 245 nt. 1, 249 nt. 12
Haymes, Brian 170 nt. 20
Healy, Nicholas 231
Hegel, Georg W. F. 86 nt. 17, 106 nt. 51, 107, 114 nt. 72, 116 nt. 79, 119, 120 nt. 87, 139 nt. 132, 140 nt. 135, 147, 150, 206, 220, 221 nt. 75, 221 nt. 77, 234 nt. 18, 254 nt. 24, 276 nt. 59
Heidegger, Martin 86 nt. 18, 99 nt. 38, 113, 114 nt. 72
Hendrix, Scott 2 nt. 2, 30 nt. 2, 43 nt. 54
Herder, Johann Gottfried 180
Herrmann, Wilhelm 80, 81, 82–93, 95, 100 nt. 40, 109 nt. 58, 110, 111 nt. 64, 121, 125, 127 nt. 105, 139, 147–8, 180, 200, 201 nt. 8, 206 nt. 25, 213, 215, 217
Higton, Mike 246, 250 nt. 13, 258 nt. 29
Hirsch, Emanuel 139, 140 nt. 135, 148, 201, 203 nt. 15, 210
Hitler, Adolf 63 nt. 29
Hofmann, E. T. A. 57
Hodge, Charles 173 nt. 22, 228 nt. 6, 270, 278 nt. 65, 278 nt. 67
Holl, Karl 81 nt. 7, 139, 140 nt. 135, 147–8
Holmes, Oliver Wendell 274–7, 279
Howe, Julia Ward 266, 272
Hudson, Winthrop 174 nt. 24
Huijgen, Arnold 44 nt. 60, 47 nt. 66, 50 nt. 70
Hunsinger, George 2 nt. 1, 56 nt. 2, 141 nt. 139
Hurtado, Larry 94 nt. 30
Hus, John 7 nt. 1, 11 nt. 11, 13 nt. 19, 29 nt. 1
Huxley, Aldous 276 nt. 59

Ishmael 36
Iwand, H. J. 100 nt. 39

Jackson, Thomas "Stonewall" 268–72
James, William 276 nt. 59

*Name Index*

Janz, Denis R. 17 nt. 34
Jenson, Robert 227, 234 nt. 18
Jeremiah (prophet) 58–9, 204, 208 nt. 34
John (apostle) 95 nt. 30
John the Baptist 64, 222
Jüngel, Eberhard 121 nt. 88

Kant, Immanuel 57, 93 nt. 29, 97, 101–10, 111 nt. 64, 112–13, 114 nt. 72, 116 nt. 79, 120 nt. 86, 121, 124 nt. 99, 125, 126 nt. 104, 127 nt. 105, 132 nt. 116, 133, 140 nt. 135, 143, 147, 150, 202, 220, 221 nt. 75, 227
Karlstadt, Andreas 20
Kierkegaard, Søren 3, 57–8, 64, 67, 73–4, 102 nt. 44, 104 nt. 50, 106, 109–10, 130, 143, 166, 240 nt. 32, 276
Kirkland, Scott 78 nt. 2
Kutter, Hermann 204

Lane, Anthony N. S. 51 nt. 73
Laplace, Pierre-Simon 276 nt. 59
Lazareth, William 45
Law, David R. 240 nt. 32
Lee, Robert E. 268 nt. 26, 272 nt. 39, 275 nt. 56
Leo X, Pope 19
Lessing, G. E. 98, 124 nt. 99, 132 nt. 116, 143, 147
Lewis, C.S. 3 nt. 3, 73 nt. 72
Lightfoot, J. B. 4
Lincoln, Abraham 266, 270–1
Lindbeck, George 227
Locke, John 97, 124 nt. 99
Lohmann, Johann F. 102 nt. 45, 104 nt. 49
Lohse, Bernhard 11 nt. 12–13, 13, 16 nt. 30, 26 nt. 54, 31 nt. 7, 38 nt. 34, 42 nt. 49, 163 nt. 6
Long, D. Stephen 110 nt. 61
Lotz, David W. 45 nt. 61
Luther, Martin 2 nt. 2, 3–4, 79 nt. 4, 81 nt. 7, 84 nt. 12, 85, 89 nt. 21, 106, 109–11, 117 nt. 80, 118, 124 nt. 99, 126 nt. 104, 127 nt. 105, 130, 132 nt. 115, 133 nt. 118, 134, 135 nt. 119, 136, 140–1, 142 nt. 143, 146 nt. 153, 147–8, 150, 152, 163 nt. 6, 174, 180 nt. 5, 189, 190 nt. 44, 204–9, 211–13, 225, 235 nt. 19, 237, 257

MacCulloch, Diarmaid 30 nt. 2, 42
MacIntyre, Alasdair 144 nt. 149, 227, 258 nt. 29
Macken, John 132 nt. 116
Malthus, Thomas R. 276 nt. 59
Martensen, Hans Lassen 204
Marx, Karl 276 nt. 59
Mather, Cotton 196
McClendon, James Wm., Jr. 245 nt. 1, 246, 249
McCormack, Bruce 82 nt. 7, 98 nt. 35, 100 nt. 40, 101 nt. 45, 106 nt. 51, 112 nt. 68, 116 nt. 79, 129 nt. 111, 208 nt. 34, 220 nt. 73
McKinnon, Alisdair 215 nt. 56
McLelland, Joseph C. 108 nt. 56
Menand, Louis 274–5, 276 nt. 59
Möhler, Johann Adam 150, 226
Moon, Lottie 174
Morgan, Robert 86 nt. 18, 111 nt. 64
Moses (prophet) 40, 41, 95, 238
Münzer, Thomas 32
Mynster, Jakob Peter 204

Natorp, Paul 125 nt. 103
Newman, John Henry 253
Newton, Isaac 127 nt. 105
Ngien, Dennis 52 nt. 76
Nicodemus 41
Nietzsche, Friedrich 99 nt. 38, 276
Noll, Mark 277 nt. 61, 278 nt. 67, 279 nt. 70
Numbers, Ronald 277

Oakes, Kenneth 87 nt. 19, 92 nt. 25, 93 nt. 28–9, 101 nt. 41, 113 nt. 70, 120 nt. 86, 121 nt. 90, 124 nt. 97
O'Callaghan, Paul 45 nt. 62
Oetinger, Friedrich Christoph 183 nt. 18
Opitz, Peter 63 nt. 29
Overbeck, Franz 57, 98, 202, 204

Paley, William 279
Paludan, Phillip 272 nt. 42
Paul (apostle) 1, 11 nt. 11, 21, 31–3, 57, 58–9, 61, 68, 89 nt. 21, 95 nt. 30, 96 nt. 33, 101, 104 nt. 48, 111 nt. 64, 118–19, 202, 204, 218, 240 nt. 31, 242
Pelikan, Jaroslav 17 nt. 34, 251 nt. 14

Peter (apostle) 21, 24 nt. 48, 237 nt. 26, 242
Peterson, Erik 135 nt. 119, 138, 206
Pickett, George 277
Plasger, Georg 158 nt. 3, 176 nt. 31
Plato 57, 107, 113 nt. 71, 117 nt. 80, 119, 197, 202
Preuss, Hans 63 nt. 29
Prierias, Silvester 7, 12
Przywara, Erich 150
Pyper, Hugh 216 nt. 56, 219 nt. 70

Rable, George C. 264, 266, 268, 276, 277
Rade, Martin 92 nt. 25
Rae, Murray 215 nt. 53, 216 nt. 56, 219 nt. 69
Ragaz, Leonhard 201 nt. 8
Rahner, Karl 23, 24
Rauschenbusch, Walter 170 nt. 19
Ream, Todd C. 248 nt. 8
Rendtorff, Trutz 97 nt. 35
Rieger, C. H. 181
Ritschl, Albrecht 85 nt. 17, 87 nt. 19, 95, 109 nt. 58, 111 nt. 64, 120 nt. 87, 130, 139, 142 nt. 143, 199, 220, 234 nt. 18
Rousseau, Jean-Jacques 132 nt. 116
Rumscheidt, Martin 212

Sadoleto, Jacopo 21, 22
Scheeben, Mathias Joseph 150
Schelling, Friedrich W. J. 106 nt. 51, 180
Schlatter, Adolf 57
Schleiermacher, Friedrich 25, 58, 79, 81 nt. 7, 84, 85 nt. 17, 87 nt. 19, 88 nt. 20, 91 nt. 23, 92 nt. 26, 95, 97, 109 nt. 58, 111 nt. 63, 119, 120 nt. 86-7, 121, 127 nt. 105, 128, 132-7, 139-40, 142 nt. 143, 145 nt. 149, 150, 157, 180, 199, 204, 206, 208 nt. 34, 209, 214, 216 nt. 58, 220, 221 nt. 75, 228, 234 nt. 18, 254 nt. 24
Scholtz. Heinrich 94 nt. 29, 99 nt. 38
Sherman, William Tecumseh 272-3, 277
Shultz, Heiko 201 nt. 7
Shurden, Walter 172 nt. 21
Smith, James K. A. 247 nt. 5
Smyth, John 174
Smyth, Thomas 265 nt. 9
Sockness, Brent W. 90 nt. 22, 127 nt. 105

Socrates 221 nt. 77
Sommerville, C. John 248 nt. 7
Sonderegger, Katherine 98 nt. 38, 132 nt. 116
Spener, Philip Jacob 181, 182 nt. 12, 183 nt. 18, 184, 186 nt. 28-9, 187-93, 197, 276 nt. 59
Stein, K. James 189
Still, Todd D. 4 nt. 5
Stoeffler, F. Ernest 182 nt. 12, 195 nt. 70
Stout, Harry S. 267 nt. 20, 271 nt. 38, 273 nt. 43, 278
Straus D. F. 86 nt. 17, 90 nt. 22, 98 nt. 38, 106 nt. 51, 126, 234 nt. 18
Strom, Jonathan 188 nt. 42
Sykes, Stephen 78 nt. 2, 121 nt. 89, 129 nt. 111

Tell, William 161
Tersteegen, Gerhard 182 nt. 12, 183 nt. 18
Til, Van 196
Tillich, Paul 80 nt. 5, 128, 137, 147, 203, 206-8, 215, 234 nt. 18
Tholuck, August 194
Tholuck, Friedrich 96 nt. 34
Thornwell, James Henry 266
Thurneysen, Eduard 56 nt. 4, 135 nt. 120, 138, 201-3, 208, 210
Troeltsch, Ernst 85, 86 nt. 18, 87 nt. 19, 88 nt. 20, 91 nt. 23, 111 nt. 64, 129, 139, 140, 200
Twain, Mark 273-4, 276, 279

van den Belt, Henk 29 nt. 1, 39 nt. 40, 49 nt. 70
Vanhoozer, Keven 46 nt. 64, 50 nt. 70-1, 52 nt. 74, 227-9
van Vlastuin, Willem 42 nt. 53

Wagner, Falk 97 nt. 35
Wallmann, Johannes 182 nt. 13
Walsh, Sylvia 219 nt. 69
Walter, Gregory 35 nt. 24
Ward, W. R. 197
Warfield, Benjamin 278 nt. 65
Webster, John 51 nt. 73, 71 nt. 67, 77 nt. 2, 98 nt. 37, 116 nt. 79, 168 nt. 14, 173 nt. 22, 230 nt. 10, 241 nt. 34, 242 nt. 36, 243 nt. 37, 245 nt. 1, 252 nt. 18

Wegscheider, Julius 140 nt. 135
Wellejus, Harald 210
Wells, Sam 249 nt. 12
Wesley, John 196
Westerholm, Martin 78 nt. 2, 103 nt. 48, 124 nt. 100, 132 nt. 116
Westhelle, Vítor 39 nt. 40
White, William S. 270
Whitefield, George 196
Williams, Roger 174
Winn, Christian T. Collins 184 nt. 19
Wisse, Maarten 51 nt. 73
Wittgenstein, Ludwig 79 nt. 3, 185 nt. 23, 196–7, 227
Wobbermin, Georg 135 nt. 119, 147
Wycliffe, John 7 n.1, 29 nt. 1

Zachhuber, Johannes 43 nt. 57, 85 nt. 17, 120 nt. 87, 254 nt. 24
Zahl, Paul 228
Ziegler, Philip 201, 214
Zinzendorf, Nicolaus 139, 182 nt. 12, 183 nt. 18, 184–6, 192, 196
Zwingli, Ulrich 2 nt. 2, 7, 10, 13 nt. 21, 20, 21 nt. 41, 55–7, 59, 84, 117 nt. 80, 150, 157, 162, 165

# SUBJECT INDEX

American Civil War 263–4, 271–4, 277–80
   American religious synthesis 263–4, 271–4, 277–80
   Confederate cause 266–8, 277
   divine providence conception 264, 267–8, 273, 275, 277–80
   prophetic judgment 270
Anabaptism 20–1, 137
anthropology 61, 122, 205, 209
apostles 20–2, 58–9, 63–5, 141, 237
atheism 117, 123–4, 266
Augustine
   doctrine of the church 7
   notion of God's glory 37–8
   soteriology and ecclesiology 26
authority. *See also* Word of God
   church teachers 70–1, 176
   papal 10, 12, 18, 42
   Scripture 11, 20, 25, 43, 47, 61–2, 66, 69–70, 143, 161–2, 187, 227, 238–9
   voice of Christ and 9, 13, 31–2, 41, 237, 270
autonomy 132, 173, 180

baptism 3, 11, 170–4, 176
Barth, Karl
   anti-apologetic stance 82, 84, 91
   anti-ideological commitments 120–1
   on Calvin 55–75, 83, 140–1, 150
   and canon 94–6
   as church theologian 97–9, 151–3
   commentary on Romans 30–1, 35, 57–8, 101, 103, 110, 118, 145, 180, 201–4, 208–10, 212, 215, 217
   Creator-creature distinction 61, 106, 109, 110 n.61
   doctrine of revelation 110, 113
   dogmatic discussion 112, 114–15
   ecclesial issues 124–5, 133–43, 147–53
   epistemological concerns 97–113, 123–33
   on estimation of Bultmann 86–90, 94–6, 101, 113–16, 119, 121, 127–30, 137, 140, 147, 179
   evaluation of Luther and Calvin 55–70, 83
   *Göttingen Dogmatics* 83 n.9, 84 n.12, 85 n.14, 85 n.16, 88 n.20, 91 n.23, 93 n.29, 94 n.30, 102 n.45, 103–4 n.48, 104–5 n.50, 107 n.53–4, 108 n.55, 109–10, 112–13, 119, 128 n.110, 139 n.134, 148, 152 n.165, 190, 206–7, 216, 217 n.61
   Herrmann tradition, inheritance of 82–93
   and historiography 78–9, 97, 119, 123, 132–3, 138–44, 147–8, 151
   Kantian and Neo-Kantianism context 97, 100–1, 103–4, 106–10, 118
   as the last Protestant 143–53
   lectures on the Reformed confessions 84, 136, 150, 157–9, 161, 183
   list of important persons 57–8
   on Luther 3, 55–75, 140, 141, 147, 148, 205, 208, 209, 213
   philosophical conceptions 101–3, 113–19
   Platonic concepts 57, 107, 113, 118–19, 197, 202
   positive estimation of Kierkegaard 203–21
   Protestantism, modern liberal 97, 133–9, 144–51
   on reading Scripture 73
   Reformed confessional identity 70–1
   rejection of hagiography of historical figures 72–5
   on Schleiermacher 58, 79, 81 n.7, 84–8, 91 n.23, 92 n.26, 95, 97, 98 n.36, 109 n.58, 111 n.64, 119, 120 n.86–7, 121, 127–8, 133–40, 142 n.143, 145 n.149, 146 n.153, 150, 157, 180, 194, 199, 204, 206, 209, 214, 220, 228

# Subject Index

theological arguments 113–17
theological genealogy of faithful witnesses 57–9
on Zwingli 56–7, 84, 150, 157
biblical theology 72, 102 n.44, 109 n.58

Calvin, John 7
  apologetics 83
  Barth's evaluation 55–75, 140–1, 150
  convictions on providence 268–70
  God's singular lordship 61
  Reformed tradition 162, 165–6, 183, 204
  on Scripture 61, 129, 152, 237–8
Christianity
  American 270, 280
  and atheism 266
  and canon 94, 129
  existential concerns 226
  historical tradition 160, 200
  image of pilgrimage 229–30
  present age 97, 133
Christian University
  central practices 251–2
  confessional task 251–3, 256–9
  future prospects 247–8
  higher education goals and assessment 245–50, 255
  intellectual and moral vigilance 251, 255, 257
  theology as a discipline/various tradition 245–7
christology 50–2, 60 n.17, 61, 79–80, 81 n.7, 84 n.12, 85, 88 n.90, 90 n.21, 92–3, 95 n.30, 102 n.45, 103–4, 109, 111 n.64, 112 n.68, 113 n.71, 118 n.83, 126 n.124, 127 n.107, 128–31, 142 n.143, 170 n.20, 172, 185, 194, 206 n.25, 213–16, 220, 221 n.77, 236, 240 n.31–2, 242
  anthropology *versus* 61
  Christ and faith 33
  Christ as the Lord of Church 13, 25
  determinations and constrictions 46
  Scripture and 40–1
  three-fold office 21–2, 25, 42, 44, 217, 237
church 1–4, 7–26, 39, 42–51, 53, 58–9, 61–75, 83, 88, 95–9, 104, 109, 118, 120, 122–5, 128, 133–53, 157–65, 169, 173–7, 181, 183, 185–94, 207, 211, 226–59, 273, 276, 279–80. *See also* ecclesiology
  absolute authority and activity of Christ 238–40
  ascended lordship 233–6
  assimilative power 240–2
  Christ's first and second advents 231–2
  eschatological location 230
  free voice of Christ 236–8
  God's economy of salvation 230–2
  Spirit's power 243–4
  transitory identity 229
  typology of models 229–30

divine economy 46, 51, 72, 173, 230
dogmatic theology 50, 70, 72
  Christian University 249
  confessionalism 158, 161, 175
  pietism 190, 192, 219
  pilgrim church 243

ecclesiology. *See also* church; Protestant ecclesial vision
  Catholic 24
  Christ and church conception 23, 81–4, 86–90, 92–5, 99, 104–6, 109, 118, 120, 122–5, 128–30, 137, 141–6
  christological 18
  corollaries 173
  epistemological concerns 227
  evangelical 26
  key convictions 14
  Luther's estimation 7–13
  meta-doctrine 227
  pilgrim church 227–31
  plurality 171–2
  positive vision 20
  postliberalism 226–7
  Reformation vision 26
  Roman Catholic doctrines 135, 226
  Schleiermacher's 25
  soteriology *versus* 19, 22, 26
evangelical theology
  christology 50–1
  church fathers 62
  church under the Lordship of Christ 16–26

confessionalism 175
ecclesial figures and movements 1–4
modern challenges 124
Pietism 185, 194–7
positive articulation 50
rival traditions 144, 146–7
Scripture principle 66–9, 148–50, 168
witness to the gospel 61

faith
cultural shifts and challenges 135–7
eschatological character 193
Kant's understanding 103, 110
objective reality 214–15
Old Testament predecessors 229
patriotism and 273–6, 278
in Pietism 182–3
Reformed identity 160, 163, 166–7
Scripture principle 61–2, 69, 143, 175, 188, 237
in *solas* 39–42, 45–52
subjectivity and 60, 179

Free Church tradition
Anabaptism 20–1, 137
confessionalism 170–5
Scripture principle 158, 161, 168, 172, 175

God's revelation 57–9, 71, 104–7, 110, 125–6, 129, 144, 146, 168, 172, 179, 205, 216, 220, 238
gospel 1, 4, 8–10, 13–17, 19–22, 25–6, 32–4, 36, 40, 45, 53, 61, 72, 94, 123, 142, 149, 152, 173, 176, 212, 219, 233, 237, 244, 249–50, 253, 255–6, 274
evangelical witness 61

hero worship 64–5, 72, 165
historical criticism 72, 75
historical study 70–5
historicism 75, 79, 85, 200, 215, 221, 270
historiography of Protestantism
present age 97
prior influences 73–4
the Reformation 133–43
Holy Scripture
authority of 62, 67

immanentalism 200, 221
inner faith 11, 166, 179
inner subjectivity 181, 184

Kant, Immanuel 124–7, 133, 143, 147, 150, 173, 202, 221
epistemological concerns 97, 126, 220, 227
on individual liberties 173
influence on Barth 57, 83, 100–22, 125
Kierkegaard, Søren 3, 57–8, 64, 67, 73–4, 276
christological conceptuality 104–9
difference between genius and apostle 63–4, 73, 166, 216
on God's revelation and salvation 143–4
indirectness and incognito, notion of 106, 109–10, 216–17
influence of Barth 58, 64, 73
notion of contemporaneity with Christ 57, 64, 67, 73

liberal tradition 78–81, 94, 96, 132, 143, 179, 199, 201, 208–9, 212
Luther, Martin 7
Christ's salvific and revelatory capacities 32–3, 43
definition of Scripture 40
distinction of Christ and church 25–6
doctrine of justification 35–6
on First Timothy 36
on Galatians 33, 38, 44
on Genesis 31, 33, 36
God's singular lordship 61
on Hebrews 40
hermeneutical program 41
interaction and influence with Zwingli and Calvin 56
on James 40
on Isaiah 32, 37
on John's Gospel 32, 34, 36, 41
on law of Moses 40
liberalism-personal historiography 79–82
on Psalms 31
on Revelation 40
on Romans 35
story of Hagar and Ishmael 36

theology of the cross 1, 9, 50, 52, 59, 85, 109–10
Word of God as proclamation 8–11, 13–15, 18–19, 21–2, 43

New Testament 30, 34, 40, 52, 123, 229

Old Testament 34, 41, 95, 229, 265

Pietism
  Barth's criticism 181–5
  branches 181
  centrality of Christ 185–92
  Protestant liberalism and 180
  religious individualism 180–1, 187
practical theology 72
Protestant ecclesial vision 7, 11–16, 18, 20, 22, 25–6, 83, 85–92, 94, 101, 103, 108, 110, 112, 114–19, 124, 137, 144, 147–50
Protestantism
  confession and theology 27, 29, 70
  disagreements about sacramental practice 20, 22, 26
  failures and weaknesses 1–2
  later conception of church 16
  re-examination of the five *solas* 29
  Scripture principle 11, 66
  *solas*, use in 29, 47–50
psychologism 79, 88, 200, 221

Reformation
  confession of 18, 56, 84, 136, 150, 157–9, 161, 183
  constructive vision 22
  convictions 149
  distinct camps 143–4
  five *solas* of 29–53
  notion of justification 19
  priesthood principle 191
  primary elements 61
  vision of the church 9, 13, 124, 137, 142, 145, 150, 188
Reformed confessions 18, 56, 84, 136, 150, 157–9, 161, 183
Reformers
  apostolic witnesses 141
  Barth's recognition 56–9

biblicism 66
Christ as the head of the church 26
confession standards 68–9, 71
disputes with Catholic opponents 22, 24
ecclesiological thought 18
as historical figures 71
nature of authority 70
notion of justification 19
practices of the church 14
Protestant disagreements 20
rejection of scholasticism 83–4
soteriological concern 7
traditions of the evangelical churches 67
unique role 64
on voice of Christ and the church, distinction 8, 21
witnesses to Scripture 75
Roman Catholicism 11–13, 16–17, 19, 22–7, 49, 62, 110, 112, 124, 134–5, 145, 150, 175, 226–7, 229, 244, 246

Schleiermacher, Friedrich
  concerns of Pietism 180, 194
  ecclesiological discussions 25
  on Old Testament's status 95
  views on theology 79, 81, 84, 97–8, 121–2, 128, 132, 199, 204, 206, 209
Scripture. *See also specific Reformers*
  authority of the 11, 20, 25, 43, 47, 61–2, 66, 69–70, 143, 161–2, 187, 227, 238–9
  evangelical theology 66–9, 148–50, 168
  hermeneutical disputes 265–6
  Luther's definition 40
Second Vatican Council 226
*solas*
  forms of exclusion 47–8, 50
  origin 29
  theological description 46
  types 29, 46, 49
*sola crux* 52
*sola fide* 8 n.4, 19 n.38, 20, 29, 39 n.40, 93, 128
*sola gratia* 8, 20, 29, 39 n.40, 51 n.73, 93 n.29
*sola scriptura* 7, 17 n.35, 19 n.38, 20, 25, 29, 39 n.40, 41 n.46, 43–4, 45 n.62, 47 n.66, 49–50 n.70, 51 n.73

*sola verbo* 46
*soli Deo gloria* 29
*solus Christus* 29, 39 n.40, 43, 45 n.62, 51 n.73, 53, 234 n.18
soteriology
    Augustine's 26
    central principle 22, 61
    critical function 19, 41–2
    reform and renewal movement 7

theology. *See also* evangelical theology
    biblical 72, 102 n.44, 109 n.58
    christocentric 149
    dogmatic 83, 85–92, 94, 101, 103, 108, 110, 112, 114–19, 124, 137, 144, 147–50
    historical 3–4
    historiography of 133–43
    liberal 147, 180
    modern period 123–32, 140, 152, 180, 217
    philosophy and 113–23
    of Pietism 188
    practical 72
    trinitarian 171, 230

Word of God 8–11, 13–15, 18–19, 21–2, 43

Zwingli, Ulrich
    Barth's view 56–7, 84, 150, 157
    vision of Church 10